A DREADFUL DECEIT

Also by Jacqueline Jones

Soldiers of Light and Love:
Northern Teachers and Georgia Blacks, 1865–1873

Labor of Love, Labor of Sorrow:
Black Women, Work, and the Family, from Slavery to the Present

The Dispossessed:
America's Underclasses from the Civil War to the Present

American Work:
Four Centuries of Black and White Labor

A Social History of the Laboring Classes
from Colonial Times to the Present

Creek Walking: Growing Up in Delaware in the 1950s

Saving Savannah: The City and the Civil War

A DREADFUL DECEIT

The MYTH *of* RACE
from the COLONIAL ERA *to*
OBAMA'S AMERICA

JACQUELINE JONES

BASIC BOOKS
A Member of the Perseus Books Group
New York

Books published by Basic Books are available at special discounts for bulk purchases in the United States by corporations, institutions, and other organizations. For more information, please contact the Special Markets Department at the Perseus Books Group, 2300 Chestnut Street, Suite 200, Philadelphia, PA 19103, or call (800) 810-4145, ext. 5000, or e mail spccial .markets@perseusbooks.com.

Designed by Trish Wilkinson
Set in 11.5 point Adobe Garamond Pro

Library of Congress Cataloging-in-Publication Data
Jones, Jacqueline, 1948-
    A dreadful deceit : the myth of race from the colonial era to Obama's America / Jacqueline Jones.
        pages cm
    Includes bibliographical references and index.
ISBN 978-0-465-03670-7 (hardback) — ISBN 978-0-465-06980-4 (e-book) 1. Race awareness—United States—History. 2. Race—Philosophy. 3. African Americans—Race identity—History. 4. African Americans—Biography. 5. United States—Race relations—History. I. Title.

E185.625.J658 2013
305.800973—dc23
                                                                                        2013031130

10 9 8 7 6 5 4 3 2 1

For Amelia

CONTENTS

INTRODUCTION

Like countless other cultures and countries throughout the world, the United States has its own creation myth—its own unique, dramatic story intended to explain where we came from and who we are today. In the case of the United States, this story holds that the nation was conceived in "racial" differences and that over the last four centuries these self-evident differences have suffused our national character and shaped our national destiny. The American creation story begins with a violent, self-inflicted wound and features subsequent incremental episodes of healing, culminating in a redemption of sorts. It is, ultimately, a triumphant narrative, one that testifies to the innate strength and moral rectitude of the American system, however imperfect its origins.

According to this myth, the first Europeans who laid eyes on Africans were struck foremost by their physical appearance—the color of their skin and the texture of their hair—and concluded that these beings constituted a lower order of humans, an inferior race destined for enslavement. During the American Revolution, patriots spoke eloquently of liberty and equality, and though their lofty rhetoric went unfulfilled, they inadvertently challenged basic forms of racial categorization. And so white Northerners, deriving inspiration from the Revolution, emancipated their own slaves and ushered in a society free of the moral stain of race-based bondage. The Civil War destroyed the system of slavery nationwide, but new theories of scientific racism gave rise to new forms of racial oppression in the North and South. Not until the Civil Rights Acts of 1964 and 1965 did the federal government dismantle state-sponsored race-based segregation and thus pave the way for better race relations. Though hardly an unmitigated triumph, the election of Barack Obama as president in 2008 signaled the dawn of a postracial society and offered a measure of the distance the country had traveled since slavery prevailed in British North America.

Yet America's creation myth is just that—a myth, one that itself rests entirely on a spurious concept: for "race" itself is a fiction, one that has no basis in biology or any long-standing, consistent usage in human culture. As employed in the popular rendition of America's national origins, the word and its various iterations mask complex historical processes that have little or nothing to do with the physical makeup of the people who controlled or suffered from those processes.

The ubiquity of the term *race* in modern discourse indicates that early-twenty-first-century Americans adhere to this creation myth with remarkable tenacity—in other words, that they believe that race is real and that race matters. In fact, however, like its worldwide counterparts, the American creation myth is the product of collective imagination, not historical fact, and it exists outside the realm of rational thought. Americans who would scoff at the notion that meaningful social or temperamental differences distinguish brown-eyed people from blue-eyed people nevertheless utter the word "race" with a casual thoughtlessness. Consequently, the word itself helps to sustain not only the creation myth but also all the human misery that the myth has wrought over the centuries. In effect, the word perpetuates—and legitimizes—the notion that some kind of inexorable primal prejudice has driven history and that, to some degree at least, the United States has always been held hostage to "racial" differences.

Certainly, the bitter legacies of historic injustices endure in concrete, blatant form. Today certain groups of people are impoverished, exploited in the workplace, or incarcerated in large numbers. This is the case not because of their "race," however, but rather because at a particular point in US history certain other groups began to invoke the myth of race in a bid for political and economic power. This myth has served as a tool that one group can use to ratchet itself into a position of greater advantage in society, and a justification for the economic inequality and the imbalance in rights and privileges that result.

Perhaps the greatest perversity of the idea of race is how meaningless it truly is. Strikingly malleable in its contours, depending on the exigencies of the moment, race is a catchall term, its insidious reach metastasizing in response to any number of competitions—for political rights, scarce resources, control over cheap labor, group security. At times, within this constellation of "racial" ideas, physical appearance receded into nothingness—for example, when the law defined a person's race according to his or her "reputation" or when a mother's legal status as a slave decreed that her offspring would remain enslaved, regardless of their own skin color.

The indistinctness of this idea has given it a twisted trajectory. Throughout American history, members of the white laboring classes witnessed firsthand the struggles of their black coworkers and rivals and yet still maintained that "race" constituted a great divide between them. After the Civil War, on the campaign stump, white politicians charged that black people were incapable of learning, even while the descendants of slaves were rapidly gaining in literacy rates compared to poor whites. In the early twenty-first century, many Americans disavow the basic premise of racial prejudice— the idea that blacks and whites were somehow fundamentally different from each other—and yet scholars, journalists, and indeed Americans from all walks of life persist in categorizing and labeling groups according to those same, discredited principles.

This book is about the way that the idea of race has been used and abused in American history. It focuses on the contradictory and inconsistent fictions of "race" that various groups of people contrived for specific political purposes. As deployed by the powerful, race serves as a rationale for brutality, and its history is ultimately a local one, best understood through the lives of individual men, women, and children. The stories included here range over time and space to consider particular, shifting processes of racial myth-making in American history: in mid-seventeenth-century Maryland; Revolutionary-era South Carolina; early-nineteenth-century Providence, Rhode Island; post–Civil War Savannah, Georgia; segregationist Mississippi; and industrial and postindustrial Detroit.

The myth of race is, at its heart, about power relations, and in order to understand how it evolved, we must avoid vague theoretical and ahistorical formulations and instead ask, Who benefited from these narratives of racial difference, and how, where, and under what conditions? Race signifies neither a biological fact nor a primal prejudice, and it lacks the coherence of a robust political ideology; rather, it is a collection of fluid, contingent mythologies borne of (among other imperatives) fighting a war, assembling a labor force, advancing the designs of demagogues, organizing a labor union, and preserving voting and public schooling as privileges reserved for some, rather than as rights shared by all.[1]

This book is about physical force flowing from the law, the barrel of a gun, or the fury of a mob; but it is also about the struggle for justice and personal dignity waged by people of African descent in America. Their fight for human rights in turn intensified policies and prejudices based on so-called racial difference. In fact, in the region that would become the United States, race initially developed as an afterthought or a reaction—an afterthought, because for several generations the exploitation of people of African heritage required no explanation, no justification beyond the raw power wielded by the captors; and a reaction, because a concerted project based on the myth of race eventually arose in response to individuals and groups such as abolitionists and civil rights activists who challenged forms of state-sanctioned violence and legal subordination that afflicted enslaved people and their descendants.

For the first century and a half or so of the British North American colonies, the fiction of race played little part in the origins and development of slavery; instead, that institution was the product of the unique vulnerability of Africans within a roiling Atlantic world of empire-building and profit-seeking. Not until the American Revolution did self-identified "white" elites perceive the need to concoct ideas of racial difference; these elites understood that the exclusion of a whole group of native-born men from the body politic demanded an explanation, a rationalization. Even then, many southern slaveholders, lording over forced-labor camps, believed they needed to justify their actions to no one; only over time did they begin to refer to their bound workforces in racial terms. Meanwhile, in the early-nineteenth-century North, race emerged as a partisan political weapon, its rhetorical contours strikingly contradictory but its legal dimensions nevertheless explicit. Discriminatory laws and mob actions promoted and enforced the insidious notion that people could be assigned to a particular racial group and thereby considered "inferior" to whites and unworthy of basic human rights. Black immiseration was part and parcel of white privilege, all in the name of—the myth of—race.

By the late twentieth century, transformations in the American political economy had solidified the historic liabilities of black men and women, now in the form of segregated neighborhoods and a particular social division of labor within a so-called color-blind nation. The election of the nation's first black president in 2008 produced an outpouring of self-congratulation among Americans who heralded the dawn of a postracial society. In fact, the recession that began that year showed that, although explicit ideas of black inferiority had receded (though not entirely disappeared) from American public discourse, African Americans continued to suffer the disastrous consequences spawned by those ideas, as evidenced by disproportionately high rates of poverty, unemployment, home foreclosures, and incarceration.

Spanning the seventeenth through the late twentieth centuries, the following six chapters highlight a number of constant themes that connect disparate times and places: the wavering class lines that blurred divisions between blacks and other people of color compared to whites of modest means; the matrix of military, political, and labor-market imperatives used to justify the denigration of people defined as "black"; the persistent, ongoing process of blaming black men and women for economic downturns and other national misfortunes; and patterns of circular and cumulative causation whereby racial mythologies gave license to practices by which blacks were marginalized and dispossessed, conditions that in turn reinforced these same mythologies.

The six stories presented here challenge the American creation myth and provide a new perspective on both the evolving notion of race and the multiple, practical uses that groups of whites found for that notion. The mysterious circumstances surrounding the death of an enslaved African named Antonio at the hands of his Dutch master in early colonial Maryland reveal the social dynamics of an Atlantic world of colliding empires. Within this world, Africans were enslaved not because of their "race" or their status as nonwhites or non-Christians; rather, Africa's diverse ethnic groups lacked membership in a robust nation-state that could rescue, protect, or redeem them on the high seas or in a foreign land. During the early years of British North American settlement, planters in the Chesapeake Bay region of Virginia and Maryland experimented with groups of laborers who were European, Native, or African, men and women set to work in the fields as bound workers, family members, sharecroppers, or hired hands. These planters were not ideologues; they embraced the institution of human bondage because it was possible and practical for them to do so, not because either visceral feelings or intellectual theories of racial difference inevitably impelled them in that direction.

By the time of the Revolution, the institution of bondage had made a small group of planters fabulously wealthy. Those in the South Carolina Lowcountry failed even to contemplate the hypocritical dimensions of their own revolutionary rhetoric of liberty and equality; they felt no compunction to rationalize human bondage, preferring to see the institution as one upon which their own self-interest depended. Slavery provided the ruling class with the labor that fueled a privileged way of life, of which richly furnished mansions, fashionable clothing, lavish dinners, and fancy carriages were key components. Race as a justification for black subordination developed only gradually as other slaveholders—Thomas Jefferson most notably—decided that revolutionary times demanded a theory of social difference that would posit black intellectual inferiority and rationalize black exclusion from the body politic of the new nation. To counter these gradually emerging ideas of racial difference, evangelical preachers such as the fugitive slave Boston King sought a wider, transnational community based on religious faith and spiritual equality among all men and women.

Meanwhile, in the post-Revolutionary North, whites of all classes and backgrounds aimed to preserve their political privileges by attaching the stigma of slavery to recently freed people of color. This contradictory, fictional narrative held that the former slaves and their descendants were by nature poor and dependent, but also at the same time predatory and dangerously capable of depriving whites of access to good jobs and even political rights. A rapidly transforming economy in the Northeast threatened the social and financial stability of white householders and provoked attacks on blacks, who served as scapegoats for the factory system's degradation of skilled labor. Elleanor Eldridge, a savvy black businesswoman of early-nineteenth-century Providence, Rhode Island, defied contemporary stereotypes of her forebears, Africans and Narragansett Indians, as lazy, promiscuous, and degenerate. At the same time, in a series of disputes over landownership, Eldridge also confounded her white supporters, who preferred to see black people as purely pathetic victims of slavery, rather than as advocates for themselves in the courts and in the marketplace. Throughout the North, white politicians hastened to encode "racial" distinctions into law, thereby excluding a whole group of free, native-born Americans from the rights of citizenship.

By the time of the Civil War, myths of race had hardened to presume a large underclass of dark-skinned menial laborers, men and women "naturally" inferior to whites in intelligence and moral sensibility. Yet these prejudices could not account for the growing number of people of African descent who were well educated and accomplished—and in some cases as "white" as white supremacists themselves. As a result, the notion of race became more flexible and abstract. Richard W. White, a Union veteran, looked "white," yet he earned for himself—through his service in the Massachusetts Fifty-fifth Regiment and his aggressive push for civil rights for former slaves—a reputation as a "black" man. White became a loyal Republican, assuming that the party of Abraham Lincoln was as dedicated to the full equality of the freedpeople as it had been to the elimination of slavery. However, by the latter part of the century, it was clear that, despite the massive loss of life during the Civil War era, the American partisan political system would fail to address, or redress, systematic forms of discrimination leveled at black people. In fact, both the Democratic and the Republican Parties catered only to their own constituents—white men who could vote—and acted on the presumption that no partisan good could come of challenging racial ideas.

From the early nineteenth century onward, control over public schooling in its various forms became a means by which whites could reserve for themselves specific privileges and economic opportunities. In the South, even rudimentary education such as literacy instruction seemed to threaten a political economy that relied on a large, subordinate agricultural labor force. In 1900 Mississippi politicians used the heavy hand of the state, and manipulated the fury of the lynch mob, to promote, once again, a baldly contradictory set of ideas—that first, black people were incapable of learning, and second, black people must be prevented from learning at all costs. William H. Holtzclaw, a Tuskegee Institute graduate, founded his own small vocational institute for blacks in the heart of rural Mississippi, only to encounter a violent hostility among whites to any plan or program that would improve the lives of black people still mired in a rural peasantry. Yet Holtzclaw's work as the principal of Utica Institute demonstrated that under certain conditions money could speak louder than racial rhetoric in shaping the relations between local store owners and their black customers, the school's staff and students. The merchants' prospect of financial gain moderated the harsh project of race that might have otherwise threatened to destroy the school. Particular racial meanings derived from local conditions in the town of Utica during the early twentieth century.

In the second half of the twentieth century, a small group of industrial workers sought to weld diverse laboring classes into a unified movement; yet they had to contend with racial ideologies that not only were well entrenched and granted "scientific" credibility, but also were perceived by whites regardless of class as necessary to their own well-being and the future well-being of their children. Transformations in the economy again produced wrenching dislocations for all workers, prompting whites to reprise their nineteenth-century practice of scapegoating blacks as the root cause of white unemployment. To counter these ideas of division and distrust, Simon P. Owens and others in his Detroit-based Marxist-humanist collective held that, as coal miners and factory workers, black people were uniquely positioned to lead the way in challenging new soul-deadening assembly-line technologies. By this time, generations of discriminatory laws and policies had produced whole communities marked by concentrated poverty—neighborhoods bereft of good schools, adequate health care, and decent jobs for men and women with little in the way of skills or formal education. In contrast to prevailing and mistaken notions of "race," Owens's focus on an entrenched division of labor as a key factor in African Americans' plight identified a determinant of intergroup differences that was at once concrete and meaningful.

Antonio, King, Eldridge, White, Holtzclaw, and Owens are the six protagonists of this book, and yet a seventh figure too plays a critical role. This book takes its title from a recurring phrase used by David Walker in his brilliant, militant polemic, *Walker's Appeal,* first published in 1829. Walker, a native of North Carolina, had been born to a free mother and an enslaved father. By the 1820s he was living in Boston and playing a leading role in the fight against slavery. His *Appeal* draws from history, political theory, and Christian theology to expose the falsity of race. Walker argued that Europeans had devised a uniquely harsh system of New World slavery for the sole purpose of forcing blacks to "dig their mines and work their farms; and thus go on enriching them, from one generation to another with our *blood* and our *tears*!!!!" Gradually, white people, he wrote, concocted lies by which they "dreadfully deceived" themselves, ruses to keep blacks in ignorance and subjection—the idea that descendants of Africans "were not of the *human* family," that they were "void of intellect," and that enslavement was their "natural condition." These notions mocked the equality of all people before God and amounted to the greatest deceit of all—that blacks "are an *inferior* and *distinctive race* of beings."[2]

Walker adamantly refused to identify himself as a member of "the negro race"; different skin colors did not imply useful or significant distinctions among groups of people, he noted. Enduring "reproach for our colour," blacks all over the country regardless of legal status remained victims of whites' avarice and fear. Even those free from the yoke of bondage encountered discriminatory laws that prevented them from getting an education and a decent job. Meanwhile, they had to suffer in silence as whites smugly dismissed their poverty as inevitable and eternal. Walker called on his black readers to throw off the cloak of servility and defend themselves against blows to the body *and* blows to the spirit—both kinds emanating from the myth of race. Prescient, he warned of a coming conflagration that would destroy the system of slavery; but like other abolitionists of the time, he failed to anticipate that, although slavery would die, "race" would survive and mutate into new and hideous shapes.[3]

In a study devoted to the resonance of race, defining the terms *white* and *black* is essential. Like notions of race, these two remarkably dichotomous descriptors emerged from a fundamental imbalance in power among social groups. On slave ships transporting men, women, and children from their homelands to the New World, European captors became white and their African captives became black. Over time these two adjectives each took on multiple meanings, with white signifying "someone free and descended from free forebears," and black signifying "someone enslaved or descended from slaves." These contrasting associations were the result of political processes, when people in power foisted a "black" identity on people devoid of legal protection, and later, when members of the latter group embraced the term "black" as an act of solidarity among themselves. The terms "black" and "white" are used throughout this book, then, with the understanding that they distinguish between groups of people according to heritage, legal status, or collective self-identification, depending on the immediate context.

In the early twenty-first century, the words "race," "racism," and "race relations" are widely used as shorthand for specific historical legacies that have nothing to do with biological determinism and everything to do with power relations. The story that unfolds in the following pages suggests that racial mythologies are best understood as a pretext for political and economic opportunism both wide ranging and specific to a particular time and place. If this explication of the American creation myth leads to one overriding conclusion, it is the power of the word "race" to distort our understanding of the past and the present—and our hopes for a more just future—in equal measure.

ONE

ANTONIO

A Killing in Early Colonial Maryland

These were the criminal charges leveled at Symon Overzee by the Maryland Provincial Court: that on September 20, 1656, at his St. John's plantation near St. Mary's City, Overzee beat a man called Antonio with a whip made of pear-tree twigs, that he poured hot lard onto Antonio's wounds, and that he then tied Antonio to a ladder and left him to die.[1]

Six months before, Antonio had arrived in Maryland, forced off a boat onto the banks of the St. Mary's River, a waterway that connected Overzee's plantation with the greater Chesapeake Bay and with the wider Atlantic world. Antonio had survived a months-long ordeal, a journey that began in his homeland, the Kongo-Angola region of West Central Africa, and took him through the coastal port of Loango to the volcanic island of St. Helena in the South Atlantic, across the ocean to the Dutch colony of New Amsterdam, and finally south to the Chesapeake. Symon Overzee had intended that Antonio join St. John's patchwork labor force of Europeans, Indians, and Africans, some free, some enslaved, others bound as indentured servants; when Antonio arrived in March 1656, these workers were preparing tobacco seedbeds in the half-cleared, stump-filled fields along the St. Mary's River. Yet Antonio declared his own intentions: at the first chance, he escaped from St. John's and lit out for the nearby woods and swamps. Caught and dragged back to the plantation, he bided his time and then ran away again, and again. In late September 1656, field workers were bent over picking hornworms off tobacco leaves and bracing themselves for the frantic harvest to come, but by then Antonio was dead.[2]

Maryland's Provincial Court proceedings typically took the form of a boisterous ritual meant to impose a measure of rough justice on all persons living within the boundaries of this raw, highly litigious outpost of the British Empire. Trials veered toward spectacle; Ebenezer Cook, a contemporary poet and cynic, contended that judges, defendants, lawyers, and jurors all dealt in "nonsense, stuff, and false quotations / With brazen Lyes and Allegations." Held during the winter slack season, when no agricultural work occupied the colonists' time, the court session of February 1659 offered a striking diversion to all. It featured no ordinary defendant, no defiant servant or downcast debtor, but rather Symon Cornelisen Overzee, one of the most prominent men in the colony. Trafficking in slaves and tobacco, he and other merchants pumped the lifeblood of commerce through the creeks and rivers of the Chesapeake region. By the time he faced public scrutiny for the drastic way he had administered what the court called the "correction" of Antonio, the thirty-one-year-old Overzee had earned a reputation as a shrewd trader who had wrested riches out of the fields and thickets of Maryland's Western Shore—no mean feat for a merchant who grew up in a comfortable home in Rotterdam. Yet according to the trial transcript, in late 1658 a fellow colonist had "informe[d] the Court ag[ain]st Mr. Symon Overzee," forcing him to defend himself against a charge of manslaughter.[3]

In November 1658 two eyewitnesses to the alleged killing, Hannah Littleworth and William Hewes, gave depositions in the august presence of Judge Philip Calvert, half brother of the colony's proprietor, Cecil Calvert, second Lord Baltimore. Littleworth offered a remarkably detailed account, even though it was recorded more than two years after the fact. She testified that at St. John's, in the morning or early afternoon of the day in question, Overzee's wife, Sarah, had acted in her husband's absence and ordered the man "commonly called Tony" to be chained up "for some misdemeanor." That afternoon Overzee returned to his fine house overlooking the river and proceeded to release Antonio from his shackles, commanding him to return to work. Yet instead of obeying his master, Antonio "layd himselfe downe & would not stirre." Overzee cut a switch out of pear-tree twigs, ordered Antonio stripped of his clothing, and "whipd him upon his bare back." Alternately observing and abetting the assault were Littleworth, a servant; Hewes, a hired man; an unnamed enslaved Indian; and Mathew Stone, brother of former governor William Stone.[4]

According to Littleworth, even after the whipping, Antonio "still re-mayned in his stubbernes & feyned himself in fitts, as hee used att for-mer times to doe," refusing to stir off the ground. Now clearly exasperated, Overzee instructed Littleworth to bring him a red-hot fire shovel with lard on it. As he began pouring the scalding fat onto Antonio's back, the shock and the pain of it finally forced the defiant man onto his feet. Overzee told the Indian standing nearby to bind Antonio's wrists with leather ties and to suspend him from a ladder leaning against the main house. "And still the negro remained mute or stubborne, & made noe signes of conform-ing himselfe to his Masters will or command." Shortly thereafter Overzee and his wife left the premises without giving the onlookers any instructions "concerning the sd negro." (Meanwhile, "a negro woman" remained in the workers' quarters and "never stird out" in the course of the afternoon—a tantalizing and unelaborated detail in Littleworth's testimony) Littleworth recalled that as a wind rose from the northwest, she realized "the negro was dying." Less than half an hour later, Antonio suffocated to death; he had been bound to the ladder between 3 and 4 in the afternoon, drawing his last breath between 6 and 7 that evening.[5]

William Hewes, the other deponent, confirmed Littleworth's basic ac-count and claimed that he at one point had been willing "to help the negro from the grownd" but that Overzee, cutting the pear twigs, threatened to run his knife through Hewes if he did. Philip Calvert asked only one di-rect question: whether or not the black man's feet remained on the ground when he was tied to the ladder. Littleworth maintained that they were, but Hewes seemed less certain. (Perhaps the justice was gauging whether or not Antonio's punishment constituted strappado, a medieval form of torture in which the victim was suspended above the ground.) And finally, Hewes confirmed that "the negro did commonly use to runne away, & absent him-self from Mr. Overzees service." That day in September, on the eve of the harvest, Overzee apparently confronted a chronic offender impervious to discipline of any kind.[6]

A few weeks after the depositions, on December 20, 1658, the Provin-cial Court formally convened at St. Clement's, a feudal manor that sprawled over 12,500 acres in northwestern St. Mary's County. Governor Josias Fen-dall and his councilors, who were serving as associate judges, were in at-tendance. Also present now was Overzee, who requested "that he may be acquitted," bringing an end to the matter. Instead, he was ordered to post a huge bond of 100,000 pounds of tobacco, the common currency of the

Chesapeake, and to appear at the next court session. The judges wanted to hear from Mathew Stone, whose testimony might elicit, in the words of the court transcriber, "some things materiall in the business."[7]

It was several weeks later, in February, when the court next met, this time in St. Mary's City, Maryland's capital, a short distance across a creek from Overzee's plantation. Maryland's attorney general proceeded to empanel a jury of twelve men and present a formal indictment of manslaughter against Overzee. Maryland planters were desperate for labor, and some routinely brutalized their workers, whether slaves, servants, or hired hands. Yet the torments inflicted upon Antonio seemed to go beyond acceptable forms of discipline: the indictment read that Overzee had tied the black man to a ladder and left his body to "hang from the Grownd exposed to the injuries of the weather, Of which stripes, melting Lard & hanging up by the wrists &c: the sd Toney wth in three howres died."[8]

The intervening months since the first hearing had worked to Overzee's advantage. Instead of calling Mathew Stone to testify, the court now decided to hear from a surprise witness—the powerful Job Chandler, a court councilor, receiver general of the colony, and Overzee's brother-in-law. Chandler spoke not about Antonio's death, but about events leading up to it, beginning in March 1656, when Antonio first arrived at St. John's. Chandler told the court that Overzee had sent Antonio to Chandler's Portobacco plantation, located north of St. Mary's City, with instructions to "give him blowes" to make him work. Yet soon the overseer there was complaining that "hee could not make him doe any thing"—even force Antonio to prepare his own food by pounding corn into hominy. Antonio managed to run away and, "lurking about the plantation," waited until the others were occupied in the fields or the cow pen before periodically returning to the house and stealing bread and meat before disappearing into the woods again. At one point he had eluded capture for about a month when a female servant happened upon him one day in Chandler's workers' quarters, eating hominy out of a pot.[9]

At the sight of the woman, Antonio fled again, only to be tracked down by dogs while he was still nearby, "amongst high weeds creeping on his hand[s] & knees," in Chandler's words. The planter found that the fugitive had an infected hand, but questioning him about the cause of the injury elicited no intelligible response. Chandler testified that he "could not with all the words & signes I could imagine understand from him how it came, for of all humane Creatures that ever I saw, I never knew such a Brute: for I could not perceive any speech or language hee had, only an ugly yelling

Brute beast like." After dressing Antonio's hand, Chandler offered him some food, which "hee eate as Ravenous as an hungry starved Dog, & after hee had eaten good part of what I gave him hee made signes that hee would be-gone," an attempted escape that Chandler thwarted with the use of a whip. Chandler ordered a servant to bind and keep watch over the offender until he could be returned to Overzee's plantation, for Antonio was, he believed, "a dangerous Rogue" who "might take some fit opportunity to doe mee, or mine, a mischief." Yet somehow, Chandler recounted, because of either the servant's negligence or the intervention of the devil, Antonio managed to free himself, a feat that, according to the planter, "did seeme very strange to mee, [he] having but one hand to do it." Chandler concluded by saying that he then returned Antonio to Overzee, who had learned of recent events from an informant, a local Pangayo Indian.[10]

According to court records, the jury deliberated for "some time" and returned its verdict: "Ignoramus"—literally, "We know nothing of it"—meaning that the jurors had decided that the evidence was insufficient to sustain the charges. The sheriff declared that anyone else with knowledge about the case should step forward and offer it now. "And noe one appear-ing, The Prisoner acquitted by Proclamation." Overzee was free to go.[11]

The trial, such as it was, had a number of curious elements—not least among them its characterization of Antonio's relationship with Overzee. The depositions provided by Littleworth and Hewes referred to Antonio as Overzee's "negro servant" and thereafter repeatedly as "the negro." In con-trast, the day that Chandler testified several weeks later, the court referred to the victim as "the said slave." No doubt Antonio *was* an enslaved worker; by definition indentured servants contracted with a master in return for their passage across the ocean and for their room and board, and as he could not speak English, Antonio could not agree to such an arrangement. The fact that Overzee was tried in court at all was notable, furthermore, for masters had considerable leeway in "disciplining" their workers. And the intimate involvement of Symon Overzee's brother-in-law in the proceedings was re-markable as well. Chandler's overseer was one of the twelve jurors deciding the case. Chandler himself shed no light on the immediate circumstances surrounding the killing, but he reinforced the view that Antonio was resis-tant to all "correction" and that he was a dangerous man, even preternatu-rally so. The day Chandler took the stand, he was also serving in his regular capacity as a councilor on the Provincial Court. Essentially, Chandler over-saw proceedings in which he was the only witness.[12]

On the surface at least, the outcome of the trial hardly appears surprising: jurors absolved a wealthy Chesapeake planter-merchant of responsibility for taking the life of an enslaved Angolan. Nevertheless, the trial remains something of a mystery. Why was a man of Overzee's stature hauled before the court at all? Did not Overzee possess the right to deal with his own slave— who, under colonial American law, constituted his personal property—any way he saw fit? What accounts for the delay in the trial, which came more than two years after the actual incident? And who was bold enough to "inform" against Overzee?

Underlying the trial were the protagonists' assumptions about the legitimacy of a labor system that granted to one group of people the power of life or death over another group. This system emerged from a militarized Atlantic world that only gradually spawned new social categories. The inhabitants of Maryland in its early, turbulent years defined themselves and others according to multiple, overlapping signifiers related to wealth, ethnicity, religious belief, and gender. In testifying about Antonio, Job Chandler had tried to impose an identity upon him, but it was not an identity the black man chose, nor was it an identity based upon the idea of "race." Rather, Chandler seemed to be drawing upon the image of the "wild man," a popular trope in Early Modern European folklore and literature. Indeed, when Chandler described Antonio as a creature crouching, menacing, and uttering incomprehensible sounds, he evoked precisely the stereotypical person who was mad, degenerate, demonic. Europeans originally devised this image to describe other Europeans—usually heretics or some other kind of dangerous being—not Africans.[13]

At this early period in Chesapeake colonial settlement, the notion of race had virtually no practical significance. In fact, Chandler made no effort to assign a "race" to Antonio, a man who was ultimately a member of only one of many groups of resistant workers in the Chesapeake. Wealthy Chesapeake planters engaged in shrewd calculations to assemble the diverse pool of subordinate labor that powered their plantations; the tobacco economy demanded men, women, and children compliant and susceptible to severe discipline regardless of their ancestry, regional loyalties, physical characteristics, or religious beliefs. No trial witnesses or justices tried to justify Antonio's enslavement and later death by invoking his alleged biological difference from, or inferiority to, Europeans.

It was his lack of political power, not his appearance or any imposed racial identity, that truly set Antonio apart in the colonial world. Ultimately, planters within the Chesapeake sought out vulnerable field workers who lacked the protection that fellow warriors, coreligionists, jurists, or sea captains might have afforded them. Indians and European servants could count on some combination of these protections. Early on, the colonists were forced to negotiate and establish diplomatic relations with powerful Native regional confederations ("nations"), making it difficult to enslave Natives for service as field workers. The well-being of English indentured servants received at least minimal consideration under the law, and these young men and women also benefited from customs that had long regulated relations between the landed gentry and their workers. In contrast, African captives had no advocate, no protector, in the New World, whether in the form of a well-armed nation-state or lawyers representing a traditional body of law. And so the English and other European groups felt free to exploit Africans and their descendants with impunity.

Local political economies and labor demands shaped by military imperatives—not racial prejudices—account for the origins of slavery in the colonies. The story of Antonio's death is a small sliver of that story, wrought in Maryland and elsewhere throughout the New World by the tangled motives flowing from commercial gain, ethnic and religious chauvinism, and aggressive empire-building on the part of Europeans as well as people indigenous to the area. Yet the enslavement of Africans was not a foregone conclusion. Antonio's suffering derived from his extreme political vulnerability compared to both European and Native laborers; at the same time, in his agony and his resistance, he remained a tangible threat to his oppressors generally and his master particularly. And so a central question remains: Why would Symon Overzee choose to bring onto his plantation a "dangerous Rogue," an "ugly yelling Brute beast like" person who might do harm to his family and inject into this precarious settlement yet another source of disorder? The answer to this question emerges out of the history of early Maryland, a place forged in violent conflict between Natives and interlopers and among the interlopers themselves.

In March 1634, more than two decades before Antonio's death, a party of about 140 English men and women disembarked from the ships *Ark* and *Dove* on an island off a fingerlike peninsula extending southeasterly from the North American mainland into the Chesapeake Bay. The passengers, exhausted from a harrowing four-month voyage on stormy seas, intended to claim the territory they called Maryland for its new proprietor, Cecil Calvert, second Lord Baltimore. Calvert's "designe" for Maryland included converting the Indians to Christianity (at least in part as a means of securing them as political and military allies) and establishing a network of feudal manors that would turn a profit and also offer religious freedom to English Protestants and Roman Catholics. Led by Cecil's brother, Lieutenant Governor Leonard Calvert, the immigrants soon realized that the place they occupied was but a tiny beachhead in a vast land of competing Native and European empires. Within this land, neither allies nor enemies were readily identifiable by their appearance, speech, or country of origin, and traders and runaway workers made a mockery of territorial boundaries that were both shifting and porous.[14]

Immediately upon their arrival, the colonists plunged headfirst into the high-stakes world of Chesapeake diplomacy, managing to strike a deal for land with the leader of a local Indian group affiliated with the Piscataway, a 7,000-person strong chiefdom that dominated the peninsula. The leader agreed to share with the newcomers a portion of the spot called Yaocamico six miles up a Potomac tributary, the St. George's River (later the St. Mary's). Apparently, he thought the interlopers would protect his people from their powerful rivals to the north and west: the Iroquois and the Susquehannock. For their part, the colonists fervently hoped that "this emperour being satisfied, the other kings [of lesser tribes] would be more peaceable." The Marylanders understood that Chesapeake Native groups were large, well organized, and armed; therefore, a combination of trade, accommodation, and physical force would prove useful in cohabiting with and exploiting these dangerous peoples and in playing one group off against another.[15]

George Calvert, first Lord Baltimore, had envisioned a New World settlement that would reward wealthy investors with expansive landholdings and lucrative public offices and serve as a rebuke to the religious wars tearing England apart. Yet the colony's founding by his son Cecil, two years after the elder Lord Baltimore's death, only inflamed existing tensions of all kinds in the Chesapeake basin. There a fierce rivalry prevailed among the Dutch, Swedes, Finns, and English for trade with multiple Indian nations. England was by no means all-powerful within this complex and often violent trading system. In fact, it was the lively Dutch port of New Amsterdam (present-day New York City) far to the north that greatly facilitated commerce among the colonists and Europe; and even in the closer English colony of Virginia, Rotterdam rivaled London as a market for staples produced in the Chesapeake.[16]

Founded a quarter of a century earlier than Maryland, Virginia had forged a successful military and diplomatic alliance with the fierce Susquehannock, facilitating a highly lucrative trade in beaver pelts. Powerful London merchants, many of whom were Protestants, had a direct interest in the trade. Jealous of their own territorial prerogatives, and respectful of the Susquehannock's hunting and fighting abilities, Virginia colonists cast a suspicious eye on their new neighbor Maryland. The Piscataway, latecomers to the beaver trade, wasted little time allying with the Marylanders, a move that threatened the delicate equilibrium between the Virginians and their own Indian trading partners. Even more alarming to Virginians were the extraordinarily sweeping powers granted to Cecil Calvert by Charles I: Calvert was essentially king of his own colony, with control over land, taxes, political appointments, judicial affairs, and religious matters—a degree of authority no longer enjoyed by any English monarch, let alone by administrators of the Crown's other North American colonies.[17]

Virginia's opposition to Maryland emanated, ominously, from within Maryland itself. Kent Island, off Maryland's Eastern Shore in the middle of the Chesapeake, was home to William Claiborne, a Virginia councilor and militant Protestant. He considered himself the indispensable pivot on which the beaver trade turned: the link among Virginians down the bay, the Susquehannock to the north, and the great Protestant merchants 3,000 miles to the east in London. To Claiborne, the founding of Maryland represented a threat of multiple dimensions: a rival for the beaver trade and for the goodwill of Indian allies, a nest of Roman Catholics bent on the subjection of all Protestants, a center of kingly privilege, and an assault on the security of his Kent Island home. Between 1635 and 1638 Claiborne and his supporters parried with a Maryland force led by Leonard Calvert and Thomas Cornwaleys, the latter an original emigrant and the colony's military commander. Marylanders, for their part, rightly feared that they would survive and prosper only to the extent that their own leaders were willing to take up gun and sword in defense of the colony.[18]

Most prominent among Maryland's fighters, the Roman Catholic Cornwaleys exemplified the combination of privilege, wealth, religious zeal, and physical aggression that played such a powerful role in shaping the early history of the colony. Born in England in 1605, the second son of Sir William Cornwaleys, Thomas took the route of many young men from distinguished families who could not expect an inheritance, a right limited to the firstborn. Cornwaleys was Maryland's leading investor and entrepreneur and an early trader in beaver pelts. He was a sworn enemy to Virginians and to Protestants, especially to men who were both. By the 1640s Cornwaleys was the richest man in Maryland, possessed of more than 8,000 acres, and he reckoned his New World success in distinctly material terms. His St. Inigoe's Creek mansion was built with 50,000 bricks, and, in his words, "furnished with plate, linen hangings, bedding, brass, pewter, and all manner of household stuff worth at least a thousand pounds, about twenty servants, a hundred cattle, a great stock of swine and goats, some sheep and horses, a new pinnance of about twenty tons beside a shallop and other small boats." Cornwaleys had much to fight for and defend.[19]

Cornwaleys had another, more perishable asset to worry about: human chattel. A portion of his wealth was derived from Maryland's slave trade, which in the colony's early years was fueled mostly by men, women, and children forcibly transported from the African continent, but also by some Natives, mostly women and children, captured by the English in battle or sold to the English by enemy tribes. Only the wealthiest colonists could afford to own, rather than lease, their laborers. As a slaveholder, Cornwaleys had a disproportionately large stake in the colony's economy, a stake that would become even greater over the coming years.

Throughout the 1640s regional religious and political hostilities simmered and periodically boiled over, with raids and revenge raids by the Susquehannock and the Piscataway upon the English and upon each other. The soldier-provocateur Cornwaleys strove to prove himself the equal of his nemesis Claiborne by conducting periodic killing sprees in the form of surprise attacks on the "enemie" Indians, thereby perpetuating the cycle of mayhem on all sides. In 1643 Cornwaleys earned accolades as, in the words of a contemporary admirer, "that noble, right valiant and politic soldier [who] killed with fifty-three of his raw and tired Marylanders twenty-nine [Susquehannock] Indians."[20]

Thus, Maryland remained literally and figuratively unsettled, and it was becoming apparent that the colony's future, if indeed it had one, lay not in acquiring a larger share of the dwindling supply of beaver pelts, but in grubbing around in the ground and growing tobacco. By 1650 depleted natural resources and intertribal wars had diminished the power of the Susquehannock, signaling a shift away from the trade in beaver pelts that had brought Indian, Virginian, and London elites together in common pursuit of material gain and diplomatic accommodation. Now arose a greater emphasis on a market economy based on tobacco and a burgeoning Indian slave trade. This latter enterprise was facilitated by a predator Indian group well armed by Kent Island's Claiborne: the Westo, who wreaked havoc by raiding Native groups for bodies to sell. Early Maryland planters considered Indians a reserve of viable subordinate laborers; captives were relatively available, cheap, and easy to acquire. Meanwhile, tobacco, with its powerful addictive and narcotic qualities, was finding favor all over Europe. Maryland settlers had begun growing the crop as early as 1636, and throughout the Chesapeake tobacco leaves already served as an official regional currency—"the Money of that Country which Answers all things," in the words of a regional booster at the time. Growing the weed necessitated cultivating diplomatic relations with Natives who could furnish slaves, but also dispossessing the Natives of their hunting grounds. For labor, Chesapeake planters primarily relied on young English men and women servants imported to grow tobacco, with the region's cash supply derived from the marketing of tobacco in Europe and the selling of enslaved Natives to the West Indies.[21]

Back in England, Lord Baltimore rightly feared for his weak and largely defenseless colony. Its fate seemed sealed in 1647 with the defeat of King Charles I and the victory of the English Parliament in the Civil War. As a royalist and a Catholic, Cecil Calvert well understood his own precariousness and that of his New World enterprise. He therefore made a bold move: upon the death of his brother Leonard, Calvert sought to secure the goodwill of the king's enemies, and ingratiate himself with Parliament, by appointing William Stone as Maryland's first Protestant governor. A resident of Virginia, Stone was a nephew of wealthy tobacco merchant Thomas Stone, whose syndicate had captured a monopoly of the Virginia tobacco trade as early as the 1630s. The new governor set about recruiting to Maryland other well-born Virginia Protestants—especially Puritans, who felt aggrieved there—and rewarding them with land and public offices. Though he claimed that he was offering refuge mainly to persecuted Puritans languishing in Anglican Virginia, in fact Stone cared less about freedom of religion and more about respectability of pedigree. Some three hundred Virginians proceeded to form a settlement to the north and west of St. Mary's on the western bank of the Chesapeake Bay, along the Severn River, a town they called Providence (the site of present-day Annapolis). With the infusion of this new blood, presumably the colony could placate Parliament and also reassure Virginia that Maryland was not in effect a Catholic mission bent on the destruction of all Protestants.[22]

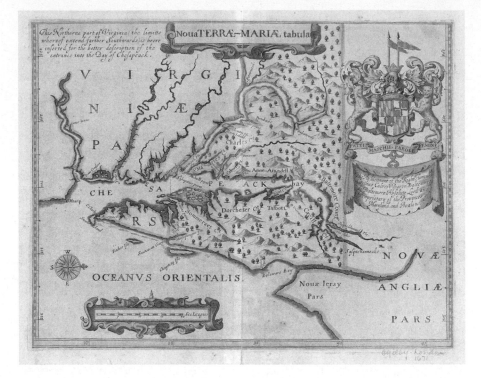

FIGURE 1.1 Oriented to show the north on the right, John Ogilby's 1671 map of Maryland was the first to provide the names of the colony's counties. Ship captains relied on this map to locate ports for picking up shipments of tobacco along the Chesapeake Bay and its tributaries. St. Mary's County, in the middle of the map, is a peninsula that lies at the confluence of the bay and the Potomac River. Despite the proximity of St. Mary's to Virginia, armed conflict among Marylanders, Virginians, Susquehannock, and Piscataway complicated trade and travel between the two places. COURTESY MARYLAND STATE ARCHIVES SPECIAL COLLECTIONS (WILLIAM T. SNYDER MAP COLLECTION). JOHN OGILBY, 1671 NOUA TERRAE-MARIAE TABULA MSA SC 2111-1-2.

Among these recruits were two young recent arrivals to Virginia named Symon Overzee and Job Chandler, both Protestants (but not Puritans). Even at this early point in their careers, the fortunes of the two men had become tightly linked. Born in 1623 in Stratford-upon-Avon, Chandler came to Virginia in the spring of 1648. He was the younger brother of influential merchant Richard Chandler, one of Lord Baltimore's associates and subsequent critics. A former apprentice to Thomas Stone, whose tobacco syndicate had benefited from strong connections with Holland's merchants, Richard was now capitalizing on his own connections with Dutch traders.[23]

Political allies of Overzee would later claim that he, too, was born in England, but in fact he grew up in a prosperous Rotterdam family. (The privileged status Overzee would come to enjoy in Maryland might have derived from Lord Baltimore's authority to proclaim anyone an English citizen.) Overzee's father, Cornelis Symonsz Overzee, a prominent ship owner, sea captain, and tobacco importer, likely traded with both Richard Chandler and Thomas Stone. As early as 1647, Symon was living up to his last name, which means "overseas" in Dutch: only twenty years old, he was actively trading as the contractor or owner of ships plying the Virginia-to-Rotterdam tobacco trade. He probably settled in Virginia around 1650, his immediate task the promotion of his father's business interests. By 1651 both Symon Overzee and Job Chandler were living in Lynnhaven, Lower Norfolk County, in the southeastern corner of Virginia, where Chandler was already serving as a county sheriff, justice of the peace, and burgess, or member of Virginia's colonial assembly. The area was the site of a thriving Dutch trading post that supplied the English planter elite with exotic foods and spirits, fine furniture, luxury goods such as linens and laces, and, for a wealthy few, enslaved workers. Shortly after their arrival in Virginia, Overzee and Chandler married two Lynnhaven women, the Thoroughgood sisters, Sarah (born in 1631) and Anne (1630), respectively. They were the daughters of Adam Thoroughgood, recently deceased, a wealthy political leader, Indian fighter, and slave trader. At the time of their marriage, the sisters were the stepdaughters of Sir Francis Yeardley, the younger son of Virginia's first governor, the Protestant George Yeardley.[24]

Symon Overzee's father-in-law was also in the process of developing deep ties to the colonial system of slavery. Born in Jamestown in 1624, Francis Yeardley had grown up in a slave-holding household. He himself was an early buyer and seller of enslaved Africans and Indians, relying on Dutch merchants for his own large bound workforce. In 1647 the twenty-one-year-old Yeardley had made an excellent match with a wealthy thirty-six-year-old Lynnhaven widow. Her new name, Sarah Offley Thoroughgood Gookin Yeardley, testified to the serial monogamy that prevailed during the early years of Chesapeake colonization, when mortality rates were high—almost three-quarters of immigrant men died before age fifty—and marriages short, an average of seven years. Francis Yeardley took up residence with his new wife at her Lynnhaven estate, where she was living with her children, including (at that point) her unmarried daughters, Sarah and Anne. After Overzee and Sarah Thoroughgood wed, Yeardley and his new son-in-law parlayed their kin relationship into a financial one. The two men jointly bought the sloop *Wittepaart* (Dutch for White Horse) from its captain, Dirck Wittepaart, and embarked on a trading business facilitated by Overzee's ties with other Dutch merchants on both sides of the Atlantic.[25]

In 1649 Lieutenant William Lewis, a Catholic landowner, signed over his patent for 2,000 acres on Portobacco Creek on Maryland's Western Shore to Overzee and Chandler jointly. Lewis had in mind the long-term interests of Maryland, and by his gift to the two Protestants he hoped to spare the colony the religious and political wars ravaging England, and the whole English Empire, at the time. Chandler also laid claim to an additional 1,200 acres of land. Arriving in 1650 with his bride, Overzee named his portion of the tract, located on Nangemy Creek near an Indian settlement of the same name, "Rotterdam." For a while at least, the Thoroughgood sisters would live on adjoining estates in Charles County.[26]

Overzee's brother-in-law was received with great fanfare in their new home. In June 1651 Maryland officials offered Chandler a uniquely obsequious welcome to the colony, hailing the arrival of "our trusty and well beloved Job Chandler," recommended by Governor Stone and surrogate of "your Brother and our good Friend Richard Chandler of London Merchant." Sweetening the deal for Job were several high-ranking political and judicial appointments conferred upon him: he would serve as a member of the Governor's Council, a small, powerful judicial body; as a county justice of the peace; and as receiver general of the colony. This last position required him to collect port duties and quitrents and entitled him to an annual salary of £100 sterling as well as 10 percent of the colony's revenue. Members of the council declared their "special trust and Confidence in your Fidelity Wisdom diligence and experience of affairs in these Parts," no doubt an exaggerated compliment to the youthful newcomer, but certainly a testament to the influence of his brother, Richard, in parliamentary politics and colonial affairs generally.[27]

Overzee's star, too, was on the rise. He and his wife soon moved from his Rotterdam holdings to a plantation called St. John's, at St. Mary's City. The move was, if nothing else, strategic, for though it took Sarah away from her sister, it made the Overzees close neighbors of Philip Calvert and Thomas Cornwaleys and brought the couple literally within shouting distance of the colonial seat of power. Yet the St. John's house itself might have been enough to draw Overzee out of the wilds of Nangemy Creek. Situated strategically above the banks of the St. Mary's and close to a millpond, the

FIGURE 1.2 An artist's rendering of St. John's, the home of Symon Overzee, where the enslaved man Antonio died in September 1656. At a time when most Maryland colonists lived in small, temporary structures, the St. John's house was exceptional for its size and gracious design and for the improved fields, gardens, and orchards that surrounded it. The site has been recreated by Historic St. Mary's City. COURTESY L. H. BARKER AND HISTORIC ST. MARY'S CITY.

one-and-a-half-story frame dwelling had been built by colonial secretary John Lewger. So commodious was the structure that at times the assembly and the general court had met there, and sheriffs and guards had lodged there with the Lewger family. For Overzee, who no doubt had been raised in material comfort surrounded by books and fine furniture and carpets, the house was a welcome and dramatic contrast to the primitive, temporary clapboard and wattle-and-daub structures that sheltered most Marylanders at the time. The Overzees took up residence on a fully improved plantation that included a freshwater spring, a tannery, pasturelands, corn and tobacco fields, and orchards. Although according to a local historian St. Mary's City could "hardly be called a Towne"—it consisted of a forge, a mill, a Catholic chapel, and a few small houses—it was the most that Maryland had to offer the couple in terms of a settlement. Yet if the move to St. John's increased Overzee's physical comfort, it also demanded that he fill a new and completely unfamiliar role: that of plantation owner and labor manager.[28]

Around this time Francis Yeardley, too, responded to Governor Stone's call for Protestants, establishing a plantation near Chandler and Overzee on Portobacco Creek and accepting political appointments. In September 1651 Yeardley and Chandler were serving together on the Governor's Council. Meanwhile, Yeardley boldly straddled Virginia and Maryland by maintaining his Lynnhaven residence, where his wife continued to live, and filling a number of local posts in Virginia. Maryland chauvinists would later charge that Yeardley had only "pretended" to settle in their colony. Yet Overzee also retained ties to Virginia, where his seafaring father was trading in tobacco and deerskins in the early 1650s, and where Symon numbered many planters among his debtors.[29]

Unlike his sons-in-law Chandler and Overzee, Yeardley had grandiose plans for the development of New World settlements, plans that presumed peaceful cohabitation with Christian Indians. Yeardley drew on his father's wealth and reputation, and on the skills of an interpreter he employed, Nathaniel Batts, to go beyond trading beaver pelts with the Susquehannock and to forge new links with Indians from the Currituck and Albemarle Sounds to the south of Virginia. In correspondence with a potential English investor, he referred to Native leaders in terms that conveyed his respect for them: these were "emperors" and "great commanders" presiding over "great nations" defended by men "valiant and fierce in fight." Yeardley defined these strange-looking people not by their skin color or their race, but by their powerful political-military associations. At the same time, he envisioned a future settlement of English-speaking, Christianized, literate Indians who would live in English-style frame houses and promote Mediterranean enterprises such as vineyards, olive trees, and silk-making. Such a scheme, Yeardley concluded, would rebound to God's glory and "England and Virginia's honor," suggesting his loyalties lay with Maryland's rival.[30]

If Yeardley and Chandler's influence in Maryland was political, Overzee's clout—such as it was—was economic. Though benefiting from his connection with Yeardley, Overzee had already built a substantial trading business of his own, partnering with influential traders in Rotterdam and Virginia, including, among the latter, Edmund Scarborough of Northampton County. In the process Overzee learned what his father already knew: that merchandizing in the age of empire was not for the risk averse. Indeed, seventeenth-century Dutch traders embraced the perils of far-flung voyages, relishing the battle against pirates, mutinous crews, and stormy weather just as they relished the battle against their own sinfulness in the sight of God. Overzee remained on the front lines of wealth creation during these uncertain times. In 1648 he lost one of his ships to the Spanish on the high seas en route to Virginia. Two years later the ship that he and Yeardley owned—originally named the *Wittepaart* but now diplomatically renamed *Virginia Merchant*—sank off the coast of New England. These setbacks failed to dampen Overzee's spirit; courting disaster and making money were part of the same impulse.[31]

Barely out of their teens, Overzee and Chandler had already given evidence of the energy and political savvy necessary to take advantage of Maryland's economic potential. Nevertheless, neither the arrival of these and other Virginia Protestants nor the forthcoming parliamentary support could guarantee Maryland the security and stability its inhabitants craved. The Chesapeake remained a site of sporadic warfare, with the Westo Indians forcing a reconfiguration of the tribes they raided for slaves, the Susquehannock terrorizing Maryland planters, and Maryland Catholics and Protestants kidnapping and assaulting each other.[32]

And then in early 1652 came a diplomatic breakthrough when the Susquehannock initiated a conditional peace with the colony. The treaty secured the territorial rights of Maryland, with the exception of Kent Island, "which belongs to Captaine Clayborne." The Indians and English agreed to retrieve fugitives for each other—"Servants belonging to the English or to the Indians [who] shall goe away or run away from either side"—with masters liable for the costs incurred in capturing them. The treaty further stipulated that any Indians who entered an English settlement must limit their delegation to no more than ten persons and must carry tokens, distributed to them earlier by the English, to identify themselves as friends. The treaty was signed, on the one hand, by Maryland officials and, on the other, by Sawahegeh, treasurer, and by a number of war captains and councilors "appointed and sent for that purpose by the Nation and State of Sasquehanogh." The agreement concluded on a hopeful note: that "these Articles and every particular of them shall be really and inviolably observed and kept and performed by the two Nations before named."[33]

For treaty purposes in 1652 at least, the English were willing to grant certain Indian tribes the status of *nation,* with all the military and political significance the term implied. These Native groups possessed the numbers and the military prowess to extract from the English a measure of fearful respect; and in fact all Indians were either allies or foes, social relations the English well understood. Absent from these considerations was any sense that the Indians were part of a homogeneous race of people. Rather, there were clear social and political divisions among various cultural groups, differences that rendered generalizing about these Native peoples difficult and indeed counterproductive for anyone on the front lines of colonial profit-seeking.

Meanwhile, together Maryland and Virginia authorities were pushing back against Parliament's stringent measures to restrict the Dutch trading presence in the Chesapeake; the colonists were torn between their loyalty to England and their commercial interests, and the latter won out over the former. The regional tobacco economy hinged on merchants such as Overzee and his network of Virginia and Dutch traders, a Rotterdam–New Amsterdam–Chesapeake connection based on a dense tangle of intermarriages that spanned the Atlantic. During this era of English civil wars and of banditry on the high seas, Chesapeake tobacco planters understood that to sell their crop abroad—that is, to survive and profit—they needed the predictable sail power that only the Dutch could provide. In 1651 Virginia's governor, William Berkeley, condemned Parliament's Navigation Acts forbidding foreign nations to trade with any English colonies. Declared the governor, "The Indians, God be blessed round about us are subdued; we can onely feare the *Londoners,* who would faine bring us to the same poverty, wherein the *Dutch* found and relieved us; [the Londoners] would take away the liberty of our consciences, and tongues, and our right of giving and selling our goods to whom we please."[34]

As a Dutch trader Overzee played an integral part in Maryland's emerging prosperity, but he was living in a struggling English community that was profoundly suspicious of foreigners—regardless of skin color—who were part of viable nation-states. This suspicion kept Overzee on the political fringes of the embattled colonial sphere he had so recently joined, even while granting him a healthy share of its profits. Unlike other prominent men, Overzee had little to do with the governance of the colony, and for one so wealthy, he was conspicuously absent from the long list of councilors, burgesses, county justices of the peace, jurors, and overseers of highways who enriched themselves by making laws and policies that favored their own financial interests. Overzee's public service stints were limited to a brief period in late April and early May 1658, when he appeared as a commissioner for St. Mary's County, appointed by Lord Baltimore, and when he twice served as a foreman of petit juries impaneled by the county. (As a native of the Netherlands, he was ineligible for political or administrative office.) Yet his regular appearances in court testify to his extraordinary economic power in a time and place where influence was measured by the number of a person's legal adversaries. Over the years Overzee confronted many dozens of debtors in county court and Provincial Court in Virginia and Maryland. No amount of tobacco— whether owed by male or female, rich or poor, young or old—was too small to be forgiven or forgotten. Moreover, his relation to Job Chandler rendered unnecessary any formal politicking on Overzee's part; in fact, the two men enjoyed an ingenious alliance based on the political power of the one and the economic prowess of the other. Theirs was the elite equivalent of a *mateship,* the contemporary term for a landholding partnership between men of modest means.[35]

Governor Stone appreciated that Symon Overzee represented an entrepreneurial moneymaking machine of sorts. Nevertheless, the governor was paying dearly for recruiting at least some of Overzee's fellow Virginia Protestants several years before. Throughout the early 1650s, pressure was building among the principled Puritans from Virginia; they chafed at taking an oath of allegiance to the Catholic Lord Baltimore, disingenuously refusing to swear "to uphold [the] Antichrist." During this newly unsettled period, some Marylanders fled to England; among them was the militant Catholic Thomas Cornwaleys.[36]

Stone and his allies clashed violently with a group of disaffected Puritans on Sunday morning, March 25, 1655. This clash, known as the Battle of Great Severn, took place at Horn Point, opposite the Puritan settlement of Providence, and brought together a total of four hundred men from both sides. Fighting alongside Stone that day were a newly commissioned Major Job

Chandler and Chandler's benefactor, William Lewis. Chandler appeared determined to remain loyal to the governor and to distance himself from the other former Virginians, men possessed of a religious zealotry that was alien to him. Stone, Chandler, and Lewis were captured in battle and, with ten others, convicted of treason and condemned to death. Stone and Chandler were spared—according to one observer "by the Petitions of the Women, with some other friends which they found there"—but Lewis was not. He and three others were executed. Eventually, Chandler paid a fine of 15,000 pounds of tobacco for his role in the rebellion.[37]

Throughout this tumultuous period, Job Chandler and Symon Overzee held onto their livelihoods, and their lives, by virtue of their relation to Yeardley and to Chandler's brother and Stone's uncle in London. The wealth that the two young men accumulated in Maryland through the 1650s can be measured any number of ways. Overzee owned several large land parcels, including the 1,000-acre Rotterdam plantation; the St. John's freehold of 200 acres, where he lived with his wife; an additional 800 acres near St. Mary's City; a plantation called Hebden's Hole, of 700 acres; and another 600 acres called Stoopside. By the mid-1650s he had expanded St. John's to include a loft, a dairy, and a quartering house where an indeterminate number of free and enslaved workers lived. He furnished the home with a rich array of cabinets, feather beds, leather chairs, trunks, and pewter and silver serving sets. His wife, Sarah, owned Holland aprons and dresses trimmed with Flanders lace, in addition to mounds of linens, blankets, and sewing materials—an abundance of finery that would one day pique the malicious envy of some of her servants.[38]

Chandler in time also accumulated enslaved workers and at least 500 acres in addition to the 1,000-acre parcel he received from William Lewis (and named Chandler's Hope). His profit-making activities included delivering Indian prisoners to county officials and sending large quantities of muskrat skins to London. Yet Chandler distinguished himself primarily not as a trader but rather as an elected official and political appointee. He was a regular on the county court circuit, hearing a veritable kaleidoscope of cases involving witchcraft, adultery, infanticide, bigamy, theft, slander, public drunkenness, and murder. Together with other judges, he sentenced offenders to a range of punishments, from a stint in the pillory or on the ducking stool, to fines, brandings—runaway workers at times had an "R" burned into their shoulders—and death by hanging. Such power apparently convinced Chandler of his own invincibility.[39]

It was Francis Yeardley who, living and politicking in two colonies at once, put into motion a series of events that would escalate into a major scandal engulfing Overzee and Chandler. This controversy, as with Overzee's later trial over the death of Antonio, would revolve around the disposition of slaves. In the winter and early spring of 1653–1654, Yeardley was in residence at his Portobacco plantation, worked by a number of enslaved Africans and Indians. By March 1654, however, Yeardley was back at his plantation in Virginia, where he received an Indian chief from the Albermarle region to the south. The chief wanted his son to be baptized and so left the youngster with his hosts "to be bred up a Christian," which, Yeardley prayed, "God grant him to become!"[40]

Yeardley's springtime absence from Maryland had worried his creditors there. In April one buyer sent a boat to Portobacco to pick up two enslaved Indian youths he had already paid for, but Yeardley was not there to make good on the transaction. If indeed the planter had intended to elude his creditors, it would not have been the first or last time a debtor had slipped away across the bay; this sort of boundary-crossing was already a time-tested way of leaving behind financial, personal, and legal obligations of all kinds. Yet Yeardley was far too wealthy to fear those whom he owed tobacco or slaves, no matter how large the debt. He left Maryland to return to the place he considered his real home. Now, however, his peripatetic existence came to an abrupt end: in February 1655, while still at his Virginia plantation, the thirty-five-year-old Yeardley died. With him expired his vision of an English-Indian cooperative in the territory that would eventually become North Carolina.[41]

In May, shortly after Yeardley's death, Chandler and Overzee took control of their late stepfather-in-law's Portobacco estate by virtue of their status as Yeardley's closest male heirs, the sons-in-law of Yeardley's widow. The local sheriff began routine proceedings to assess the estate so that all its creditors with outstanding claims could be compensated. Yet in a deft act of sabotage, Chandler, in his capacity as councilor, ordered the sheriff to refrain from securing the plantation and to stay away from it until further notice. At this point Overzee brought in one of his sloops and spirited off the plantation the most valuable movable property, the enslaved workers, depositing them at St. John's so that they could be fed before being sent, and presumably sold, away. Later one of Yeardley's creditors would state the case against the two: "The One [Chandler] having protected the sd Estate contrary to the Legall Course of Attachment, & after delivered it up, &

permitted it to be exported," acting in concert with "the other" (Overzee), who "knowingly ayding & assisting by his Sloope & man to the exportation of the same, & victualing them att his own howse, when they were going out of the province." As a result, "the said Partys are since enriched, by the sd Estate." It is unclear whether or not either Chandler or Overzee knew the identity of all the claimants on Yeardley's estate. If they did know, their underhanded appropriation of the assets was reckless in the extreme. If they did not, they would soon pay for their ignorance.[42]

While this legal clash between one of Yeardley's creditors and the Overzee-Chandler mateship was unfolding, a slave ship docked at the Dutch colony of New Amsterdam to the north. In November 1654 Dirck Wittepaart and a partner had received permission from Amsterdam authorities to sail their ship *Wittepaart* to Africa and take on human cargo for the slave trade. (This ship is not to be confused with an earlier ship of the same name that Wittepaart had previously sold to Overzee and Yardley.) In September 1655 the vessel docked in New Amsterdam and deposited 391 traumatized men, women, and children into slave pens. Residents of the city could not help but note the vessel's arrival: the overwhelming stench of human waste emanating from the hold permeated the whole harbor. Sixty-four of the total 455 persons wedged in the hold of the ship had perished between the West African port of Loango, in the Kongo-Angola region, and New Amsterdam.[43]

The *Wittepaart* was the first ship to dock at the Dutch seaport for the express purpose of selling slaves. Soon after the ship arrived, the city council expressed alarm—not at the savagery of the slave trade, but at the quick sale of people who had "been transported and carried hence without the Hon'ble Company or the inhabitants of this province having derived any revenue or benefit therefrom." The result was "An Ordinance Imposing a Duty on Exported Slaves," New Amsterdam's first tax on the sale of human beings.[44]

Among the buyers who paid the extraordinarily large sum of 1,200 florins (on average) for each captive was Virginia merchant Edmund Scarborough, who regularly traded between the Chesapeake and New Amsterdam. Scarborough was Virginia's equivalent of Maryland's Thomas Cornwaleys: a New World planter-entrepreneur possessed of many thousands of acres (in Scarborough's case, 30,000 on Virginia's Eastern Shore) who combined political influence with a savvy business sense and unapologetic aggression toward any Indians he considered threatening to his enterprises. In April 1651 Scarborough had rallied his neighbors with reckless bravado, formed his own militia, and conducted an unprovoked attack on a band of Eastern Shore Pocomoke with whom the English were at peace. The massacre horrified Virginia authorities struggling to coexist with the many Indians who literally surrounded them.[45]

Among his purchase of forty-one men and women at New Amsterdam, Scarborough reserved at least some for his own large salt works, manned eventually by thirty enslaved laborers. Some of the other slaves would go to his daughters, Tabitha, age eighteen (and recently married), and Matilda, twelve. The Africans whom Scarborough bought had remained in Manhattan for seven months after their arrival; a one-month voyage to Virginia would have them arriving in March 1656. Sure enough, on the 27th of that month, Scarborough's daughters received a patent of 3,500 acres of land in Northampton County, Virginia, as a routine reward for transporting into the colony seventy laborers.[46]

Sometime during that month, Antonio also arrived on Symon Overzee's plantation. The timing of Antonio's arrival, coincident with the arrival of the Scarborough slaves, and the active trade relations among a group that included Scarborough and Overzee suggest that the enslaved man had been on board the *Wittepaart*. And the owner of the vessel was almost certainly the same captain who had piloted the ship of the same name that Overzee and Yeardley bought in 1650, revealing another connection between Overzee and the slaves brought south to the Chesapeake by Scarborough.

The three-hundred-day voyage of the Dutch slave ship *Wittepaart* originated in Texel, the Netherlands, in November 1654 and took on slaves in Loango, stopping along the way in St. Helena before arriving at New Amsterdam on September 15, 1655. Yet even this minimal information opens a wider window onto Antonio's life in Kongo-Angola and the Chesapeake.

Slave traders prized young men trained as soldiers, men healthy and strong enough to withstand the horrific Middle Passage and attract buyers of sturdy field workers, so there is a strong likelihood that Antonio's previous life had involved some form of military service for his own tribal group. Like many other persons captured in this region of West Africa in the mid-seventeenth century, Antonio might have hailed from the Ubangi River and learned the trades of metalworking or pottery-making. Or he might have mined for gold, iron, or copper or made a living as a fisherman. This last kind of job would have provided him with the skills to survive for weeks at a time in the dense latticework of creeks and rivers on Maryland's Western Shore, as he would do toward the end of his captivity.

There is a strong likelihood, too, that civil unrest in Africa had propelled Antonio into slavery. During the 1650s the Kongo-Angola region witnessed a bloody competition among the English, French, and Dutch to displace Portuguese traders and missionaries. Antonio might have been sold by his kin or convicted for a crime; but more likely he was the victim of a raid that was merely a pretext for kidnapping human beings. Many captives from this area were given Portuguese names (such as his). And, significantly, a considerable number were Christian, testifying to the labors of Catholic missionaries in that part of Africa since the latter part of the fifteenth century and to the decision among certain Kongo leaders to embrace the new faith on behalf of themselves and their people.[47]

Antonio belonged to one of the many dozens, even hundreds, of cultural groups throughout this region of West Central Africa, and he spoke a language that was not understood by his European captors or even, probably, by many of his fellow captives. On board the *Wittepaart* he had become black and African—crude labels deployed by the white captain and crew to distinguish themselves from people bound for sale. In what was a floating prison–*cum*–torture chamber, the more than four hundred men, women, and children had been packed tightly, forced to lie together in their own urine, excrement, blood, and vomit. The ordeal sometimes served to forge rudimentary social bonds among people who had no preexisting connections apart from the hue of their skin and a vulnerability to warriors and slave traders in their homelands. Shipboard rebellions were neither uncommon nor often successful; but they led to pidgin languages that enabled the captives to transcend their diverse ethnic identities, thus welding together disparate peoples in opposition to white men. More often, however, the Middle Passage devastated those Africans who survived it, stripping them of hope and any sense of belonging or protection. The routine rape of women captives and the torture, dismemberment, and murder of troublemakers were institutionalized forms of terror practiced by captains, strategies calculated to turn soldiers and freeborn men and women into slaves. The stench that emanated from the *Wittepaart* in New Amsterdam harbor gave fulsome expression to the combined horrors suffered by the captives.[48]

By the time he was forced onto Symon Overzee's plantation, Antonio had endured the disintegration of a number of communities of which he was a part—in his homeland, on the forced march to the sea, aboard the slaver, during the seven cold months in New Amsterdam, and, finally, on Scarborough's ship bound for the Chesapeake. And now in Maryland, Overzee and Chandler were trying to force Antonio to till the soil, a task reserved for women in his homeland and one avoided by all English colonists who could afford to do so. At St. John's, he refused to bend to the will of his captors; he ran away.[49]

Tobacco was a labor-intensive crop that required heavy hoeing, stoop labor, and a timely harvest. Mid-seventeenth-century Chesapeake planters experimented with various kinds of workers whose productivity could be regulated by some combination of kinship obligation, physical force, and legal sanction. The system admitted few tangible incentives that would have prompted field hands to toil willingly in the heat and humidity of midsummer. Most landowners therefore considered a matrix of factors in their search for a compliant labor force—a suitable combination of bound and free, young and old, male and female, English, Indian, and African workers. Overzee, Chandler, and other Chesapeake planters had little choice but to use trial and error to cobble together workforces consisting of young immigrants from Europe, mostly England; forced immigrants from Africa; Indians of enemy tribes; and nearby poor but independent householders. Some of these workers toiled as indentured servants, others as wage earners, sharecroppers, or renters. Some Indians and Africans were held as slaves. Yet it was difficult to correlate a specific ethnic group, or a specific skin color, with a specific legal status.[50]

African workers were relatively rare in the Chesapeake during these years; they were expensive to buy, and they were likely to fall ill and die soon after enslavement there, making an investment in them a risky venture indeed. In 1650 the region was home to only 1,700 persons of African descent (about 10 percent of the total population), some of them servants, some of them free, and others enslaved. Passengers aboard the *Ark,* the ship that had deposited Maryland's original settlers on the continent in 1634, included Mathias de Sousa, an indentured servant of African-Portuguese descent; within four years of his arrival in the colony he had become free, a mariner and a fur trader, and, remarkably (in 1642), a member of the colonial assembly of freemen. Those planters leading the way by introducing enslaved Africans into their workforces were mainly Dutch merchants. Signaling their great wealth, Francis Yeardley, Symon Overzee, and Job Chandler all used enslaved laborers on their Maryland plantations at a time when most of their neighbors were relying on white indentured servants. (Among Overzee's slaves were two Indian youths, a boy and a girl.) Some owners exploited Africans for the skills they had acquired in their homeland: Edmund Scarborough later wrote that his enslaved "Angolas" knew how to work metals, make pots, weave mats and clothing, and rotate crops. Granted some control over their own energies, they chose to raise pigs, sheep, and chickens.[51]

At least two other persons of African descent worked on Overzee's St. John's plantation, including the anonymous black woman, perhaps a domestic, who remained in the quartering house and "never stird out" the day Antonio was killed. She remains an enigma: Was she indifferent to, contemptuous of, Antonio? Overwhelmed with pity but fearful for her own safety? John Babtista, described in Maryland court records as "A moore of Barbary," also worked for Overzee as a servant in Virginia in the late 1640s, perhaps as a way to repay a debt for some linen that he owed Overzee's father. Babtista's name was his insurance policy at a time when Christian converts could still distinguish themselves from most enslaved Africans. Symon sold the remaining time on this man's contract to another planter, who tried to hold him against his will past his indenture. The English-speaking Babtista sued, left his new master, and emigrated from Virginia to Maryland, where he began working as a servant for the younger Overzee again. Overzee granted Babtista his freedom on March 1, 1656, just a few weeks before Antonio arrived at St. John's, though this act failed to resolve either Babtista's legal status or the compensation due him; both matters remained in litigation for years. Still, persons of African descent occupied a variety of legal statuses in mid-seventeenth-century Maryland.[52]

Throughout this period European travel writers showed great interest in the Chesapeake's Africans and Indians alike, in some cases generalizing about particular groups' distinctive physical appearance and reproductive potential. Yet in separating friend from foe and identifying potential workers, English colonists found themselves forced to deal in local realities, not in theoretical or ideological abstractions. These local realities, moreover, worked to the Indians' advantage—and worked against Africans.

Together with other planters, Overzee desperately needed compliant laborers, but he was not so foolish to think that dark-skinned, non-English-speaking, pagan Natives afforded a limitless reservoir of tobacco hands. The Susquehannock held out little promise as field laborers, bound or otherwise. As long as the beaver trade was viable, Indians were trading partners and diplomatic allies; but even with the rise of tobacco, and the ruthless efficiency with which the Westo captured and enslaved weaker groups, planters used discretion in exploiting Indians as workers. Indians tended to vanish into the forests or serve as a provocation to their countrymen to kill English masters. Overzee directed an enslaved Indian, probably the youth he owned, to bind Antonio right before he whipped him. Planters were willing to traffic in a young male Indian slave or two at a time, but adults could fetch higher prices in the Caribbean. In its relatively weak and defenseless state, then, Maryland could not afford to aggravate either the Piscataway or the Susquehannock by enslaving as many local Natives as its labor-intensive staple-crop economy might require.[53]

The English remained ambivalent about the roles and uses of Indians in general: Were they to be hounded as heathens or cultivated as political allies? Poet Ebenezer Cook expressed the confusion by referring to Indians in general as "courteous devils." Most Natives eschewed what the English considered decent clothing, and the warriors made themselves look fearsome by painting their faces red, green, white, and black. Noting their strange appearance, their "black, long and harsh hair," and bizarre tattoos, another contemporary Marylander, George Alsop, highlighted their odd and frightful practices: "Singing (or rather howling out) . . . bellowing in a strange and confused manner," they remained terrifying creatures, a people of devil worshippers, "strange to behold."[54]

At the same time, Indians maintained powerful military and political confederations and eagerly embraced trade, activities the English appreciated. Indeed, noted Alsop, "where they [Indians] spy profit sailing towards them with the wings of a prosperous gale, there they become much familiar" to the English. In addition, Francis Yeardley's scheme for a productive colony of Indians testified to his confidence that they could be converted from pagan hunters to sedentary Christian farmers. At times it even seemed as if Indian allies were the least of the colony's enemies. Virginia Protestants now living in Maryland and chafing under the requirement that they take an oath of allegiance to the Calverts charged that Indians "judged to be heathen" in fact "exceeded in kindness, in courtesies, in love, and mercy, unto them," than those "mad, rash rulers of Mariland." Various ethnic and political identities existed only in relation to one another.[55]

Indian men proved useful as hirelings, and they welcomed payment for hunting wolves; harvesting the rich bounty of the Chesapeake—blue crabs and terrapins, deer, fish, and fowl; tracking down cattle and hogs; retrieving criminals and runaway workers; and (depending on their point of

origin) trafficking in slaves. The Pangayo Indian who reported to Overzee on Antonio's whereabouts lived in Zachaia Swamp, east of Portobacco
Creek. He no doubt counted on some kind of reward for the information.
For colonists, the issue of arming Indians presented a dilemma: whether to
supply "friend" Indians with guns and ammunition so that they could hunt
and protect the English from "enemy" Indians, or whether to deny these
ostensible friends firearms on the theory that all Indians were dangerous.
In general, though, Maryland Natives tried to keep their distance from the
colonists in both cultural and physical terms; the Piscataway, for example,
stayed to themselves in a village in the northwestern part of the colony.[56]

As they set about establishing their Maryland plantations, Chandler and
Overzee pondered the best way to manage workers set to any number of
tasks that were invariably some combination of disagreeable, difficult, and
unfamiliar. At St. John's between 1650 and 1658, Overzee employed at
least twelve indentured servants, two sharecroppers, a renter, four slaves (Indian and African), and four builder-carpenters (and probably many more
of each of these groups). His heedless treatment of Antonio indicates that
he was on his way to owning more slaves, which rich men did because they
could afford to do so. Slave owning was an unpredictable investment: high
mortality rates among "unseasoned" slaves (those imported directly from
Africa, without exposure to the brutality and New World diseases characteristic of bondage in the Caribbean) could overshadow their potential as
long-term bound workers, and only the wealthiest landowners could afford
to take this risk. Overzee knew he would never find enough workers to
satisfy St. John's demand, for the land was almost limitless, and the hands
necessary to chop down trees, construct fences and dwellings, and plant
and harvest crops were scarce.[57]

The mid-1650s posed special challenges for planter colonists in Maryland;
years of political and military conflict in their homeland had taken a toll on
the supply of young English indentured servants. By this time a chronic labor shortage had become acute, the result of Maryland's poor reputation as
a settlement and a workplace. Large numbers of servants contracted malaria,
diphtheria, or typhoid during the deadly summer "seasoning time" (when
newcomers either succumbed to or survived New World diseases) soon after
their arrival. In the fields they took their lives in their hands, ever on the watch
for Indian enemies and Virginia raiders alike. Some stumps they girdled, in
the Indian manner, a method that killed the trees and allowed daylight to
stream through the branches onto the rows of tobacco or below; but other

trees they had to chop down for lumber for fences, houses, and outbuildings. Coming from a place where forests were the province of gentleman hunters, and where ordinary folk collected firewood from the "lops" on the ground, these English folk had no experience felling trees, nor did they know which implement to use—hatchet or saw or felling ax, pick, or small ax—or how to use it. Young men toiling in the forests wounded themselves or expired, crushed under falling trees. The enforced pace of the February-to-December tobacco cycle of planting, hoeing, weeding, worming, harvesting, and processing left all hands exhausted, suffering from sunburn and mosquito and snake bites. Consumption of the beverage of choice—alcohol in the form of hard cider—meant that most stumbled through the forests in a sweat-soaked haze throughout the summer and early fall. Sundown brought only more work for the famished: the pounding of corn into hominy, a task that demanded considerable time and upper body strength.[58]

Women servants employed in the fields felt especially aggrieved. For English women, such labor outside of harvest time carried a stigma associated with, in the words of one of Overzee's neighbors, "wenches that are Nasty, beastly, and not fit to be employed in housewifely tasks." A Maryland man of modest means named John Nicholls contracted with Thomas Cornwaleys and placed his daughter Hester in Cornwaleys's household, anticipating that the great man's wife would train the ten-year-old to be a lady's maid. Instead, Cornwaleys deemed the girl "a Rude Raw ill bred Childe" and put her to work in the fields. Mortified, Nicholls petitioned the court that she "may not be mad[e] a Slave a tearme soe scandalous that if admitted to be the Condition or title of the Apprentices of this Province will be soe destructive as noe free borne Christians will ever be induced to come over as servants." After a trial, the jury ruled in Nicholls's favor, though it is unclear whether their chief concern was the welfare and reputation of little Hester or the public-relations disaster that her continued "enslavement" would entail. Cornwaleys railed against the "weake and Ignorant" members of the jury, his social inferiors; the master of twenty servants, he claimed he had taken in the girl, "soe useless a Servant," only as a matter of charity.[59]

At the same time, masters did not enjoy full license to push indentured servants to the limits of human endurance the way they could with slaves. In the Chesapeake, planters had to abide by traditional English custom and give English workers the right to rest on the Sabbath and a half day on Saturday. Courts considered indentured servants' demands for adequate amounts of English food and drink to be legitimate and responded accordingly when young men and women were bold enough to press their claims with legal authorities. Indeed, as English citizens, even these downtrodden workers had access to the judicial system to varying degrees. At least some brave servants and concerned neighbors alike were willing to file grievances in county courts alleging "hard usage" on the part of a master or mistress; their boldness suggests that such rights were a brake on unbridled "corrective" violence. Those grievances yield a catalog of abuses the justices considered unacceptable according to English standards: young men and women starved nigh unto death, deprived of adequate clothing, beaten and mutilated, their wounds or illnesses left untreated to the point where, in the words of the court, "the voyce of the People Crieth shame."[60]

To many masters, the need to grow great quantities of tobacco seemed at odds with a customary judicial system that exerted some control over the deployment and discipline of English indentured servants. Seeking to provide some measure of protection to these young people, the Maryland assembly tried to systematize the terms of servants who arrived without prearranged indentures: those twenty years and older would serve four years; those between twelve and sixteen, seven years; and those younger than twelve, until they were twenty-one. Also, throughout most of the seventeenth century servants could count on receiving "freedom dues" at the end of their terms; for the men, that meant a cloth suit, canvas drawers, shoes, socks, hat or cap, felling ax and weeding hoe, two shirts, and corn and for the women, clothing, corn, and 40 shillings in cash or goods. Until 1682 the men were additionally entitled to fifty acres of land, but only if they could locate a parcel for sale and afford to hire a surveyor. The labor turnover that flowed from the limited terms of servants meant that masters had constantly to replenish their workforces.[61]

These conditions lessened the value of indentured servants in the eyes of their masters and bolstered the case for using slaves—at least among those men who could afford to buy them. By the time Symon Overzee became a planter, slavery had been a feature of New World colonization for more than a century; his father might have had a direct hand in the slave trade linking Angola to the sugar colony of Pernambuco, Brazil, which the Dutch had wrested from the Portuguese in 1630. And Overzee only had to look to the example set by his wealthy neighbors to understand which forms of labor were most cost-effective in the long run.[62]

Nevertheless, local politics played out in the short run and at times interfered with the grand designs of the powerful. Increasingly, wealthy planters aimed to use more enslaved workers outside the reach of English law and fewer rebellious indentured servants bent on using the law to their own advantage. Yet even men and women freed from indentured service could aggravate their former masters and mistresses in a way that diluted the everyday power of the elite. In the 1650s Maryland still offered relative promise for householders of modest means. In contrast to Virginia, where elites early wielded unchecked power, through the 1650s the Calverts' colony could boast at least modest rates of upward mobility. Most former servants either entered the ranks of the small landowning class or readily found jobs as sharecroppers or, if skilled in a trade, wage earners. They were required to be neither wealthy nor literate to fill the large number of local offices that maintained civil order in the beleaguered colony.[63]

For example, both Daniel Clocker and his wife, Mary, rose from servitude to become respected members of Maryland society. A carpenter, Daniel had once served Thomas Cornwaleys. Mary's first husband had freed her by buying the time remaining on her indenture from her mistress. Former servants such as the Clockers might embrace the perquisites of freedom and in the process refuse to defer to their social betters, a possibility that Symon Overzee would soon realize to his sorrow. English servants were troublesome workers, and as they aged and became free, they remained troublesome to their former masters and mistresses.[64]

———————

Owners need not fear that their slaves might one day challenge them in court. Yet the management of enslaved men and women, at once so valuable and so vulnerable, could still prove exceedingly difficult, as Overzee well understood from his frustrated attempts to monitor Antonio's labor and even his whereabouts.

Why Overzee killed Antonio remains a mystery. Raised in a privileged urban household, Overzee as a youth presumably neither witnessed nor participated in the beating to death of a recalcitrant worker. Yet carving a plantation out of the forests of Maryland was an inherently corrupting enterprise, demanding varying degrees of ruthlessness from all who engaged in it. Moreover, in 1656 political pressures on Overzee were intensifying all around. A recent precipitous decline in the price of Dutch East India stock ruined a large number of shareholders, and Overzee and his father might have been among them. Closer to home, Symon had lost several of his most influential patrons, including William Lewis, executed for his role in the Battle of Great Severn, and Francis Yeardley, who died in 1655. Two years later Overzee's mother-in-law, Sarah Yeardley, also died. Meanwhile, the English and Dutch had entered into yet another naval war, a conflict that reverberated throughout the colonies. New Amsterdam officials were aggressively pressing their claims in the Delaware Bay region, and their designs reached deep into Maryland territory. As an informal emissary of Dutch imperialists, Symon Overzee must have been keenly aware of his own shaky political status in the English colony.[65]

Or perhaps these larger issues were irrelevant. Perhaps for a young rich man used to getting his way, Antonio's violent resistance was just too much to bear. Or Sarah Overzee's role in the killing might have indicated tensions between husband and wife. Did one or both of them judge her decision to chain Antonio for "some misdemeanor" to be inappropriate—either because it was not within her purview to discipline a slave or because her husband had delegated to her a responsibility she found distasteful? Did his wife's hand in this awful business reflect poorly on Overzee as a master and a husband? Certainly, Antonio posed a real threat to the couple: he was a volatile and unpredictable stranger. To keep him at St. John's was to fracture whatever well-ordered household the couple hoped to create or maintain.

Quite aside from the circumstances surrounding Antonio's death, the trial turned out to be a staged performance among Maryland elites competing among themselves for land, labor, and political influence. Developments during the intervening months before the public testimony of servant Hannah Littleworth and hired worker William Hewes offer clues as to why and when the proceeding occurred and what it meant. Overzee continued to haul his debtors into court, as Maryland went through yet another period of political turmoil. In July 1656 the disaffected Puritan migrants from Virginia managed to wrangle an appointment as governor for Josias Fendall, a Protestant ally of William Stone and a veteran of the Battle of Great Severn. Fendall immediately antagonized powerful men in the colony, including those who claimed that God would "sooner condemn a man for killing a Negro or an Indian than for killing Captain Fendall." Thomas Gerrard, the lord of St. Clement's Manor, now for some reason switched his allegiance and challenged the Calverts and the new governor Fendall.[66]

During these months the Provincial Court considered a number of dramatic cases involving the selling, buying, "entertaining," and punishing of servants, including high-profile trials of abusive masters. Late summer and early fall brought sensational proceedings against John Dandy, charged with murdering Henry Gouge. The body of Gouge, a twenty-year-old servant, had been found naked, lying facedown in a creek, in July 1657. One witness recalled that when he saw the corpse being dragged out of the water, Dandy had remarked "that he [Dandy] Should come into a great Deale of trouble about this boy." Testimony from Dandy's neighbors and other servants revealed that Gouge had endured beatings for years; he suffered from a head wound and from bruised and bloody ears that made one witness wonder whether "the ratts [had eaten] off his Eares." If nothing else, the Dandy case showed that authorities could act with dispatch if inclined to do so: Gouge's body was found on July 7, and Dandy was jailed within a month. The trial began on September 23, and Dandy was hanged two weeks later.[67]

Around this time Symon Overzee evinced a new and striking legal vulnerability to both his debtors and creditors, a remarkable array of men and women, some of them former servants using the law to advance their claims and embarrass their social betters. Over the next two years he would become a litigant in at least ninety cases. On March 25, 1658, he was probably taken aback when the attorney for the estate of one of his deceased hirelings, carpenter John Crabtree, not only sued him for unpaid wages, but also read a statement that the carpenter had written several years before. (He had died in 1655.) Overzee had just appeared in court to sue five of his own debtors, but in a turnaround he now found himself forced to listen to Crabtree's words, which were both apologetic and defiant. Crabtree had written, "Sir you know I have bene a great while without my pay, wch hath bene a great hinderance to mee in settling my family." He continued, "Therefore I hope I shall bee noe longer delayed: for I doe not love trouble if I can avoid it." Yet three years later Overzee still had not settled.[68]

In April the court ruled that Overzee and Chandler, despite their alleged undermining of the local sheriff charged with managing the estate of their deceased mother-in-law, did in fact possess the right to Francis Yeardley's holdings because they were the assignees of Yeardley's widow. The court's decision opened the way for Yeardley's creditors to sue the estate, and one person immediately came forward. After a four-year absence, a newly married Thomas Cornwaleys had returned to Maryland from England. Putting his affairs in order, he immediately filed a suit charging that he had paid Yeardley and his Indian interpreter Nathaniel Batt 5,000 pounds of tobacco in December 1653 in exchange for the delivery of two enslaved Indian youths, but did not receive them when he went to fetch them several months later.

Cornwaleys demanded his due from Yeardley's estate and went on to level charges against both Chandler and Overzee, whom he believed conspired to move the most valuable property, its enslaved laborers, off the plantation before creditors could stake their claims. By this time Cornwaleys had reestablished himself in Maryland, now as attorney general and second in command to the governor, and had resumed his place as a burgess, a provincial judge, and an active litigant suing his many debtors.[69]

At this point Overzee began to play a more active role in local governance, as indicated by his service as foreman of two juries in late April 1658. The next month Governor Fendall was presiding over the Provincial Court when Overzee was appointed commissioner for St. Mary's County, reciting the oath, "You shall doe equall right, to the poore, as to the rich, to the best of yor Cunning, witt, & power, & after the presedents & Customes of this province, & Acts of Assembly thereof made." Another justice appointed at this time was an ambitious newcomer named William Barton.[70]

Overzee and Chandler scrambled to counter Cornwaleys's suit and his allegation that the enslaved workers were still in the two men's possession, presumably at Overzee's St. John's plantation. In September Chandler appeared in court to suggest that Cornwaleys's attorney had had plenty of time to make a claim on behalf of his client, but failed to do so. During the court session of October 5–7, Chandler and Overzee could not miss the signs that together, for the first time in their careers, they were fair game for a host of litigants, even though Chandler was currently sitting as a justice with Governor Fendall, Philip Calvert, and former governor William Stone. The governor by this time had many bitter enemies. On October 5 Thomas Gerrard, a member of the council and the lord of St. Clement's Manor, denounced Fendall; as a group the justices in turn accused Gerrard of engaging in drunken and lewd behavior and slandering his fellow councilors, including Chandler.[71]

Suddenly, Overzee's legal difficulties were overshadowed by another, more profound source of woe. Within a few days of this court session, Overzee's twenty-seven-year-old wife, Sarah, died in childbirth, and shortly thereafter, in a matter of hours or a couple of days, so did the couple's newborn baby. On Sunday morning, October 9, as Sarah Overzee's body was being carried to the church to be buried, two workers sought to take advantage of the household's distress. The hired wet-nurse for the baby, Mary Clocker, together with Mary Williams, the wife of one of Overzee's sharecroppers, began to ransack the bedchamber of the deceased woman.

Over the next few days the two Marys carried off an astounding amount of staples and goods, including soap, laces, clothing, linens, thread, buttons, handkerchiefs, and pecks of corn, not neglecting to throw in a pair of tweezers in their haste. Subsequent testimony revealed that Job Chandler, visiting or residing upstairs in the loft of the house that Sunday, had given Mary Williams the storehouse keys. She told him that she needed some spices to add to a pudding she was making, but instead she used the keys to open Sarah Overzee's "great Dutch trunk." She and Clocker hid a large, loot-filled pillowcase in a tree in the forest; however, before the goods could be fenced by Clocker's son Thomas Courtney, the cache was discovered by two children. By early November (between the October and December court sessions), witnesses were already giving depositions in preparation for a trial against Williams, Clocker, and Courtney.[72]

If Overzee and Chandler thought that Cornwaleys would let slide a relatively modest case involving 5,000 pounds of tobacco, or take pity on Overzee because of the recent loss of his wife, they were mistaken. On the first day of December, Cornwaleys appeared in court to offer a detailed chronology of the events of four and a half years before, when he contracted with Yeardley and Batt for the two enslaved Indians. He charged that the widow Yeardley hatched the plot when she heard that he was on his way back to Virginia from England; presumably, she urged her sons-in-law to take a sloop and remove "all the visible Estate of th sd Yardley," including "the sd negro's." Cornwaleys wanted not just his money back, but also answers: Who hired or borrowed the sloop for this venture? Were the crewmen engaged by the month? Who fed them? The court ordered that the two defendants appear at the next session and "putt in their answers upon oath."[73]

It is here that Antonio makes his first appearance in the existing court records, for the following day, December 2, William Barton, fifty-three years old and a landowner residing at St. Clement's Manor, "informe[d] the Court agst Mr Symon Ouerzee, for that the sd Ouerzee correcting his negro seruant the sd negro dyed under his sd correction." Entered into the record were the depositions of Littleworth and Hewes, taken on November 27, indicating that the case had been set in motion even before Barton lodged the formal charges.[74]

Barton had come to Maryland in 1654 from England with his wife and two children, and within just a few years he had done well for himself. He fought in the Battle of Great Severn, winning the favor of Lord Baltimore, and bought a freehold at St. Clements, which by this time had fallen on hard times in the absence of viable tenants. Though Barton arrived in Maryland as a mariner with no title, within a decade he was calling himself a "gentleman" and living in "Barton's Hall." Unlike most of the other St. Clement's freeholders, who eschewed public service, Barton embraced the political life of the manor and the county. Beginning in 1655, he served as a justice for St. Mary's County, and he would soon be named bailiff of St. Clement's. For his start on the road to economic independence and political respectability, Barton owed a debt to Thomas Gerrard, the contentious lord of St. Clement's Manor, who by this time had developed a deep hatred toward both Governor Fendall and Job Chandler.[75]

In his capacity as justice of the peace, Barton no doubt had the right to offer a presentment against a defendant, but the question remains why he did so. Symon Overzee had just recently lost his wife, and the death of Antonio was more than two years in the past. Still, it is difficult to ignore the timing of the case, coming as it did in the middle of Cornwaleys's suit against Overzee and Chandler and Thomas Gerrard's feud with Fendall, Chandler, and the other councilors. In "presenting" the case against Overzee, Barton could ingratiate himself with his patron, Gerrard, and with Cornwaleys, both of whom had a vested interest in seeing Chandler and Overzee humbled.

It is therefore likely that the trial over Antonio's death was largely—if not purely—a piece of political theater meant to rankle Overzee. No one was claiming that Antonio was one of the pilfered Yeardley slaves. More likely, Antonio was a proxy for the group ultimately disposed of by Overzee. Furthermore, by forcing the Dutch planter to stand trial for the death of Antonio, Cornwaleys could highlight his own reputation as a killer; he could claim that when *he* killed men, it was Indians or other enemies of Maryland, not a man bound to a ladder, with his hands tied above him.

At the next court session, on February 24, 1659, the manslaughter trial was not exactly perfunctory, but it did not appear to be a serious attempt to hold Overzee to account for his role in the death of Antonio. At that session Chandler tried his best to absolve his brother-in-law of the charge of undue "correction," ignoring the particular circumstances surrounding the torture of the enslaved man. Moreover, the court failed to call one of the material eyewitnesses, Mathew Stone, despite its announced intention to do so.

Though acquitted, Overzee was not yet free and clear. The same day the jury rendered its Ignoramus verdict in the manslaughter case, Cornwaleys once again demanded satisfaction from the brothers-in-law. Chandler claimed that he had never seen in writing the allegations against him and asked for more time, which the court granted. This request marked a brief interlude between Chandler and Overzee's trial and the impaneling of a jury in yet another major case: the trial of Mary Clocker and John and Mary Williams for theft and Thomas Courtney as accessory after the fact.[76]

This trial played out like a melodrama, with a large cast and a riveting narrative: the deceased mother and child, their bodies barely cold in the ground; the anguished John Williams professing ignorance of his wife's alleged crime; the tale of the two children coming upon the pillowcase in the hollow of a tree; and the duplicitous Mary Clocker, whose tragically brief service as wet-nurse only heightened the suspicions against her. Mary Williams threw herself on the mercy of the court and confessed, adding details about the frantic moment when she and Clocker were standing in the bedchamber where Mistress Overzee had just expired, throwing as much stuff as they could in bags and looking over their shoulder in case Job Chandler should enter the room. Williams told the court that she worried that someone would recognize and identify the goods, to which the other Mary retorted, "Hang him (as she conceaves Mr. Overzee) rather than ever hee shall have them, I will burne them, & further sayd shee would bury them in a Case in the Grownd." Williams also testified that Clocker said that Overzee already had enough linens—"there were enough about the howse"—and would not miss what she took.[77]

As Clocker, Williams, and Courtney's trial proceeded, Chandler prepared to counter Cornwaleys's allegations against him and Overzee. On Monday, February 28, Chandler finally responded to Cornwaleys's charges about the removal of the Yeardley slaves, declaring that he "utterly denyeth" all of them and reminding listeners of his own loyal service to the Calverts at the Battle of Great Severn (a point unrelated to the case at hand, as the jury may have noted). He claimed that Yeardley's assets were not removed until a year and a half after their owner's death, giving the plaintiff plenty of time to press his case. Chandler also argued that the property in question had originally belonged to Sarah Yeardley and remained hers during the course of the marriage; therefore, Cornwaleys had no claim on the estate while she was alive. As her sons-in-law, he (Chandler) and Overzee were now the rightful heirs of all that remained. Overzee spoke next and disputed the claim that he was guilty of "ayding & assisting to the exportation of the Estate of Col Yeardley." Overzee admitted that he had hired a sloop at the request of Sarah Yeardley—she wanted the Portobacco crop delivered to her in Virginia—and that at some point the boat "by distresse of weather, putt in here att St. Maries" at his own house while he was absent. He said the cargo included "Corn, Tob[acco] & Negroes," but denied that he had stolen the property from the disputed estate.[78]

Overzee had just finished defending himself when he faced a fresh round of accusations: Daniel Clocker claimed that Overzee was now reneging on a promise that, in the event Mary Clocker was found guilty and brought "upon the stage" (i.e., the gallows), the planter would use his influence to spare her life in return for 3,000 pounds of tobacco that Clocker would pay him. Certainly, the former servant showed a great deal of nerve in suing the victim of his wife's criminal behavior. Overzee countered that Clocker possessed "an ill intent [acting] out of mere malice & spleen."[79]

March brought a resolution to three cases. Overzee countersued Cornwaleys for a two-year-old debt of 3,370 pounds of tobacco and won at trial, with his attorney, Philip Land, sitting on the jury. In the suit Cornwaleys brought against Overzee and Chandler, the court ordered the two defendants to repay debts owed by Yeardley and to compensate the plaintiff with 5,000 pounds of tobacco per a December 1653 agreement between Francis Yeardley and Cornwaleys. Governor Fendall declared John and Mary Williams and Mary Clocker guilty and sentenced them to hang, and he ordered that Thomas Courtney receive thirty lashes with the whip. However, the next day the governor spared Clocker and the Williamses from the hangman's noose. In observance of the death of Oliver Cromwell (in September of the previous year) and the rise of his son Richard to the Lord Protectorate of England, Fendall pardoned all those recently convicted of capital crimes.[80]

Within a month Overzee was back in court, this time battling two of his former employees: Hugh Bevins, a carpenter, and John Williams, recently spared from execution, both claiming Overzee owed them money. On April 25 the planter requested a jury trial to resolve the charges that Daniel Clocker brought against him; this jury, like the one that had decided his fate in the manslaughter trial, came back with a verdict of Ignoramus, absolving Overzee of defrauding Clocker of 3,000 pounds of tobacco. After a few months, however, Clocker returned, this time to hold Chandler (presumably as Overzee's agent) accountable for failing to pay the full amount due him for making Mrs. Overzee's coffin and, incredibly, due his wife for delivering Mrs. Overzee of her child and nursing her baby. Clocker complained that Mary had forfeited a considerable share of her income by attending to the deceased during the height of the busy dairying season, failing to mention that his wife had been convicted of ransacking the dead woman's bedchamber. Still, the court awarded Clocker a judgment of 500 pounds of tobacco, bringing to a close the former servant's effort (most likely successful) to aggravate both great men, Overzee and Chandler.[81]

From late spring through the fall, Overzee and Chandler jointly began to dispose of some of their holdings, renting out and signing over land on Portobacco Creek and elsewhere. Like Thomas Gerrard, they were anxious about the shortage of both servants and tenants and hoping to raise some cash from the sale of land. Chandler apparently was putting his financial and legal affairs in order; in August he drew up his will, listing as executors "brother-in-law Symon Overzee, friend & brother" and William Stone.[82]

By September 1659 Overzee had remarried, this time to twenty-five-year-old Elizabeth Willoughby, who, like his first wife, came from a prominent Lower Norfolk County, Virginia, family. At the end of the month the newlyweds entertained some distinguished visitors: Bohemian-born Augustine Herman, one of Overzee's trading partners, and another man, Resolved Waldron. Herman and Waldron had journeyed south in a leaky canoe from New Amsterdam to survey territory. On behalf of Governor Peter Stuyvesant (Herman's brother-in-law), they aimed to assess the viability of English settlements, dispute the original claims made by Lord Baltimore, and demand territorial concessions from Maryland. Making their way south, the two men had crossed multiple shifting boundaries established by competing groups of Indians and Europeans, and encountered a number of fugitive servants eager to escape to, in Herman's words, a "strange nation" rather than serve their allotted time for a master.[83]

Overzee welcomed the travelers to St. John's, and a few days after their arrival, he took them across the creek to Philip Calvert's home, where they pored over maps and argued over the relative merits of claims by the Dutch, French, English, and Swedes. On October 6 Overzee appeared at a session of the Provincial Court to "English" (translate from Dutch into English) the official documents sent by Stuyvesant to Fendall. Predictably, Herman and Waldron failed to receive a sympathetic hearing for their case, which challenged the right of the English to settle anywhere between the Delaware and Chesapeake Bays. At the same time, perhaps remarkably, their host had managed to reclaim—or perhaps maintain—his high standing within Maryland society.[84]

Antonio's killer had rebounded after an intense period of nasty litigation against him over a five-month period from December 1658 through April 1659. Symon Overzee's thick skin had served him well during his multiple interlocking trials—both legal and personal—and he had emerged from this period to relish his role as host of and mediator for the Dutch ambassadors. A Protestant from Rotterdam, he had negotiated the treacherous religious politics in an English colony and retained his standing as a wealthy man of considerable influence in Maryland.

He was, in fact, an emblematic colonial trader. Writing in 1666, George Alsop ruminated on the transformation of Europeans into American colonists. Whether from the effects of the saltiness of the ocean they had once traversed, or "the remote Clyme where they now inhabit," these men became "a more acute people in general, in matters of Trade and Commerce, than in any other place of the world; and by their crafty and sure bargaining, do often overreach the raw and unexperienced merchant." Alsop added, "He that undertakes Merchants employment for Mary-Land, must have more of Knave in him than Fool" and indulge neither his conscience nor his desire to impress other people with his wealth. Rather, he "must be a man of solid confidence," pursuing his economic interest with a grim determination. Unlike his father-in-law, Yeardley, Overzee was no religious visionary; his lodestar was raw power—as a master, within his own household; as a planter, within the colony of Maryland; as a merchant, with trading partners regardless of nationality on the high seas. Accordingly, he probed for and exploited any point of vulnerability among workers and legal and political antagonists. Antonio, for all his suffering, had been only one of the many unfortunates in Maryland to get in the way of Overzee's relentless drive for financial gain.[85]

Overzee had played fast and loose with the law, and he prospered accordingly, though his wealth did not come easily and his authority was not absolute. In the 1650s St. John's plantation was a site of fraught encounters among people of English, Dutch, Angolan, and Pangayo descent, a site where the imperatives of military conquest, labor shortages, and international commerce shaped relations between masters and workers. Yet these relations had not yet crystallized into a rigid system of human bondage. Though Overzee was a wealthy and influential European, he nonetheless could be hauled into court for killing an Angolan. And it is unclear whether the benefits of enslaving men and women outweighed the costs, for that process came at a high price in terms of the master's peace of mind and his sense of well-being and safety for his family.

Slavery resulted from a complex calculus of the security and financial costs and benefits flowing from several different kinds and ethnicities of workers. Most profoundly, the Byzantine politics of New World empire-building revealed that Antonio remained uniquely defenseless, but not because of his skin color or what the English judged to be his strange customs, unintelligible speech patterns, volatile temperament, or recalcitrance in the fields. Rather, within the Atlantic world he lacked an advocate in the form of an Indian confederacy or a European nation-state. Abused workers from places other than Africa could count on countrymen or coreligionists to provide them with at least a minimal amount of protection in the fields, forests, courts, and colonial assembly. Because of their nationality, English servants possessed basic rights (though those rights were often honored in the breach), whereas Indians and Africans were utterly without rights by comparison. Neither group had been party to the generations-long process of negotiation between the English landed gentry and their field workers, a negotiation that had yielded legal protections for impoverished white men and women. Both groups were also subjected to the stereotypes and prejudices of their colonial neighbors. If the English considered Africans exotic, they held essentially the same views of Indians. Both groups of dark-skinned people appeared wild and unpredictable, easily seduced by the devil.[86]

Ultimately, the defining difference between Indians and Africans, no less significant for its obviousness, was that Indians were native to the continent and organized into nations and confederations, political entities that the English understood and, for a while at least, respected. In the colonies Europeans remained suspicious of all Indians, but they did not reify them; rather, some were "friends" and some were "enemies." It was the slave traders in Africa who had to worry about diplomatic and economic relations with various African groups; New World planters had the luxury of contending with persons from that continent as bound workers only, not as diplomats, leaders, or organized bands of warriors.

In time, of course, this relative disparity would change. By the end of the seventeenth century, Maryland colonists saw Indians less as military allies and more as human barriers to the cultivation of their cash crop; in 1695 the governor authorized his council to seize Piscataway land to "occasion a greater quantity of Tobacco to be made." Indians would be forced to supply the land, and Africans the labor, in pursuit of profits.[87]

Overzee and his neighbors understood that they did not have to fear retribution from armed men seeking vengeance for the death of Antonio, for no nation of military consequence could claim the victim as its own. Yet in 1656 the idea that all black people belonged in slavery, a notion that would come to dominate American public life, was hardly a foregone conclusion. In the Atlantic world, variations in languages, religious beliefs, and military prowess were ingredients in a transnational competition for power, and fixed forms of identity were anathema to the competitors. Neither ethnicity nor skin color correlated precisely with a specific legal status; Africans and persons of African descent worked as slaves, but also as freemen and freewomen and as servants, indentured or otherwise. Similarly, some Indians were hirelings and others slaves. Colonists used the word *slave* itself with a remarkable amount of imprecision. In 1638 the word first appeared in official Maryland records, but it was unclear whether the term referred to enslaved Indians or Africans; and it was not unusual for some (such as Hester Nicholls's father) to refer to badly exploited young people as "white slaves" or even "white Negroes." Ethnicity remained a key signifier: Edmund Scarborough described his slaves as Angolans, not Africans; Chesapeake colonists called themselves English, not Europeans; Marylanders allied with the Piscataway, not with Indians.[88]

In fact, the aggravation felt by Overzee and Chandler in disciplining Antonio did not bode well for the expansion of African slavery as an institution. Enslaved laborers were expensive, and if they ran away or died, a master's considerable investment went with them. Perhaps Overzee had received Antonio as a gift from Scarborough or Dirck Wittepaart, the captain of the ship of the same name. If so, Overzee had no financial investment—just his reputation as a master—to protect. At the same time, colonists in general were frightened by the Indians and Africans who cohabited with them; English masters found it difficult enough living among countrymen and -women with whom they shared no kin ties—profane young people who drank, fornicated, shirked work, and stole all manner of goods, the "loathsome, stinking" servants who threatened the moral no less than physical health of entire households. Then, too, Chandler believed that Antonio was fully capable of doing his family harm, certainly an argument against introducing larger numbers of Africans into these isolated plantations. Yet despite the potential danger they represented, recalcitrant enslaved men and women were too valuable as substantial financial investments to incarcerate or execute—in most cases, at least.[89]

Throughout this period Maryland colonists initially found paganism a convenient rationale for enslaving Indians and Africans; hence, the religious conversion of those groups represented a formidable obstacle to solidifying the institution of bondage. In the seventeenth century Catholic missionaries were proselytizing among Kongo-Angola groups, Jesuit priests and men like Francis Yeardley were envisioning the peaceful cohabitation of the English and newly converted Indians, and some Africans and Indians were embracing Christianity on their own. In the eyes of masters and mistresses, such developments might serve to reflect the glory of God and render Africans more familiar to the English, but converting workers did not lessen the demand for their labor. And, of course, in claiming time off for the Sabbath and other ways to participate in the community of Christian believers, enslaved workers would have explicitly challenged their own uniquely subordinate status.

In 1664 a Maryland law stipulated that enslaved workers would retain their status for life, and that the children of white women and enslaved black men would be born as, and remain, slaves. Seven years later colonial legislators wrote into law a new kind of person—the enslaved Christian devoid of all rights—four years after Virginia had passed a similar statute. The colonists in general feared that the process of religious conversion could potentially deprive them of a vast number of laborers, now baptized. Lawmakers shifted from a religious rationale for slavery to a legal one and in the process reassured planters that they could proselytize among their enslaved workers without fear that such apparent solicitude would result in their freedom. Ten years later the colony decreed that the legal status of a child derived from the status of his or her mother, reversing an English precedent. This 1681 law allowed planters to sexually abuse enslaved women and at the same time replenish their own bound labor force with children born to such forced unions. Late-seventeenth-century legal developments thus signaled that justifications for slavery remained fluid, and that neither legal authorities nor planters were deploying the notion of racial differences as a rationale for the subordination of black people. Indeed, the light-skinned offspring of masters and enslaved women mocked the very notion that slavery was created as, or remained, a "racial" institution.

As denizens of an Atlantic world, the English routinely encountered people with "natural" skin colors along a broad spectrum from "white" to "black." In the Chesapeake the English confronted coreligionists darkened by the sun who had so transformed themselves, in the words of a contemporary Virginia colonist, "both in complexion and habite" that they were recognizable only by their speech. The term *mulatto* at this point in colonial American history referred not to a Greek or a Turk or a member of any other particular established ethnic group, but rather to a person who blended national identities and thus lacked one of his or her own. This increasingly lax approach to defining ethnicity culminated in a system of identification that erased national origins altogether in favor of an either-or classification. Soon Europeans would use the word *white* to describe themselves, no matter their nationality or, for that matter, their skin color; and *negro* or *black* would mean "slave," no matter the person's ethnicity.[90]

A number of factors contributed to the codification of African slavery in the New World in the period after Antonio's death. Most Chesapeake planters were neither ideologues nor idealists; they were entrepreneurs bent on making money and thus willing, if reluctantly so, to cohabit with suspect and even menacing peoples. In the late seventeenth century, a shortage of English indentured servants, combined with more favorable mortality rates for seasoned Africans, made slavery more profitable for colonial householders, even those of modest means. And the fact that enslaved women could reproduce the plantation workforce helped to shift the economic calculus from servitude to bondage.

Eventually, planters would justify the system of slavery with theories of racial difference, theories that their colonial forebears had no incentive to create or invoke. British North American slavery evolved from a struggle for empire and a quest for mastery in the fields, and racial prejudice was more of an afterthought than a cause.

———————

At the February 14, 1660, session of the Provincial Court held at St. Clement's Manor, a desperate Gregory Murrell charged that one Nicholas Morris of Virginia was harassing him for nonpayment of a debt. Murrell had already spent 102 days in debtor's jail, but at his trial Morris did not appear, and so the charges were dropped. When Morris subsequently revived his pursuit of Murrell, the defendant hired Symon Overzee as his attorney. This time around it was Overzee who failed to appear at the hearing. The court record reads, cryptically, "The sd Mr Symon Overzee dying (in a manner) sodenly, not making any Will." At the time of his death, in January or February 1660, Overzee was thirty-one years old.[91]

People either die or they do not die. How does a person die "in a manner"? The absence of an inquest suggests that local authorities did not suspect foul play. Perhaps Overzee drowned, or perhaps he succumbed quickly to one of the many fevers or gastrointestinal illnesses that took so many colonists to an early grave.[92]

Within a few months of Overzee's death, Job Chandler died, too. His last appearance at council was on June 4, 1659. The landholdings the brothers-in-law owned jointly (granted by William Lewis) came into the sole possession of Chandler's children, leaving them wealthy indeed.[93]

In early Maryland multiple conflicts divided Indians from Europeans, Susquehannock from Piscataway, English from Dutch, Protestants from Catholics, and workers from masters and mistresses. Regardless of ethnicity or skin color, the hirelings, servants, and enslaved workers of the colony who chopped its trees and tilled its soil were susceptible to harsh working conditions and punishments. Yet the unique forms of torment inflicted on Antonio are not difficult to pinpoint. Antonio's fate was sealed when he was forced on board the *Wittepaart,* for he died thousands of miles from his native land, tortured to death by a man whose language he did not understand, and buried without the funerary rites customary to his people. His country-men and -women had no opportunity to mourn him, redeem him, or seek justice in his name. In the coming years landowning colonists would devise elaborate rationalizations for the brutality that lay at the heart of slavery; but in the late 1650s Symon Overzee and Job Chandler thought or cared little beyond the facts that Antonio appeared to pose a danger to themselves and their families and that he refused to work in the fields.

TWO

BOSTON KING

Self-Interested Patriotism in
Revolutionary-Era South Carolina

In 1798, some fifteen years after the close of the American Revolutionary War, a pious man named Boston King sat down to write his life story. Now thirty-eight years old, he had spent the previous two decades searching for a community of like-minded souls bound by transcendent notions of earthly and spiritual equality. Through the years that quest took King from his native South Carolina to New York City; to Nova Scotia; and then to Sierra Leone, on the west coast of Africa; and from there to London and finally back to Sierra Leone. Born a slave, King freed himself by successfully eluding the treacherous reach of American patriots and British Redcoats alike. As a literate preacher of the Christian gospel, he defied both these combatants, who saw him and other persons of African descent only as laborers to be exploited in pursuit of white people's own divergent self-interests. In South Carolina the Revolution amounted to a contest over who would control the bodies of enslaved men and women, a struggle that turned on realities of military might. In the eyes of King, slaveholders had squandered the truly revolutionary potential of the war, instead indulging in a cynical, if hard-won, celebration of their right to hold onto their own property—the men, women, and children they owned.

King's autobiography described a life's journey toward freedom that was both temporal and spiritual. He had grown up twenty-eight miles from

Charles Town, South Carolina, on the plantation of his owner, prominent patriot Richard Waring. The plantation sat in the heart of the South Carolina Lowcountry, a fertile region where indigo and rice production enriched a few slaveholders but proved deadly to the thousands of enslaved people who toiled there. King's father, a native of Africa, worked as a cattle driver, and his mother, he wrote, labored as a seamstress and also attended "upon those that were sick, having some knowledge of the virtue of herbs, which she learned from the Indians." One day when he was twelve, minding cattle for his master, King underwent the first of a series of religious revelations: "It pleased GOD to alarm me by a remarkable dream. . . . I saw millions of millions of souls; some of whom ascended up to heaven; while others were rejected, and fell into the greatest confusion and despair." A few years later he found himself apprenticed to a builder and "was beat and tortured most cruelly," unable to work for weeks at a time. When the British invaded South Carolina in 1780, he fled to Charles Town, to "throw myself into the hands of the English. They received me readily, and I began to feel the happiness of liberty, of which I knew nothing before." King's brief sojourn in the city was not without its hardships, however: he contracted smallpox, and he "was much grieved at first, to be obliged to leave my friends, and reside among strangers." Later King would express gratitude for "the blessing of the Lord," not the British, for his recovery from smallpox and his deliverance from slavery.[1]

That summer Boston King had joined diverse black fugitives converging in war-ravaged Charles Town. Streaming into the city from the killing fields of the Lowcountry rice kingdom, and from hiding places in remote marshlands, came hundreds of black people seeking refuge and paid labor. On their bodies were inscribed personal histories: scars from beatings and bouts of smallpox, and tribal marks from the Angola, Eboe, Fulow, and Guinea regions of Africa, long-lost homelands. Light-skinned well-dressed native English speakers, ladies' maids and gentlemen's valets, mingled with ragged, dark-skinned speakers of Gullah, a pidgin language. Together they were fleeing from proud patriots, from die-hard Tories, and from men and women whose loyalties bent with the stiff gale winds of war sweeping over the city and its hinterland. Boston King was a seeker after liberty, and in that respect he had imbibed the particular spirit of this revolutionary age. At the same time, though, he and other fugitives were, like Antonio more than a century before, partaking of a generations-long rebellion against tyranny in a most vicious form—the tyranny wielded by slaveholders.[2]

Some whites in South Carolina and elsewhere termed blacks a "Nation within a Nation," a "separate people" by virtue of their common plight. Yet if such a black "nation" did exist in the Lowcountry, it was hardly a stable one. Black people possessed many roles and identities rather than a single one. Some were imposed upon them, but others they chose for themselves, all within a colonial system shaped by the imperial imperatives of the British Crown. Hence, enslaved laborers were articles of commerce, bought and sold by traffickers in human flesh; producers of the profitable staple crops rice and indigo; service workers for wealthy consumers of luxury goods; petty marketers within the local economy; members of families and communities of extended kin; and some, at least, sisters and brothers in Jesus Christ together with their oppressors throughout the Western world.[3]

The American Revolution spawned any number of homespun and learned theorists of republican values, but most South Carolinians regardless of skin color saw the conflict primarily as a means to pursue their self-interests, variously defined. Wealthy whites aimed to preserve their "liberty" by protecting their property, whether in the form of human bodies, gracious mansions, or rice plantations sprawling over thousands of acres. For their part, Boston King and his black Lowcountry compatriots sought to deprive the Americans and the British and their respective armies of the one resource they craved in equal measure: the labor of slaves.

South Carolina planters, together with their counterparts throughout eighteenth-century colonial America, stereotyped Africans according to their tribal origins but refrained from attaching any racial characteristics to Africans and their descendants generally. Like their Maryland predecessors, Lowcountry elites maintained order through violence and state-sponsored terror; they saw no need to justify bondage in racial terms because local critics of bondage—mostly the enslaved themselves—were for the most part weak and lacking in both basic legal rights and firearms. At the same time, in echoes of the roiling politics of the seventeenth-century Chesapeake, Lowcountry planters perceived enslaved workers as situated on a continuum of potentially dangerous undesirables that included Native groups and impoverished men and women of the planters' own ethnic heritage. Nevertheless, the institution of slavery produced an overarching dichotomy between "white" (the free) and "black" (the enslaved), a dichotomy that stigmatized even those people of color who were free. Overall, though, South Carolina elites believed that enslaved workers were subversive not because they were of a certain race, but because their current circumstances and historic grievances made them so.

In the years before the Revolution, South Carolinians remained determined to resist the growing calls among northern whites to consider slavery a humanitarian issue, a matter of morality. Rather, they sought to turn the issue on its head and claim that the institution was good and right because it ensured them a particularly genteel, "English" existence. For planters and Charles Town merchants, a claim to equality with the British gentry depended on an existence that only slave labor could ensure. Hence, the trappings of wealth—including the large numbers of retainers to build fine homes and to serve, cook, scrub, and sew within them—constituted an argument that the colonists deserved a place of respect and political equality within the empire.

Nevertheless, if slavery was the foundation of Carolina's "civilized" way of life, it was also the greatest threat to that way of life. The two archetypal enemies of the institution of slavery, bloodthirsty field hands on the one hand and evangelicals preaching the equality of all God's children on the other, posed a distinct danger to white people regardless of status—the former because they threatened whites with bodily harm, the latter because they challenged an entire political economy built on the oppression of a particular group of people. No wonder, then, that within the South Carolina General Assembly as well as the gracious drawing rooms of Charles Town mansions, discussions of slavery turned on rational questions of profit, and also on rational fears of self-preservation, a form of "self-interest" shaped by the viscera as well as the ledger book.[4]

For the 100,000 blacks who lived in the Lowcountry, a series of ongoing wartime catastrophes defined their own interests and created a chaotic mix of peril and promise. When war came to South Carolina in 1775, some fugitives joined long-standing colonies of runaway slaves deep in remote stands of live oaks and tall pines. Other men and women, "carried off" or "driven off" by British or American soldiers, were forced to dig trenches and build fortifications for white men on both sides of the conflict. The fighting gave some blacks the opportunity to carve new lives out of the turmoil of war. The successful British assault on Charles Town in the spring of 1780 inflamed the surrounding countryside, as lines between patriots and American-born loyalists blurred, leading to raids and counterraids by rogue bands of armed men and swelling a refugee population of blacks and whites. Boston King took advantage of these upheavals to make his way into the city, freeing himself, at least temporarily, in the process. Meanwhile, the Crown's men were quashing slave uprisings on estates seized from rebel owners. By this time the plantation system had utterly collapsed, as slaves abandoned the cultivation of staple crops. Mounted black men became a military force to be reckoned with in a time and place where food, guns, horses, and black bodies were prized commodities, the currency of a war-torn realm.

Lowcountry blacks, fully one-half of whom in 1775 were African born, inhabited a land of profane and sacred dimensions. In the deadly rice swamps, they toiled under the exploitative task system, forced to grow and process most of their own food. Waterways along the coast served as conduits of information and commerce, as avenues of escape, and, within the African American spiritual world, as a link between the living and the dead. Enslaved people struggled to harvest the fruits of their own labor, engage in trade, and pray and live out their family lives on their own terms. For these reasons, some blacks remained rooted to their home quarters, especially after the formation of local militias drained white men from the plantations. Nevertheless, by 1781 warfare had brought a halt to much food production. In the fertile Lowcountry, teeming with fish, shellfish, deer, and fowl, the final chapter of the conflict was written on the gaunt faces of people who were starving to death.[5]

Meanwhile, British forces of occupation were conducting bloody forays outside Charles Town, scouring the countryside for garden truck and livestock. Yet as in all wars, material deprivation was unevenly distributed. During the last week of January 1782, a favored few of the British officers in the city received handwritten invitations to a ball that Thursday evening. Braving unusually cold weather, the guests who gathered at the fashionable address of 99 Meeting Street found the dance to be an exotic, and no doubt erotic, affair. Their hostesses, three enslaved women, had appropriated from their (presumably absent) mistresses the white women's silk dresses, powdered makeup, sense of social grace, and even names. Calling themselves Hagar Russell, Isabella Pinckney, and Mary Fraser, they arrived at the party in handsome carriages and joined their guests in a sumptuous repast, dancing until 4 in the morning. Yet like the broader history of Charles Town, this elegant affair masked the rot that lay just beneath the surface.[6]

The three hostesses no doubt welcomed a respite from their usual lot that winter—perhaps days spent polishing silver, dusting mahogany furniture, attending to the personal needs of fastidious mistresses, or laundering the clothes of British soldiers. They were probably light-skinned ladies' maids and grateful for a night of dressing up, dancing, and flirting. Predictably, not every white person was amused. Three weeks after the event, an indignant Charles Town merchant, Daniel Stevens, relayed to a northern friend a detailed description of what he called the "Ethiopan Ball." He fumed, "Those shameless tyrants," the British officers, "dress'd up in taste, with the richest silks, and false rolls on their heads, powder'd up in the most pompous manner" the enslaved women and then "drove [them] through streets in pomp alongside of them." Stevens neglected to mention to his friend that before the British arrived, the city's elite men had routinely attended the same sort of gatherings. A visitor to Charles Town four years before had been struck by a South Carolina "peculiarity," namely, "the 'black dances' as they are called; which are given by Negro and Mulatto women, to which they invite white gentlemen." In any case, Daniel Stevens was now offering up his patriotic if salacious and wholly disingenuous description of the Ethiopian Ball to indict what he called the "state of shame and perfidy [of] the officers of that once great Nation [Britain]."[7]

Outside the rarified atmosphere of 99 Meeting Street, the city's shops reflected the ironies of the war's impact. Now that the occupation had opened trade with England again, the well-stocked shelves of mercantile houses displayed a striking array of newly imported goods. Wealthy women perused shell jewelry and ivory combs, feathered plumes, looking glasses, tea tables, and a wide selection of fabrics, from German linens to flannels, linseys, and Yorkshire cloths. In contrast, the central marketplace, where old, young, rich, and poor shopped for food, had only limited, exorbitantly high-priced items for sale: trout, clams, oysters, eggs, geese, turkeys, peas, and okra supplied by enterprising black women and men skilled in trading and smuggling.[8]

It is unknown whether Charles Town's British commander, Lieutenant General Alexander Leslie, attended the Ethiopian Ball. If invited, he might have felt conflicted. He certainly needed a diversion, no matter how brief, from his woes, but he had recently received orders from the British Army's headquarters in New York to economize on the garrison's expenses, which were spiraling out of control. And for British officers generally, a winter's night of conviviality could not ease their anxieties. News of the stunning defeat of Lord Cornwallis at Yorktown in October 1781 had reached South Carolina a month later. The rebel victory emboldened the enemies of the king and inspired many halfhearted loyalists to abandon him—in some cases, once again, for their allegiances to either side remained unsteady throughout the war. Leslie informed his superiors glumly, "In short the whole of the Country are against us." Meeting in Jacksonborough a mere thirty-six miles to the south was the South Carolina General Assembly, the provincial congress that South Carolinians had formed to govern their state after the Royal governor, Lord William Campbell, had disbanded the original, Crown-controlled body. Meanwhile, the British lacked the horses they needed to fight and forage for food.[9]

Called to justify the garrison's lavish spending—greater even than that of British headquarters in New York City—Leslie could only point to the expense of feeding and sheltering an estimated 4,000 people, including troops, black workers, and large numbers of refugees, these last two groups deserving of support because of "their Misery and helpless situation." Loyalists who had scattered to New York, East Florida, and the West Indies when rebels had first seized the city six years earlier, at the start of the war, were now returning home and looking to Leslie for sinecures that would allow them to sustain their large entourages and lavish way of life. Those loyal to the king who had stayed and endured the depredations of the rebels were demanding exorbitant compensation for their confiscated estates. Rawlins Lowndes, a former rebel but now one of several "sudden Converts to Royalty," offered Leslie a meticulous accounting of all he had lost in the last two years. Previously, Lowndes's holdings had produced annually 1,000 barrels of rice, worth £15,000, and he had earned £3,000 from rentals of his several Charles Town properties. Now, he lamented, "my houses have been taken from me for public uses, and are gone so much to decay they are not fit to be let . . . [and] I have from various causes lost upwards of 80 of my best slaves."[10]

Leslie had other worries besides the staggering claims submitted to him by entitled planters. Hessian mercenaries recruited to fight alongside the British had been forming "too many [local] connections" and deserting, melting into the hinterland; replacement recruits were expensive. And Indians, too, were making insistent demands: in late December Leslie had received from the southern superintendent of Indians a bill for the extraordinary sum of £11,000, this over and above the £5,000 the agent had recently spent for cash and gifts, resources ultimately wasted on inconstant allies. If the price racked up for a series of dinners held in Savannah for Chocktaw Indian chiefs and warriors was any indication, His Majesty's money was going for copious amounts of alcohol consumed from bowls of punch and bottles of wine, porter, grog, and, one evening, a keg of rum to bring the gathering to an end, in the words of a British Indian agent, "and send them [the Indian guests] to Camp they being drunk."[11]

In Leslie's mind, the only truly commendable person in the Charles Town garrison was the resourceful Lieutenant Colonel James Moncrief, head of engineers and hero of the siege of the city two years before. Moncrief did not attend the Ethiopian Ball; at the time he was in Savannah, Georgia, strengthening that city's defenses. Throughout the two-and-a-half-year occupation of Charles Town, he orchestrated the labor of hundreds of black men and women in the city and on the coastal islands guarding the harbor. He was, in Leslie's estimation, a man of "excellent judgment" who had performed admirably under the most trying circumstances. Moncrief actually produced something of value for the Crown, and his skillful management of the region's most precious resource—labor—made him infinitely more valuable than faithless troops, spoiled loyalists, and endlessly demanding Indian nations.[12]

Had they known of Leslie's distress during the winter and early spring of 1782, his enemies might have taken heart. Still, patriot planters found little in the state's prospects to cheer them. As early as 1775, they had watched as groups of their enslaved workers fled to the British on the largely mistaken assumption that enemies of their owners were their friends. By 1780 at least some of these black men and women were laboring under the direct supervision of Moncrief in Charles Town. Arthur Middleton, a wealthy slave owner and signer of the Declaration of Independence, knew firsthand the toll the war had taken on the holdings of planters. More radical than his father, Henry Middleton, an early president of the Continental Congress, the forty-year old Arthur remained an unwavering patriot throughout the war despite his material losses: in early 1776 fifty of his enslaved workers, including John Banbury, thirty-one, and his African-born wife, Lucy, had fled his plantation. Middleton's former enslaved workers were now earning wages in the British Army's Engineer Department and the Royal Artillery.[13]

The Middletons and their neighbors understood that the war was being fought by ever-shifting factions unpredictable in their motives and actions—backcountry settlers, rival Indian tribes, loyalists, substantial numbers straddling both sides, and, most menacingly of all, the thousands of black men and women in their midst, a subversive force in the heart of American territory. Black men, many of whom had once been subjugated and brutalized by the very revolutionaries who now claimed to be fighting in the name of liberty, were aiding the British directly as spies and guides, but some were acting under no white man's orders. Arthur Middleton was relieved when on February 10, 1781, the South Carolina General Assembly rejected a recent proposal introduced by one of their own, young Colonel John Laurens, to enlist the state's slaves for battle. The proposal had prompted a mixture of derision and alarm among the delegates, and they voted the measure down decisively. Governor John Matthews instead authorized the military use of blacks as servants, wagoners, and skilled laborers for purposes of the colony's defense.[14]

By this time a vicious guerrilla war was engulfing the backcountry, as food shortages gave rise to bands of black and white renegades who had no politics, just a murderous rage for revenge and greed for the spoils of war. The numbers told a larger story: in 1780 South Carolina alone accounted for fully two-thirds of all patriot battlefield deaths and 90 percent of all patriots wounded. The take-no-prisoners policies on both sides yielded a grim litany of summary executions, burned estates, and kidnapped slaves. Military discipline was nonexistent. Patriot general Nathanael Greene lamented the condition of his threadbare, mutinous force, two-thirds of whom, he believed, were "totally unfit for duty." By the spring of 1782 the exhausted rebels, like their antagonists, were contending with "mutinies" and "conspiracies" among troops who, deprived of pay and food, were resorting to banditry. North Carolina officials could not resist taunting their proud neighbors to the south, rice-rich men who now groaned under "all the calamities which can be apprehended from an Insolent Relentless Irritated, and Rapacious enemy, from your own Slaves armed against their former masters, [and] from the Savages [Indians] excited to make bloody and merciless dispositions and . . . to make their force and ferocity as effectual against you as possible."[15]

Despite the bitter clash between the British and the Americans over the nature of empire, for the most part officers on both sides shared similar views of enslaved people, whom they perceived primarily as so many cards in a deck—to be shuffled from one place to another, used, or discarded as wartime strategy demanded. In November 1775 Virginia's royal governor, Lord Dunmore, had issued a proclamation promising freedom to slaves who would leave their masters and join the British forces. This move alerted American military officials to the revolutionary and devastating potential of enslaved men as both fighters and laborers for the British. And soon after, the Continental Army and some northern states enlisted enslaved men in their ranks and then emancipated them. Yet these moves were less expressions of principle than they were political ploys (on the part of Dunmore) and troop-recruitment efforts (among northern patriots). Overall, manpower shortages were the critical factor affecting policies toward and ideas about blacks. In South Carolina virtually no men of influence bothered to address the humanitarian dimensions of bondage. At the same time, many enslaved people, like Boston King, took their chances; if they could not find freedom on the Lowcountry battleground, they would at least try to seek out a better life than they had known before. In contrast to their patriotic owners, whose views of freedom were distinctly exclusionary and self-referential, these enslaved people became principled seekers after liberty.[16]

Throughout the South dire, immediate labor demands shaped the priorities of politicians and military officers; fighting over territory became a means of pursuing variable notions of patriot and British self-interest. Both sets of combatants, however, contended with a hostile terrain and with black workers of varying degrees of usefulness. The lush Lowcountry mocked conventions of eighteenth-century warfare: military engineers on both sides had to transport fieldpieces, cannons, and troops over territory intercut with unbridged creeks and rivers. Soldier-workers expended thousands of man-hours in an effort to fortify redoubts and batteries in danger of sinking into the soft, marshy soil. The British siege of Charles Town had amounted to a clash between two undermanned armies rushing to reconfigure the terrain to their own purposes. In the end, the major players had not been the commanding generals, Henry Clinton for the British and Benjamin Lincoln for the Americans, but their respective engineers—Moncrief of the Royal Engineers and Frenchman Louis le Beque de Presle, Chevalier Du Portail, head of the Continental Military Engineering Corps. In fact, however, Du Portail arrived late on the scene and then only to advise Lincoln to evacuate the poorly fortified Charles Town immediately.[17]

On December 24, 1779, a British fleet of sixty-one ships carrying 7,584 men had set sail from New York; stormy weather slowed the progress of the convoy and also resulted in the loss of ships bearing Hessian soldiers and horses for cavalry and other purposes. The delay of the fleet on its way down the coast gave the Americans some time to assemble a black workforce intended to bolster Fort Moultrie (named for General William Moultrie) at the mouth of Charles Town Harbor. The General Assembly hastily took up the question of the "raising of a Black Corps to be annexed to the army," with much of the ensuing debate focused on the definition of "pioneers," "fatigue men," "oarsmen," and "mariners," the categories of labor to which the men would be limited. The assembly called for the impressment of 2,000 blacks between the ages of eighteen and forty. The number of enslaved men actually volunteered by their owners amounted to only a fraction of that number—perhaps 600. Faced with a critical labor shortage, General Lincoln would periodically go to the city's outlying fortifications and take up a pick and shovel, rallying his men and reminding them that the cause would be won by those who dug most energetically in the dirt. Meanwhile, morale remained low among the troops, wracked by smallpox, hunger, and intense dislike for the Massachusetts-born Lincoln, and there was, according to one deflated patriot, "no Rum or Sperits of any kind which they hanker after so much."[18]

The British feared that "our long voyage and unavoidable delays since have given the rebels time to fortify Charlestown towards the land, a labour their numbers in Negroes has greatly facilitated," in the words of General Clinton. Yet his troops gained some advantage by their arduous slog through the lowlands. The first approach of the British fleet had set off a massive exodus among thousands of enslaved rice laborers along the Ashley and Cooper Rivers, many of them traveling by water toward the coast. On June 30, 1779, Clinton made his own Dunmore-esque proclamation, promising every black person who abandoned the rebels "full Security to follow within these Lines, any Occupation which he shall think proper." Certainly, his words suggested that fugitives would not be reenslaved in the process. Yet British officers on the march were quick to take advantage of men and women refugees; each regiment received ten blacks who could be put to work cooking, washing clothes, and otherwise serving their new would-be masters.[19]

By March 7 the British, largely unimpeded, had begun erecting batteries along the Ashley River, relying on black men as pilots and as sources of military intelligence and muscle power. Blacks guided troops around the Lowcountry cypress marshes and seemingly impenetrable undergrowths of yucca and hollies and piloted supply ships through mazes of rivers. Sent out to forage, British scouting parties that lacked the guidance of local blacks lost their way and spent the night camped out, shivering, in deep stands of

Sea Island oaks, black gums, and tupelos. More fortunate troops were led by runaway slaves to the expansive plantations of some of the Lowcountry's most ardent patriots, including Rawlins Lowndes, Ralph Izard, and the Middletons. The foreigners marveled at the impressive Georgian-style houses and formal gardens before looting stores of Madeira and fine wines and pocketing shoe buckles and watches. They could not help but contrast the planters' wealth to the impoverished condition of their enslaved workers, for standing in the shadow of brick mansions were dwellings of earthen walls covered with thatched palmetto roofs.[20]

The British needed all the military support they could get, and the brief appearance of a Lower Creek sachem named Ravening Wolf gave hope that, in the words of Hessian captain Johann Ewald, the chief would reassure upcountry Native groups that the "English army . . . was in such a condition that it was worth the trouble for these nations to venture further into an alliance with the English." The sight of Ravening Wolf, clad in sandals and a long shirt but no breeches or stockings, caused quite a stir among the soldiers. His clothing and adornments suggested the ambivalent nature of Indian self-interest—dependence on whites for trade, but also a desire to remain independent of them. According to Ewald, the chief had a ring through his nose, and he had daubed his face with red paint. "On his chest he wore a ring-shaped silver collar and around both arms silver shields fastened with red ribbons, which were gifts from England and on which the monogram 'George Rex' was engraved." In the end, though, the chief seemed more curious about the Hessians' long beards ("put on merely for ornament," he thought) than serious about offering any real aid to the Crown.[21]

Chief Engineer Moncrief had no illusions about the task before him. He had won accolades for his successful defense of Savannah against French and Continental forces in the fall of 1779. From that campaign, he understood that the assault on Charles Town depended upon the number of men he could bring under his control and the ability of those men to transport huge amounts of equipment over water-soaked terrain. He relied chiefly on sailors and on blacks assembled from a variety of places, including 120 "Black Pioneers," a group of black fatigue workers organized by the army and sent south with the fleet from New York City, and laborers attached to the British occupying forces in nearby Savannah. Gradually, he integrated into his corps the fugitives making their way toward British lines; their intimate familiarity with the waterscape and their long years of working in marshland proved a boon to him. By April 1, with an estimated 3,000 men at his disposal, Moncrief was supervising the rapid construction of new redoubts as well as assembling various pieces of offensive equipment. Working in cold rainy weather, blacks tore down local buildings and out of the wood fashioned several mantlets, portable screens used to shield soldiers; each one required eighteen men to carry it. They built abatises, obstacles formed from tree branches with their ends sharpened and placed in a ditch at the base of a battery. They dug trenches, drained swamps, and constructed sandbag trestles, fascines, and pontoon bridges to traverse ten different rivers, each a laborious undertaking. To compensate for the loss of the horses at sea, Moncrief put black men to work dragging cannons, munitions, entrenching tools, and provisions through the soft, silty marshes. Encircling the city to the west, a force 134 strong used a contraption made of two wheels on the front and wooden rollers on the back to transport cannons and flatboats overland from the Ashley to the Cooper River.[22]

The British then proceeded to launch a barrage of cannon fire toward Charles Town, raining death and destruction on its defenders. At the same time, within the city black people were proving subversive to the American cause. Some managed to flee and give the British information on recent troop movements and the devastation wrought by the shelling. On April 17 one neighborhood burst into flames, not from British shells but from a fire that began when a group of enslaved men who had been boiling pitch abandoned their post. Whites attributed the conflagration to an "accident." The climax to the siege came on May 10 when Fort Moultrie's defenders surrendered at the sight of the advancing enemy.[23]

Not every self-proclaimed patriot had stayed to defend the city. Soon after the war began in 1776, Boston King's owner had hired him out to a series of Charles Town tradesmen, white men who beat him nigh unto death. By this time Richard Waring himself had taken up residence in the city, but when he heard that the British invaders were on the march, he removed his entire household back to the countryside, a safe distance from the port city. It was in late spring 1780 that King once again feared for his life—this time because another slave to whom he had lent a horse failed to return it—and he made his way to Charles Town to try his luck with the British. King's motives were not political or ideological but self-preservative. And indeed the same could be said of Waring, whose commitment to the patriot cause was only as strong as the American military presence in his immediate neighborhood.[24]

The occupying British Army had to deal with the uncertain loyalties of American soldiers and civilians alike. For military officials, the first order of business was to economize and send 2,000 enemy soldiers back to their homes, "on parole," extracting from them an unenforceable promise that they would not take up arms against the Crown again. Eventually, the authorities would also pack off twenty-nine prominent Charles Town patriots, ridding themselves of, in the words of one British officer, "some of the most dangerous, hardened, and perverse Rebels that ever existed." One sympathetic patriot reported that the exiles, sent to detention in St. Augustine, Florida, complained loudly when they found themselves in decidedly less than luxurious quarters, "compelled to do the most menial Offices, yet could scarcely procure the plainest Necessaries of Life." In contrast, hundreds of merchants and artisans eager to resume trade remained in Charles Town; they, together with several leading rebels, Henry Middleton among them, reversed course and took a renewed oath of allegiance to the king, becoming the "protection gentry." David Ramsay, a patriot and historian of the war, condemned them as weak-willed cowards: "Several who had lived in ease and affluence from the produce of their lands, cultivated by their slaves, had not fortitude enough to dare to be poor."[25]

When General Leslie sat down on June 3 to outline his plans for the occupation, he wrote this under the word "Negroes": "There are so many different Interests to attend to in the Arrangements required." He wanted to respect the property rights of loyalist planters and return enslaved men and women to their rightful owners. As for runaways who had deprived the rebels of their labor, after serving the British "faithfully during the war [they] are entitled to their Freedom." Until then, they should work in the various military departments "with adequate Pay, Provisions and Cloathing." Yet despite Leslie's pointed policies, the city's black population continued to "go about uncontrolled, to the distress of the [white] inhabitants, the detriment of the government, and in direct violation of orders."[26]

Not even a raging smallpox epidemic, "which sweeps them away in great numbers," in the words of a British officer, could discourage hundreds of blacks from coming into the city. (Boston King had managed to survive after going for several days without food and water and thanked God for sending a British soldier who revived him.) Leslie's chief concern was to slow the number of black in-migrants. At one point he intercepted seven hundred blacks en route downriver; believing they were infected with smallpox, he decided to "distribute them about the Rebell Plantations," a deadly form of germ warfare that relied on black bodies as agents of disease. In June he rejoiced when an estimated five hundred black men, women, and children left with Clinton as part of a thirty-ship fleet bound for New York City; some had attached themselves to Hessian officers, and others had joined—or been forced to join—the Black Pioneers. Taking the pox with them, more South Carolina blacks would follow Cornwallis north in the fall of 1781 en route to his fateful encounter at Yorktown.[27]

Efforts to stem the tide of humanity coming in from the countryside included a short-lived initiative to force fugitives to labor on the sequestered estates of the rebels. In an ambitious plan, the British aimed to hire 100 white men to oversee 5,000 blacks considered still enslaved, now to the Crown; but the steady incursion of American forces, combined with the decayed nature of many plantations, their fields weed choked and irrigation systems destroyed, halted that experiment. As the American army moved closer to Charles Town and overran these broken-down estates in 1781, the British officer in charge of the project admitted defeat, as he was "compelled . . . to abandon every hope of effecting His purpose; and behold with extreme regret, the product of His unremitting labor, become a most Material acquisition to the Enemy."[28]

The prospect of cash wages paid by the British proved a powerful lure for field hands and skilled carpenters, English speakers and non-English speakers, people running away from an owner or toward a place of unknown possibilities. In January 1781 a master advertised for a runaway, enslaved carpenter Hercules, and acknowledged that "he is frequently seen in Charlestown, where he may endeavor to get employ." (The ad ended with the somewhat plaintive words, "If Hercules returns of his own accord, he shall be forgiven.") Some fugitives opted for self-reinvention. The owner of a runaway named Titus suggested that he was well equipped for city life: "He may alter his name, speaks bad English, and can (tho' very cunning and artful) pass for a fool."[29]

Once in the city, many blacks found themselves subject to multiple forms of coercion, for their bodies carried a high market value throughout the years of the Revolution. Privateers plying the coastline offered escaped slaves jobs as pilots or crew members; some of these offers were legitimate, and others were mere pretexts for kidnappers to sell men and women in the Caribbean islands. British and Hessian officers and their wives, and even ordinary enlisted men, could now afford their own personal valets, hairdressers, and cooks and considered these workers to be status symbols of the highest order. Loyalists decamping to London or elsewhere succumbed to the temptation to take with them enslaved servants accustomed to the everyday rituals of the elite. And displaying black retainers remained a prized perquisite for the occupiers: Lieutenant Governor William Bull, complaining of kidney stones, traveled through the streets on a litter borne by four enslaved men.[30]

Like the Americans, the British acknowledged that black labor was "so necessary in every branch of employment." One of many military departments in the city, the Ordnance Department, used 800 workers. In the spring of 1781 the Engineering Department, Commissary General, Quarter Master General, Barracks Master, Royal Artillery, and General Hospital were employing at least 515 men, 141 women, and 15 children, almost all of whom still had an owner attached to their names. Some toiled as servants, sawyers, carpenters, smiths, and teamsters. Others were set to cleaning the filthy streets and maintaining the one hundred commercial buildings now quartering troops.[31]

Moncrief successfully attracted and kept black workers of both sexes, perhaps because of his willingness to see that they were decently clothed and paid in cash, though at rates less than those for white laborers. He provided blankets, shirts, shoes, suits, and dresses for hundreds and employed a full-time tailor to sew garments out of white plains and blue duffels in addition to the customary osnaburg called "Negro cloth." Some employees, such as boatmen Cupid, Alex, Troy, Will, Abraham, and Jack and chain drivers Tom, Peter, Mingo, Glasgow, and Cudjo, pocketed their pay directly. Others, presumably still enslaved by loyalist masters, received food, clothing, and shelter while their owners showed up periodically to claim their wages.[32]

In occupied Charles Town, familiar communities of blacks reconvened and new communities coalesced. While he was in the city, Boston King might have encountered the other Waring slaves, Mathias, Tom, Peter, and Scipio, who were now working for the British Quarter Master. Phillis Clark of South Carolina met her future husband, Pompey, who had come south with the British from the North, when both were working in the Hospital Department. An unknown number of men and women had attached themselves to Moncrief since his defense of Savannah in 1779. Among those now under his supervision were twenty of General William Moultrie's slaves: Sally, Fanny, Daphne, Abba, Nappy, Molly, Flora, Peggy, Rachel, Mariane, Peggy, Lindy, Ealy, Bob, Prince, Cyrus, John, Sharper, and two men named Jemmy. Some workers had remained in the city after their patriot owners were paroled or exiled, and others had joined the ranks of refugees fleeing their masters in the countryside.

David George and his wife were among those black people who followed a circuitous route to Charles Town. Born around 1740 in Essex County, Virginia, of African parents, George had fled from a cruel master and found his way south to the Savannah River, where he was enslaved by Creek Indians for three years. A charismatic black preacher named George Liele inspired George to believe that he had "found great blessing and mercy from the Lord." Determined to devote his life to his newfound Christian faith, George felt "so overcome that I could not wait upon my master." Defying whites who sought to silence these evangelical preachers "lest they furnish us with too much knowledge," George learned to read and interpret the Bible for himself. He began to minister to Liele's congregation in Savannah (from which grew the first African Baptist Church in North America), at the same time keeping a butcher's stall and trading in hogs. When the British captured that town in 1779, George's wife found work as a laundress for General Clinton, "and out of the little she got maintained us." The Georges were probably among the many blacks who accompanied Clinton on his triumphal entry into Charles Town.[33]

Drawing on skills characteristic of West African cultures and honed under slavery, many black men and women participated in a robust local economy driven by a shortage of food and by an expanding demand for domestic and military labor. In February 1781 British officials publicized regulations for the public marketplace, a long list revealing of blacks' resourcefulness generally and black women's historic role as traders more particularly. Black men with access to some sort of conveyance possessed considerable advantages in this economy. The Barrack Office routinely sent out calls for wood and for owners of wagons, carts, and "small VESSELS and Craft." Because privateers had seized British fishing boats, the garrison remained dependent on the black men and women who could bring in fish and truck from the surrounding area. City authorities complained about the high prices that teamsters exacted for their services; the Board of Police established "Rates of Cartage: for wood, lumber, salt, lime, and shingles" in an effort to stem the traders' "desire of inordinate gain" and tendencies toward "engrossing."[34]

In Charles Town and the surrounding Lowcountry, traffickers smuggled goods and food in from the hinterland via boat, carriage, horse, and oxen, facilitating a viable informal economy that benefited whites and blacks alike. Authorities called in vain for consumers to refrain from buying from soldiers who did not have written permission from their commanding officer to trade or barter. Still, many blacks found willing partners in homesick foreign troops eager to ransack private homes and strip them of everything from tablecloths and pillowcases to silver tea sets. Lively local markets, whether legal or illegal, reflected a larger breakdown in military discipline. One officer advertised in the local paper, "I do hereby give notice to all deserters from the regiment under my command that if they will return to their duty, by joining their corps . . . they will be pardoned for all past offences."[35]

To the extent that they could get rice, vegetables, and fish in to the Charles Town market, black men and women could turn to their own advantage "deranged estates"—that is, those abandoned by whites in the interior and on the Sea Islands. Patriot general Francis Marion condemned the trade in provisions originating along Wamboo River and Goose Creek, but he despaired of curtailing it, for such a move would require him to "tak[e] every person adjacent to town and make them prisoners, or keep them a great distance from their plantations, and remove all their possessions." Throughout the Lowcountry, clusters of black men and women staged their own quiet revolution when they planted gardens and fished, intending to earn some money by marketing any surplus no matter how small.[36]

For all military and political officials, entrepreneurial activity on the part of blacks assumed a conspiratorial cast, leading to calls for the summary execution of those caught carrying provisions of any kind or engaging in the "shameful commerce" of purloined horses. Writing from the rural outpost of Uxbridge in August 1782, Governor Matthews reported to Marion that American cavalry were derelict in allowing the "dozen or twenty negroes to come out almost every night in the week, and carry off cattle, horses, and anything else they want, within twelve or fifteen miles of their camp." Because of this "villainous" activity, "the Charlestown markets are now daily supplied with the greatest plenty of everything they want," he claimed with some exaggeration.[37]

White revolutionaries showed little appreciation for blacks' own brand of insurgent independence. Rebel planters were constantly denouncing British soldiers who sought to "steal all the [blacks] they can, and carry them off" or who incited workers to "desert" their masters—men, women, and children whom the Red Coats would either sell or put to work. Patriots rarely acknowledged that some of those "carried off" might have gone willingly; instead, they saw blacks in general as dupes of the British. The king's forces wished that it were so—that the blacks who sought shelter with the British were biddable and compliant. In fact, behind British lines some refugees found paid work but others faced reenslavement, which quickly soured the willingness of many blacks to devote themselves wholly to the British cause. Army employees had to wear regimental identification badges, while the provost marshal would "flog out of the encampment all those who are not Mark'd agreeable to Orders." Officers were "to execute on the Spot any Negro who is found quitting the Line of March in search of plunder." However, plunderers were not easily separated from soldiers. Mounted black cowboys drove cattle for the advancing army, and black "Dragoons" (as many as one hundred at a time) engaged in "bush fighting" against the rebels. Governor Matthews authorized the execution of all blacks "taken in arms" whether aiding the British or operating on their own, for, he wrote, "exemplary punishments on such notorious offenders will have a very salutary effect."[38]

Less liberators, the British remained the enemies of black people's enemies. Boston King left Charles Town to accompany a British raiding party outside the city and began to work for a British captain, supplying him with fish. The officer asked him, "How would you like me to be your master?" King escaped from this man and attached himself to another officer, risking his life to retrieve military intelligence and warn British troops of an imminent patriot attack. At one point, making his way back to the camp, he heard approaching American soldiers and, fearing detection, "fell flat upon my face till they were gone by." Once again, he believed, God had interceded: "I then arose, and praised the Name of the Lord for his great mercy, and again pursued my journey." For his courage he earned "3 shillings and many fine promises, which were all that I ever received for this service from him [the second officer]."[39]

In contrast to single men like King, who had responsibility only for himself when he fled from his master, many families tried to remain in familiar surroundings; there husbands and wives tended their gardens and chickens, cows, and pigs and protected the modest stores of household goods they had accumulated. Those still under the nominal supervision of a white man either ignored his orders or negotiated for more favorable treatment. When the British swept through the Ashepoo region, "they took with them" (in the words of planter Thomas Pinckney) nineteen blacks, among them "the hardy boys." Those who remained "are now perfectly free to live on the best produce of the plantation"—that is, the produce they themselves had grown. As for the overseer, they "pay no attention to his orders."[40]

Predictably, compared to their British counterparts, American officers were just as rapacious in their exploitation of black men, women, and children. In December 1781 General Greene highlighted the governing principle shaping military and labor deployment: "The natural strength of this country in point of numbers, appears to me to consist more in the blacks, than the whites." The Americans put blacks to work as cooks and valets, like the slave Billy, who, according to a patriot officer, was "well known throughout the army, making himself useful in shaving, and dressing the hair of many officers," and as ransom, like "one negro man, named Doctor," whom General Thomas Sumter held, along with a horse, a saddle and bridle, a cutlass, and nineteen silver dollars, all for the use of the revolutionaries' cause until their owners could prove that they were not allied with the British.[41]

The Americans also used black men's bodies as an inducement for militiamen to volunteer. A plan first proposed in 1779, the so-called Sumter's Law, would give "a negro bounty" to each recruit because efforts to draft men had failed miserably. Similar plans were proposed throughout the war to reward men who raised and commanded their own troops, and one in April 1781 provided that South Carolina allow each colonel of a new regiment "to receive three grown negroes and one small negro; Major to receive three grown negroes; Lieutenants one large and one small negro; the staff, one large and one small negro; the sergeants, one and one quarter negro, each private, one grown negro." (Children under ten years and adults over forty were deemed one-half a person.) In May 1782 Governor Matthews wrote to General Marion and asked him "whether it will be best to sell the negroes, and recruit with money, or continue on the old plan of recruiting with negroes." Cash was more portable, and less truculent, than black people.[42]

Patriot troop recruitment efforts reflected the shortage of Lowcountry whites available for service and the resistance of nonslaveholders to join the fight. Early in the conflict Charles Town elites understood that white men of modest means did not necessarily share their animus toward the highhandedness of the Crown. On the eve of the war, settlers in the fast-growing backcountry hailed from Virginia and North Carolina, while others were German and Scots-Irish immigrants who now feared the patriot cause would endanger their land grants. All remained at perpetual risk of Indian raids. In 1775 a prominent planter, William Henry Drayton, together with a Presbyterian minister, the Reverend William Tennent, traveled west of Charles Town and conducted a series of political rallies–*cum*–religious revivals to bring settlers there into the patriot fold. These efforts availed little; Drayton especially had little experience dealing with people whom he considered the ruder sort, those who used horses instead of enslaved workers in the fields. Tennent's unctuous sermons also aroused suspicions among folk wary of the motives and manners of Lowcountry aristocrats.[43]

For elites, the war brought into sharp relief the unpredictability of various Indian tribes and poor white men as well as slaves. Soon after the conflict started, the Americans were aiming to pry the Cherokee away from their historic allies, the British, and to secure the military support of other Native groups. When the Catawba sent two of their men to Charles Town to inquire about the nature of the emerging conflict, members of the patriot Council of Safety told them that "our brothers on the other side of the water wanted to take our property from us without our consent, and that we expected their warriors would join ours." Predictably, this paean to American property rights failed to move Native warriors. When pleading failed, total war followed. Drayton, an emissary to the Cherokee, was frustrated by the hostile reception he received from them. In July 1776 he issued a "word to the wise" to upcountry military officers: "It is expected you make smooth work as you go—that is you cut up every Indian corn-field, and burn every Indian town—and that every Indian taken shall be the slave and property of the taker; that the nation be extirpated, and the lands become the property of the public." Before long this scorched-earth policy led to the dispossession of all Cherokee east of the South Carolina mountains.[44]

During this period of strife, the state was forced to relinquish its claim as a place of "civilization" and refinement. By 1782 the backcountry, much of it engulfed in flames, had dissolved into anarchy, with courts closing and lynch mobs stepping into the breach. Large numbers of American militiamen deserted. Stationed at St. David's on the Great Pee Dee River, an American officer denounced the plundering and other depredations "perpetrated by a banditti of the most desperate villains and mulattoes, immediately bordering on our settlements." Despite atrocities so "fierce and cruel," in the words of a judge, the governor felt compelled to "open a Treaty with these very Murderers," which allowed the miscreants a pardon and the privilege of living at home. For the great planters, the carnage confirmed their view of a region populated by uncivilized backwoodsmen, settlers untamed by wealth borne of the profits from slavery.[45]

The western part of the state remained a nest of menacing Natives and fugitives. Prominent planter and slave trader Henry Laurens cited what he considered British forces' craven manipulation of both groups: "Excited by rewards & promises[,] the Savages of the Wilderness & the Negro Slaves" had been propelled to what he called "an indiscriminate Butchery of Men

Women & Children." From the outset of the war, South Carolina leaders had fretted about securing the cooperation of diverse Indian nations, groups that respected no colonial boundaries but had proved profitable trading partners. Lowcountry patriots recognized that, in the words of John Rutledge (Governor Matthew's predecessor), "diplomacy" with certain Native groups took the form of "Donations" over and above "the Emoluments of Trade." Among those donations, ammunition and guns were high on the Indians' list of prized articles. Like Marylanders a century and a half before, South Carolinians faced a balancing act: to provide weapons, in the words of an official 1775 declaration, "with such a quantity as might, in some degree, satisfy their urgent wants, but could not incite, by enabling, them to commit hostilities." For their part, most tribes, and factions of tribes, found they could play the combatants against each other and also profit handsomely by demanding guns and alcohol. As a result, American officials shared with their British counterparts the view that Indians in general remained insatiable for gifts and ever ungrateful.[46]

In early 1782 military desertions increased the pressure on both sides to arm slaves as uniformed soldiers. The British had put guns in the hands of black men who stormed Savannah in 1778 and then protected it from French forces a year later, and had also authorized the Black Dragoons to conduct raiding parties. By March Moncrief and Leslie were contemplating a formal "brigade of negroes." Moncrief reminded his superiors of "the many advantages which His Majesty's service has derived from their [blacks'] labor in carrying on the different works in this and the province of Georgia." He recommended that his superiors now arm them and presumably grant them their freedom in return. Leslie concurred, "as it appears to me a measure that will soon become indispensably necessary shou'd the war continue to be carried on in this part of America." As to who should command this new armed force, Leslie suggested Moncrief as "a very proper person to be at their head, being well acquainted with their disposition, and in the highest estimation amongst them."[47]

Patriots, however, continued to be far more reluctant than the British to accept black soldiers into their ranks. Earlier in the century, in their battles against Indians and the French and Spaniards, South Carolina colonial officials had enlisted blacks, finding these soldiers "necessary, but very dangerous domestics." General Lincoln had proposed arming slaves in anticipation of the British siege of Charles Town, a plan countered by the governor at the time, John Rutledge, who insisted that if these servile men were to be mobilized at all, it would be "as a corps of able bodied men accustomed to labor." Overwhelmingly, South Carolina patriots believed enlisting blacks was a disastrous idea. Remarking on the threat posed by blacks in the Revolutionary era, one rebel later wrote, "All subordination being destroyed, they became insolent and rapacious, and in some instances exceeded the British in their plundering and devastations."[48]

On the subject of black soldiers, Rhode Island native Nathanael Greene reduced the question to one of bodies and dollars only. He told Governor Rutledge, "The number of whites in this state are too small, and the state of your finances too low, to attempt to raise a force in any other way." Greene continued, "That they would make good Soldiers I have not the least doubt and I am persuaded the State has it not in its power to give sufficient reinforcements without incorporating them." Quickly rebuffed by the South Carolina General Assembly, the general agreed to settle for 440 black wagoners, pioneers, artificers, and personal servants. At the same time, he believed that unless blacks had an "interest" in their own continuing servitude, they would be "of little benefit, and by no means depended on" in the larger war against Britain. He proposed "that the public cloathe them, and that the negroes be allowed the same wages allowed by Congress to the soldiers of the Continental army." Greene noted that opposition to this plan stemmed not from the expense "but from an apprehension of the consequences."[49]

"An apprehension of the consequences": the imperatives of military mobilization only intensified whites' raw fear of the black people who lived in their midst. And, indeed, it was that fear that had made all of South Carolina an armed camp long before the start of the Revolutionary War, one menaced as much from the inside as from the outside.

––––––––––

On Sunday morning, September 9, 1739, almost sixty years before Boston King wrote his autobiography, twenty enslaved men, "some Angola Negroes," who had been set to work repairing the roads near Stono, reconfigured themselves into a band of rebels under the leadership of an enslaved man named Jemmy. In a bid to make their way to the Spanish outpost of St. Augustine in present-day Florida, and to the freedom promised to all runaways there, they broke into a store and made off with firearms and powder. Then they headed southward, ransacking and burning houses and killing white men, women, and children. Soon other blacks joined the band, and, according to a contemporary account, "they calling out Liberty, marched on with colors displayed, and two Drums beating." Out on the road, Lieutenant Governor William Bull unwittingly happened upon the insurrectionists, but he managed to escape and raise the alarm. In the end, the blacks killed twenty-five whites, and forty-five slaves paid with their lives for what came to be known as the Stono Rebellion.[50]

Here was Symon Overzee and Job Chandler's worst nightmare come to pass: a whole host of Angolans slaughtering their masters. With the aid of "several Indians" (offered food in return for their services), white responders shot and killed some of the blacks on sight and later executed others. Still, the planters of the region would congratulate themselves that "notwithstanding the Provocation they had received from so many Murders, they did not torture one Negroe, but only put him to an easy death."[51]

William Bull attributed the revolt among what he called "domestic enemies" to "a slack inspection" of enslaved men who "had been very indiscreetly assembled and encamped for several nights." Yet Stono was no spontaneous uprising. Rather, the rebels had sought to exploit the tensions gripping South Carolina whites in the summer and early fall of that year—a yellow fever epidemic in Charles Town, the prospect of an impending war with Spain. The conspirators hailed mainly from Kongo-Angola, and their martial tactics—the drums beating, white flags flying—reflected both West African military traditions and contemporary Christian iconography. In the five years preceding the rebellion, six out of ten of all the enslaved workers imported into South Carolina had come from Kongo-Angola, where Catholicism had taken hold nearly a century before.[52]

South Carolina's highly profitable staples of rice and indigo exacted a price of eternal vigilance on the part of slave masters and mistresses who lived there. Whites' anxieties were legion. Africans brought with them contagious, ill-defined diseases, "distempers." And the costliness of their bodies produced a growing, crushing debt for individual planters and for the whole colony because South Carolina's exports of deer skins, tar and turpentine, and rice and indigo could not match the value of imported slaves and luxury goods. In the 1730s traders had overseen the sale of 17,323 slaves on the docks at Charles Town, 16,280 of whom had come directly from Africa, the others from ports in the Caribbean. Like Symon Overzee's Antonio, Jemmy and other perpetrators of the Stono Rebellion had no recorded last names, and they represented the radical potential of runaways to wreak havoc on the established order. South Carolina's royal governor was

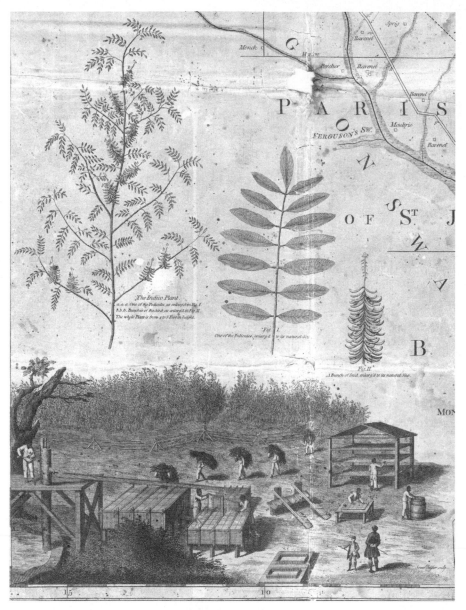

FIGURE 2.1 This detail from a 1773 map of St. Stephen's Parish in Craven County, South Carolina, shows enslaved workers making dye from indigo. The picture suggests the variety of tasks that slaves were forced to perform, from cultivating and harvesting the indigo plant to chopping down trees, clearing fields, constructing fences, and building the wooden apparatus used to produce the dye from the plant. Similarly, rice cultivation necessitated complex irrigation systems that slaves were forced to engineer, build, and maintain. USED WITH PERMISSION FROM THE JOHN HOPE FRANKLIN RESEARCH CENTER, DAVID M. RUBENSTEIN RARE BOOK AND MANUSCRIPT LIBRARY, DUKE UNIVERSITY.

convinced that "our Negroes are . . . more dreadfull to our safety than any Spanish invaders." As the black population grew, so did the danger posed by conspirators; at the time of Stono, the colony had 39,155 slaves and only half as many whites. Some Lowcountry parishes were more than 90 percent black.[53]

Authorities reacted decisively to Stono. Delegates to the General Assembly struggled to put into words their terror: "On this Occasion every Breast was filled with Concern. Evil brought Home to us within our very Doors awakened the Attention of the most Unthinking. Every one that had any Relation, any Tie of nature; every one that had a Life to lose were in the most sensible manner shocked at such Danger daily hanging over their Heads." Authorities mobilized armed patrols in the countryside and scout boats along the coast and bolstered a police watch to scour back alleys, gardens, and service buildings in Charles Town. They banned the use of drums, associated with secret messages and criminal behavior, and—inferring that African-born slaves were more dangerous than their American-born counterparts—slapped a prohibitively high tariff on imported slaves, reducing direct imports of Africans to only 1,356 (out of a total of 1,562 slaves) for the entire decade of the 1740s. (Despite this effort, between 1706 and 1776 Charles Town traders sold 93,843 slaves, about half of all Africans imported into the British North American colonies.) Owners sought to deal swiftly with runaways—many of them valuable, able-bodied young men— by selling them to the Caribbean islands. Nevertheless, the colony would remain in a perpetual state of unease. Cried the lawmakers, "With regret we bewailed our peculiar Case, that we would not enjoy the Benefits of Peace like the rest of Mankind and that our own Industry should be the Means of taking from us all the Sweets of Life and of rendering us liable to the Loss of our Lives and Fortunes."[54]

In response to real and perceived threats from the blacks who surrounded them, officials devised a series of punishments that in their cruelty reflected the deep, pervasive fear shared by Lowcountry whites who considered themselves beleaguered within their own homeland. Executions and forms of torture became public spectacles: black men and women were hanged, their heads severed and placed on poles for all to see. Strung up and suspended from the ground, they endured (or not) two hundred lashings at a time, with vinegar or salt rubbed into the bloody wounds. They were burned alive, branded, gibbeted, or hung in chains until dead, mutilated and castrated, buried alive.[55]

Whites took offense at unfamiliar cultural forms they deemed inherently menacing. Blacks' distinctive language, Gullah (perhaps a form of "Angola"), a pidgin that melded African grammar with English vocabulary, provided a means of communication incomprehensible to most whites. In the quarters black men and women observed traditional forms of song and dance under the cover of darkness. Secret mutual-aid and benevolent societies; the practice of herbal medicine, which (it was feared) could lead to the poisoning of masters and mistresses; incessant drum beating; the strange sounds and body movements that accompanied worship and funeral services—all of these West African traditions seemed threatening to masters and mistresses. And when an Anglican missionary described Lowcountry blacks in 1740 as "a Nation within a Nation," he alluded to blacks' cultural bonds *and* to their impulse for collective self-defense against white people's violent aggression.[56]

As the number of slaves increased in South Carolina, so, too, did whites' fears of blacks as a homogeneous, uniformly threatening people. In characterizing all blacks in this way, South Carolinians unconsciously mimicked Job Chandler's use of the European trope of the wild man during Antonio's trial in the previous century. At the same time, these white colonists also invoked an English legal precedent that had allowed for the economic subjugation of impoverished peoples more generally. Reflecting the influence of the sugar colony of Barbados, South Carolina's initial slave law of 1712 referred to blacks as "of barbarous, wild, savage natures"; the legislation echoed a 1547 English statute designed to punish and keep in check vagrant peasants, who, shunning productive labor, would supposedly steal and also threaten their social betters with bodily harm. To enslave a whole group of people, and their offspring as well, was to address a perennial challenge faced by the English propertied classes in the midst of widespread underemployment—countering the criminal behavior of highwaymen and pickpockets who robbed and assaulted rather than working. By harnessing the energies of the poor, vagrant laws and systems of bondage could yield predictable reserves of labor and discourage the mayhem wrought by the dispossessed upon the wealthy. Based on the rule of law, which at least recognized the basic humanity of landless countrymen and -women, that project had been stable enough in England, but in the New World it provoked the resistance of enslaved peoples and the apprehension of whites who could not control them.[57]

Not all British colonial authorities were willing to assume the public security risks that came with human bondage. Georgia, founded in 1733 as a barrier between the English of South Carolina and the Spanish of East Florida, initially banned slavery on the theory that the institution would discourage white settlers from working hard enough to tame the coastal swamps and inland hardwood forests. From Virginia came a voice of experience, wealthy planter William Byrd II, who urged the Georgia Trustees to stick to their principles, for slaves would "blow up the pride, & ruin the industry of our white people, who seeing a rank of poor creatures below them, detest work for fear it should make them look like slaves." Also, according to Byrd, it was likely that a black man "of desperate courage" would "kindle a servile war . . . before any opposition could be formed against him, and tinge our rivers as wide as they are with blood." Byrd had predicted Jemmy of Stono. Nevertheless, in 1749 the Trustees bowed to the demands of Georgia's whites, who insisted that slaves toil as field hands only and remain under the close supervision of an overseer. Presumably, enslaved artisans and domestics, who had relative freedom to ply their trades on a day-to-day basis, would threaten the colony's order. The hot, muggy climate and the arduous work of clearing the land had convinced the new settlers of the "Impossibility of white men being asked to work here and live" without the labor of slaves.[58]

Exhibiting none of Georgia's hesitation about slavery, South Carolina quickly transformed itself from a rough-hewn backwater colony devoted to lumbering and cattle ranching, where enslaved workers and free white colonists labored together in the woods, to a staple-crop powerhouse that contributed to Britain's riches. Contemporaries called the rice swamps the "Golden Mines" of Carolina—literally, the equivalent of the Brazilian gold mines for the Portuguese and, more prosaically, the Chesapeake tobacco fields for the great planters of Virginia and Maryland. And just as in South America's infamous mines, the human price of the rice economy was enormous: cultivation of the staple was, in the words of one contemporary observer, "*a killing work for the negroes.*" Virtually all survivors of the Middle Passage suffered emotional trauma and damaged immune systems, conditions that shattered women's fertility. Toiling in soggy fields during the height of summer, rushing to harvest the crop in fall, working in the cold muck in winter, blacks of all ages suffered high mortality rates. Elderly workers and pregnant and nursing mothers could not always complete their task of one-quarter acre a day in the allotted time; they relied on the help of younger hands or endured the lash. Because of a genetic-based immunity, some West African groups were resistant to the mosquito-borne diseases, such as malaria and yellow fever, that ravaged white populations in South Carolina. At the same time, workers contracted pneumonia and tuberculosis from toiling in the cold and in standing water, gastrointestinal ailments brought on by drinking polluted water, and anemia from subsisting on protein-deficient diets. On some plantations more than half of all babies were dead within a year of their birth, a condition that reflected the work demands placed upon women during the latter stages of pregnancy.[59]

Some enslaved men and women could work in the afternoons for themselves, but others had only Saturday afternoons and Sundays. Lowcountry blacks considered their own time to be their "right," a chance to fish, tend gardens, and raise chickens. Black women who traveled routinely between plantation and city market embodied the Gullah entrepreneurial impulse characteristic of West Africa and the Caribbean. The resulting trading networks facilitated communication among plantations, leading whites to see trading as a means of circulating goods and provisions but also of spreading rumors among workers and news of sinister plots. Throughout the eighteenth century a series of slave uprisings and conspiracy scares highlighted the sources of subversion embedded in the plantation system.[60]

In Charles Town whites might grudgingly tolerate a familiar black woman hawking her wares on a city sidewalk or in the public marketplace, but they took a decidedly dimmer view of groups of enslaved men and women gathering together for any reason. This principle extended to religious worship as well as to clandestine exchanges of stolen goods. Carolina masters remained suspicious of Christianity as a potentially explosive set of beliefs, whether propounded by Anglican missionaries, whom the slaves mostly ignored, or the more egalitarian-minded evangelical preachers, whom the slaves at times found compelling. Some of the latter, who preached loudly about the miserable plight of people treated worse than livestock, attracted a following in the quarters and in cramped meeting places in Charles Town. Ideas that glorified the brotherhood and sisterhood of the spirit could inspire a worker's resistance in the fields or a cook's effort to administer a deadly potion as part of an evening meal. The newly Christianized David George wrote of his religious conversion, "I felt my own plague, and I was so overcome that I could not wait upon my master." Instead, "I felt myself at the disposal of sovereign mercy." Boston King's early vision, of a fiery world where millions of souls ascended to heaven but others suffered rejection, revealed his faith in an apocalypse that would affect all people on the basis of the depth of their piety, rather than on the color of their skin.[61]

The Lowcountry was a site of considerable religious diversity, with elites embracing the formality of the Church of England and poor whites and enslaved workers finding in the sermons of Baptists and Methodists an uplifting, egalitarian message of deliverance and redemption. Some African-born Muslim men and women tried mightily to retain cultural practices related to diet and worship, though the slave system was not hospitable to traditions that mandated either specific foods or prayer at certain times of the day. Some Angolans tried to adhere to their Catholic faith as they had practiced it in their homeland. Yet regardless of their ethnicity, many enslaved men and women were receptive to evangelical precepts that gave rise to the celebration of eternal life over death. They also embraced literacy as a means to unlock sacred texts and found appealing those Christian beliefs that stressed an afterlife, the omnipotence of the spirit, and the convergence of supernatural and natural worlds. Like West Africans, enslaved Lowcountry men and women honored the symbolic and real properties of waterways as revealed in the ritual of baptism and the stories of runaways: According to a Gullah saying, "The sea brought us, the sea shall take us back"—to Africa, to their ancestors, to God.[62]

Surrounded by what William Bull called "domestic enemies," coastal whites lived as a people constantly besieged. Moreover, when the great rice planters gazed westward, they saw the upcountry borderlands populated by enemy Indians whom they called "savages" and friendly Indians who were a "strainge copper collour'd gentry," as well as fugitive slaves and white men restive in their powerlessness in the colonial assembly. Still, throughout the eighteenth century the lords of the rice kingdom prospered, adding to their wealth in land, slaves, and money. Together with lawyers and merchants, they consolidated their power by dominating political offices and by forming dense extended familial ties through endogamous marriage practices. In 1750 Charles Town was the richest settlement in the British North American colonies. The Lowcountry now resembled the West Indies with its staple-crop monoculture, enslaved majority, and tiny, wealthy elite.[63]

South Carolina planters sought to fashion themselves as English men and women living abroad, expressing their "Englishness" in a variety of ways: the men by sitting in the assembly with their hats on and by challenging the king's prerogatives; the women by following the latest Continental fashions in ladies' clothing and replicating London social etiquette. The Charles Town aristocracy hosted highly ritualized tea parties and elaborate dinners; enjoyed concerts, operatic performances, the theater, and dance assemblies;

and gambled on games of chance and horse races during the winter social season. Planters considered themselves cosmopolitan; they regularly traveled to the North, the Caribbean, and England with tutors, nurses, cooks, laundresses, valets, and footmen in tow. Despite the Lowcountry heat and humidity, they wore heavy English garments and at times ate heavy English food. Apparently no self-imposed form of physical discomfort was too great to bear in service to English modes of dress and diet.[64]

The colonists' appropriation of British material and political culture was decidedly selective—for example, they chose not to emulate the 1772 Somerset decision that essentially abolished slavery on English soil. In fact, it was through *things* that the colonists most forcefully expressed their identity and contrasted themselves to black and red "savages" and impoverished white reprobates in the backcountry. With its eight wharves handling the cargoes of as many as three hundred ships at a time, Charles Town was the center of an extensive luxury trade in furnishings, clothing, and carriages, and the way of life among its most privileged residents was encapsulated in the frequently invoked word "opulent." Planters' wives amused themselves shopping for colorful silk and satin fabrics, smooth and shiny, and dainty shoes with silver buckles, in contrast to the drab, coarse garments worn by barefoot enslaved men and women. Daniel Stevens's displeasure at the Ethiopian Ball stemmed at least in part from the jarring sight of black women in such rich clothing.[65]

Rice and indigo produced high rates of human misery but also the cash and credit necessary to build magnificent plantation houses such as Drayton Hall and Middleton Place and the elaborately furnished Charles Town houses to which the grandees and their families repaired for much of the year. Yet black people's labor was necessary not only to *buy* a luxurious way of life, but also to *maintain* it. Indeed, wealth had little value without an enormous retinue of enslaved people to care for immense dwellings and serve the white people who lived there. Domestics emptied chamber pots and cleaned up the vomit and excrement of the ill. Laundresses faced a mountain of clothing and table and bed linens to be washed and ironed. Personal valets attended to men who demanded to be shaved, their hair dressed and wigs powdered. Seamstresses and ladies' maids served mistresses seemingly unable to adjust their own corsets, wigs, and hooped petticoats by themselves. Carpenters serviced delicate carriages and phaetons, and footmen remained on call at all hours. In this world of fine things, an elaborate afternoon meal for twenty guests became not only a social event, but also an expression of a man's status and his competitive instincts. Enslaved cooks and their helpers spent hours hauling water, stoking fires, gutting fish, plucking chickens, shucking oysters, peeling onions, seasoning meats, and then assembling, boiling, stewing, frying, roasting, and baking the many delicacies that made up a Lowcountry supper. Enslaved waiters served the multiple courses that followed, contending with an array of soup bowls and dinner plates, butter boats, fruit and dessert plates, salt dishes, and changing glasses for each new wine and eating utensils for each new course. The end of the meal brought relaxed conversation for the guests, but for those in the kitchen hours of washing, drying, and storing all the silverware, dishes, glasses, pots, and provisions in their proper places.[66]

In England free white servants performed all these many tasks. In South Carolina the national or ethnic heritage of plantation laborers was irrelevant to the tasks at hand, but of course critical to keeping those laborers in a state of subjection. The net result of the social system was that Carolina elites lived in fear for their lives in a way that their English counterparts did not. Luxury was its own liability, for if wealthy whites expected to surround themselves with fine things, they had no choice but to rely on the daily labors of real and potential thieves and murderers.

As a matter of principle as well as practice, consumption drew the ire of a small number of critics, who understood the political and security risks associated with compulsive, competitive buying. During the 1769 debate over the nonimportation agreements (which would bar the sale of English luxury items and other imports from the mother country), Reverend Tennent chastised Charles Town women, so attached to the status and sociability of what he contemptuously called "their darling tea-dish ceremony." Radical patriot Christopher Gadsden pointed out the irony of protests against taxation when in fact "it is but a burden arising voluntarily from an indulgence in foreign articles, nine-tenths, in general, I believe . . . superfluous[,] and luxuries." In fact, he claimed, this devotion to expensive things was a form of dependence that flew in the face of republican simplicity, for "if there is anything that deserves the name of the Great Whore of Babylon, it is certainly her ladyship, Trade." In the same spirit, some northern visitors to Charles Town attributed the intellectual shallowness of their hosts to their love of fine things. According to Josiah Quincy Jr., "The luxury, dissipation, life, sentiments and manners of the leading people naturally tend to make them neglect, despise and be careless of the true interests of mankind in general." Ebenezer Hazard saw the Lowcountry rich as "haughty and insolent," lording over poor whites who were just as indolent as they and appearing "to pay more attention to dress than any thing else."[67]

A widespread view held that the black population was highly combustible, susceptible to leaders who might at any time draw the disaffected together and thereby ignite them. By the 1770s, however, Lowcountry elites had made a calculated decision to tolerate a certain amount of threat to maintain the vibrancy of commerce and their own privileged way of life. City jurors exclaimed in 1774 that "Negroes in Charles-town are become so obscene in their language, so irregular and disorderly in their conduct, and so superfluous in their Numbers," revealing the cultural contradictions of slavery within an acquisitive society. Like the colony at large, which contained 100,000 slaves and 90,000 whites, Charles Town had more blacks than whites among its 14,000 souls. On any given day, many black people went about their jobs with no owner in sight; these were slaves who hired themselves out or did errands at their mistress's bidding and fugitives who sought out urban anonymity. In a city where one out of every thirteen structures was a grog shop, liquor purveyors did a brisk business selling to whomever had the money to buy, even on Sundays. An underground economy flourished in rum and stolen goods, bringing together blacks and whites who bartered and exchanged the snuffboxes, watches, and clothing pilfered from wealthy men and women. In multiple ways, then, marketing—and its corollary, stealing—undermined the ideal of a static, hierarchical society.[68]

The fragile hegemony that South Carolina elites had established over a rapidly growing subordinate black population was repeatedly tested, however, in the buildup to the Revolutionary War. For whites, crises stemming from threats real and imagined arose with striking frequency in the third quarter of the eighteenth century, as black people "mimick'd their betters in crying out 'Liberty,'" in the words of an alarmed Henry Laurens. Increasing numbers of black men and women were embracing Christianity and calling for an end to the tyranny of the body over the spirit. In March 1759 a black man named Philip Johns (or Jones) recounted his vision of white people under the earth and of a sword going "through the Land[;] it should shine with their blood." Johns, apparently inspired by the millennialist exhortations of an Anglican cleric in Charles Town, told his followers "that God Almighty had given much for them to do . . . for killing the Buckras [i.e., Whites]," according to a witness. Johns was executed. In the fall of 1765 news that the Crown was going to require the use of stamped paper for official and commercial transactions provoked consternation among whites, who now feared that their own protests against English authority would give license to violence-prone slaves to do the same. Around this time authorities gibbeted alive two black men accused of poisoning their master.[69]

Having witnessed the carnage of Stono firsthand, Lieutenant Governor Bull reiterated his warning that "the cause of our danger is domestic, and interwoven with almost all the employments of our lives and so ought to be our attention to the remedy." By 1775 white paranoia leavened with the provocations of emboldened black preachers had proved an explosive mix throughout the Georgia and South Carolina Lowcountry. Swift retribution was the watchword—two black men accused of arson and poisoning were burned alive in Savannah, and in Charles Town a free black pilot named Jerry was tried, convicted, and hanged for allegedly fomenting an insurrection among slaves, his body then "burned to ashes." A white physician condemned what he saw as a rush to judgment in this case and remarked after the hanging, "Jerry met death like a man and a Christian, avowing his innocence to the last moment of his life. . . . Surely, there is no murder so cruel and dangerous as that committed under the appearance of law and justice." In November of that year black men forced to labor on harbor fortifications threw down their shovels and congregated on Sullivan's Island with the intention of seeking refuge on a British ship. A slave rebellion was truly under way, with at least some of the rebels drawing upon time-honored Christian precepts infused with contemporary revolutionary rhetoric—to whites, a frightening combination if there ever was one. More disquietingly, by this time armed conflict between patriots and British troops had flared up in the North, and white South Carolinians expressed well-founded anxieties about whether the war, when it arrived, would threaten their tenuous grip on newly energized black chattel.[70]

For the first three years of the conflict, South Carolina saw little in the way of combat. After fending off a clumsy assault by British forces in June 1776, however, Charles Town authorities confronted a startling new reality: business had stalled, and on the countryside the mobilization of militiamen had deprived plantations of overseers, halting the production of rice. Still, the aggravations faced by patriotic planters had little to do with British forces far away. Rather, their human property was giving them renewed trouble. Masters such as Isaac McPherson of Stono found themselves now forced to bargain with enslaved workers; his newly purchased "negro fellow well known in this town named Tom, a carpenter by trade," decided to take off because, according to McPherson, "he does not chuse to live in the country." The white man promised Tom, "so the said fellow may be satisfied," that he "could look for another master," an indication that McPherson was willing to be accommodating as long as he could somehow get his money back. The institution of slavery, defined by plantation discipline, was disintegrating.[71]

In the city poorly disciplined American troops and resourceful blacks were already causing an uproar. In June 1777 General Marion expressed gratitude to a group of white women who planned to host a dinner for the soldiers, but he could only hope that "the men will behave with sobriety and decency to those ladies who have been so kind as to give them so genteel a treat; for soldiers being seen in the street drunk or riotous, will be scandal to the regiment, and prevent any farther notice being taken of them." In the winter of 1779 Charles Pinckney Jr. wrote to his wife that he and others were at a loss about how to "oblige the militia to do their duty." Indeed, the volunteers' unruly behavior had "roused the spirit as well as the indignation of the House so much at the conduct of their fellow-citizens" that legislators were considering subjecting the men to martial law. Black people, meanwhile, were supplying the city with poultry, corn, and other provisions brought in from the islands and coming to dominate the city's wartime economy as draymen and hawkers and suppliers of fish and game. Throughout the Lowcountry, enslaved men and women were engaging in kinds of trading and risk-taking that their owners could well understand and to a degree at least appreciate. Yet a common love of liberty among the owned and the owners remained a self-evident truth quite lost on planters and slave traders.[72]

The Revolutionary War had no discernible impact on Lowcountry whites' commitment to slavery. If anything, the uprisings and defections that whites had witnessed during the war had bolstered their resolve to strengthen the institution of bondage, a goal that necessitated turning southern states into militarized entities. In 1787, four years after the war's end, former governor John Rutledge sought to consolidate South Carolina's gains during the Revolution by defending the international slave trade at the new republic's Constitutional Convention. He and others crafted the US Constitution as a proslavery document in which trading in human bodies amounted merely to the "importation of such persons as the several states shall think proper to admit." To a colleague from Maryland, who argued that it was "inconsistent with the principles of the Revolution, and dishonorable to the American character, to have such a feature [slavery] in the Constitution," the South Carolinian retorted, "Religion and humanity had nothing to do with this question; interest alone is the governing principle with nations." Rutledge suggested that if Northerners would only "consult their interest, they will not oppose the increase of slaves, which will increase the commodities of which they will become the carriers." He was correct in predicting that the Union as a whole would continue to support at least the domestic slave trade, and that northern merchants would continue to prosper from slavery in the South. As for limits on the trade, Rutledge made clear his constituents' opposition: "The people of the slave States will never be such fools to give up so important an interest."[73]

Rutledge, like many other whites who supported slavery, possessed only a selective understanding of human liberty. A representative South Carolinian, he had begun his political career at age twenty-one when he became a member of the colony's General Assembly. He served as a delegate to the First Continental Congress (in 1774), president of the lower house of the legislature (1778), and governor of the state (1778–1782). He eventually resumed his seat in the assembly and went on to represent the state at the Constitutional Convention in 1787. He ended his career with a brief stint as chief justice of the South Carolina Supreme Court. His older brother Edward was a signer of the Declaration of Independence and a fierce critic of anyone who proposed to arm the slaves. Both Rutledges were wealthy slaveholders. John spoke on behalf of all patriot planters when he likened the subordination of the colonies to the Crown to a process of enslavement. Addressing the General Assembly in April 1776, he declared that "no man, who is worthy of life, liberty, or property," would fail to join the cause when he realized that the only choices were "absolute unconditional submission, and the most abject slavery, or, a defence becoming men born to freedom." All over South Carolina white men were rallying to the cry "We rather choose to die Freemen than to live Slaves, bound by Laws in the formation of which we have no participation."[74]

Rutledge and other patriots rested their case for independence on the principle of self-interest; they spoke and wrote much about the loss of their own liberties, a prospect made all the more horrifying by their intimate familiarity with bondage. Yet those fears provoked virtually no doubts about the institution of slavery per se. In their failure to connect their own grievances against unbridled authority with the grievances of their enslaved workers, revolutionary South Carolinians were not so hypocritical as they were oblivious to the glaring contradiction: for them, self-interest was all, and a common humanity counted for nothing. Moreover, in the process of defending the South's commitment to slavery, Rutledge made no attempt to claim that the enslaved themselves deserved such treatment by virtue of their race or anything else; the institution of bondage existed because white men profited from it and relied upon it, not because people of African descent were fit for no better.[75]

Like their claims for liberty, patriots' defense of slavery rested on a basic assumption about their rights as Englishmen—rights that Africans and their descendants conspicuously lacked. When John Rutledge and other planters cited "natural rights" as a justification for rebellion, they tended to affix the qualifier "for Englishmen" only. During the Stamp Act crisis of 1765, which spurred the colonists to demand "no taxation without representation," soon-to-be patriots pointed out that it was not all people, but only "British subjects" who were "entitled to the inestimable rights of the same laws and customs, founded on the reason and common sense of mankind." In one of the opening rhetorical salvos of the Revolution, William Henry Drayton (writing as "Freeman") likewise claimed that what he called "the fundamental right of Englishmen is that *residuum* of natural liberty, which is not required by the laws of society to be sacrificed to public convenience." Drayton indignantly asked, "Why should not the English Colonists in America, enjoy the same national rights, which the English Colonists in Ireland possess?" The Americans were certainly not calling for the political equality of children with their parents, wives with their husbands, or enslaved men and women with their masters. Nor did Rutledge and his peers aspire to a form of democracy that would presume the equality of the Lowcountry elite with the backcountry rabble. Some hierarchies and forms of subjection were "natural" and just, whereas others were "unnatural" and unjust. To the South Carolinians, then, their birthright as Englishmen—and not some putative universal humanity—allowed them to lay claim to freedom from the Crown.[76]

At the same time that Revolutionary Lowcountry leaders were promoting their own self-interest, few could plead ignorance of contemporary antislavery arguments. One such argument came in the form of the bold actions of their own slaves who absconded during the war. Another came in

FIGURE 2.2 A notice published on April 26, 1760, in the Charles Town *Gazette* by Henry Laurens's firm, Austin, Laurens & Appleby, one of the colony's leading importers of slaves and exporters of rice, indigo, deerskins, and naval stores. The advertisement seeks to allay planters' fears that, along with slaves, they would be introducing the scourge of smallpox into their households. Planters understood that they paid a high price for the colony's dependence on slavery: their own indebtedness and widespread fears of disease, as well as violent resistance and rebellion on the part of their bound workers. COURTESY NEW YORK PUBLIC LIBRARY.

the form of John Laurens's pleadings to his well-born neighbors. The outspoken Laurens was no wide-eyed evangelical preacher or crackpot visionary. Born in 1754, the son of Henry Laurens, one of the wealthiest men in the British North American colonies, John studied in Geneva and London between 1772 and 1776 and returned home a confirmed patriot. In 1777 he became an aide-de-camp of General Washington. While serving in the northern theater of war, he took note of the heroic actions of black soldiers who had enlisted in the Continental Army and in state regiments sponsored by New York and Rhode Island. Gradually, he devised a plan radical in its simplicity: to turn slaves into soldiers and emancipate them for their service. His father expressed skepticism: "I abhor slavery," the older man wrote in 1776, but as for emancipation, "great powers oppose me—the Laws & Customs of my Country, my own & the avarice of my Country Men. What will my children say, if I deprive them of so much estate?"[77]

In 1778 he had his answer to that question, when John Laurens requested his father "cede me a number of your able bodied men slaves, instead of leaving me a fortune." In asking for an early inheritance consisting of human property instead of money, John aimed to mold these black men into a fighting force of honorable men. Such an effort, he believed, would "bring about a two-fold good; first, I would advance those who are unjustly deprived of the rights of mankind to a state which would be a proper gradation between abject slavery and perfect liberty, and besides I would reinforce the defenders of liberty with a number of gallant soldiers." John Laurens believed that his father's enslaved laborers had the potential to represent the American cause with distinction. Despite their currently debased condition, blacks were, he wrote, "capable of aspiring to the rights of men by noble exertions, if some friend of mankind would point the road, and give them a prospect of success." Laurens was horrified that rebels against the Crown would continue to enrich themselves and indulge their tastes for fine things by colluding in "the bloody wars excited in Africa," wars intended "to furnish America with the slaves—the groans of despairing multitudes, toiling for the luxuries of merciless tyrants."[78]

John Laurens presented his plan to enlist and then emancipate slaves before the South Carolina General Assembly (of which he was a member), where it was summarily crushed. Laurens had fully expected "that monstrous popular prejudice, open-mouthed against me," but he failed to anticipate the extent of the scorn that the elite would heap upon him; its members made certain, in his father's words, that his "black Air Castle is blown up, with contemptuous huzzas," not once but twice. In successive debates the question turned on blacks' potential for violence, rather than on any putative shortcomings among them in terms of their temperamental or intellectual capacity for freedom. In early 1782 the General Assembly defeated the proposal for the second and last time. Christopher Gadsden condemned the scheme as a "very dangerous and impolitic step." Overall, planters "received [it] with horror," in the words of patriot David Ramsay. Remarking on the

100 votes against the measure and the 12 or 15 in favor of it, Edward Rutledge, "very much alarmed on the Occasion," expressed relief: "Upon a fair full Argument, people in general returned to their Senses, & the Business ended." John Laurens died on August 27, 1782, killed during one of the last and largely meaningless skirmishes between American troops and British soldiers outside Charles Town. His proposal had gone down amid cries of ridicule and derision, but the assemblymen believed they had given those ideas a "fair full Argument" before rejecting them.[79]

Whites' resistance to black liberty remained entrenched throughout the war and its aftermath; yet at least some slaveholders came to believe that the Revolutionary project mandated that Americans devise some rationale to justify the harsh exploitation of blacks as well as their exclusion from the body politic. Virginia's Thomas Jefferson, architect of the nation's conception of liberty and a slaveholder himself, speculated about whether black people were inherently less intelligent and imaginative than whites, and whether they could and should be barred from civic life on that basis. Jefferson certainly understood that blacks' historic grievances set them apart from whites; their resentments were real and well founded. At the same time, he set about generalizing about all "black" people, even as increasing numbers (his own children among them) had both African and European ancestry. In contrast, his South Carolina counterparts developed no theories of black inferiority, for they were not in the business (as Jefferson was) of reconciling Enlightenment theories of liberty with self-interested theories of the limits of liberty. Rather, Lowcountry planters saw enslaved people on a continuum of dangerous groups whose interests were antithetical to their own. If blacks were commodities, they nonetheless also exhibited behaviors that likened them to Indians and impoverished whites, other groups at odds with propertied white men.[80]

All three of these subordinate groups proved resistant to discipline and disruptive of the established order. Skin color alone did not connote inferiority in either intelligence or resourcefulness. Enslaved people were (according to their masters) smart and artful in the crafts of deceit and disguise. Indians were barbarous savages, and yet their "natural" impulses made them "politic, warlike, and jealous of their independence." Backcountry whites as a group were little better than "horse thieves," the "scum of the universe," with the traders among them "a Shame to Humanity, and the Disgrace of Christianity." John Rutledge called them "a pack of beggars." At times poor white militiamen seemed incorrigible, and in fact the complaints about insubordinate troops echoed complaints about recalcitrant slaves. According to one officer, "When a soldier shows so great a contempt of discipline as to break through the orders that are issued, he is easily led on to commit the greatest offenses"—stealing, succumbing to drink, and "meanly skulking from his duty," chief among them. When in the summer of 1782 Governor Matthews had complained to Arthur Middleton that "relaxness in discipline . . . has really grown into licentiousness," he was referring to American troops, but he just as well could have been referring to slaves. By that time so many militiamen were deserting and "refus[ing] to do their duty" that officers were reporting them "collectively," rather than individually by name.[81]

By this time black men and women were weighing their options as the British prepared to evacuate Charles Town. Victorious patriot masters had been reduced to cajoling and threatening fugitives who were pondering whether to stay in familiar surroundings or to cast their lot with the departing British. Using "every argument" he could think of, Christopher Gadsden finally promised his escaped slaves Billy, Sam, and Nancy that they would receive a "pardon" if they returned to him; at the same time, he was secretly arranging for them to be "taken immediately into custody" if they did not comply. In early November a board of examiners gave 260 laborers the choice of either returning to their owners or, on the basis of British lieutenant colonel James Moncrief's testimony, receiving a British certificate of protection from the claims of their former masters, having been deemed (in official parlance) "obnoxious" to their owners by virtue of their service to the British. Moncrief was hoping to send some of this latter group to St. Lucia as military laborers. Gadsden eventually cornered several blacks he knew—perhaps his own former slaves on the British payroll, including Caesar, a laborer for the Artillery Corps, and Scipio, who worked for the Quarter Master General. He reported, though, they "told me with an air of insolence they were not going back."[82]

British officer Alexander Leslie, now a general, assumed the daunting task of categorizing workers as he contemplated freeing some of them: "sequestered" workers who had belonged to rebel owners and lived on plantations now abandoned, and blacks who were either the legal property of loyalists or attached to soldiers or civilians as "servants." Admitting he was "embarrassed how to dispose" of the sequestered slaves, Leslie was hoping to raise some cash by selling them. By far the largest proportion of the estimated 9,000 blacks to leave the city with the British were slaves of loyalists bound for East Florida, the West Indies, or England. As for the rest, the Americans demanded that Leslie return to their original owners all black men, women, and children held by the Crown either as waged or as enslaved laborers. Leslie agreed at first, and then reneged, on the pretext that his adversaries were still holding three captured British soldiers. Even as he was winding down operations, he needed black workers for the massive undertaking of removing troops, horses, provisions, and artillery to the new British garrison in Halifax; because many soldiers were ill, blacks had to fill their places. Meanwhile, Moncrief ordered his workers to dismantle the same batteries they had recently built, lest the Americans try to attack the departing fleet. In fact, the evacuation that day was uneventful; apparently the Americans feared the departing enemy would torch the city if provoked.[83]

Many blacks formerly belonging to patriots remained enslaved, now beholden to new loyalist owners. Leslie acknowledged that "officers long in this country look on negroes as their property . . . and every officer wishes to include his slave into the number to be brought off. They pretend them spys, or guides, and of course obnoxious, or under promises of freedom" from some high-ranking general. Some black people, including Mary Postell, who had worked under Moncrief's supervision and was now preparing to leave the city on her own, decided to attach themselves as "servants" to departing loyalists. In contrast, other blacks slipped away from their masters who were preparing to board ship. Of the 5,327 black men and women who left Charles Town on December 14, perhaps 1,200 were free or of an indeterminate status.[84]

Forming a small sample of enslaved men and women who scattered outside South Carolina in the final stages of the war, workers from the wealthy—and revolutionary—Middleton family left for Georgia, East Florida, Jamaica, St. John, Indian Territory, and New York. Some died en route to these places; for others these disparate destinations were only way stations. On December 14 fifty of Charles Town's black emigrants sailed for New York City. There they met hundreds of formerly enslaved South Carolinians who had converged from different places in the course of the war. Some had come north with the British—in August 1776, in the wake of the initial, failed assault on Charles Town; with General Clinton, after the successful siege of 1780; or on any one of the numerous transports that sailed between the two port cities between 1780 and 1782. Others had escaped from owners who had resettled temporarily in Virginia (where authorities exempted slave imports from a per capita tax) or Philadelphia.[85]

New York was a magnet for fugitives, a place where they might find paid employment and a measure of safety. Some former Lowcountry slaves labored for the Black Pioneers as teamsters, carpenters, and longshoremen, building temporary housing for the troops and transporting large quantities of tents, baggage, clothing, and artillery off and on ships. They also found jobs cleaning streets, shoeing horses, and repairing wagons. With an estimated 50,000 loyalist refugees and 18,000 provincial, British, and German soldiers, the city afforded plentiful work for black women as domestics and cooks and, predictably, as hostesses of so-called Ethiopian Balls. Yet like Charles Town, New York offered only temporary security for many fugitives.[86]

Sometime before 1782 Boston King had boarded a British man-of-war sailing from Charles Town and disembarked in New York, where he tried to find work as a carpenter. He later recalled, "But for want of tools [I] was obliged to relinquish it, and enter in [domestic] service." It was around this time that he met his soon-to-be wife, Violet, a dozen years older than he was and the former slave of a Wilmington, North Carolina, owner. The couple moved to New Jersey, where King labored for a series of white men who paid him little or nothing at all; out of desperation he went to work on a pilot boat and then a whale boat. In his misery, he wrote, "I called to remembrance the great deliverances the Lord had wrought for me, and besought him to save me this once, and I would serve him all the days of my life." Seeing a young friend brutally punished, King determined to free himself once again, and using a stolen boat, he and Violet managed to escape to New York. There he met long-lost acquaintances, presumably men and women he had known from South Carolina, who now "rejoiced to see me once more restored to liberty, and joined me in praising the Lord for his mercy and goodness."[87]

In 1783 a rumor swept through the city that the British intended to return all slaves to their masters. According to King, "This dreadful rumour filled us all with inexpressible anguish and terror, especially when we saw our masters coming from Virginia, North-Carolina, and other parts, and seizing upon their slaves in the streets of New-York, or even dragging them out of their beds." Among the persistent owners was South Carolina's Rawlins Lowndes, who managed to track down a black woman working for the New York Engineer Department. Rawlins appealed to the highest echelons of British command, claiming that that the woman "had raised his children and had the care of their infancy." When questioned, however, she gave an account that differed "materially" from that of Lowndes, but a British officer eventually handed her over to the white man. Other perils awaited blacks who had taken refuge in the northern city. New York's thriving slave market catered especially to departing loyalists who wanted to take with them experienced house servants. Some former slaves who had made the arduous journey to New York on foot now found themselves sold and forcibly transported to London or Jamaica.[88]

Fears of reenslavement help to account for the 1,136 men, 914 women, and 740 children who sailed from New York from April through November of 1783; most (2,775) were bound for Nova Scotia. Some, like Boston King, received from British general Samuel Birch a certificate of protection, "which dispelled all our fears, and filled us with gratitude." Together with 133 other black people, he and his wife were aboard *L'Abondance* when it departed in July for Port Roseway. The passengers hailed from states up and down the Eastern Seaboard. One county in particular was overrepresented—Norfolk, Virginia, with at least some of the blacks former slaves of the Willoughbys, probably descendants of the family of Symon Overzee's second wife.[89]

Of the 418 South Carolina blacks who left New York during the final months of the British occupation—including 21 free people of color and 397 former slaves representing almost 300 different owners—only a few went, in the parlance of British emigration officials, "on their own bottom," that is, unencumbered by potential claims on their bodies. General George Washington was outraged at what he considered the flagrant theft of valuable property belonging to the victorious Americans, a violation of the Treaty of Paris the year before. Still, it was black people's value as laborers, more than any considerations of humanity or justice, that motivated British officials to help them escape from New York. The last boat to sail for Nova Scotia left shortly after the official evacuation of troops, for blacks had been forced to play a major part in the garrison's final, concerted wartime effort—to remove men, horses, livestock, and military equipment out of the city. The British had even decided to dismantle a whole fort and take the pieces with them, and for this particular effort, too, they had to rely on black workers.[90]

Washington's protests, and his largely thwarted attempt to restore his compatriots' lost property, account for the personal descriptions of emigrants that read like truncated advertisements for fugitive slaves; British officials thought they might someday have to calculate the value of each person and compensate former American owners. Thus, Boston King, then twenty-three, was described as a "stout fellow" and Violet, thirty-five, as a "stout wench." Arthur Middleton lost John Banbury, thirty-eight, and his wife, Lucy, forty, also a "stout fellow" and "a stout wench," respectively. Henry Middleton lost Harry, fifty, "worn out," and Sarah, twenty-five, "stout wench with a child 6 months old." Among the ten persons formerly belonging to Henry and his sons Arthur and Thomas were three (George, Bob, and John) now attached to Hessian officers and two (Charles Middleton and Thomas Thompson) claimed by loyalists, John Nash and a Mr. Ellis, respectively. Other black émigrés belonged to generals, lieutenants, cornets, captains, majors, and even a trumpeter.[91]

The Nova Scotia–bound group was only a small fraction of South Carolina fugitives, yet they were representative of those buffeted by wartime upheavals. David George and Boston King would spread the gospel in Canada and beyond. Some émigrés, like Dinah Mitchel, thirty, traveling with her baby and with her son, Frank, ten, had managed to stay together with at least one kin member. The group as a whole had a more balanced sex ratio (60 men to 40 women) than that of short-distance runaways, suggesting that more families had fled intact during the Revolution, compared to the prevalence of single male runways under slavery. Some had escaped from their owners as many as eight years before, when the royal governor took his leave from South Carolina, but others did not break free until the last boat left Charles Town in December 1783. Some assumed new names. Of the 274 who listed a last name, 155 (56 percent) gave a name different from that of their former master. In other cases the last name was an approximation of the owner's. Thus, General Benjamin Huger's slave Ned became Ned Ugee, and Henry Middleton's Henry became Henry Minton.

For the British, Nova Scotia was a relatively close destination to store equipment for future expeditions and to provide homesteads for disbanded troops. Officers were awarded land grants of two hundred acres each; privates, fifty acres. Some black people qualified for twenty acres each, but of the 3,550 blacks transported to Canada, only one-tenth ever received land. Finding themselves on rocky, forested soil, they had to make do with the axes and spades allotted to them; they could cut trees, but without saws they could not plane them into boards. Most barely survived the stormy winter living in hovels made of saplings covered with bark. White settlers, no doubt bitter about their own plight, subjected blacks to draconian punishments for minor infractions: two hundred lashes for petty larceny, hanging for stealing a bag of potatoes. Here were black men and women who had literally slaved for the British during the war, who had a rightful claim to British citizenship, and now had no hope of wringing a livelihood from Nova Scotia's snow-covered landscape. Mary Postell had worked for Moncrief in Charles Town and agreed to work as a servant for loyalist Jesse Gray. He claimed her as a slave, paid her nothing, and sold her two children. Suing for her freedom, she had her lawyer call to the court Scipio Waring, who had worked with her in Charles Town. While Waring was testifying on her behalf, his house burned to the ground in a fire that also killed his child. The judges in the case ultimately vindicated Gray and his claim on Mary Postell.[92]

Boston King and David George attempted to transform tiny black settlements in Nova Scotia from outposts of suffering into congregations of believers, King for the Methodists and George for the Baptists. In the new settlement of Birch Town, Violet King led the way for her husband. Later, he expressed gratitude that her conversion had "set her soul at perfect liberty." He wrote, "The joy and happiness which she now experienced, were too great to be concealed and she was enabled to testify on the goodness and living kindness of the Lord, [with] such liveliness and power, that many were convinced of her testimony, and sincerely sought the Lord." By 1785 Boston King had embarked on his own mission to bring nonbelievers to God. Yet preaching did not earn him money; and as time went on and the residents of Birch Town "killed and [ate] their dogs and cats; and poverty and distress prevailed on every side," he sought work as a chest-maker, a fisherman, and a seaman. In the process, he found himself thrown on the mercy of white men who used the Lord's name in vain with impunity.[93]

In spreading the Gospel, David George also "found the white people were against me," and though his Shelburne church had grown from several dozen members within a few months, he could not feed his wife and children. When he addressed a congregation of both blacks and whites, he roused the ire of his white neighbors. Throughout the province disbanded soldiers grew increasingly hostile toward the blacks in their midst, men and women who would work for starvation wages and who demanded equality with white people. George and his family had to flee Shelburne when forty or fifty former soldiers "came with the tackle of ships, and turned my dwelling house, and every one of [his black neighbors'] houses, quite over, and the meeting house they would have burned down, had not the ringleader of the mob himself prevented it." George continued to preach, even when a mob "came and beat me with sticks and drove me into the swamp." He eventually removed his family to Birch Town.[94]

In 1792 King and George's village furnished half of all the Nova Scotia recruits to a new colony on the coast of West Africa, Sierra Leone, established five years before as a haven for freed slaves. Boston King joined the emigrants in hope of "contributing to the best of my poor ability, in spreading the knowledge of Christianity in that country." In February 1792 fifteen ships carried 1,196 people, fully one-third of the Canadian Maritime black population, to Freetown, a port on the Atlantic Ocean. Among the blacks relocating were a number from South Carolina in addition to King and David George. Several, including Lucy Banbury, John Kizell, and Frank Peters, now returned to the continent of their birth. There, the self-proclaimed "Nova Scotians" forged a new identity for themselves, as "Africans" who were also Christians, a chosen people fierce in their defiance of craven white authorities in the United States and other places throughout the Atlantic world. Yet rent by internal disputes and the contempt of white officials, beset by conflicts with surrounding Native groups, and decimated by disease and extreme weather—Violet King was one of the early casualties—the colony faltered and gradually lost its idealism.[95]

Within a few years, denominational rivals George and King had traveled separately from Sierra Leone to England, where they told their dramatic stories of flight and faith and became objects of curiosity among white clergy and intellectuals. For King, preaching in an English church allowed him to see the congregants as his brothers and sisters in Christ and to overcome his "uneasy distrust and shyness" toward whites (whom he pointedly refrained from calling "our enemies") in general. Here finally was a community of the spirit where distinctions based on skin color and ethnicity receded and different groups of people embraced a common humanity. In 1796, after a two-year stay in England, King returned to Sierra Leone, where he remarried and resumed his evangelizing among a Native group, the Sherbro. He and his second wife died six years later.[96]

The American Revolution had highlighted deep fissures among groups of people who called themselves "white," at the same time making manifest the basic values shared by whites and blacks alike. Boston King was a risk-taker, a quality prized by the planters who invested so much money in land and slaves in the hope of a great return. Black people, too, were savvy traders and lovers of fine clothes. The gruesome deaths that awaited black preachers of the Gospel were testament to the power of ideas that bound together the enslaved and their masters as fellow Christians. The light skin color of increasing numbers of black workers challenged the idea that Africans and their descendants remained a group apart from all whites and exposed the falsity of the notion of enslaved peoples as a separate "race." Nevertheless, ultimately, white South Carolinians lacked empathy, or, to use an eighteenth-century term, "sensibility"—a modern view of the world that would have allowed them to rise above their own narrowly defined interests and appreciate the sufferings of other men and women. Black people were exploited by wealthy slaveholders because that exploitation was critical to whites' identity, status, and physical comfort and because they had the means—the power and the money—to do so. Like seventeenth-century Maryland planters, South Carolinians saw no need to offer an intellectual rationalization for slavery to themselves or anyone else.[97]

For the southern states generally, the end of the war meant the simultaneous expansion of "liberty" and slavery, as staple-crop cotton agriculture spread into the upcountry, beyond the Appalachian Mountains. Seeking new markets, fresh lands, and "efficient" cultivation techniques, planters presided over an explosion in the number of slaves through natural reproduction and reopened avenues of importation, eventually "re-Africanizing" the Lower South workforce. Annual cotton exports climbed, from 10,000 pounds in 1790 to 6 million pounds ten years later. By 1810 half of all enslaved laborers in the state toiled west of the Lowcountry and a unified class of white men presided over a slave owners' republic. Within a couple of decades South Carolinians would be forced to defend their "peculiar institution" against increasingly vocal northern abolitionists, and only then would the sons and daughters of patriots begin to invoke the so-called imperatives of race to justify their own freedom at the expense of the enslaved.[98]

A year after the withdrawal of British forces, the city of Charleston (renamed in 1783 to downplay the significance of the monarch that it originally intended to honor) enacted "An Ordinance for the better ordering and governing of Negroes, and of other Slaves, and of Free Negroes, Mulattoes and Mustizoes, within the City of Charleston." The law amounted to a long list of familiar complaints about unruly men and women of color—regardless of legal status or phenotype—hiring themselves out unsupervised, trading in the market and throughout the city street without a license, renting rooms and keeping shops on their own, fencing goods, and assembling freely "for the purpose of merriment during all hours of the day and night." The law's stipulation that no more than seven male slaves gather together at any one time failed to stem the rumor or threat of slave conspiracies. In the event of any real or suspected rebellion, South Carolina elites, like other Southerners, would abandon their states' rights principles and demand that federal troops come to their aid.[99]

Whether in the North or South, the new states were united in their desire for cheap labor, in their fear of impoverished "disorderly" people, and in their conviction that the nation was a "white" one: the Naturalization Act of 1790 decreed that only "free white people" could enter the country and aspire to citizenship. The act signaled the demise of indentured servitude and other forms of bound labor among whites and the simultaneous elevation of slavery as a labor system apart from all others. This original codification of citizenship, then, made explicit the categorization of all blacks, whether enslaved or free, as outsiders deprived of even the hope of political equality and protection under the law. The Revolution had fortified the institution of bondage and highlighted the legal liabilities of all people of African descent residing in this newly independent nation, even if their forebears also included Europeans or Native Americans. Indeed, the white supremacist impulses of Lowcountry planters were less a regional aberration of an otherwise glorious cause than a variation on a national theme that shaped the contours of the new republic everywhere and the contours of the nation for generations to come.

THREE

ELLEANOR ELDRIDGE

"Complexional Hindrance" in Antebellum Rhode Island

Demolishing a house with one's bare hands in a matter of minutes takes considerable effort; the task is, by definition, hard work. Demolishing several houses by hand over a few hours takes not only hard work, but also a concerted sense of purpose, especially if the perpetrators are determined to destroy a whole community and not just the buildings that compose it. Eyewitnesses to the destruction of the Providence, Rhode Island, neighborhood known as Hard Scrabble on the night of Wednesday, October 18, 1824, provided a vivid account of the physical exertion necessary to this grim undertaking. The men who caused the mayhem, together with their lawyers, testified to the political will that drove this perverse kind of "work."

That night a mob of several dozen young men labored mightily to dismantle seven of Hard Scrabble's buildings and damage several others. Jesse Sweet, owner of a dwelling left "badly shattered" by the attack, recalled, "It was pretty hard work to pull the houses down," and "those engaged appeared to labour hard." One of these "workers," Nathaniel Metcalf, "made himself very busy," in Sweet's words, and another, Oliver Cummins, boasted that "he had worked like a good fellow." A town watchman observed what he called "the proceedings" by "keeping as still as possible"; he returned the next morning and found the area "a complete ruin, the houses demolished, the inhabitants without shelter and everything in ruins."[1]

Providence authorities called the event a "riot" perpetrated by a "mob" against the tiny community, which consisted of no more than twenty structures. Located in the northwestern corner of the city, the ramshackle neighborhood of Hard Scrabble was a place where sailors, construction workers, and other patrons of its "halls" and "disorderly houses" (small shops and brothels) could dance all night to the fiddle and tambourine and find cheap lodgings, food, alcohol, and sex. Yet far from a spontaneous riot, the proceedings that night in October reveal a considerable amount of purposeful labor, a planned attack on what respectable folk considered a noisy, disreputable place, a "notorious nuisance." Assembling at 7:30 in the evening, the fifty to sixty men who reduced Hard Scrabble to splinters used their hands to rip studs and joists from the buildings; but the rioters had also come armed with clubs and axes, the better to chop off shingles and split beams, and with their own lanterns, the better to assess the task before them on a moonless night. Exhausted from their labors, the rioters at one point "took a vote and finally concluded to adjourn until Saturday evening," a nod to democracy in action.[2]

In antebellum New England white men took up bricks and cudgels in brutal attacks on individual blacks and on whole black communities in what was at heart a fierce, local competition for what many considered to be finite resources: jobs, real estate, public schooling, political rights. At the same time, northern white men were relying on the lawmaker's handiwork and the lawyer's brief to craft new ideas about free people of color generally, men and women only recently emancipated from slavery. These emerging ideas held that even free blacks remained "naturally" poor and inclined toward criminal behavior. Whites regardless of class or ethnic loyalties fashioned their own identity by contrasting themselves to blacks—hence, the democratic spirit of the rioters, convinced of their own righteousness and secure in the conviction that they were doing white people's work on that dark night in 1824.

Authorities brought to trial the men who had labored so hard to destroy Hard Scrabble, but the proceedings denied justice to the victims of the mob's fury. During Oliver Cummins's trial, attorney Joseph L. Tillinghast spent less time defending his client than he did condemning the black people who lived, labored, and allegedly squandered their money in Hard Scrabble. Tillinghast considered it obvious that "we must all agree the destruction of this place is a benefit to the morals of the community," for it was a refuge of prostitutes, thieves, and fencers of stolen goods. Rather than subject the defendants to the humiliation of a trial, the lawyer intoned, the upright citizens of Providence should applaud them for their "meritorious and praiseworthy act." In his summation, Tillinghast announced with feeling, "Gentlemen of the Jury—The renowned city of *Hard-Scrabble* lies buried in its magnificent ruins! Like the ancient Babylon it has fallen with all its graven images, its tables of impure oblation, its idolatrous rights and sacrifices."[3]

Attempting to counter Tillinghast's bombastic appeal, Attorney General Dutee J. Pearce pointed out that if outraged persons were determined to shut down a brothel, they possessed the legal and peaceful means to do so. Nevertheless, the all-white jury acquitted Cummins. They found Metcalf and one other defendant guilty but recommended the two be discharged anyway, and the presiding justices obliged. Pearce then dropped all charges against several other men.[4]

Despite the moral panic stoked by Providence authorities, Hard Scrabble was not an all-black enclave, nor was it primarily a site of vice and crime. Black and white shopkeepers, seamen, and laborers lived there, as did whites and people of Narragansett Indian descent, all patrons of the neighborhood's refreshment stands and grog shops. Some boardinghouse owners served as go-betweens for their customers looking for work and ship captains looking for crew members, making Hard Scrabble a rough sort of labor exchange. Attracted to its cheap land and rents, poor people and their families built modest dwellings or occupied close quarters in its shanties and tenements. Jesse Sweet, who testified against Cummins and other defendants, was white. At the same time, the court denied a voice—either individual or collective—to Hard Scrabble residents like Christopher Hall and other people of color who lost their "halls" and homes to the ax-wielders. True, men and women of various ancestry worked, ate, fought, danced, and fornicated together in Hard Scrabble, which was at heart a boisterous, impoverished community, but it was also home to industrious laborers who could afford no better.[5]

Nevertheless, local newspapers (as well as defense lawyers) framed the night of violence in a way that produced a dramatic narrative of respectable white men purging Providence of disorderly blacks—presumably all former slaves unable to lay claim to a glorious recent past of fighting against and triumphing over British rule. In the months before the riot, the *Providence Gazette* had alerted its readers to what it considered an alarming inmigration of poor blacks into the city, vagrants the paper described as eager to "live on the labours and earnings of others, and to riot in dissipation and idleness." Residents must do their "duty," warned the editors of the paper, so that "the number of these locusts, who consume the fruits of industry and labours of our citizens, may be easily ascertained, and they will be driven from our confines."[6]

Popular hostility toward Hard Scrabble posited contradictory claims: black parasites feeding off an honest white citizenry but also rapacious black predators wresting privileges from white rivals. The tensions that animated the Hard Scrabble mob had provoked violence elsewhere in Providence in the days leading up to the incident. On a downtown bridge the Sunday before the riot, black and white youths had fought each other in a pitched battle, throwing bricks and wielding clubs and bludgeons. Apparently, the whites were responding to a provocation by blacks, who were, according to another local paper, the *Beacon,* "determined that they would possess and maintain the side walk, at all hazards, and had declared that they would not yield an inch to any 'white face' whoever he might be." Sidewalks were a relatively recent innovation in Providence, but white pedestrians had wasted little time seizing the inside of the walkway, forcing black men, women, and children into the muddy, carcass-strewn, excrement-littered center of the street. According to the *Beacon,* the Sunday night fight "ended with a victory most signal and complete on the part of the negroes," a win "that may embolden them to make a more formidable effort to gain an ascendancy over the town." Whites therefore should seek to control these "cast-off and out-lawed" intruders, the *Beacon* urged, so that blacks would no longer find in Providence "an asylum safe and secure, in which they can dwell and riot without undergoing the fatigue of labour."[7]

The Hard Scrabble rioters had intended to dispossess modest black householders and shopkeepers and force them to flee. Widower Christopher Hall supported his children by chopping wood; he was, in the words of one who knew him, "a pious man, bearing a good character." The mob dismantled his house, leaving only the roof intact, and then seized his possessions, carrying them to nearby Pawtucket and selling them at auction. Defiantly, the black man returned to his wrecked dwelling, pulled the roof down over his cellar, and lived the winter with his children in this covered hole in the ground. A group of white women offered to care for his children, but he refused. A year and a half later Hall took his family and immigrated to Liberia under the auspices of the American Colonization Society (ACS), founded in 1816 to sponsor the settlement of free people of color and former slaves in Africa. In contrast to colonization efforts in Sierra Leone borne of abolitionists' revolutionary fervor the century before, the ACS operated under the assumption that blacks, now labeled by many white Americans an inferior "race," could not and should not live in the United States as a truly free people. Most northern blacks condemned the ACS; they sought full citizenship rights in the United States rather than deportation masquerading as repatriation.[8]

It was the plight of Christopher Hall and his children, not the carousing of midnight revelers, that revealed most starkly the hardships of black people in Providence and other northern communities in the 1820s. Throughout the post-Revolutionary North, with the practice of slavery codified in the country's new Constitution but challenged by an increasing number of free blacks and their allies, many states passed legislation that would provide for eventual emancipation. However, these states also offset abolitionist legislation with "Black Codes" that denied blacks fundamental rights and limited their opportunities to work and to move in search of work. In 1784 Rhode Island had provided for the gradual freeing of its slaves. Yet Providence continued to "warn out" (i.e., turn away) recent black in-migrants, to pass ordinances targeting black drinkers and prostitutes specifically, and to bar black children from public schools whether or not their parents were taxpaying homeowners. In the face of demands from propertied blacks that their children be allowed to attend the public schools—because "taxation and representation went together"—city authorities in 1800 stopped taxing black householders altogether. Two years before the Hard Scrabble incident, the state had also disenfranchised black male property owners, seen as swing voters in closely divided elections. Like other northern states that revoked black male suffrage in the early nineteenth century, Rhode Island feared that granting black men citizenship rights would only accelerate rates of black in-migration. Cried a state legislator, "Shall a nigger be allowed to go to the polls and tie my vote? No, Mr. Speaker, it can't be."[9]

Many northern whites regarded free blacks as a social oxymoron of sorts. Since the vast majority of them were poor, whites assumed they must have been unprepared for freedom, and this view simultaneously reflected and reinforced a discriminatory social division of labor in the North. To be sure, such stereotypes also benefited in material ways the whites who held them. By keeping blacks in menial jobs permanently, whites might reserve new and better opportunities for themselves and ensure that someone else did the ill-paying, disagreeable work. In the 1820s Providence was a bustling center of transatlantic commerce and also an engine of broader regional industrial development fueled by textile mills and other manufacturing establishments throughout New England. Yet employers refused to hire blacks as machine operatives or as skilled workers. Most blacks scrounged for a living, the men as seamen, teamsters, manual laborers, peddlers, errand runners, servants, and scavengers; the women as laundresses and cooks. Compared to the colonial period, when many enslaved workers possessed specialized skills, in the increasingly industrialized early Republic fewer and fewer blacks were producing any tangible objects; instead, they sailed, hauled, scrubbed, chopped wood, cooked, watered down the streets, and whitewashed buildings. That so many waited for work on street corners and bridges, or worked outside for wages as peddlers and street cleaners, or went door-to-door to beg for jobs or hawk their services as night men and chimney sweeps, made them vulnerable to routine harassment from whites. William J. Brown, a black community leader, noted that he and his neighbors "had little or no protection" as they wended their way through the gauntlet of whites lining Providence streets; mobs were "the order of the day, and the poor colored people were the sufferers." While the vast majority of emancipated black people remained poor, the rest of the region—and nation—celebrated dynamic growth and "progress."[10]

The attack on Hard Scrabble demonstrated nothing less than whites' attempts to purge Providence of black people altogether; by this time, according to the emerging white "racial" imagination, the former slaves and their descendants had already rendered themselves superfluous to the body politic and to the new industrial system. Some Hard Scrabble rioters worked hard that night out of sheer exhilaration, for the hurrahs of the crowd and the thrill of it all, but others labored out of fear and anger. In the Northeast the factory system signaled disruptions to deep-seated forms of authority within families and also within the political arena. Fathers must now yield to the mill owners who employed their children and enforced a harsh industrial work discipline. Unskilled whites found themselves for the first time thrust into competition with free people of color vying for jobs as canal diggers and railroad construction workers. At the same time, the 1820s and 1830s marked a transition in the nation's political system, with traditional modes of deference giving way to the more popular styles of campaigning represented by the election of Andrew Jackson to the presidency in 1828. In many parts of the country a newly broadened suffrage presented a distinct challenge to elites, who were accustomed to governing without courting the votes of ordinary men. Nevertheless, Rhode Island maintained uniquely onerous property qualifications for voting: in 1830 more than two-thirds of the state's white men lacked the right to vote, a high number at odds with the new ideal of universal (white male) suffrage.[11]

Members of the self-proclaimed respectable laboring classes aspired to full citizenship rights, in the process distancing themselves from the unruly mix of toilers who spent their days doing ill-paid work outside and their nights carousing in places like Hard Scrabble. Presumably, the disorderly black poor represented a profound threat to prosperity and to America's vibrant new democracy. Not surprisingly, while Joseph L. Tillinghast was representing the Hard Scrabble defendants, he was planning to run for political office. In his condemnation of black vice, Tillinghast played to the all-white jury, but also to a larger constituency of conservative farmers and anxious tradesmen who now fell back on their skin color, ethnicity, and family history to distinguish themselves from their fellow Americans. This process of differentiation relied on the idea of race and on legislation to enforce that idea.[12]

Southern colonial planters had lacked the incentive to construct a rhetorical or legal apparatus to justify slavery; their power came from the barrel of a gun and the handle of a whip. In contrast, antebellum northern whites launched a concerted project to impose "order" on newly freed slaves by devising racial ideologies and enshrining those ideologies in discriminatory laws. Race was not only a means of categorizing people. It was also a multi-pronged strategy consisting of mob actions, pseudo-scientific pronouncements, legal statutes, and barriers to good jobs—in other words, one group's plan of action for retaining and strengthening its economic and political power at another's expense. Whites had much to gain from such ploys; in that regard racial ideologies were a rational response to rivalry among groups, a means to protect the privileges that derived from a particular ancestry if not a particular skin color. At the same time, these whites assumed that political rights were precious, finite resources and that to the degree that blacks benefited from equality, whites would suffer accordingly.[13]

Throughout the North a strident campaign to cordon off and demean the "colored" population forced black men and women to seek out each other and to build a base for political activism. If white church congregants confined blacks to upstairs galleries, if white officials barred black children from the public schools, if white Freemasons refused to admit blacks into their ranks, then "black" or "African" institutions would fill the void. By the 1820s Providence whites were watching with a mixture of amusement and alarm as people of color began to cluster in specific neighborhoods.

Some Providence blacks were managing to buy property and open small shops; like their white counterparts, they formed the temperance and literary societies that were the hallmark of an emerging middle class regardless of color. They also established the African Meeting House, the Meeting Street School for Colored Children, the African Greys (a militia group), debating associations, and black Freemasons lodges. This last institution in particular, a transnational fraternal order, sought to bind together black men of talent wherever they lived. The black Masons forged wider connections among people of African descent all over the United States and the Atlantic world, with what members called their "brothers in affliction." The group evoked natural and universal rights in its call for equality among all people and in its efforts to promote responsible leadership on the part of black men.[14]

In Providence blacks' indignant public voice and their presence on the streets and in the white imagination were out of all proportion to their numbers—in 1824, the year that Hard Scrabble was attacked, the city's black population was only 1,200 out of a total of 16,000. Through their writings, former slaves and their descendants angrily explicated new ideologies of racial differences and policies of racial exclusion. Yet they failed to agree on a concrete plan to combat a rising, regionwide tide of antiblack violence. Speaking to a Providence audience on Thanksgiving Day, 1828, Boston black preacher Hosea Easton, like a substantial contingent of black and white "friends of the colored people," urged his listeners to *earn* the respect of whites: "It is no time, my young friends, to spend your time in the dance-hall. It is no time to exercise your ability in gambling. But you must lay aside all unnecessary diversion, and alter your courses. Come out of this degrading course of life; Distinguish yourselves as pious, industrious, and intelligent men and women." This course, according to Easton, "will demand respect from those who exalt themselves above you."[15]

Not all black writers and activists agreed that their community must prove itself worthy of citizenship rights. And certainly if blacks at times exhibited raucous or untoward behavior, so, too, did many whites (the Hard Scrabble rioters constituting a notable example). In 1829 David Walker, then living in Boston, published his *Appeal,* a lengthy tract in which he argued that plantation slavery in the South and the sources of black misery in the so-called free North were part of a single unified system of violent labor exploitation masked as obeisance to race. Writing as an evangelical Christian and as a member of the Freemasons, Walker damned white hypocrites for making American blacks "the most wretched, degraded, and abject set of beings that ever lived since the world began." He ridiculed religious and other "scientific" justifications for black oppression, citing Thomas Jefferson and other theorists in this regard; these ideas, he wrote, were little more than a ruse designed to keep black men, women, and children hard at work "as slaves and *beasts of burden.*" Walker was one of his generation's most prescient and insightful critics of the nascent ideas of racial difference concocted by self-identified whites against descendants of Africans—the notion that blacks were by nature lacking in intelligence, morals, and industry. After depriving black people of schooling and access to the trades and factory work, whites claimed, perversely, that black's impoverished state was right because it was "natural."[16]

Walker simultaneously excoriated those blacks who offered what he called only "a groveling servile and abject submission to the lash of tyrants," North and South—especially the black men of the "free" states content with "*wielding the razor and cleaning boots and shoes.*" And he issued a not-so-veiled threat: "The whites want slaves, and want us for their slaves, but some of them will curse the day they ever saw us."[17]

Walker's words had an ominously prophetic ring: in late summer 1831 Providence newspaper readers learned of Nat Turner's revolt in Southampton, Virginia, when rebellious slaves and free people of color murdered an estimated sixty whites. Authorities executed Turner and fifty-five of his presumed coconspirators, and white mobs killed as many as two hundred more blacks. In the words of the *Providence Patriot/Columbian Phoenix,* the white victims had been sacrificed "to the savage ferocity of demons in human shape." Compounding whites' anxiety was the fact that some people who shared their skin color were also beginning to take up the rebels' cause, if not their violent methods. Earlier that year Boston abolitionist William Lloyd Garrison had founded a newspaper, *The Liberator,* dedicated to the immediate eradication of slavery. Conservative congregational clergymen, textile mill owners, and the white laboring classes came together to oppose the emerging abolitionist movement, which, they feared, sought to cut off the flow of raw cotton northward and send millions of slaves pouring into northern cities. Whites had no trouble linking what they considered the seditious rantings of Garrison and Walker to the carnage unleashed by Turner and his followers.[18]

In Providence the four-day Olney's Lane (or Snow Town) riot in September 1831 gave dramatic expression to whites' collective anxieties—and to the limits that authorities were willing to place on white mobs like the one that had destroyed Hard Scrabble. City officials described the Olney's Lane neighborhood in familiar terms, as a place inhabited by "idle blacks, of the lowest stamp," a place of "midnight revels, the succession of severe and bloody affrays, and of the frequent, bold and open riots, carrying fear and alarm into numerous respectable families." On the evening of Wednesday, September 21, a group of six or seven seamen on shore leave from the Swedish ship *Lion* set out looking for trouble and perhaps for a particular black man, Richard Johnson, owner of a modest "cooky stand," a site of raucous entertainments and frequent fistfights. A subsequent investigation highlighted the discordant noises that marked the ensuing melee—Johnson's anguished cry, "Is this the way blacks are to live, to be obliged to defend themselves from stones?" and the crack of his pistol when he fired in defense of his establishment and killed one of the *Lion*'s crew. The seamen beckoned onlookers to join them, and "a great noise was made, the crowd singing and shouting" as they proceeded to tear down several buildings.[19]

The robust response of law enforcement authorities revealed that Olney's Lane was no mere encore of Hard Scrabble. An estimated one thousand would-be troublemakers regrouped on Thursday night and, with alarm bells ringing in the background, fought with police officers and a hastily assembled militia force. After using axes, fire hooks, and clubs to tear down ten houses in Olney's Lane, the rioters moved on to Snow Town, another small black neighborhood to the west, and continued their work of demolition. As the battle continued on Saturday night, 130 militiamen found themselves "assailed by stones or brick bats, and constantly insulted by shouts, hisses, and execrations." Crowd members roared their rage as the soldiers fired a warning volley over their heads. A sheriff directed the militia captain to fire, eliciting the cry, "Fire and be damned!" Within minutes four white men—a shoemaker, a paper hanger, a bookbinder, and a sailor—lay dead or dying.[20]

On Sunday Joseph L. Tillinghast, selfsame lawyer for the Hard Scrabble defendants seven years before and now speaker of the state House of Representatives, moderated an emergency Providence town meeting. This time he offered no words of praise for the presumed defenders of the city's morality. Instead, he condemned the "disorderly and riotous conduct of the mob" and lauded the "forbearance, moderation and firmness of both the civil and military authorities." Among the wrecked buildings were two brothels, but the mob had gone too far and also attacked the holdings of prominent men, merchants, and absentee slumlords. According to the resolutions passed by the meeting over which Tillinghast presided, "It was no excuse for a mob, that the houses they assailed were inhabited by persons of ill fame, or that their tenants had on another occasion acted improperly or illegally." The rioters had targeted law enforcement officers as well as militiamen and damaged or destroyed property belonging to leading men of the city. Within weeks officials had instituted administrative changes that would presumably allow them to respond more quickly to civil crises such as Olney's Lane.[21]

By the mid-1830s it was apparent that the American political party system could no longer contain conflicts springing from "racial," no less than class or ethnic, animosities. These tensions were metastasizing, finding expression in social and cultural forums as well as the political arena. Between 1834 and 1837 abolitionists traveled around the countryside collecting signatures on antislavery petitions and exhorting townspeople to form their own antislavery societies. These same years in Philadelphia, New York, Cincinnati, and other cities, angry mobs screaming, "Amalgamation!"—a rallying cry among whites opposed to black equality and to black political action in any form—pillaged black neighborhoods, burned schools and churches, and beat men, women, and children. Among many whites, the carnage hardened their conviction that blacks remained a group apart, unworthy of even basic civil protections. Indeed, keeping black newcomers out, and driving current black residents out, amounted to an act of white "self-preservation."[22]

In calmer moments Providence whites acknowledged that, in the words of the *Gazette* after Hard Scrabble, it was unfair "to condemn our black population in the gross. They do not merit indiscriminate censure; and many of them, from long residence, are known to be sober, industrious and respectable citizens." Yet many whites considered black property owners to be just as much a "nuisance" as their lewd and drunken counterparts. It was strivers such as William Brown—mariner, shoemaker, self-taught bookkeeper, churchgoer, and founder of self-improvement societies—who led organized resistance against white prejudice and the self-fulfilling policies it spawned.[23]

For all black men and women determined to avoid exorbitant rents and buy their own home, David Walker had offered a cautionary tale about "a poor man of colour, who labored night and day, to acquire a little money, and having acquired it, he invested it in a small piece of land, and got him a house erected thereon," only to be "cheated out of his property by a white man, and driven out of door!" Continued Walker, "Can a man of colour buy a piece of land and keep it peaceably? Will not some white man try to get it from him, even if it is a *mud hole*?" Walker's story revealed the well-founded conviction among blacks, then and since, that raising themselves up in society would prove a Sisyphean task so long as they lacked equal protection under the law.[24]

The tribulations of one Providence woman of African and Narragansett descent seemed to offer ready testimony to the truth of Walker's words. Though associated with various "disorderly" elements merely by virtue of her dark skin, Elleanor Eldridge had kept a far distance from Hard Scrabble and Olney's Lane in both a literal and a figurative sense. In 1824 Eldridge was thirty-nine years old, the owner of a small house in rural Warwick, Rhode Island, and a more substantial one in a largely white Providence neighborhood. She was the antithesis of the noisome pest denounced by whites. A wage earner since the age of ten, she had over the years amassed impressive real estate holdings by dint of hard work as a cow drover, egg gatherer, spinner, weaver, dairy maid, laundress, wallpaper hanger, painter, domestic servant, nurse, soap boiler, and whitewasher. Nevertheless, in the mid-1830s she fell prey to white men who intended to deprive her of the hard-won fruits of her own labor. They wielded not axes or clubs but sheriffs' orders and judges' decrees. And they targeted her not because of her actions or character but because of an imposed racial identity that made her uniquely vulnerable under the law and that lumped her together with all the other industrious blacks who so threatened the privileged position enjoyed by white men and women.

Yet Eldridge did not play the role of victim well. In fact, she was also thoroughly and willingly enmeshed in the hard-edged financial world of Jacksonian America as a house-rich, cash-poor owner of rental properties; an enterprising businesswoman; a speculator in city lots; a debtor adding mortgage upon mortgage; and a self-taught litigator meeting suit with countersuit. From this perspective, Eldridge was not the poor woman of color so cruelly exploited by white sheriffs, judges, and businessmen; instead, she was just one among many speculators of the day engaging in risky financial behavior and paying the price for her own carelessness in managing money.

In 1838 Eldridge formed a serendipitous partnership with one of her employers, a thirty-three-year old white writer, Frances Harriet Whipple. Together, they produced the *Memoirs of Elleanor Eldridge,* hoping to sell enough copies so that Eldridge could pay her debts and offer a public rebuke to those who had wronged her. The two women wrote Eldridge's life story to appeal to a narrow segment of the New England book-buying population: men and women of abolitionist sympathies, particularly well-to-do white

Elleanor Eldridge.

FIGURE 3.1 The Frontispiece of *Memoirs of Elleanor Eldridge,* published in 1838 in Providence, Rhode Island, by B. T. Albro. Eldridge holds a tool used in her trades of whitewashing and paper hanging. Her unadorned personal appearance, including her short hair and simple shawl, suggests that she and Frances Whipple wanted to present her to readers of the *Memoirs* as a hard-working woman eschewing fashionable clothing and other forms of ornamentation. COURTESY RHODE ISLAND HISTORICAL SOCIETY.

women disapproving of what they considered the cruel, money-driven labor relations besetting the Northeast. In the end, though, Eldridge confounded her white enemies and friends alike, for she conformed to none of the contradictory stereotypes of black people that constituted the rhetorical basis of so much violence, as well as so much "benevolent reform," in antebellum America. She was, ultimately, her own woman, not nearly as vulnerable as her adversaries assumed, but not nearly as free to shape her own destiny as she herself presumed.[25]

It appears at first an unlikely collaboration, the pairing of the daughter of a former slave with the daughter of one of Rhode Island's oldest (colonial) families. Though separated by twenty years in age, and by strikingly divergent forms of life work, Elleanor Eldridge and Frances Whipple found fertile common ground, which Whipple highlighted, if only obliquely, in the *Memoirs*. Both women claimed descent from Revolutionary War soldiers, both endured family crises that threw them into the workforce at an early age, and both suffered the untimely loss of loved ones. Eldridge eschewed politics; she wanted to make money by working and renting out the tenement rooms she owned, and she was willing to master the intricacies of property law to do so. In contrast, Whipple was bent on exposing a dominant white-male culture that seemed to denigrate the "female" values of love, cooperation, and generosity; she aimed to shame men who put their "souls in their pocket"—that is, men who sold their moral instincts for a few coins or ignored these instincts when it suited their personal interests.[26]

The *Memoirs* revealed Whipple's dilemma: on the one hand, she aimed to condemn the heartlessness of Eldridge's tormenters, and on the other, she had to detail Eldridge's plight, which ultimately flowed from the older woman's own aggressive, speculative impulses. Juxtaposed to Whipple's bland praises of long-suffering womanhood were her own complicated retellings of Eldridge's financial dealings and role as a savvy businesswoman–*cum*–self-taught lawyer. One sympathetic person who read the book and met its subject noted as much, suggesting that the sentimental story as written by Whipple contrasted with Eldridge's bold style of self-aggrandizement.[27]

Of course, the *Memoirs* itself was a moneymaking venture. A group of nineteen white women, current and former employers of Eldridge over a thirty-year period, sponsored the book and an 1842 sequel by offering testimonials to her good character. Eight editions of the *Memoirs* were published between 1838 and 1847. When Whipple began the book, she was already an experienced writer determined to make a living with her pen; in 1829 she had edited her own short-lived periodical called the *Original,* a collection of sketches, poems, and short stories. Within a few years she was publishing pieces in Garrison's *Liberator.* Whipple surely understood that the *Memoirs* would succeed—would sell—to the extent she could attract white female readers, an audience she knew well. So she couched the narrative in the language of a clear-cut morality tale, with an exemplary heroine and a large cast of male villains. Readers would derive from the story of what Whipple called this "indigent and obscure" woman universal life lessons in justice.[28]

At the same time, the book did not promote standard sentimental fare. Eldridge was childless, and she claimed no membership in a particular church or even religious denomination. Though Whipple sprinkled her text liberally with quotations from the Bible, God was not the prime force here: people were. On the surface at least, Eldridge seemed free of the patriarchal imperative enforced by fathers, husbands, and preachers. And Whipple underscored a potentially radical theme made explicit on the front cover with a quotation from Shakespeare's *Merchant of Venice:*

> *O that estates, degrees, and offices*
> *Were not derived corruptly! And that clear honor*
> *Were purchased by the merit of the wearer!*
> *How many, then, should cover, that stand bare?"*[29]

Whipple was suggesting that white men's so-called popular politics was corrupt because it excluded virtuous white women and people of color. Yet she failed to recognize a larger political truth: the depth of black people's enforced dependence on well-meaning employers and benefactors such as herself. More generally, these patron-client relations contradicted the prevailing individualistic, meritocratic spirit of the age. Many blacks of comfortable means could hardly claim to be "self-made" so reliant were they on whites for jobs, loans, and acts of legal intercession.

The *Memoirs* contained a number of inconsistencies, omissions, and verifiable errors. Whipple referred to and quoted from correspondence and manuscripts, "Elleanor's documents," which she purportedly consulted, but in other places she implied Eldridge was illiterate (she was not). Whipple took liberties, considerable liberties in some cases, and her chronology was faulty. Eldridge's memory probably failed her at times, and at others she and Whipple may have calculated that fiction would serve their cause better than fact. Yet census data, court and tax records, private correspondence, and newspaper accounts, among other sources, confirm the basic outlines of Eldridge's labors and her unhappy encounters with the local court system as presented in the *Memoirs*. And one of the striking aspects of her story was her relative residential stability: her family of origin is documented by the 1790 and 1800 federal censuses, and she herself, as household head and Providence resident, appears in every census from 1820 to 1860.[30]

Eldridge reported her birth date as March 25, 1785, in Warwick, Rhode Island, a town situated on a "neck" in Narragansett Bay, a dairy district seven miles south of Providence. Whipple began Eldridge's story by confronting forthrightly destructive prejudices as they affected both blacks and Indians: "Elleanor Eldridge, on the one hand, is the inheritess of African blood, with all its heirship of wo[e] and shame; and the subject of wrong and banishment by her Indian maternity on the other. . . . It seems, indeed, as if the wrongs and persecutions of both races had fallen on Elleanor." There followed an account of the capture of Eldridge's paternal grandparents and their offspring, including her father, Robin, and his siblings, by slave traders in the Congo River region of West Africa, the place of origin of Antonio and the Stono rebels.[31]

In Whipple's account, Eldridge's grandfather, the "simple-hearted" Congo chieftain Dick, together with his wife and small children, were "induced . . . to come on board an American slaver, under pretence of trade." Suddenly, the crew surreptitiously weighed anchored and set sail out to sea. In short order the family "were chained, and ordered below; where the sight of hundreds of wretches, stolen, wronged, wretched as themselves, only showed them that they were lost forever." As for the Middle Passage, "No tongue can depict the horrors of that passage." Arriving in the colonies, the human cargo was "presented for sale, more than half brutalized for the brutal market," the father's "pride crushed, and his hopes forever extinguished." The slave market, suggested Whipple, was a creature of its masters' cynical calculation and unspeakable cruelty—a formulation that echoed her critique of employer-employee relations generally.[32]

Certainly, the Rhode Island slave market was a root cause of Eldridge's plight and that of her ancestors. For eighty years, beginning in 1727, merchants in Newport and Providence were key players in the American slave trade, despite a state ban against the trade legislated (and promoted by the state's Quakers) in 1787. Fully one-sixth of all Africans imported to British North America arrived through Rhode Island ports. Based on Elleanor's age and birth order, it is possible that her grandparents were captured in the 1740s, a time when Newport was taking the lead in the notorious Atlantic "triangle trade" that cycled sugar, rum, and human bodies from the Caribbean to the United States to Africa. However, it is highly unlikely that chieftain Dick would have been so gullible as to take his family aboard any kind of foreign ship lying off the coast or in one of the Congo's inland waterways. By the mid-eighteenth century, the Congo region was thoroughly militarized, its politics and economy corrupted by the stealing, buying, and transporting of slaves; virtually all native men, especially "chieftains," would have participated in, witnessed, or at least heard about both the fierce fighting and the depredations of human trafficking that had engulfed that part of Africa.[33]

Dick's three sons, Dick, George, and Robin (sometimes Robert), grew up in bondage, as did most other Rhode Island blacks at the time. On the eve of the Revolution, the Narragansett region of southwestern Rhode Island had exceptionally large numbers of enslaved persons compared to the rest of New England; in towns such as South and North Kingston one-third of all white families owned slaves. In Warwick, Kent County, where Eldridge's father lived, nearly one-fifth did; indeed, Eldridge was a common name in Warwick, and Robin probably acquired his surname from a master there. Throughout New England and the Mid-Atlantic, black men like Robin were well integrated into a dynamic economy as skilled craftsmen and farm laborers and were often given whites' family names as an acknowledgment of their inclusion—however patronizing and incomplete—in whites' social world.[34]

At the beginning of the American Revolution, Robin and his two brothers joined the patriot cause and thus, in Whipple's words, "presented themselves as candidates for liberty." Perhaps they joined the First Rhode Island Battalion, the only patriot regiment consisting entirely of men of color. (Their names are not on extant rosters, though that does not rule out the possibility that they served, or fought, in some capacity.) In return for volunteering, the Eldridge brothers, wrote Whipple, were "promised their freedom, with the additional premium of 200 acres of land in the Mohawk country [in western New York State], apiece." At the end of the war, the three "were pronounced

FIGURE 3.2 A French Army officer who fought at Yorktown on the side of the patriots sketched these four Continental Army soldiers in 1781. On the left is a black private from the First Rhode Island Regiment, which included several companies of black soldiers (among them, perhaps, Elleanor Eldridge's father, Robin, and two uncles). Also pictured are a white private, a rifleman, and an artilleryman. Black veterans of the war belied white men's later claims to an exclusive Revolutionary heritage. COURTESY JOHN HAY LIBRARY SPECIAL COLLECTIONS, BROWN UNIVERSITY.

FREE; but their services were paid in the old Continental money, the depreciation, and final ruin of which, left them no wealth but the one priceless gem, LIBERTY." Penniless, they were unable to claim the land owed them, a promise betrayed by Congress, which had stipulated "that all soldiers' children who were left incapable of providing for themselves, should 'inherit the promises' due to their fathers." Later in life Elleanor, according to Whipple, saw a public notice to that effect and tried to make a legal claim on behalf of her siblings, but to no avail.[35]

Whipple noted that during their time in the army, Robin Eldridge and his comrades "literally left foot-prints of blood, upon the rough flint, and the crusted snow," perhaps a reference to the ill-fated Oswego campaign of February 1783. Crossing a frozen lake to attack a British trading post, black soldiers from Rhode Island and New York endured bitter cold and many suffered from frostbite. Yet the promises of two hundred acres of "Mohawk lands" are suspect: only New York authorities could confer grants of land in their state, and then only upon New York soldiers, though Rhode Islanders reasonably might have assumed that they were entitled to such a reward as well. In dismissing the troops under his command at Saratoga in June 1783, Rhode Island's Colonel Jeremiah Olney regretted "that such faithful service has heretofore been so illy rewarded, and painful is it to him to see the officers and men retire from the field without any pay, or even their accounts settled and the balances due ascertained."[36]

In embellishing these stories of enslavement and Revolutionary War military service, Whipple wanted to show that the love of freedom was by no means the exclusive province of whites, a point not all that obvious to readers saturated with images of blacks unable or unwilling to provide for themselves. She wrote, "Oh LIBERTY! What power dwells in the softest whisper of thy syllables, acting like magic upon the human soul!" These stories also served to refute the white workers bent on contrasting their own Revolutionary War heritage with blacks' history of slavish dependence. One contemporary critic of the American Colonization Society made the astute observation that blacks' skin color was not "the sole source of the universal prejudice against the descendants of Africa, though undoubtedly it has served to strengthen and perpetuate it." Rather, "the name of the negro has, in this country, always been associated with slavery, and the word slave is, and ever has been, a term of reproach all over the world." It was this association—of blacks with slavery only—that Whipple sought to dispute in her account of Elleanor's father and uncles.[37]

Robin Eldridge went into the war a married man. After he returned to Warwick, he and his wife, Hannah Prophet, settled near at a place called Apponaug, "where," Whipple wrote, "by his honesty, industry, and general good character, he was always held in esteem." There he bought a piece of land, built a house, raised a family, and remained self-supporting. Whipple reported that Hannah Prophet was the daughter of Mary Fuller, a Narragansett Indian, and of Thomas Prophet, an enslaved man whose freedom she bought. In what would have been a practice not uncommon at the time, Mary might have raised the money for Thomas's purchase price by selling some of the property she owned. By the mid-eighteenth century the Narragansett were impoverished, overwhelmed by debts incurred while indulging in English goods and vices such as alcohol. In 1780 less than six hundred Indians were just barely managing to survive on reservation lands, and others were leading a peripatetic existence, searching for jobs throughout New England—the men as farm tenants, servants, sailors, and day laborers; the women as traders of cranberries and cheese and hawkers of brooms and baskets. In Narragansett country a radically unbalanced sex ratio in favor of women (2:1) made Indian-black unions predictable, if not strictly necessary. In the eyes of whites, patterns of intermarriage and forcible displacement had effaced the Narragansett's historic identity, transforming them into "people of color" virtually indistinguishable from blacks in terms of the stigmas attached to them—as unsettled, slothful, and depraved.[38]

Much about Eldridge's background remains a mystery—whether she was indeed the granddaughter of the Narragansett Mary Fuller, whether she spoke or understood Algonkian, and whether she considered herself black. In the course of the *Memoirs,* she visited with Massachusetts relatives, including her mother's only sister, and stayed in touch with two of her Prophet cousins, Jeremiah and Lucy. It is impossible, though, to tell if she was closer to one side of her family than to the other—her African grandfather or her Indian grandmother—or to neither or both. At any rate, in her ambitions to accumulate property and profits, Eldridge partook of a thorough "Americanness" that transcended ethnic or "racial" identity.[39]

When the US Census was taken for the first time in 1790, "Robin Eldrich," a free man of color, was heading a six-person household in Warwick, a household at least partially supported by his wife, Hannah, a laundress. The couple had nine children; Elleanor, the youngest, was one of five who survived. That year Warwick had a population of 2,493 persons, including 35 slaves and 224 free persons of color. In 1790 Hannah died, a traumatic event for her daughter, who within a few years was placed as a servant in the home of one of her mother's former employers, the wealthy Joseph Baker of Warwick.[40]

Thus, at a tender age Elleanor Eldridge, like many other black children of the time, entered the world of paid labor, but not before, according to Whipple, she showed her mettle by "making a definite BARGAIN" with the Bakers: "She fixed her price at 25 cents per week, and agreed to work for one year." Whipple gave an emotional account of Elleanor's parting from her family: "The sundering of family ties is always painful; and I have often thought that among the poor it is eminently so." Elleanor tore herself away from her baby brother (probably George, born in 1791 to Robin and his new wife, Betsey), who called out, "Don't go, Nelly!" What a revelation for white readers—that for the Eldridges, neither their modest circumstances nor the color of their skin diminished family feeling.[41]

Whipple described Elleanor's time with the Bakers as pleasurable, but not because of any intrinsic goodness embedded in the master-servant relationship. In this respect the author alluded to "the servant problem" at a time when native-born white women were shunning the job as inherently degrading. According to Whipple, the Bakers treated Elleanor as one of their own children and received her cheerful cooperation in return. This blissful state of affairs illustrated the principle that, as Whipple ruminated, "kind and judicious masters and mistresses, generally are blessed with efficient and faithful servants." In contrast, more typical families considered their servants "*the mere instruments of their own selfish gratification . . .* the mere appendages of luxury"; these families did not care if their employees were "left to their own wayward courses, often [to] sink into depravity and vice, when a little kindness and good feeling, a little affectionate interest and judicious advice, might restrain and save them."[42]

During the nearly six years she worked for the Bakers, Elleanor learned "all the varieties of house-work, and every kind of spinning," Whipple explained. When Elleanor was fourteen (in 1799), she also became expert in "plain, double, and ornamental weaving" and made carpets, coverlets, damask, and bed ticking. Like most urban women of her day, Whipple possessed no such skills herself, and she was correct in suggesting that this form of double weaving was "a very difficult and complicated process," an art and a mystery. Though Elleanor lacked any formal education, and indeed "her powers had never been disciplined by any course of study," she nevertheless, in Whipple's words, demonstrated "great mechanical genius, or to speak phrenologically . . . her 'constructiveness,' 'comparison,' and 'calculation' are well developed."[43]

By pronouncing Elleanor a "mechanical genius," Whipple paid homage to the resourcefulness of rural New England women and at the same time (perhaps inadvertently) highlighted the exclusion of African Americans from textile mill work, and indeed factory work of all kinds. The early Rhode Island textile mills employed mostly white children and women, an acknowledgment that making cloth was white women's work and that, in some respects at least, machine-tending was but an extension of household industry. By the 1830s factories throughout the Northeast were hiring an eclectic labor force of male and female, young and old, native-born and immigrant workers. Yet black and Narragansett men, women, and children were conspicuous for their absence from these work sites; machine operatives were "modern" workers, while people of color continued to perform task-oriented labor in white households or out-of-doors.[44]

Whipple paired the description of Eldridge's mechanical genius with details of her success as a dairywoman employed by another prominent

Warwick family, that of Captain Benjamin Greene, from 1803 to 1811. At the Greenes' she did spinning for a year and then assumed responsibility for more than two dozen cows, making "from four to five thousand weight of cheese annually" and winning prizes for the quality of her work. Though spinning, weaving, milking, and cheese-making were "not very poetical" subjects, Whipple declared, "they are important, as giving a distinct idea of the capacity, which early distinguished our subject."[45]

In 1800 Elleanor was the only person of color in the Joseph Baker household; when she moved to Captain Greene's soon after, census records suggest that was again the case. During the colonial period many enslaved New Englanders lived in white households apart from other blacks—in contrast to the South, where those whites who owned slaves often required them to live in separate quarters. In 1774 nearly half of all Rhode Island slave-holding families included only one black person. Whipple herself mentioned no other blacks in Elleanor's life besides her immediate family from the time she left her family at age ten until she emerged as "quite a belle" nine years later. It was then she began to attract suitors and to accompany her half brother George to the annual Negro Election festivals that were common in certain New England towns. The June festivities drew people of color from scattered workplaces to come together to dance, prance, drink, and show off their finery; the songs and musical instruments were loud and distinctively African in origin, the costumes brightly colored and fanciful. The men elected a leader, a "governor," and other informal officials to serve as judges throughout the year. While Elleanor was working for the Greene family, George was elected governor of Warwick's black community three successive years. Meanwhile, whites gathered to gawk and to ridicule what they considered the foolish pretenses of their slaves and servants. For their part, black people aimed to make a mockery of those who believed in their own racial superiority.[46]

That George Eldridge was elected governor three times in a row speaks to his relative influence in the Warwick community, perhaps a reflection of his father's good name and status as a Revolutionary War veteran. Whipple suggested that Elleanor thereby occupied "the very highest niche of the [colored] aristocracy," appearing on George's arm dressed in a way that befitted "the sister of 'His Excellency'": "On some of these occasions she wore a lilac silk; on others a nice worked cambric; then again a rich silk, of a delicate sky blue color; and always with a proper garniture of ribbons, ornaments, laces, &c-." Perhaps her fine clothing was part of her own wardrobe, or a gift from the Greenes for the day, for by dressing elaborately, by "shining in borrowed plumage," celebrants reflected the wealth of the households where they labored.[47]

Disingenuously, Whipple begged the reader's forgiveness for offering details of Elleanor's dresses and accessories, but she also suggested that "no fair reader" would blame her for an "honorable exactness" on the subject of clothing. Here the author ran the risk of portraying her heroine as a stereotypical black woman frittering away what little money she earned in a misguided effort to imitate her fashionable social betters. Similarly, in describing Elleanor as a sought-after belle and a "buxom lassie," Whipple presented her as a sexual being in a way that on the surface at least ran counter to her image as a diligent worker.[48]

It was in the lengthy passages describing Elleanor's love interest, a cousin named Christopher G, that Whipple succumbed most noticeably to sentiment: "There was the due proportion of fear, hope, doubt, ecstasy, and moonlight; together with the proper infusion of sighs, tears, &c" during the meetings of the two lovers ("I feel myself justified in calling them so"). Whether Christopher G, a seaman, actually existed is unknown. Real or not, he was representative of the many black men who sailed up and down the East Coast in the first years of the nineteenth century. In Whipple's telling, his wooing of Elleanor spanned at least six years, only a few days of which he apparently spent in her company or even on dry land. Shipping out of Providence and Newport, he traveled to the West Indies, Ireland, England, and Russia. Some of these destinations were unintended; writing from Guadeloupe (again, this according to Whipple), and several years later from Archangel (Arkhangelsk), Russia, he reported that he had been held against his will by British ship captains and crews.[49]

Soon after Elleanor developed an attachment to Christopher, her father died. (Noted Whipple, perhaps thinking of her own father, a less than dutiful breadwinner, "Robin Eldridge had the art, which many white fathers have not, that of commanding, at once, respect and affection.") Learning that the disposition of the estate "could not be settled, without some legal advices" (presumably, information about her father's finances) from her sister Fettina, now living in Adams, in western Massachusetts, Elleanor in the fall of 1806 took a temporary leave from the Greene family and traveled the 180 miles to Adams on foot. Adams was also home to Elleanor's aunt, her mother Hannah's only sister, and a number of cousins, all of whom were, according to Whipple, "respectable." Such kin networks bound together people of color throughout New England; former slaves, with their newfound mobility, took advantage of such connections to further family ties and to find jobs. Elleanor quickly found work as a weaver and also "made quite a sensation among the colored beaux of Adams." The following spring she returned to Warwick, now in possession of letters giving her power of attorney over her father's estate. At Captain Greene's house, she took up weaving again and over the next few years tried to take her mind off her beloved Christopher.[50]

Around 1811, wrote Whipple almost perfunctorily, "there was a long period of alternating hopes, doubts, and distressing fears. Then came the heart-rending intelligence, of shipwreck, and death." Elleanor's "lover," it seems, had been lost at sea. She lived the rest of her life a single woman, loyal to Christopher with her "faithful heart." Through this story Whipple was likely hoping that she could count on the sympathies of the growing number of never-married women in New England; some might relate to Elleanor's heartbreak because their "single blessedness" was a product not so much of their own choice as of demographic changes that left the region with a surplus of women when young (white) men migrated west in large numbers. Yet other women, inspired by stirrings of democratic individualism, might have chosen never to marry in order to remain free of legal constraints that kept a woman from running a business or buying property on her own. Whether intentional or not, Elleanor's status as a single woman would open up this second path to her.[51]

The *Memoirs* revealed Elleanor Eldridge through descriptions of her work, and her good works, rather than through her own words. Toward the end Whipple offered a rare quotation—this in response to "our young and romantic readers . . . curious to know why Elleanor never married." Whipple reported that "she says she has determined to profit by the advice of her aunt, who told her never to marry, because it involved such A WASTE OF TIME: for, said she, [and here apparently quoting Eldridge quoting her aunt] 'while my young mistress was courting and marrying, I knit five pairs of stockings.'" Overall, though, Eldridge offered up little of herself in the narrative, focused as it was on her wage-earning activities, relations with family members, and legal bouts with devious officials and heartless creditors.[52]

By the midpoint of the *Memoirs,* Whipple had established Eldridge not only as the granddaughter and daughter of slaves, but also as the daughter of a Revolutionary War soldier. Her life thus far, according to Whipple, testified to the universal virtues of respectable New England womanhood, for Eldridge was a devoted family member, a skilled weaver, and the heartbroken object of the affections of a young man, now deceased. And so few "fair readers" could have anticipated the heroine's energetic burst of deal-making soon to come; as it turned out, this mechanical genius had a head for numbers, and she was determined to make her business sense pay. Her success would reflect her ability to cultivate relations with well-to-do white patrons and present herself as a creditworthy, hardworking woman—in other words, to escape from the stigma of race insofar as such an escape was possible in the nineteenth-century North.

In 1812 Captain Greene died, and subsequent "alterations" in his family prompted the twenty-seven-year-old Elleanor to leave and move in with her sister Letisse in Warwick. She thus joined a pronounced exodus among blacks from the homes of their employers and former owners to their own households. For many former slaves, establishing their own homes apart from their former masters, and owning a small piece of property, demonstrated that they were free persons with a tangible, if modest stake in society. The local Court of Probate had appointed Letisse as guardian of her younger siblings now that both parents were deceased. Together Letisse and Elleanor "entered into a miscellaneous business" that consisted of weaving, spinning, laundering, nursing, and boiling soap. This last item they carried to Providence to sell in the market. Such miscellaneous pursuits were common among free people of color forced into low-paying, seasonal jobs and could provide women such as Elleanor and Letisse with a crucial—if meager—supplemental income.[53]

Without a family to support, and now living apart from her white employers, Elleanor managed to save enough money to purchase a small house; it provided her with shelter and a steady income because she rented parts of it to tenants for $40 a year. And as long as she was living in Warwick, she served as dutiful maiden aunt, at times helping out in George's household—for example, when his whole family became gravely ill and his wife and several children died. In 1815, however, Elleanor moved to Providence at the behest of another sister; it is possible that through her soap-selling business in that city she came to understand the opportunities, at once vast and circumscribed, that awaited her there.[54]

The bustling city where Elleanor Eldridge made her new home was only a matter of miles from Warwick, but in its economy and character it offered a striking contrast to the sleepy agricultural village she had just left. The Embargo of 1807 and the War of 1812 had temporarily hobbled the growth of Providence as a port, but those interruptions in foreign trade also stimulated domestic manufactures; now the city and its environs were transformed into the cradle of several simultaneous early Republic "revolutions"—in industry, transportation, and the commercial market. By 1815, within a thirty-mile radius of the city, workers operating 140,000 spindles in 165 mills were weaving 29,000 bales of southern cotton into 28 million yards of cloth. Meanwhile, municipal authorities were embarking on a building spree, reconstructing the wharves, bridges, and buildings destroyed by the Great Gale of 1815 and sponsoring a number of public works projects, such as the reclamation of marshlands west of the river in 1817 and the installation of sidewalks in the early 1820s. A canal linking Providence to Worcester was completed over a three-year period, 1825 to 1828, and a railroad linking Providence to Boston began operations in 1835; both projects provided jobs for hundreds of workers. Meanwhile, wood remained the city's greatest source of energy, increasing the demand for choppers and haulers exponentially.[55]

As the city's economy expanded, so did its population. From 1800 to 1870 the city grew by an average 36 percent each decade—in the 1820s by 43 percent, the result of multiple urban in-migrations and foreign immigrations. Rural folk abandoned the countryside in response to periodic depressions and freakish weather—the hurricane of 1815 and the unseasonably dry and cold summer of 1816—that took a toll on many farmers and day laborers. Beginning in the late 1820s Irish immigrants arrived to take factory jobs. Sawyers, construction workers, and seamen passing through the city found cheap rooms in places like Hard Scrabble and Olney's Lane.[56]

The perceived large influx of black newcomers to Providence galvanized white residents. In the fall of 1821 the author of a letter to the editor of the *Gazette* decried the "vicious and disorderly" black population now allegedly "flooding" into the city and supposedly causing "strong and faithful" white laborers to flee. Foreshadowing the antiblack tirades surrounding the Hard Scrabble riot, the writer suggested that "some strong measures should be adopted to rid the town of blacks who have no legal settlement, or are not *actually employed by the month or year, in the service of some white inhabitant.*"[57]

For some enterprising individuals, however, the city's swelling population afforded opportunity for material gain. Throughout this period Elleanor Eldridge and other landlords aimed to profit from the more than 1,800 free people of color seeking jobs and places to live in Providence. She was also responding to the labor and consumer demands of wealthy merchants and lawyers and members of the emerging middle class. Around 1815 she "commenced a new course of business, viz—white-washing, papering and painting," Whipple wrote. (Eldridge apparently gave up weaving for good; the textile mills proliferating on the countryside were producing cloth more quickly and cheaply than she could make it.) Eldridge's decision revealed a keen appreciation for emerging markets. Prosperous households were stocking their pantries with a rich array of imported foods and buying luxury consumer goods from far-flung corners of the world—silks and window screens from China, honey and pineapples from Cuba, and other exotic items from Europe, Brazil, and India. They were also decorating their brick Colonial and Federal-style mansions with "elegant paper hangings," including those made in France with fancy landscape prints and borders to match. For the duration of her working career, Eldridge offered a variety of services while working for many homeowners and landlords. The portrait of her in the *Memoirs* frontispiece showed her holding the tool of her trades: a long-handled brush used for papering and whitewashing. With her short curly hair, simple dress and shawl, and serious demeanor, she was the embodiment of probity. Yet an equally evocative portrait would have had her clutching a sheaf of legal papers and mortgage notes, for Eldridge's business sensibilities had by this time landed her in court.[58]

During the winter months Eldridge often worked as a domestic in a hotel, boardinghouse, or private family. Among her employers were Henry Mathewson, a well-known ship captain who traded along the coast of South America; Davis Dyer, a merchant who specialized in goods as varied as clover seed, Madeira wine, and North Carolina hams; Gravener Taft, a teacher in the city's first public school, opened in 1800; Nathan Waterman Jackson, the city's longtime town clerk (from 1799 to 1829); and Gamaliel Church, a US Customs inspector. Mathewson and Dyer were also landlords; they probably hired Eldridge to work on the houses they rented to tenants. Whipple remarked of these employers, "ELLEANOR HAS ALWAYS LIVED WITH GOOD PEOPLE." By highlighting this connection between Elleanor and some of the city's most prominent families, Whipple implied that her subject routinely interacted in a responsible way with employers of good character and morals. As a free woman, Eldridge had earned their respect as well as their patronage, no mean feat for a woman born to a father born a slave.[59]

In the winter of 1819 Eldridge consented to accompany a Miss Jane C to New York City, but there she fell ill ("occasioned by the damps of the basement kitchen") and could do no work. Jane C hired a nurse to attend to Eldridge, and she also paid for "two of the most skillful physicians the city afforded." By April the patient, who seemed to be suffering from "a malignant fever, of a typhus kind," was well enough to return to Providence. And yet in a remarkable development, according to Whipple, Miss C paid not only Eldridge's medical fees, but also "THE FULL AMOUNT OF HER WAGES FOR THE WHOLE TIME, as if she had always been in actual service." Whipple praised such "disinterested benevolence," in response to which "human nature feels itself exalted, and begins to learn its own divinity." To rest and recuperate fully, Elleanor decided she must return to Warwick, and it was there on August 7 that the census taker found her in the house she owned (it was assessed at $350). Her brother George lived in his own house on one side of her, and her brother Jetter headed his own household and lived in her house as a tenant.[60]

Sometime in the spring or early summer of 1820, Elleanor had a most unpleasant encounter with the law that revealed her enduring reliance on the white men who were her employer-patrons. On July 26 the *Providence Patriot* ran a "public notice" stating that a person recently convicted of petty theft in Cranston had described his accomplice, and as a result "Eleanor Eldridge, a woman of colour, was arrested." She was interviewed and released, but the incident prompted "certificates" from "several gentlemen in whose families she had worked in this town, desirous of dissipating any injurious impression which might be made by the above occurrence." Among the letter writers were those whose names were published in the notice: Nathan W. Jackson, Gravener Taft, and Gamaliel Church, all of whom attested to "her good conduct, honesty and industry, while employed by them." Without the testimonials of these men, Eldridge might have been sent to the city workhouse or endured a public whipping in the State House yard. For obvious reasons, the *Memoirs* made no mention of Eldridge's humiliating arrest and interrogation.[61]

Eldridge was not able to avoid controversy for long, however, and not all of it seems to have been unjust. As Whipple delved into Eldridge's investments and legal woes, she did not stint on the financial details. However, throughout this part of the story she got the chronology wrong and con-sistently portrayed Eldridge as an innocent victim when in fact court and legal documents suggest she had assumed more risk than she could handle. In that respect Eldridge was not unlike many other speculators, then and since, who borrowed more freely than they should have. One of Whipple's contemporaries, who later wrote a biographical sketch of her, alluded to Eldridge's considerable property holdings, "of which she had been perhaps legally, but at all events unfairly, deprived."[62]

In 1826 (Whipple gave the date as 1822), Elleanor, "Single Woman of Colour," took $100 in her savings, borrowed about $1,600 from an unknown individual or individuals, and bought a 50- by 130-foot lot "together with a certain wooden Building erected for a Dwelling House" in Providence. (Nathan W. Jackson, the town clerk who had testified to Eldridge's good character six years before, recorded the deed.) Soon she added an addition on either side and set up housekeeping for herself in one of them. She rented out the rest of the house to tenants for a total of $150 a year. It was in this Spring Street dwelling that she would live for much of the rest of her life. Whipple described the dwelling, "with its two wings, and its four chimneys," as wearing "quite an imposing aspect" and "a fine establishment" with a "pleasant little garden-spot." It accommodated as many as ten residents—Eldridge and three families of two to three persons each. Such cramped quarters were customary for black families, who, regardless of size, were used to occupying only one or two rooms.[63]

The relatively large sums of money associated with Eldridge's real estate investments are noteworthy. For a humble laboring woman, she was remarkable for hoarding cash and securing loans, from $200 to $1,500 at a time, from private creditors, probably her male employers or the husbands of her female employers. She apparently eschewed the siren call of consumer goods; if she needed to impress someone—a judge, for example—she borrowed a fancy horse and carriage from an employer. Perhaps the fact that her father was a homeowner convinced her of the lasting value of real estate: her holdings would not only put a roof over her head, but also pay her a regular dividend, and their value would appreciate as the demand for housing grew apace.[64]

In the late 1820s Eldridge took out more loans, including one from George Carder, a bank director and attorney who apparently specialized in real estate cases; he lived in Apponaug, where Elleanor had grown up. She probably knew him, and members of her family had probably worked for him for years. He charged Eldridge 10 percent interest and told her that she need pay only the interest on the loan each year. What Eldridge did with the money is unclear, but she does not seem to have used it to expand her latest property, for the number of tenants there remained unchanged during this time. In 1830 she was living in her Spring Street house, along with eight black tenants: two single men, Abraham Rooms and Richard McKim; Noah Howland, a seaman and head of a household of three; and Samuel Shoffield, head of a household of five. Most of her immediate neighbors were white. It was around this time that Elleanor served as executor of the estate of Lucy Gardner, a woman of color, who had died in the early fall of 1830; as required by law, a "notice" ran in a local paper, informing creditors of Gardner's death and requesting them to submit their claims to "the subscriber"—Eldridge—"for settlement." Elleanor was educating herself about property law.[65]

Whipple had Eldridge "again seized with the typhus fever" in September 1831, the month of the Olney's Lane violence. (Presumably, Providence readers in 1838 remembered that cataclysmic event, and Whipple intended to show that Eldridge had no connection to it.) After spending six weeks in Warwick, Elleanor and the widowed George decided to journey again to Adams, where she could recover in the company of her relatives. Around this time, though, she defaulted on one of her loans; a judge ordered her to pay $57.45 and court costs of $4.57.[66]

En route to Adams, Elleanor and George stopped at a Hadley, Massachusetts, inn for the night, but she felt so unwell they decided not to continue and stayed another day. Other patrons of the establishment believed that Elleanor was ill, deathly so, and, in Whipple's words, "the reader will subsequently find, how all Elleanor's troubles sprang from the wanton carelessness of those, who so busily circulated the story of her death." George and his half sister finally made their way to Adams, where he spent the winter cutting wood and courting his cousin, Ruth Jacobs. It was not until the spring that George and Elleanor, along with Ruth, returned to Providence. Whipple described a scene in which Elleanor went across the street to buy bread, only to be confronted by the baker's son, who, astonished, exclaimed, "Is that you Ellen? Why I thought you was—dead!" To which she replied, "No; I am not dead . . . but I am hungry. Give me some bread, quick!" The boy then screamed, "Don't come any nearer!—don't Ellen, if you *be* Ellen—cause–cause—I don't like dead folks!"[67]

Despite the dramatic details of this story, it is possible that Whipple needed to fabricate a tale of Eldridge's absence from Providence in order to make credible—and even more perfidious—the actions of creditors and law enforcement authorities during the intervening months. Whipple also seemed to be reminding her readers of the invidious nature of gossip. Eldridge's legal woes might have stemmed from the malicious rumor of her death, or she might in fact have made herself vulnerable to the depredations of white creditors and the sheriff simply by owing so much money and then leaving town for an extended period of time. Regardless, the white men who pursued her in court must have been taken aback at the aggressive way she defended herself.[68]

Soon after returning to Providence, Elleanor discovered that John Carder, a Warwick innkeeper and brother of George Carder, had recalled the full amount of the loan given her by his brother on such favorable terms. In her absence John convinced the sheriff to repossess her house. This development should have impressed upon Eldridge the dangers of leaving Providence for any length of time when creditors were expecting her to be more attentive to her finances, but apparently it did not.[69]

Around this time—after her return from Adams in April 1832—Elleanor found herself back in court, this time as an advocate for her half brother. In Whipple's words, George Eldridge had been accused of "having horse-whipped, and of otherwise barbarously treating a man upon the highway," one Samuel Gorton, a member of a prominent white Warwick family. The actual indictment read that on April 4, 1832, "with force of arms" George Eldridge committed an assault on Gorton that "did bruise and wound" him with "malice aforethought to kill and murder." Elleanor visited George in the jail in East Greenwich, where she found him "in a state of great distress," anxious about the well-being of his family. (And in fact the 1830 census shows that the thirty-nine-year old "George Eldred" was head of a household of eight, three children and four other adults, one of whom was presumably his new bride, Ruth.) To secure George's freedom, Elleanor was, in Whipple's recounting, ready to risk all, for "was there any thing in the abstract possession of money, houses, or lands, that could, for one moment, be weighed against it? She thought not." Whipple claimed Elleanor posted a $500 bond for George and oversaw his defense, with its "considerable cost and trouble."[70]

In February 1833, in her own hand, Elleanor wrote to Attorney General Albert C. Greene (kin to Benjamin Greene), notifying him that her brother's lawyer, none other than Joseph L. Tillinghast of Hard Scrabble trial fame, was ill and thus unable to appear in court. There are several possible reasons that the vociferous defender of the 1824 rioters agreed to take the case. Eldridge might have been paying him his standard fee. Or the several of his female relatives who were sponsors of the *Memoirs* might have urged him to work pro bono or for a reduced fee. In the absence of Tillinghast, Elleanor requested a continuance of the case and added, "I will holde My Self heretofore bound for Costs, etc."[71]

In August 1833 at least twenty-four people appeared as witnesses in the Kent County Court of Common Pleas in response to a summons from the deputy sheriff. A number of those who showed up in court were close neighbors of either Carder or Gorton or George Eldridge. It is likely then that both Elleanor and George had established client-patron relations with George Carder over the years. Living not far from Benjamin Greene, Carder knew and trusted Elleanor well enough to lend her money, and he felt favorably enough toward her half brother both to post bail for him and to testify on his behalf at the trial. George Eldridge was ultimately declared not guilty, though whether or not through Elleanor's efforts, as Whipple claimed, is unknown. Certainly, Tillinghast's involvement in the case must have been a boon to the defendant; few other blacks accused of crimes could count on such a high-profile defense lawyer.[72]

Over the next two years Eldridge's financial woes mounted, thanks in part to a falling out with one of her old allies. Returning home after a stint as a nurse and domestic servant in Promfret, Connecticut, she found out that her home had been seized to pay the ten-year-old, $250 loan from George Carder. Whipple denounced the seizure as a "wanton destruction of property"—the sale of a house valued at several thousand dollars, all for a $250 loan! Nevertheless, court records indicate that Eldridge had indeed defaulted on the original loan. John Carder was suing her in January 1835 because she had not repaid the money owed his brother. When she could not come up with the amount of the loan, plus court costs, the sheriff auctioned off her house on September 12 to thirty-one-year-old Benjamin Balch, a baker, for about $1,700. Balch proceeded to demolish the two additions Eldridge had put on the structure and to evict her tenants. Whipple reported, "Ellen, in a single moment, by a single stroke of the hammer [was] deprived of the fruits of all her honest and severe labors." With her tenants "compelled to find shelter in barns and out-houses, or even in the woods," a creditor, sheriff, and buyer, all supposedly "honorable" men, had managed to effect a Hard Scrabble riot in miniature.[73]

Eldridge, probably with the aid of her employers, decided to challenge Balch in court. By May 1836 Tillinghast was about to launch a (successful) run for the US House of Representatives, but he agreed to represent her in *Elleanor Eldridge v. Benjamin Balch*. Eldridge also enlisted the services of Attorney General Greene. Observed a contemporary, Greene had "assisted her, as did many of the best citizens of Providence, to whom she was well known." Greene suggested that the auction of her house might have violated the law if it had not been announced three times in public, or in the local papers, before the sale.[74]

In a case heard by the Court of Common Pleas in January 1837, Eldridge charged that Balch "with force and arms has broken & entered" her house and that the sale itself had not been properly advertised. When Sheriff Mann insisted that he had indeed posted the requisite notice, three other witnesses disputed his contention, but, according to Whipple, "it was found that the oaths of common men could not be taken against that of the High Sheriff. So the case was decided against the plaintiff."[75]

Certainly, any debtor would have despaired at this point. Yet in Whipple's recounting, Eldridge proceeded to hire two men (whom she "fee'd liberally") to search the city for evidence that the sheriff had placed notices of the sale in three places: "But no person could be found, who had either seen them, or heard of their being seen. A fine advertisement, truly!" And what accounted for this outrage? Whipple answered her own question: "THE OWNER OF THE PROPERTY WAS A LABORING COLORED WOMAN." Around this time, however, Balch decided to be done with the wrangling and to make a tidy profit in the process. So he offered to sell the house back to Eldridge for $2,100, plus two years' worth of rent, prompting her to seek yet another loan. Impatient, Balch now informed her that the price would be $2,300 and, soon after that, $2500 plus six months' rent. He was claiming that he had made certain "repairs and alterations" for which he was owed compensation. He was even threatening to charge *her* rent because her furniture had remained in the house all this time. Sheriff Mann seized the furniture, and he would have sold it had not a mysterious benefactor—according to Whipple, "a gentleman who had the management of [Eldridge's] business"—reached a settlement with Balch. Recovering her property, Eldridge once again plunged headlong into debt. And so she was in straitened circumstances in 1838 when Whipple offered to tell her story about how she became "a prey to the wanton carelessness, if not the willful and deliberate wickedness, of men, who SHOULD have been the very last to have seized the spoils of the weak."[76]

In her dealings with white authorities, Elleanor had defied not only the stereotypes of black women as poor and dependent, but also the reality that made most of them vulnerable under the law. If creditors had thought her an easy mark—someone unable to afford legal counsel, someone from whom they could strip all earthly belongings on the pretext of recalling a loan—they were mistaken. And throughout this period she called upon her employers for support that went well beyond the financial and in fact made a dramatic statement about her respectability and her creditworthiness. Eldridge thus eluded the usual, and disastrous, effects of the race project in Providence, a project designed by whites to keep blacks in poverty. At the same time, among her many business ventures, her partnership with former employer Frances Whipple stands out for its sheer audacity, for Eldridge desired not just public vindication, but also the money that such a partnership could earn her. She showed, then, that she possessed both the nerve and the entrepreneurial spirit to make whites pay handsomely—not, in this case, for a stint of whitewashing or painting, but for her own carefully constructed life story.

––––––––––––

By the time the *Memoirs* appeared in print, Eldridge had established herself as a skillful navigator of local judicial and law enforcement bureaucracies. She had apparently looked into the possibility that her father had been due a grant of land by virtue of his status as a veteran of the Revolutionary War. After his death, she served as executrix of his estate. With the help of patrons, she had defended herself against charges that she was an accomplice to theft, and she had played a part in (if not managed) the proceedings that eventually won George Eldridge's acquittal at trial. She had signed legal documents, issued promissory notes, secured loans and mortgages, and benefited from the legal counsel of one of the most influential men in the city when she sued Balch for breach of contract and Sheriff Mann for dereliction of duty. She had enlisted the help of the state attorney general and hired two investigators to expose the sheriff as a liar. Thus, Whipple's assertion that white men had taken advantage "of her ignorance of business, and her situation as an unprotected colored woman" was true only to a degree. And at the least, Elleanor had learned to exploit the complexities of white patron–black client relationships, a dexterity that must have amazed her creditors.[77]

Eldridge would have been counting on the publication of the *Memoirs* to pay off her considerable debts, and, if Tillinghast had not provided his services pro bono, recoup her considerable legal fees. Whipple, for her part, aimed to register her own outrage over the case, which she considered a betrayal of the "simplest and most evident principles of justice." By publicizing Elleanor's ordeal, she could at least expose what she considered the gratuitous spite that underlay the act: "By the common laws of HONOR, it is cowardice to strike the unarmed and the weak. By the same rule, HE WHO INJURES THE DEFENCELESS, ADDS MEANNESS TO THE CRIME."[78]

Whipple had an additional aim with the *Memoirs:* to provide "the colored population, an example of industry and untiring perseverance, every way worthy of their regard and earnest attention." In her view, the long-term remedies to Eldridge's dreadful predicament were that white men become more moral and less "mean" and that black people become more moral and less frivolous in their pursuits. This proposition, put forth by a number of black and white men and women (including the Reverend Hosea Easton), remained doubtful, however, because whites of varying political persuasion looked askance at all blacks, whether impoverished or comfortable in their circumstances, whether rowdy or respectable. William Brown expressed the conundrum facing blacks in Providence, and elsewhere in the North: "If you were well dressed they would insult you for that, and if you were ragged you would surely be insulted for being so; because as peaceable as you could be there was no shield for you." Brown also maintained that people of color had no legal recourse unless they had "some white gentleman that would take up their case for them." Yet Eldridge was not shy in demanding her due from white women and men who were indeed in a position to "shield" her.[79]

Eldridge left no record of her views of her benefactors, either the nineteen sponsors who arranged for the publication of her two books or the readers who bought them. As for the views of her supporters toward *her,* some evidence suggests that even her most public advocates found her too assertive, making bold claims upon their dollars as well as their praise. For whites of different political bents, she represented an enigma of sorts. An independent businesswoman, she established her own household at a time when white housewives were lamenting that the departure of live-in domestics made it difficult to maintain their own homes. An owner of a substantial amount of property, she was hardly the abject bondwoman immortalized in abolitionist literature. The abuse she suffered at the hands of white men came in the form of eviction notes and recalled loans, not beatings or sexual assault. In fact, with their blinkered gaze focused on the horrors of southern slavery, many white abolitionists failed to see the burdens shouldered by people of color in the North.

A small book that sold for 50¢, the *Memoirs* was a popular success, going through eight printings within the ten years of its publication and selling perhaps as many as 2,000 copies, a substantial number for the times. Eldridge herself went on a wintertime book tour in 1838–1839, visiting New York City; Philadelphia; Boston, Fall River, and Nantucket, Massachusetts; and Bristol, Warren, and Newport, Rhode Island. Apparently, many literate, book-buying Northeasterners were eager to read Eldridge's story and the revelations it provided.[80]

The white women who supported the book's publication seem to be a case in point. Considered together, Eldridge's sponsors constituted a Providence women's reform association in microcosm, their status and impulses similar to those of other women active in the many other overlapping groups at the time: the Providence Employment Society to benefit wage-earning women, Providence Ladies Anti-Slavery Society, Providence Association for the Benefit of Colored Children, Providence Society for the Relief of Indigent Women and Children, and the Providence Female Charitable Society. All the sponsors belonged to families in relatively comfortable circumstances, and most of the women had employed Eldridge in some capacity. Several had joined with other members of either their immediate or extended families, and others lived together in the same building or next door to each other. Their husbands belonged to interlocking networks of bank directors, merchants, and public officials, though a few made their living as skilled tradesmen (one as a shoemaker) and others owned paper-hanging or painting businesses. The fact that so many sponsors had surnames that were also Providence street names—Cushing, Olney, Arnold, Chandler, Rhodes, Williams, Thurber, and Lockwood—indicates that they, like Frances Whipple, were members of long-established Rhode Island families.[81]

The sponsors might have had no broader agenda than to lend their names to an effort designed to benefit a longtime, loyal employee. Several women had suffered a personal loss that perhaps made them more sympathetic to the tribulations of a single woman forced to fend for herself; more than half were widows, at least some of whom had had difficult dealings with lawyers, mortgagors, and other creditors in the process of sorting out their late husband's estate. Three sponsors (Mary T. Gladding, Elizabeth G. Chandler, and Amey A. Arnold) were related to Joseph Tillinghast; after his death in 1844, they would be listed as direct heirs. That he should defend the destroyers of Hard Scrabble, defend city authorities after Olney's Lane, and defend George and Elleanor Eldridge in court perhaps points to his consistent stance in favor of social order and respectable individuals.[82]

More obvious is the reason that William Lloyd Garrison opened the pages of *The Liberator* to Eldridge's story, as he would first do for Whipple's writings on her behalf. *The Liberator* published her poem "Hard Fate of Poor Ellen" in which Whipple pleaded with her readers:

> *Sweet sympathy! O, shed one tear!*
> *Humanity! Pray loud your aid;*
> *And, if you're not rewarded here,*
> *In heaven you will be over-paid.*

Whipple portrayed Eldridge as a pathetic victim of rapacious white men, much like an enslaved woman of the South. *The Liberator* also ran lengthy advertisements for the *Memoirs* and publicized Eldridge's book tour. In the November 30, 1838, issue, Garrison offered a lengthy, glowing testimonial for both Eldridge and the "attractive narrative" she was selling: "Elleanor belongs to that race which a republican and Christian people (alas! What a mockery of terms!) have for two hundred years classed among the brute creation, and treated with utmost barbarity." Recounting her legal woes, Garrison noted that "all the fruits of a life of industry and prudence [were] wrested from her by fraud and violence."[83]

Yet Eldridge never conformed to northern whites' views of the suffering slave, and even some dedicated abolitionists found fault with the book itself and with her insistent prodding for money. In New Bedford, after hearing her speak, one audience member opined that the book might have been more effective "had it been written in the plain common sense style in which the subject of it narrates it." This person also criticized Eldridge for not seeking out the formal schooling that might have helped her avoid legal trouble in the first place. In response, she said that she was too old to worry about education: "My head is too full now."[84]

In late 1838 Garrison confided in a letter to one of his friends in Providence that he found Eldridge's appeals grating. She was, he felt, "in affluent circumstances." And he found "her heart set upon the perishable things of earth," rather than devoted to more principled matters. His recent notice in the paper, he admitted, though "cheerfully written," nonetheless "was extorted by her importunity." Eldridge, it seems, had asked Garrison to come to her defense, and although he had obliged, he resented both the pressure and the woman who exerted it. Unlike the bruised slave, she was not an obvious or appropriate object of charity. Furthermore, she had an outsized sense of her own self-importance, according to Garrison, owing to "bad advisers [presumably Whipple], who have led her to think that her case is one of *national* importance, and that abolitionists universally would bestir themselves mightily on her behalf!" Meanwhile, even his public endorsement had failed to move more than forty copies of the two hundred books he had in his office. Her promise "to return shortly, and bring another trunk full with her" filled him with dread.[85]

That Eldridge generated such antipathy even among her ostensible allies speaks to the complicated racial ideologies that dominated post-Revolutionary America. Garrison remained fixated on the image of the slave writhing under the sting of an owner's whip; like many other white abolitionists, he saw no connection between slavery in the South and black poverty in the North. Black writers pointed out that even many "friends of the Negro" refrained from hiring blacks in any but the most menial capacity. No matter how stridently abolitionists denounced slavery, they seemed to take for granted a social division of labor that confined all black people regardless of ambitions or talents to ill-paid labor. Almost all whites ignored the relationship between the exclusion of blacks from new (if exploitative) jobs in an expanding economy and their exclusion from citizenship rights.[86]

Eldridge was remarkable for her bold, even brazen, efforts to bend local labor and real estate markets to her will, and it was no wonder that these efforts drew scorn from whites of divergent classes, cultures, and political beliefs. Whether high-minded abolitionists or employers of ill-paid black menials, whites expected obsequious expressions of gratitude from a group of people only just released from slavery. In antebellum New England few whites could imagine the former slaves as independent actors, as advocates for their own hard-won self-interests. The collusion of white workers and elites kept blacks confined to lowly, dangerous labor. As a woman and an entrepreneur, Elleanor Eldridge had no trouble distancing herself from the blacks who confronted Providence whites on the sidewalk, or who fought them on a downtown bridge with bricks and bludgeons; such violent forms of self-defense only confirmed in the minds of whites that blacks were prone to violence and other forms of criminal behavior. And so whites—

FIGURE 3.3 This iconic image of a slave first appeared in the 1780s as the seal of England's Society for the Abolition of Slavery. In the United States the image was popularized through abolitionist publications such as a broadside of John Greenleaf Whittier's 1837 poem "Our Countrymen in Chains." The image endured after emancipation, when whites in the North and South persisted in seeing descendants of Africans as servile men and women beseeching whites (or government officials) for aid. LIBRARY OF CONGRESS.

surrounded by a group of people toiling at ill-paid tasks, the men deprived of the right to vote and the women limited to domestic service—devised a racial ideology from a harsh reality, an ideology that justified the immiseration of black men, women, and children, all in the name of racial difference.

In 1842 Whipple published another book on Eldridge's behalf, this one titled *Elleanor's Second Book* and sponsored by eleven women, five of whom
overlapped with the previous group. Whipple assured her readers that "our
dark friend" was still trying to pay off Balch and that on his way out of
the house (he had occupied it for three months, from August to November
1838), he had pilfered fireplace grates and uprooted several bushes from
the yard. In fact, Eldridge had arrived home from her book tour and immediately initiated a fresh round of challenges to Balch. This time she had
another, equally prominent lawyer on the case: Gamaliel Dwight, secretary
of the Rhode Island Bar Association. Eldridge's plans for the house now included improvements for her tenants. And her exhausting court appearances
had not dampened her enthusiasm for financial transactions or diminished
such opportunities: Balch's former partner was eager to hire her "bake-
house" (presumably a part of the house). Eldridge reported to Whipple, "I
have let it for good rent."[87]

The *Second Book* offered little new information about Eldridge; it summarized the *Memoirs* and included short stories exposing the indignities
visited upon poor but honest mill workers, pieces that had been published
before. And the *Second Book* had a slap-dash feel about it, perhaps because
Whipple's attention was elsewhere. In July 1842 she had wed artist Charles
Green (she was thirty-seven, and he was twenty-four). She continued to
write for abolitionist and temperance magazines and had recently completed a novel, *The Mechanic.* Moreover, a violent upheaval in Rhode Island
politics was now claiming much of Frances Whipple Green's emotional and
literary energies and in the process upending her views about black people's
relation to their "true" friends.[88]

Rhode Island's white workingmen had been agitating for changes in the
state's suffrage laws since the 1830s. In 1841 a group calling itself the Suffrage Association began planning a "people's convention" to write a new state
constitution, a "people's constitution," that would enfranchise white men
who did not own property. The association opposed black suffrage, even
among home owners, because, in the words of one of its members, "we know
that, as a general rule . . . it might be too great a shock to public sentiment
to allow colored men the privilege." Arrayed against these insurgents—called
Dorrites, after their leader, Thomas Dorr—were men calling themselves
the Law and Order Party. Also called Charterites, this group supported the
original 1663 Royal charter, a document that decreed that only substantial
householders could participate in politics.[89]

Apparently, some light-skinned black men managed to vote for delegates to the People's Convention, but overall the gathering—like the leaders who dominated it—favored a whites-only policy. Newly arrived in Providence, a black preacher named Alexander Crummell appeared before the October convention and presented a petition that expressed black people's collective ire. The association's high-minded rhetoric purporting to represent all "citizens" was sullied by a blatant antiblack bias: "To pair citizenship with color corrupts the purity of Republican Faith," the petitioners declared. Representing the nearly half of all black Providence men who by this time owned their own homes, the petitioners felt compelled to refute various arguments that they were not worthy of the vote:

> Is justification of our disfranchisement sought in our want of christian character? We point to our churches as our reputation. In our want of intelligence? We refer not merely to the schools supported by the State, for our advantage; but to the private schools, well filled and sustained, and taught by competent teachers of our own people. Is our industry questioned? This day, were there no complexional hindrance, we could present a more than proportionate number of our people, who might immediately, according to the freeholders' qualification, become voters.[90]

Democracy eventually won out in the Rhode Island dispute, but its reach remained limited. In the spring of 1842 state authorities representing the "Charter" government declared the Dorrites guilty of treason and sought to suppress a popular uprising throughout the state, including an alternative "People's" government. Among those quashing the Dorrites by force—Dorr was eventually imprisoned for several months—were the African Greys, who had volunteered to assist 3,500 white militiamen in the effort. And for the first time Providence authorities opened the ranks of the City Guard to blacks. To reward black men for their service in the so-called Dorr War, a new constitution would grant the franchise to propertied black men. All native-born landless men in the state could vote if they owned $134 worth of personal property, performed a day's worth of militia service, or paid a $1 poll tax. (The Suffrage Association responded by denouncing the Law and Order Party as the "Nigger Party.") However, the vast majority of Irish immigrants could not meet these requirements and remained disenfranchised. Throughout the Dorr rebellion, no one ever suggested that Elleanor Eldridge, or any other woman for that matter, be allowed to vote. In 1845 her taxable holdings amounted to $4,500.[91]

White women were active in the Suffrage Association, and Whipple Green became a foot soldier in the cause. Caught up in the ferment, she contributed the best way she knew how—by writing. In her new magazine, *Wampanoag and Operative's Journal,* she claimed that by excluding black men, the Dorrites had "forfeited the esteem and confidence of all the true and consistent friends of freedom."[92]

Yet when the dust cleared and the Charterites emerged victorious, Whipple Green proceeded to denounce what she considered to be the blatant manipulation of blacks by the Law and Order Party. In her history of the conflict, *Might and Right,* she condemned the imprisonment of Dorr and his followers, and she took to task abolitionists for withholding their support from the Suffrage Association: "I have yet to learn that black men are better than white men, or that their rights are any more sacred." She wrote, "They made the colored men voters, not because it was their *right,* but because *they needed their help.*" As for the black man who would sell his political soul for favors from antidemocratic forces, "I would tell him that he is a DUPE." She failed to appreciate the awful dilemma faced by black householders in Providence: to cast their lot with the white laboring classes, most of whom were rabidly hostile to all people of color, or to acquiesce in the patron-client relationships established with wealthy whites over the years. To understand the alliance between men of color and elites, she need only to have looked at her own sponsorship of Elleanor Eldridge.[93]

The People's Convention and its aftermath did expand the bounds of political participation for Rhode Island's propertied black men to a degree. As many as one thousand of them were enfranchised as a result of the new constitution, and they became a key constituency of the Whig Party machine. In local and state contests throughout the 1840s, they confirmed the worst fears of the Dorrites and served as decisive swing voters, representing as they did 2 percent of the total Rhode Island population of 108,837. However, state and national political systems remained biased against the broader cause of black civil rights. Though official recognition of the African Greys was notable, overall Rhode Island's black men gained little for their affiliation with the Whigs. And in 1848 their partisan loyalties led them to vote for slaveholder Zachary Taylor over Free Soil candidate Martin Van Buren, who opposed the territorial expansion of slavery. For blacks, political elections offered a poor vehicle for expressing moral principles.[94]

In 1847 forty-two-year-old Frances Whipple Green divorced her husband of five years on grounds of abandonment and "acts of extreme cruelty and gross misbehavior . . . repugnant to, and in violation of the marriage contract." By this time her interests had shifted to Spiritualism, a positing of the unity of the material and spiritual worlds, and she was trying to make a living by writing and speaking on the subject. In 1861 she moved to California, and the following year she married sixty-year-old William Creighton McDougall, a miner and a politician. In the 1870s she and her husband moved around mining camps east of San Francisco. While he panned for gold, she kept house and wrote on spiritualism, California botany, and recent history. In 1871 she published a lengthy newspaper piece, "The Donner Tragedy: A Thrilling Chapter in Our Pioneer History." She died in Oakland in 1878.[95]

During Elleanor Eldridge's lifetime, Rhode Island's political economy threw in stark relief the rivalry among laboring blacks and whites for public resources, including tax-supported schools. Inevitably, it was the whites—more numerous and with political influence—whose claims for those resources were heard most loudly, for blacks as a group were the constituency of no party or politician.

When members of the Providence Mechanics' Association met in October 1831, soon after the Olney's Lane riot, their main purpose was to call for a ten-hour workday not only for themselves but also for their children, whom they hoped would be able to go to public school: "We acknowledge the charity of Rhode Island citizens and manufacturers, in appropriating funding for free and public schools, and we wish to have our children reap their proportion of the benefit." Toiling for up to fourteen hours a day left no time for nine- and ten-year-old factory workers to attend classes during the day or night.[96]

In Rhode Island white children occupied the front lines of the Industrial Revolution (they made up 40 percent of the early workforce; most of the rest were women). These children labored for long hours in poorly lit, claustrophobic mills scattered throughout the state. Employers valued children for the cheapness of their wages, which averaged 75¢ to $2 a week; for their obedience—they were accustomed to taking orders from their fathers; and for their malleability, because they had no choice but to conform to factory regulations or suffer fines or pay cuts in the process. However, this process of inculcating in children the virtues of punctuality and industrial-work discipline in general was an uneven one. Some fathers objected to challenges to their own authority and spoke out against conditions endured by sons and daughters who toiled as machine tenders in the heat and dampness of the mills in summer and in the cold by candlelight after dark in the winter. Shop-floor bosses varied in their attentiveness to the safety concerns of a workplace where children were replacing bobbins, surrounded by whirring wheels and gear shafts and flying shuttles. Nevertheless, Rhode Island was the last New England state to mandate compulsory school attendance (in 1883), reflecting the integral role of children in the industrial labor force.[97]

As the common schools broadened their reach among whites, drawing in immigrants and the urban poor, violence against black schools and their teachers intensified proportionately. Educational reformers promoted public schools as an agent of the new industrial order, a guarantor of uniform instruction and a marker of eventual, full citizenship rights for the children who attended them. The threat to white privilege posed by black education was evident in the lengths to which mobs would go in preventing black pupils from learning—anything, anywhere. In 1833 in Canterbury, Connecticut, a white woman named Prudence Crandall had opened a school for both black and white children; threats forced her to dismiss the whites and teach black girls only. Local whites expressed their continued displeasure: shopkeepers refused to sell to Crandall or her seventeen pupils; townspeople poisoned the school's well and set fire to the building; the local sheriff arrested and jailed Crandall for violating a recently passed law that made it illegal to teach blacks from out of state. Frances Whipple had penned a poem of protest, unsurprisingly, published in *The Liberator* as an "Address to Miss Prudence Crandall": "Heroic Woman! Daring pioneer / In the great cause of mental liberty!"[98]

Many whites believed that citizenship rights were finite: supposedly, the more "mental liberty" granted to blacks in the public schools, the less "mental liberty" enjoyed by whites. A leading opponent of the Canterbury school, Andrew Judson, member of the American Colonization Society and aspiring politician (he was elected to the US House of Representatives in 1835), spoke for many whites seemingly undisturbed by their blatantly contradictory views of blacks: "The colored people can never rise from their menial condition in our country," he declared, and then added, "they ought not to be permitted to rise here." Here, then, were the cruel ironies of northern prejudice: whites charged, on the one hand, that black people were incapable of learning and exercising citizenship rights and, on the other, that they were all too capable of learning and politicking and threatening white privilege in the process. A northern abolitionist named James Freeman Clarke pointed out that white politicians went out of their way to ingratiate themselves with their constituents by "attacking the unpopular and defenceless colored man." Blacks' vulnerability derived from a legal system that deprived them of basic protections, and such discrimination in turn spawned contempt. Noted Clarke of whites' attitudes toward blacks, "We dislike them because we are unjust to them."[99]

The promise of equality enshrined within the four walls of the schoolroom was not lost on blacks in Providence. The city's public school system, founded in 1800, suggested a future meritocracy, where opportunity based on talent and hard work would erase arbitrary forms of privilege, such as the one represented by the strange and shifting idea of race. In 1857 a group of black men petitioned the Rhode Island General Assembly, protesting the city's segregated black schools, opened in 1838: they "set us apart, make us a proscribed class, and thereby cause us to feel that we have separate interests and not alike concerned and interested in whatever pertains to the interests of the State." Denying black children a public education, the petitioners pointed out, caused "us to be regarded in the eyes of the community as an inferior, a despised class to be looked down upon; and thus blunt our patriotism." More generally, barriers to "rising" provoked anger and frustration among blacks all over the North. Providence black leader William Brown noted, "To drive a carriage, carry a market basket after the boss, and brush his boots, or saw wood and run errands, was as high as a colored man could rise." In the 1850s blacks in Providence were still barred from factory work and absent from the city's list of professions such as lawyer, druggist, merchant, and professor. Still, when the city's public schools integrated in 1857, not all black residents were enthusiastic; some lamented the loss of teaching positions and the loss of control over a pivotal community institution.[100]

Yet Elleanor Eldridge *had* managed to rise without much, if any, in the way of formal education. Unlike a black teacher or preacher, she was not dependent on impoverished pupils, congregants, or customers for her livelihood. In a city where nearly nine out of ten black women were working as menials, she had managed to accumulate a substantial amount of property by dint of hard work and an uncanny ability to navigate the state's law enforcement and judicial systems. At the same time, she was forced to rely on white patron-employers, who provided her with credit, legal assistance, and sponsorship of the *Memoirs*.

Eldridge's bouts with the law had not taken away her appetite for risk-taking. In 1847, several years after she had claimed her head was "too full" for schooling, she bought a lot next door to her Spring Street house for $2,000, paying $500 in cash and securing a mortgage for $1,500. Three years later she was living in her house, along with seventy-one-year old Mary Carpenter, a cook. Three other households made their home in separate apartments, including Thomas and Cornelia Case; laborer Stephen Brown and his wife, Anna, and one-year-old Susan Johnson; Sarah Smith and (perhaps her sons) David, a laborer, and Ira. Ten years later Mary Carpenter was living next door in Eldridge's other house and Eldridge had new tenants under her own roof: Mary J. Randolph, a washerwoman, and her daughter Mary J.; and Rosannah Carpenter, a cook.[101]

Eldridge died of tuberculosis on June 24, 1862, at the age of seventy-six. Public officials recorded her death and listed her parents as "Robert (c[olored])" and Hannah Eldridge. With her real estate holdings of $4,800, she was the wealthiest black woman in Providence and within the black community second in wealth only to Manuel Fenner, a horse farrier and veterinarian. Two siblings and four nieces and nephews were her heirs. In 1860 one sister, Roby (Roba) Potter, was living in South Adams and still working as a domestic servant at the age of eighty-two and another, Dorcas Rosser, aged sixty-seven, lived in Warwick. Elleanor's nieces included Lettice Peck, living in San Francisco with her white husband, a cook; Jane Lloyd, a washerwoman in Buffalo; Julia Hoose, married to a farmer in Lanesborough, Massachusetts; and Abby Ann Lewis, married to a Providence barber. Her nephews included Robert M. Eldridge, a sailor and farm laborer, and George, a miner, both of Warwick. When she died, Robert and George together sold her house for $4,500 to the local surveyor of highways. A contemporary biographer of Frances Whipple Green McDougall wrote that Eldridge "lived to a good old age, a respected and respectable woman, tall and erect as the young oak in the native forest of Rhode Island, through which her grandmother had wandered among the last of a race now unknown."[102]

By this time Providence was attracting few black migrants; compared to Boston, it was a particularly inhospitable place for them. Immigrants were joining the ranks of the Rhode Island industrial workforce, but few of these white newcomers could vote because they lacked means to purchase enough property to meet the $134 threshold. Thus, in the 1860s foreign-born voters numbered only 1,260 (out of 37,394 immigrants residing in the state), while the black population of less than 4,000 accounted for 1,000 voters.

This contrast in voting rights exacerbated Irish animosity toward blacks, even though, on the surface at least, the Irish shared obvious liabilities with many blacks: both groups faced discrimination from native-born whites, most members of both groups remained confined to low-paying jobs, and both had suffered from a centuries-long form of slavery—in the case of the Irish, subjugation to the British Crown. Nevertheless, Irish newcomers retained substantial advantages in politics, job-seeking, and business; for example, they replaced blacks on public works construction projects, and qualified for liquor licenses where blacks were not allowed to buy such licenses. In their distress, the Irish would see blacks not as compatriots but as competitors for scarce resources—and for citizenship rights.[103]

Within this contentious political climate, academic debates over "scientific" racial ideologies played only a minor but supporting role. In Providence antiblack laws and policies emerged from conflicts over jobs, schools, the ballot box, and the inside of the sidewalk, not from abstract theories of racial difference. Still, local papers might occasionally run pieces summarizing scholarly studies of the world's races. Around the time of the Hard Scrabble riot, the *Rhode Island American* saw fit to print an article on William Smellie's "five varieties of the human race." First published in Edinburgh in 1790, Smellie's *Philosophy of Natural History* described the African "race" as "remarkable for its black colour, curled hair, flat nose, compressed cranium, and large lips. The individuals belonging to it are nearly all in an uncivilized state, and have an apparent inferiority in intellectual capacity." In contrast, the "Caucasian race" was "distinguished by the fine form of the head and the great beauty of the features . . . distinguished in arts, arms, learning, sciences, and civilization."[104]

In the North some black clergymen disputed the very idea of race as an affront to the Christian spirit, but only a few ordinary blacks had the luxury of time to ponder the intellectual underpinnings of race. One was David Walker, and another was George Henry, a ship captain. Born in the South in 1819, Henry settled in Providence. He argued against race, pointing out that, because all mankind was descended from Adam, meaningful "racial" differences were nonexistent. God was the arbiter of all social relations, Henry wrote in a letter to a local paper: "Now Mr. Editor, where did you get your race from? If it is a different race from mine[?] Please tell me and the world, and if you cannot answer this question, never let me hear any more howls from your paper about races." He noted that extrapolating racial difference from skin color made no sense from a theoretical or practical point of view, for neither a capacity for citizenship nor a proclivity for godliness flowed from such a superficial characteristic.[105]

By casting former slaves as by nature perpetually poor and disorderly, northern politicians and members of the white laboring classes conjured a fiction to justify the suffering of men and women who were no longer deprived of power through other, simpler means—the institution of bondage. This fiction contrived a threat called "racial." Ideologues argued that blacks lacked the requisite intelligence and moral character to use their freedom well, but the actions of mobs to deny blacks access to the ballot, schools, and good jobs spoke louder than the words that posited racial difference. In this respect, the local project of discrimination carried on by the whites of Providence and its environs foreshadowed a national project of the 1860s and beyond, one embraced by whites of varying political persuasions who claimed that former slaves and their descendants posed a threat to whites' rights and livelihoods.

With some notable exceptions, abolitionists and fighters for equal rights took for granted the "complexional hindrance" that, according to the petitioners to the People's Convention, stymied all men and women of color in their bid for American citizenship. Yet even though blacks might have been one people in terms of their history and the opprobrium they endured collectively, they were hardly one people in "complexion."

FOUR

RICHARD W. WHITE

"Racial" Politics in Post–Civil War Savannah

Late in the morning of Tuesday, January 26, 1869, in Wright Square, the heart of Savannah, a man named Richard W. White approached the park amid a commotion. A large number of black men and women, all of them rice workers, were spilling out of the courthouse, adjacent to the square to the west. Dressed in the rude clothing of field hands, and speaking Geechee, a pidgin language unknown to city folk, these workers had arrived earlier that day from the Ogeechee River district to hear public testimony against several of their neighbors charged by officials with "insurrection against the lawful authorities of the state of Georgia." The Ogeechee proceedings had begun at 9 and ended at 11, when the next case, with Richard White as the defendant, was to start. Although his name was by this time a familiar one in Savannah politics, to the workers he would have appeared to be just another white man, with dark hair and dark eyes but a light complexion—hardly distinguishable from his paper-toting lawyers, all of them well dressed, with soft, callous-free hands. Yet like the reputed Ogeechee insurgents, this former Ohio school-master offered a potent threat to the established political order.[1]

Beginning in mid-January, for fourteen consecutive weekdays, the city had been transfixed by wild tales of the "Ogeechee Troubles"—according to authorities, a violent uprising on the part of rice workers near Savannah. In the courthouse black spectators were confined to the gallery and first-floor aisles, while whites sat in the downstairs seats and murmured to themselves about the several alleged ringleaders, whom they judged a "hard-looking crowd, the countenance of some of them being particularly bad." Those people unable to squeeze into the courthouse could read about each day's proceedings in the local newspaper, with the story invariably headlined "The Ogeechee Insurrection!"[2]

In December 1868 several hundred freedmen in the Ogeechee River district had allegedly armed themselves with muskets, bayonets, and swords, defying white landowners and claiming as their own the rice crop they had planted, tended, and harvested. Former slaves emancipated by the Thirteenth Amendment three years before, these rice workers continued to toil in the same fields, now bound by landlessness rather than shackles and chains. Prosecutors in Savannah claimed that, the month before, the alleged insurrectionists had loaded their flatboats and, under the cover of darkness, spirited the rice away to remote hiding places. Threatening to dump an overseer in the swamp and leave his body as carrion for the buzzards, they vowed to "fight knee-deep in blood" and expel all white men from the region—in the words of one white eyewitness, "That as long as they could see a man with straight hair he should not stay in the Ogeechee." Other sensational (and suspect) testimony featured mysterious signals exchanged among the defendants and menacing drumbeats punctuating the stillness of the flat, expansive midwinter rice fields. At the conclusion of the trial, six of the original seventeen defendants would be found guilty and given long sentences of hard labor, but the fact that Georgia's governor pardoned all of them in the summer of 1869 indicated the Ogeechee Rebellion was largely a product of white authorities' fevered imaginations.[3]

Richard W. White was at the center of another court case, *Clements v. White*. This one overlapped with the Ogeechee hearings and ran from January through March. His trial lacked a dramatic narrative shaped by gunshot blasts and rebellious field hands; instead it revolved around history, politics, and constitutional law. Yet most whites would have agreed that the outcome of this case had the potential to shake the state of Georgia to its core, owing to one simple fact: a black man had won a local election in Savannah.

At least Savannah whites *thought* he was black. Now prosecutors had to prove it in court. The case that began on January 26 culminated in a trial on March 22, 1869, when district court judge William Schley convened a jury to answer the question, Was Richard W. White, clerk of the Chatham County Superior Court, black or white? Specifically, was he a "person of color," having "in his veins one-eighth of negro, or African, blood"?[4]

"THE FIRST VOTE."—DRAWN BY A. R. WAUD.—[SEE NEXT PAGE.]

FIGURE 4.1 Alfred R. Waud's drawing "The First Vote" appeared in the November 16, 1867, issue of *Harper's Weekly* and depicts four southern black men casting ballots for the first time. Richard W. White won election to the Savannah judicial clerkship the following April. Here, Waud suggests that voting was an orderly process, when in fact white registrars, poll watchers, police, and working-class men devised a variety of tactics to prevent black men from participating in the political process at the ballot box and elsewhere. LIBRARY OF CONGRESS.

Jurors' answer to that deceptively simple question would determine whether White could remain in his newly elected post. In April the year before, the twenty-nine-year-old White had won election to the clerkship with 9,782 votes to the 2,712 votes of his opponent, William J. Clements. Whites in Chatham County had moved swiftly to unseat the new clerk. In

May members of an all-white grand jury indicted White on a trumped-up case of larceny; their aim was to intimidate him and to register the outrage of former Confederates who had been forced to sit out the election on the sidelines, stripped of the right to vote by congressional mandate for their bloody attempt to destroy the Union by force of arms. White spent a night in jail until he could post bond. A few months later Clements, a forty-nine-year-old store clerk, sued to assume the job the voters had denied him, charging that Georgia law prohibited black men from running for or serving in public office.[5]

Georgia's antebellum laws were predictably silent on the issue of black officeholders, and after the Civil War most of the Georgia political elite considered black citizenship rights to be unsettled questions still subject to debate in the courtroom and state legislature. And yet within the previous eight years, the Union had vanquished the Confederacy in the American Civil War, at a price of 700,000 lives; congressional legislation (in March 1867) had enfranchised black men in the former Confederacy; and the requisite number of states had ratified the Fourteenth Amendment to the Constitution (in July 1868), which guaranteed black people the status of citizens for the first time. Nevertheless, Georgia's whites were determined to use state courts to halt the erosion of their own power that was sure to follow from black men's inclusion in the electorate. Through the spring and into the summer of 1869, the questions of Richard White's "race" and his eligibility for office produced more than one hundred pages of testimony, cross-examination, and, ultimately, opinions of a state superior court judge and three Georgia State Supreme Court justices. And yet even before the court could render its decision, a political revolution was well under way in Georgia.

To northern visitors staying in one of Savannah's elegant hotels and luxuriating in the mild winter weather, the city presented an appearance of busyness and prosperity. Caught up in the social season, the well-to-do kept themselves occupied with private parties, charity benefits, horse races at the Thunderbolt track right outside town, and a variety of offerings at the Theatre Comique—comedies, farces, pantomimes, and "negro melodies." The docks along the Savannah River were humming with activity as longshoremen loaded three-hundred-pound bales of cotton into holds of ships bound for the North and for Europe. The whole city was "cotton mad," according to the *Savannah Morning News,* with factors and traders anxiously following the international markets each day. Savannah had regained its leading place as a southern port, second only to New Orleans and ahead of antebellum archrival Charleston.[6]

Despite these seeming signs of normalcy, the *Clements* case revealed the dramatic way the war had transformed the city's politics. Richard White and the Ogeechee defendants were among the agents of that transformation— and the presence of the defendants' supporters in the courthouse on Wright Square testified to the end of slavery and the beginning of a contentious new politics in the postwar South.

Judge Schley and Clements's attorneys were initially taken aback at the prospect of having to prove that White was indeed black. On March 4 White and his legal team issued a demurrer in response to a demand from the state's solicitor general that he vacate his duly elected position immediately; the defendant was "not confessing or admitting any of the allegations in the said Information to be true," the document asserted. Schley immediately issued an opinion from the bench stating that Georgia state law, by not expressly granting the right of black men to hold office, prohibited them from doing so, but the judge needed a jury to decide White's race. White was a relative newcomer to the city, from unknown parts and of unknown lineage, so producing his kin as evidence one way or another was not an option. Instead, Clements's attorneys would have to come up with some creative arguments to prove that a man who looked white was in fact black.[7]

———————

Ideologies of race had remained in flux in the South throughout the Civil War era. Before the war some proslavery men, like their Revolutionary-era South Carolina forebears, considered insulting the notion that they must defend bondage, an institution they considered self-evidently normal and useful. In the words of a prominent editor, "As Southerners, as Americans, as MEN, we deny the right of being *called to account* for our institutions, our policy, our laws, or our government." Yet under increasing pressure from northern abolitionists, planters had developed a rationale for slavery, a justification that bridged the past views of Thomas Jefferson and the future views of social-scientific racists. According to antebellum southern elites, blacks were unable to care for themselves; like adolescents, they could not resist the temptations to drink, steal, and sing and dance the time away if left to their own irresponsible devices. One planter spoke for the members of his class when he argued that "anatomical peculiarities" of the Negro, chief among them deficiencies in the brain, "give to him those mental and moral characteristics that distinguish him from the more perfect and intellectual of the races." Slavery was thus a necessary institution, providing care and protection for a group of dependents who lacked the discipline to engage in productive labor on their own.[8]

With the war years came a brief challenge to this view, as Confederate military authorities condemned blacks for their perfidious efforts to undermine the fight against the Union; enslaved workers were now "intelligent beings" making use of "information well calculated to aid the enemy." These blacks were guilty of "furnishing the enemy with aid & comfort, & for acting as Spies and traitors" and pursuing *cheap goods, freedom, and paid labor,*" in the words of one group of outraged Georgia planters living not far from Savannah. The mythical childlike slave now gave way to the mythical bloodthirsty subversive, a throwback to the colonial period.[9]

The end of the war brought yet another iteration of "racial" imperatives, this one positing that blacks were congenitally unfit for freedom, and hence easily duped by white politicians—in this case, leaders of the Republican Party. Ironically, this new ideology of race echoed the views of whites in the postemancipation North, who had earlier in the century claimed that black people could not use their freedom well—that the former slaves would not work of their own volition and that, unless treated harshly by employers and public officials, they would soon descend into shiftlessness and criminality. By definition, then, according to this view, free people of color represented a threat to the well-being of white folk. Whites in both sections of the country embraced this myth because it served as a convenient justification not only for denying blacks the right to vote and send their children to school, but also for denying them basic protections under the law, even when attacked by whites as individuals or in mobs. The freedpeople of Savannah thus shared with the enslaved men and women of the seventeenth-century Chesapeake vulnerability to the depredations of masters and employers, of political leaders and legal authorities.

In the wake of the destruction of slavery, unrepentant Confederates continued to organize their world around what they considered the verities of race. An editor of the Savannah *Daily News and Herald* reacted with disbelief to a piece of postwar legislation protecting the rights of former slaves or their descendants or anyone else "who does not belong to the so-called white race." Filed by Massachusetts senator Charles Sumner, the bill posed a challenge to the very idea of racial classifications, which provoked an outraged response from the editor: "Is the man '*daft*'? Does he dispute the existence of *races* among men? Is he, himself, only '*called*' and *not* a white man or of the white race?"[10]

The notion of racial differences between blacks and whites would provide a guiding principle for postwar political relations and create a social superstructure to replace the legal institution of slavery. Southern yeoman farmers could ignore the material similarities between themselves and freedpeople and embrace a notion of whiteness that guaranteed them considerable privileges, and legal rights, without altering their lowly class status. Politicians could appeal to their impoverished white neighbors and exalt solidarity among white men, all the while exploiting the labor of tenants, sharecroppers, and field hands regardless of color. Yet despite (or perhaps because of) the widespread acceptance of the notion of race, that notion did not necessarily lend itself to proof—or to rational discussion for that matter.

Richard White's trial revealed the unease of southern whites forced to defend via evidence produced in a courtroom their efforts to subordinate all black people. Under slavery, the legal status of the mother determined the liabilities of a son or daughter, regardless of the skin color of either parent or child. Now Georgia whites confronted the daunting task of enshrining a new form of subordination—discrimination against freedpeople—into a new code of laws and a new set of social norms targeting former slaves. Richard White's trial was a proving ground for these new codes and for a new racial ideology southern whites hoped might preserve their long-standing traditions of slavery—in practice, if not in name.

Clements's attorneys called four witnesses whom he hoped might prove White's "blackness." Albert Jackson, the white voter registrar in Savannah, claimed that prior to the election he had posted a list of voters in a public place, putting a "c" for "colored" next to White's name, a designation that White had not challenged. Richard Mimms, a black man, swore that White had told him that before the war he had "made his escape from a master or a guardian." Next called to the stand, a local white Republican politician named A. N. Wilson said that the first time he had seen White, in the fall of 1867, he was delivering a speech in favor of nominating an equal number of whites and blacks as delegates to the upcoming state constitutional convention; such a stance, Wilson believed, indicated that White was speaking "in behalf of the colored part of the Convention." And finally, a white physician, Dr. Easton Yonge, testified that he had listed White as a mulatto on an insurance policy for the defendant's wife, a form that White had signed without protest. Proclaiming himself an expert in the "science of Ethnology," Yonge declared that "any intelligent person" could tell "the difference between a white man and a person of color, from observation."[11]

Yonge was mistaken in assuming that White's race was apparent from observation. Jackson, the registrar, testified that he had "seen Spaniards and Italians as dark as White." Jackson had only affixed a "c" next to the defendant's name because, he said, "I believe White is reputed a person of color." And, in fact, the whole trial revolved around not the color of White's skin, but the nature of his "reputation."[12]

In a stunning admission of the arbitrariness of racial classifications, Judge Schley assured members of the jury that they could take into account the role of "general hearsay" in deciding a person's race. So now the jury must consider "the reputation of the person in his community, that is what he says of himself—what others say of him—his associates, and his general reputation as such in the community in which he resides, &c, in order to determine as to his being a white man, or a person of color." For the purposes of White's trial, race would be a matter not of ethnicity, or heritage, or appearance, or biology. It would be, purely and simply, a social fiction—one without any appreciable basis in physical reality.[13]

White's lawyers decided that they would deny their client was black and force the other side to prove otherwise. Yet in the end they had no choice but to try to counter Clements's claims, and so they argued that White was white, but even if he were not, citizenship as a legal status was indivisible: if a man could vote, he must also be able to run for election. The state constitution barred certain men from office, including those convicted of a felony, treason, embezzlement of public funds, and malfeasance in office, or those who were "idiots or insane persons." Black men as a group were not included on that list.[14]

It was undeniable that White had allied himself openly with Savannah's former slaves and free people of color in seeking to organize a local branch of the Republican Party. Over the previous couple of years he had appealed loudly and insistently to potential political supporters; the local newspapers, for different reasons, were willing enough to publicize his efforts. The jury's verdict, announced on April 1, was therefore predictable: "We, the Jury, find that the Defendant has one-eighth of African blood in his veins, and is a colored man under the laws of Georgia." Such a determination was a lie: not a witness or a lawyer or a juror or probably even White himself knew the identity of all his great-grandparents. Nevertheless, Schley affirmed in his final judgment a key point made by the prosecution: that "evidence of general reputation, reputed ownership, public rumor, general notoriety, and the like, though composed of the speech of third persons, not under oath, is original evidence, and not hearsay." Richard White was black, in other words, because other people said he was.[15]

The larger question by which the case came to be known—"Can a Negro Hold Office in Georgia?"—examined legal questions that went to the heart of the meaning of the Civil War. Although the Fourteenth Amendment had granted black people citizenship, white men in Georgia believed they could legitimately claim a superior brand of citizenship. The state of Georgia now had a new constitution, approved by the voters in 1868; this document enfranchised black men, but it did not grant them the specific right to hold office—a lack of specificity that allowed white Georgians to press their own political interests on their "reconstructed" state.

In fact, unrepentant Confederates retained enough power at the local and state levels to stymie even the most basic revisions of customary legal practice. Soon after the end of the war, the Georgia legislature sent a number of former rebels to Congress, including Alexander Stephens, the former vice president of the Confederacy. In response to this and other affronts to the memory of the Union dead, Congress instituted a series of initiatives known collectively as Radical Reconstruction, which, among other directives, mandated the enfranchisement of southern black men. The April 1868 southern state and local elections—the first since Radical Reconstruction began—resulted in Richard White's winning the clerkship and nearly thirty black men gaining seats in the Georgia state legislature. Yet in September Democrats in that body, with the support of some white Republicans, had voted to expel all duly elected black state representatives and senators. Regardless of political affiliation, white men seemed to agree that they could live with black enfranchisement as long as black men could not hold office. When *Clements v. White* commenced in early 1869, all black Savannahians were barred from serving on juries or on the police force and only one, Richard White, held office at any level of the city or county government. Instead of reflecting the county's changing voter demographics, the city's government looked much like it had in previous years: a former Confederate who had successfully run the Union blockade occupied the mayor's office, and several of the twelve city aldermen were holdovers from the antebellum and war years.[16]

To Savannah's elite, White was a cipher; he had taken up residence in the city sometime in 1866 or 1867 without announcing where he had come from or who his forebears were. He openly allied himself with the Republican Party, whose most famous member—the recently deceased President Abraham Lincoln—had made the party's name synonymous with abolitionism and black rights. At the same time, a number of notable white "traitors" to their race were also Republicans, White's attorneys among them.[17]

Judge Schley's ruling in White's case would not be the end of the matter, however. Rather than ceding his position as clerk of the Chatham County Superior Court, White appealed the case to Georgia's highest court. In his *Clements v. White* decision, Supreme Court chief justice Joseph Brown held that the Fourteenth Amendment granted blacks citizenship rights and those rights included the right to hold office. Brown, the state's wartime Democratic governor, had switched his allegiance to the Republicans following the South's surrender; he understood that, at least for the time being, the party of Lincoln was in the ascendancy in national politics. A few weeks before, in March, Republican Ulysses S. Grant had assumed the presidency, and the Republican-majority Congress had refused to count Georgia's electoral votes, citing widespread fraud in the November 1868 election. Later, in a candid moment, Brown would declare his firm belief that blacks as a "morally delinquent" group should be barred from elective office; he maintained that the neoslavery forms of labor discipline prevailing throughout the Georgia countryside served as a wholesome corrective for freedpeople, now rescued from "idleness and dissipation, and thieving."[18]

Brown was joined in his opinion by Justice H. K. McCay, but the third justice, Hiram Warner, filed a dissenting opinion upholding the lower court ruling and agreeing with the reasoning of Judge Schley that "the legal right of [black men] to hold office has never been affirmatively expressed." Despite their disagreements, the justices were able to find common ground and issue a joint opinion. They concurred with Schley and with Clements's attorneys that "pedigree, relationship and race may be proven by evidence of reputation among those who know the person whose pedigree or race is in question." At the same time, they also agreed that Schley had erred in his instructions to the jury by declaring as fact White's ineligibility for office and that therefore his ruling in the case should be overturned.[19]

For his part, Richard White seemed poised to profit from a time and place open to challenges to antebellum and wartime notions of race. Over the course of his lifetime he created for himself a malleable past: at one time or another he claimed, or others claimed for him, that he had been born in South Carolina or Virginia or Kansas or Ohio; that he was black, white, or Native American. A poet and lover of nature, he nonetheless considered his service as a Union soldier to be the defining experience of his life. With his light skin color, this newcomer to Savannah was bent on finding out how far the son of an enslaved woman could navigate through the treacherous politics of the postwar South. In the end, his adopted city offered only a constricted arena for a man defined as black, no matter his boundless talent for politicking and self-invention.

Richard W. White spent his formative years in the company of abolitionists in rural and small-town Ohio. Sometime before mid-October 1850, a white Quaker family living on a farm near the small town of Smithfield in Jefferson County adopted the youth into its household. The Ballinger family, migrants from Maryland, included William, age ninety-three, and his unmarried children Samuel, forty, Mary, thirty-seven, and Rebecca, thirty-five. One of them told a census taker that the boy living with them had been born twelve years before in Virginia. It is probable that the Ballingers gave White his name, a nod to his light complexion, though the census taker marked him "B" for "Black." Later, in the 1860s, White would report that he had been born in 1840 in, variously, Columbia, South Carolina, and in the area east of Columbia, Sumter District, and that his father, Thomas P. Cleaveland, was a native of France and his mother, Sarah, a native of Louisiana.[20]

White likely came to Ohio from a Virginia slave plantation. Jefferson County, Ohio, just across the Ohio River from Virginia, was well known for its Underground Railroad stations, which provided safe havens for runaway slaves. One busy crossing was the town of Steubenville, a few miles northeast of Smithfield. Certainly, the Ballingers would have been taking a great risk by harboring an escaped slave. In September 1850 Congress had passed the Fugitive Slave Act, criminalizing efforts to help enslaved persons flee from the South, efforts that included hiding someone in a cellar or attic or, perhaps, in the case of a person who looked white, harboring him or her in plain sight. More generally, Ohio served as a destination not only for fugitive slaves, but also for children fathered by slaveholders and enslaved women. Some of these children were brought north by abolitionists, and others were sent to Ohio by their fathers, white men who wanted their offspring off the plantation and out of the South. Richard White was too young to have made his escape from slavery on his own, but it is possible that his relatives had found their way to Jefferson County and lacked the means to care for him.[21]

Some adoptive or "patron" families chose to educate their charges, and in 1858 the twenty-year-old Richard spent the fall semester studying at Oberlin College, a place derided by critics as "that old buzzards' nest where the negroes who arrive over the Underground Railroad are regarded as dear children." Founded in 1832, the college put its radical abolitionist ideals into practice by admitting black and white women and men. In 1860 it enrolled 422 blacks: 212 women and 210 men. Within a few years of leaving Oberlin, White was teaching school in Salem, Columbiana County, due north of Smithfield. Salem, too, was a junction on the Underground Railroad and home of the *Anti-Slavery Bugle,* a publication of the Western Anti-Slavery Society.[22]

Settling in Salem together were a number of black Virginians, carpenters, barbers, whitewashers, draymen, and stock dealers who could afford to spare their children from labor and send them to a local common school taught by one of their own. Still, life was by no means secure for these transplanted Southerners, who accounted for fully three-quarters of Ohio's black population by 1860. The state swarmed with "man stealers"—kidnappers and slave catchers from the bordering states of Kentucky and Virginia. Bent on raiding farmhouses and country inns, these men searched for runaways and even free people of color, anyone vulnerable enough to be exchanged for a reward or sold on the auction block. Hardworking men and women, many fugitives from slavery and others born free, vanished without a trace after the sudden appearance of a professional bounty hunter in the area, while others only narrowly escaped being sold (back) into slavery.[23]

The personal insecurity endured by all people of color regardless of legal status shaped the African American community in Ohio. One of its best known leaders was John Mercer Langston, a man who would come to play a significant role in Richard White's life. Born in 1829 in Louisa County, Virginia, Langston was the son of Ralph Quarles, a slave owner, and Lucy Jane

Langston, an enslaved woman whom Quarles freed in 1806. After the death of their father in 1833, John and his three brothers moved to Chillicothe, Ohio. At the age of fourteen, he enrolled in Oberlin College and earned a BA in 1849 and an MA in theology three years later. In 1856 Langston and his new wife settled in Oberlin, where he became active in education and politics, pressing for the enfranchisement of black men. Scouring the state, he identified promising black students for Oberlin and paid tuition bills for some of them, including, perhaps, Richard White, who turned over $12 to the Oberlin treasurer in November 1858. The Langstons boarded a number of black Oberlin students, several of whom seem to have been the sons of slave owners; Richard White might have been one of them. From 1860 to 1862 Langston served as secretary of the state school board and spent a great deal of time visiting public schools and promoting integrated education as a critical component of American democracy.[24]

From the start of the Civil War in April 1861, abolitionists in Ohio and elsewhere saw the conflict as a righteous battle to free the slaves. Yet not all whites agreed that blacks enslaved or free had a direct role to play in this conflict. Conventional wisdom held that, by definition, soldiering was an affair of honor reserved for white men, though, according to some whites, light-skinned persons of mixed parentage might qualify given the exigencies of war. One Ohio white man wrote to the US secretary of war in the summer of 1861, expressing his support for the formation of an Ohio regiment "consisting of 1000 *colored men*, three-fourths of whom are bright mulattoes." Nevertheless, the vast majority of white Northerners rejected the idea that blacks might contribute to the conflict. One Cincinnati police officer angrily told John Mercer Langston that the war was irrelevant to black people: "It was a *white man's fight, with which niggers had nothing to do.*" In the summer of 1862, stung by widespread white opposition to black soldiers, Langston began to lay the foundation for a vigorous military recruiting effort among Ohio black men. President Lincoln released the Emancipation Proclamation on January 1, 1863, and shortly thereafter Massachusetts governor John A. Andrew announced that his state would sponsor all-black regiments filled with men from all over the North. Blacks would now join the great war of liberation as uniformed fighting men.[25]

Traveling throughout Ohio, to cities, small towns, and farm areas, Langston spoke at numerous "war meetings" and repeated the promise he had exacted in writing from Andrew and, eventually, from Ohio governor David Tod: that, in Tod's words of May 16, 1863, "the pay, bounty, clothing and term of enlistment will be the same for colored troops as for white troops." By May 1863 Langston and a fellow Ohio recruiter, brother-in-law O. S. B. Wall, had successfully filled one regiment, the famous Fifty-fourth Massachusetts, and started on another, the Fifty-fifth Massachusetts. Within just a couple of weeks, the Fifty-fifth, too, was ready, with one-third of its recruits coming from the state of Ohio. Among those recruits was Richard W. White.[26]

White journeyed east with other "Westerners"—black men from the Midwest—and arrived at Camp Meigs in Readville, near Boston, in late May. On May 31 he formally enlisted in Company D of the Fifty-fifth for a three-year term, and received a bounty payment of $50. Likely owing to his stint in college, which was rare among Americans of any background, he was immediately promoted to sergeant, one of forty-five such noncommissioned officers in eleven companies, A through K. White listed his occupation as teacher and his birthplace as Columbia, South Carolina.[27]

On May 28, under the leadership of Colonel Robert Gould Shaw, the Fifty-fourth Massachusetts left Boston for the South, receiving a boisterous send-off from the city. At Camp Meigs members of the newly constituted Fifty-fifth moved into the barracks vacated by the Fifty-fourth and immediately embarked on a rigid schedule of drills and fatigue work, their labors a source of great curiosity among whites in the neighborhood. Trained and armed with old-fashioned Springfield muskets, the Fifty-fifth departed Readville on July 21; the regiment included 767 privates, 18 musicians, 64 corporals, 45 sergeants, 9 lieutenants, 5 captains, and 4 staff and 2 field officers. Half of the enlisted men were "of mixed blood," and one-third were literate. With the exception of one chaplain and a few sergeants, all the officers were white. Apparently, many of the black men, unlike the average recruit, joined out of idealistic motives. Burt Green Wilder, a young white doctor in training, marveled at the men's decorum, writing, "These negroes are very nice folk. They don't drink, swear, or quarrel as much as the white soldiers I have seen thus far."[28]

The regiment left Boston under less than auspicious circumstances, the men's high spirits tempered by news of the Fifty-fourth's recent assault on Battery Wagner in Charleston Harbor; the battle cost that regiment 272 casualties, including the death of Shaw. The Confederates dumped his corpse into a trench with those of his men. A southern officer declared with grim satisfaction, "We have buried him with his niggers." On the day of departure, the Fifty-fifth was supposed to parade through Boston, but a downpour quashed those plans. And at the last minute the regiment also had to forego traveling through New York City. A few days earlier New York had witnessed horrific riots instigated by white men who objected to a newly instituted Union military draft; turning their wrath on black men, women, and children, whom they blamed for the war, the rioters burned the Colored Orphan Asylum and randomly killed black people who crossed their path. The death toll stood in the hundreds, the number of wounded in the thousands. Colonel Charles B. Fox of the Fifty-fifth regretted that New Yorkers would have no opportunity to see his "thoroughly drilled and disciplined colored regiment, marching firmly and boldly, as they had a right to do, through New-York streets." Instead, the Fifty-fifth went directly south, the men crammed into a ship built to transport no more than six hundred passengers; the eight hundred soldiers slept scattered on the decks or wedged together in the hold.[29]

The men spent the next several months on the islands off the coast of South Carolina—first Morris, then Folly—where, according to White, they were "worked almost to death" from the beginning. Black recruits had taken up arms more than two years into the war, after the Union had already established control over large swaths of the rebellious South. Now, in the summer of 1863, the imperatives of military occupation mandated that the energies of the Fifty-fifth be devoted largely to manual labor carried out in all-day rotating shifts: building bridges and wharves, felling trees, guarding railway lines, mounting siege guns, digging trenches, erecting fortifications, and loading and unloading stores and ammunition. The sultry heat and torrential rains of a Lowcountry summer, together with contaminated drinking supplies and punishing work demands, took a physical toll on many. Moreover, the fact that white regiments in the area were largely exempt from performing fatigue work and waiting on white officers angered the black soldiers. In its first seven weeks of service, the Fifty-fifth lost twelve men to disease and the effects of what even the white officers were calling "excessive" duties.[30]

For all its hardships, army life appealed to Richard White. With its strict daily routines from dawn reveille through evening drills, and its precise, gridlike layout, the camp offered at least the feel and appearance of orderliness. At the same time, for a young man raised by a farm family (at one point he listed his prewar occupation as cattle drover), camp life was exhilarating and even exotic. During the war the Fifty-fifth lived near and fought with regiments from New York composed of German and Irish immigrants. White found the sandhills of Folly Island to be bleak and barren, and the heat and humidity were literal killers, but when he was later deployed to

Florida, he appreciated the lush landscape and the "deep-voiced thunder" and "moaning sea," which, he wrote, spoke to him and preached "God's sermons."[31]

White must have pondered the historic forces that had thrust him so violently into the same despised group as the other descendants of Africans he encountered for the first time in the army. At least one soldier in the Fifty-fifth, a man born in Africa, still bore tribal facial etchings from his native land. Some of White's comrades had been enslaved, and others had been born free. Some had dark skin, and others, like White, had pale skin. Soldiers in the first southern Union black regiment, the First South Carolina (later the Thirty-third United States Colored Troops), also camped in the vicinity of the Fifty-fifth. Black refugees fleeing the mainland were a constant presence on the island; many had been impressed by Confederate officials to repair railroads and fortify defensive batteries around Charleston. The descendants of South Carolina's Revolutionary-era slaves, these men and women sang their traditional songs for the soldiers and sometimes brought or sold them fruit, chickens, and eggs. Yet they still spoke Gullah, a language no Northerners could readily understand, and in their distress they aroused in White memories of times he could only dimly recall, if at all, from his own childhood in slavery. Just what did he share with these men and women? Nothing more or less than an overarching political vulnerability traced back to enslaved forebears, a political and historical status that was nonetheless expressed in racial terms.[32]

Despite Burt Wilder's first impressions, the Fifty-fifth did indeed include gamblers, drinkers, and carousers in its ranks. Yet recruits also spent time debating the meaning of the war, writing letters home, reading black newspapers such as the *Christian Recorder* and the *Anglo-African,* and forming literary societies among themselves. Using New England primers supplied by the Freedmen's Aid Commission, the noncommissioned black officers took the lead in instructing their comrades as well as the refugees who had found their way into camp. In January 1864 the Fifty-fifth formed a school committee to solicit funds from sympathetic Northerners and conduct classes for the regiment's soldiers each morning. No doubt the young schoolteacher from Ohio played a part in these efforts.[33]

By this time White had been promoted (on December 13) to commissary sergeant, a lowly position in the military hierarchy but a sign that he had found favor with the white officers. The small circle of noncommissioned black officers consisted of well-educated men, many of whom were light in

FIGURE 4.2 Second Lieutenant James Monroe Trotter (1842–1892) of Company G, Fifth-fifth Massachusetts Regiment, is pictured here c. 1865. In several respects Trotter's early life, service in the army, and subsequent political career paralleled those of Richard W. White. Born in Mississippi to an enslaved woman and her owner, Trotter taught in Ohio common schools before joining the Fifth-fifth. Both he and White were eventually promoted to second lieutenant. After the war Trotter moved to Boston, where he joined the Republican Party and became the first black person to be hired by that city's US Postal Service. Unlike White, however, when Trotter was passed over for job promotions, he bolted the party and became an active Democrat. His son William Monroe Trotter (1872–1934) had an illustrious career as an influential newspaper editor and civil rights activist. COLLECTION OF THE GETTYSBURG NATIONAL MILITARY PARK MUSEUM.

color. One member of this circle was James M. Trotter, who had much in common with White. Born in Mississippi in 1842, Trotter was the son of a slaveholder and an enslaved woman; his mother took her two sons, James and Charles, and escaped to Cincinnati via the Underground Railroad. A talented musician, James had received teacher education training at a private academy in Ohio, and in the Fifty-fifth he was prominent among the school instructors. Noncommissioned officers in general enjoyed a special status: they organized the camp schools and mediated between the well-to-do white commissioned officers and the recruits, many from impoverished families.[34]

In late January 1864, White wrote a letter that was published by the *Christian Recorder* in its February 4 issue. The *Recorder* was the organ of the African Methodist Episcopal Church and, at the time, the nation's oldest black publication. White reported to readers in the North that "the men are generally well at this time, quite as much as could be expected under the circumstances that surround us." Those circumstances included heavy fatigue duty, as well as the taunts they had to endure from white soldiers stationed near them on Folly Island. He wrote, "When we first landed on this island, we were liable to be insulted by any of the white soldiers," but now, "thank God, that is about played out, and they have come to see that they are bound to treat us as men and soldiers, fighting for the same cause indirectly, if not directly."[35]

White's overall positive account of the regiment's progress was surprising given the other circumstances he mentioned in his letter: "I suppose you would like to hear how we are getting along for moncy, as you well know that we have not been paid yet." The shock had come soon after the initial deployment of the Fifty-fourth and Fifty-fifth Massachusetts regiments: instead of the $13 monthly pay, plus clothing, earned by white privates and corporals, black soldiers would receive only $10, and $3 of that amount would be deducted for the cost of their uniforms. Black sergeants made less than white privates. In December 1863 the state of Massachusetts offered to make up the difference for the black soldiers, but Northerners in both regiments rejected the idea. They argued that all the men should refuse any pay until they received the same as their white counterparts. Wrote one soldier, "No chance for promotion, no money for our families, and we are little better than an armed band of laborers with rusty muskets and bright spades."[36]

The pay issue provoked a great deal of bitterness, and protests took a variety of forms. Some men, like White, wrote to northern publications to alert readers to the outrage. Trotter contacted prominent abolitionists. The Fifty-fifth formed a committee to raise the issue formally with the regiment's colonel, Alfred Hartwell, whom they knew to be sympathetic, but his superiors dismissed his pleas on their behalf. In November 1863 men in the Third South Carolina Volunteers, almost all of them former slaves and stationed on the South Carolina Sea Islands, followed the lead of Sergeant

William Walker of that unit and stacked their arms as a sign of protest, vowing that they would not go back to work until they were paid fairly. Officers charged Walker with mutiny and, after a court-martial trial, executed him in front of his brigade in February 1864.[37]

In July seventy-four of White's comrades in Company D of the Fifty-fifth signed a letter addressed directly to President Lincoln and written by one of their members, John F. Shorter. The signatories pointed out that they had enlisted with the assurance that their pay would be "on the same footing of Similar Corps of the Regular Army." Explaining their decision to forego diminished paychecks, they wrote, "To us money is no object" because "we came to fight For Liberty justice &equality. These are gifts we Prise more Highly than Gold." They reminded the president that they had spent thirteen months in the field "cheerfully & willingly Doing our duty most faithfully in the Trenches Fatiegue Duty in Camp and conspicuous valor & endurance in battle as our Past History will Show."[38]

The army's unequal pay policies had a crushing effect on families and friends back home. As the men of Company D noted, "We left our Homes our Famileys Friends & Relatives most Dear to take as it ware our Lives in our Hands To Do Battle for God & Liberty." For married recruits, the ensuing hardships endured by their wives and children clouded the decision to refuse all pay until this wrong could be righted. Rachel Ann Wicker, the wife of William Wicker, a thirty-two-year-old farmer from Troy, Ohio, described her frustration in a letter addressed to "Mr. President Andrew." (Governor Andrew of Massachusetts passed it along to Lincoln in Washington.) Wicker demanded "to know the reason why our husbands and sons who enlisted in the 55 Massichusette regiment have not Bin paid off." She wrote, "I wish you if you please to Answer this Letter and tell me Why it is that you Still insist upon them takeing 7 dollars a month when you give the Poorest White regiment that has went out 16 dollars"? In Washington Treasury and War Department officials remained unmoved.[39]

Stationed on the coast not far from Charleston, Company D saw limited battlefield action in the spring of 1864. Together with other regiments, the company's members skirmished periodically with the enemy, made brief raids into the interior for bricks and provisions, and succumbed in large numbers to epidemics and blistering heat. Throughout this time White no doubt relished his role as correspondent for northern publications, whose editors appreciated his keen powers of observation inflected with literary sensibilities. He was unusual among the Fifty-fifth's war correspondents in including samples of his poetry in dispatches home. He felt moved by a kind of pantheism that no single religious domination could capture, and nature was his muse. The voices of the dead communicated to him through the forces of wind and sea:

> *They sing sweet tunes in muffled lanes,*
> *Where piles of runnet leaves are strewn,*
> *Or pierce my soul with nameless pains,*
> *Of carol sweet as birds in June.*

Perhaps reflecting his Quaker upbringing, White wrote that God spoke not through the biblical exegesis of the clergy, but through the "tiny lips of simple flowers."[40]

In May he wrote a letter that he knew the *Christian Recorder* would never publish and sent it instead to the *Anglo-African,* a secular publication. In it he declared the willingness of all black men to sacrifice and suffer "if, by so doing we can, in the end, gain our freedom and that of three million and a half slaves, who have been for the last two hundred years enslaved by the government and religion of this country." He went on: "I say religion, for the Christianity of the nation has done more to uphold slavery than any other one thing." It was the soldiers of the Fifty-fifth who were doing God's work "to win a free country to leave as an inheritance to their children, where no slave clanks his chains, and no mother weeps for her babe forever doomed to slavery's hell."[41]

White was proud to represent both Massachusetts and Ohio in the Fifty-fifth. Yet on July 28 he wrote to a Kansas army general in a clear, firm hand and asked to join a new "Battery of Colored men to be commanded by Colored Officers" in that state. He felt "great interest in this movement," he continued, "first because I am a colored man, and second because I have been a citizen of the state of Kansas." He concluded, "I therefore most humbly hope if you can do anything to assist me to get transferred from this Rgt to your Battery you will do so." Major R. H. Hunt, in charge of organizing "U.S. Colored artillery light," appended a brief observation to White's letter, and noted, "Judging from the letter this man is an intelligent negro, and would doubtless make a good officer; and as vacancies still exist respectfully recommend his transfer." Nothing ever came of White's request, though clearly he ached to achieve a more formal leadership role in the army.[42]

Finally, a congressional act reinstated black soldiers' back pay, but only retroactively to January 1, 1864, and only for those who could swear they had been free before the war. In September the men of the Fifty-fourth and the Fifty-fifth were paid, and together they sent more than $60,000 home. On Monday, October 10, members of the Fifty-fifth celebrated their hard-won but long-deferred compensation, and Sergeant Richard White was one of the featured speakers in a program that included music by the regimental band and the singing of "Vive L'America." A comrade provided an enthusiastic account of the proceedings in a letter to the *Christian Recorder,* noting rather cryptically, "Sergt. White gave us one of those solid and manly speeches that Western [i.e., Midwestern] men know so well how to make. It was easy to see that he meant all he said, and that he meant a great deal." White was finding a respectful audience among other freedom fighters.[43]

The Fifty-fifth engaged the enemy in only one major encounter, the Battle of Honey Hill on November 30, near Grahamville, South Carolina, not far from the coast. Under a hot sun and bereft of artillery support, the men rushed Confederate lines, charging through a narrow road bounded by underbrush set afire and running through a hail of bullets, canister, and cannon. It is possible, though, that during this battle White was at home in Ohio. On October 24 he had received approval for a thirty-day furlough that was intended, in the words of his superior officer, "for the purpose of visiting his parents, who are quite sick in Salem, Columbiana County, Ohio." The officer supported the request by accounting for all the men who remained on duty—817—and by adding, "Sergt White has always performed his duties in an exemplary manner and is well worthy of this indulgence." It is possible that White indeed returned to Salem, where he had taught and where, perhaps, his birth parents lived. In any case, it is unclear whether White left immediately for the North after the 24th and returned right before the battle or whether his departure was delayed for a week or more, sparing him the fight.[44]

In mid-January 1865 members of the Fifty-fifth moved to the mainland of Georgia. There they savored the victory of General William Tecumseh Sherman, who had completed his five-week-long trek across the state, culminating in a triumphant entry into Savannah on December 21. The Fifty-fifth performed garrison duty for Sherman's troops (who had never before seen black men in uniform) and took in the sights and sounds of a city that was but a weed-choked, dilapidated shell of its former proud self. John H. Jenkins, a thirty-eight-year-old soldier from Boston, acknowledged that "Gen. Sherman says he will not fight with [i.e., use] our colored troops," but Jenkins, over-come with exhaustion, chose to ignore the insult: "I have had my share of fighting, so he can take his white men and fight as much as he likes, as long as he lets John alone." Stationed at Forts Barton and Jackson near Thunderbolt, a few miles outside the city, the men of the Fifty-fifth spent part of their days in Savannah. They were among the first black troops whom Georgia whites laid eyes on. James Trotter reported, "Ours is the only colored Regt. so near Savannah and, of course, [we] create much sensation among the Georgians. They have great fear of our troops and are trembling because of our proximity and the expectation of our coming to town to them was [as] Belshazzar reads the handwriting on the wall."[45]

In mid-February the Fifty-fifth advanced north and entered Charleston the day after the retreating Confederate Army had destroyed the city's cot-ton warehouses, arsenals, bridges, military supplies, and even ironclad ships in the harbor. On February 19 crowds of black men, women, and children lined the streets of the still-smoldering city and roared their approval at the sight of the uniformed men of the Fifty-fifth, now conquering heroes. "Cheers, blessings, prayers, and songs were heard on every side. Men and women crowded to shake hands with men and officers." An elderly woman declared, "Bress de Lord, I'se waited for ye, and prayed for ye, long time, and I knowed you'd come, and ye has come at last." Certainly, this heartfelt re-ception made a lasting impression on Richard White, weary but euphoric in the now-vanquished cradle of secessionism. Meanwhile, for the few whites who had stayed in the city and hidden behind closed doors, the sight of black men in uniform was too much for them to bear. As a *New York Times* reporter noted with some understatement, "They [the whites] had an oppor-tunity of observing that the colored soldiers were slaves no longer." If before this moment White had been inclined to cast his lifelong lot with the former slaves of the South, this thrilling scene—the whites indoors and sullen, the blacks outside and exultant—might have solidified his decision.[46]

The Fifty-fifth could only briefly savor the moment, for its members spent much of the next several months in a downpour, slogging over muddy roads and through swampland in the South Carolina interior, rebuilding bridges and trestles, foraging for food, and skirmishing with Confederate stragglers and guerrillas. During the spring and early summer, the regiment passed through a devastated landscape littered with burned rice mills and bridges, ruined fields, rotting animal corpses, and the bleached bones of fallen comrades. Juxtaposed with these dismal sights, though, were more

FIGURE 4.3 The caption for this drawing published in the March 18, 1865, issue of *Harper's Weekly* reads, "'Marching On!'—The Fifty-Fifth Massachusetts Colored Regiment Singing John Brown's March in the Streets of Charleston, February 21, 1865." African Americans thronged the streets to welcome the city's liberators, most of whom were black men from Massachusetts and Ohio. The stirring scene no doubt made a deep impression on the soldiers themselves, including young Richard W. White. LIBRARY OF CONGRESS.

hopeful signs: large numbers of black refugees on their way to the coast, determined to make new lives for themselves. On April 11, 1865, the day that Robert E. Lee was surrendering his army to General Ulysses S. Grant in Virginia, the men of the Fifty-fifth came upon a mile-long "refugee train" composed of approximately 2,000 people and their wagons. They were, in the words of Colonel Fox, "new and old, fit and unfit, patched up, nailed up, tied up, and pegged up." Women carrying children in their arms and heavy bundles on their heads helped to form a latter-day Exodus of biblical proportions. At the end of each day songs of jubilation rang out amid the roadside campfires, praise to God and to the "Black Yankees" who had delivered these refugees from bondage.[47]

On April 14 the Fifty-fifth was camped near Charleston, where a grand celebration marked the end of four long, bloody years of fighting. A number of northern luminaries, including abolitionist William Lloyd Garrison, addressed throngs at Fort Sumter, where the conflict had ignited. But, ominously, northern officers kept black would-be revelers from attending the festivities. Just five days later an assassin took the life of Abraham Lincoln. Charleston, at least the part composed of African Americans and northern whites, plunged into mourning.[48]

In late April James M. Trotter received a commission as a second lieutenant, a belated and bittersweet recognition of his leadership in the Fifty-fifth. The regiment was breaking up, but not before Company D was detailed as provost guard at Orangeburg, northwest of Charleston and halfway between that city and Columbia. Captain Charles C. Soule had been appointed chairman of the Orangeburg Commission on Contracts, a federal agency established to promote labor contracts between freedpeople and white landowners. Black men and women, however, had their own priorities: they were in the process of reconstituting family groups scattered before the war and ensuring that they would be able to provide for themselves out of the reach of white landowners.[49]

Soule and other white officials mistook the restlessness among Orangeburg blacks as signs of lawlessness, blaming the ensuing disorder on "the advice of many of the colored soldiers," Northerners who pressed upon these simple people "false and exaggerated ideas of freedom." Alarmingly, the freedpeople seemed to trust only "people of their own color, and believe that the [white] officers who have addressed them are rebels in disguise." Freedom meant "law, order, and hard labor," in Soule's words. He predicted that "ignorant and degraded" blacks would prove to be the biggest obstacle to successful postwar reconstruction, which he defined as the revival the staple-crop economy.[50]

In a speech to an outdoor assembly of freedmen and freedwomen, Soule outlined a plan that Richard White no doubt found deeply troubling. Soule declared to his listeners, "You are now free, but you must know the only difference you can feel yet, between slavery and freedom, is neither you nor your children can be bought or sold." Landowners would compensate their workers not with cash wages but with food, clothing, and shelter. Men and women must return to the fields and labor from dawn to dusk, keeping at their tasks and seeking the permission of their employer to leave "even to nurse a child or to go and visit a wife or husband." Above all, black people must remember that they were poor and their employers rich; this fact should temper their dangerously exaggerated views of freedom.[51]

The men of the Fifty-fifth spent time in or near Charleston for brief periods throughout February, March, and April before finally convening in that city for the last time in August. The regiment was formally mustered out of the service on August 29, 1865, but not before the company physician, Dr. Wilder, under orders, took the men's body measurements. An anthropologist would later use the data to argue for the racial distinctiveness of blacks.[52]

It is possible that within this relatively short period White had been able to grasp the extent of the great competing historic forces sweeping over the city and the South Carolina Lowcountry: the former slaves' struggle for freedom and self-determination pushing back against whites' attempts to reassert the control they had lost during the war. As soon as northern troops, including the Fifty-fifth, entered Charleston, local black leaders set about establishing schools, opening and reopening businesses, forming a Union League loyal to the federal government, and assembling in mass meetings to debate political strategy for the future. At the same time, an estimated 30,000 black men, women, and children were settling on the Sea Islands, planting small patches of corn and vegetables, and peddling chickens and eggs to Union soldiers stationed nearby.[53]

Company D sailed out of Charleston Harbor on September 14, 1865. Stormy seas and lightning strikes on the ship's masts made the weeklong trip back to Boston a harrowing one. And then early in October Richard White received his own commission as a second lieutenant. He could have interpreted this delayed promotion either as a grave insult, a pathetic gesture that came after the end of hostilities, or a great personal victory, given that so few black soldiers ever achieved such an honor. Overall, only one hundred black men received commissions during the war, and fully two-thirds of those were members of the Louisiana Native Guard, many well educated and light-skinned. Of the six men who had served with Massachusetts regiments and received commissions, all but one had to wait until the summer of 1865. Like White, most were Northerners, free before the war.[54]

Soule believed that only white Northerners, men of stern business principles untainted by romantic notions of black equality, could "bring order out of this chaos." He would not have approved of the decision by one of his own men from Company D to settle permanently among the region's former slaves. Yet as early as the spring of 1864, Richard White had signaled his intentions: "Do not think I am over zealous in the work; for I think I can see a bright future opening up to our people and I am determined to fight and do all in my power to hasten the day of universal freedom." By the fall of 1865 Second Lieutenant White had proved himself smart and disciplined. He had survived the war with life and limb and reputation intact. He had served honorably, a good soldier with the soul of a poet who deferred to his white superiors. And so, determined to help forge a new South out of the war-torn old one, he charged headlong into the turbulent world of postbellum southern politics.[55]

Within a few months after his discharge from the army, Richard White returned to Charleston, where chimneys stood as lone sentinels among the ruins of crumbling walls and scorched buildings. The detritus of war mirrored a larger demographic disaster, for the white South had lost a whole generation of men—more than one-fifth of the white adult male population—and hundreds of thousands of people uprooted from their homes were suffering from hunger and disease. Freedpeople from the interior were streaming to the islands or crowding into Charleston for safety. The churning refugee populations were emblematic of the unsettled nature of the political economy throughout the coastal region.[56]

Rising from the ruins of Charleston, a jubilant black population enlivened the city. Black women promenaded and flaunted their richly colored clothing and the veils that had been denied most of them under slavery (all but the handful of hostesses of "Ethiopian Balls"). In time-honored tradition, black hucksters continued to wend their way through the streets calling out their wares: berries, shrimp, bread, peanuts, candy, and beer made out of herbs. A cadre of well-educated, light-skinned free men of color sought to seize control of the city's politics. Hailing from a small town in Ohio, White was no doubt alive to the promise of Charleston, for here was a place ripe with possibilities for an idealistic young man. On May 30, 1866, he opened an account at the Charleston branch of the Freedman's Savings Bank, created by Congress in late 1865 to encourage black veterans to save their wartime earnings.[57]

White probably arrived in Charleston sometime in late 1865 or early 1866 intending to teach in the schools sponsored by the United States Freedmen's Bureau, a government agency created in 1865 to facilitate the transition from slavery to freedom among the 3.5 million freedpeople in the South. John Ogden, the bureau's education superintendent in 1866, thought highly of White, writing in June 1868 to John Mercer Langston, "You will not forget Mr. White's matter. I wish it could be so arranged that he could be placed in this work permanently. He is too valuable a man to be consigned to a mere clerkship." White himself at some point apparently felt that he was too valuable a man to be consigned to a mere schoolmaster's post. Although he might have decided to relocate permanently to the South in order to teach, he soon realized that his political acumen and his public speaking talents fitted him for a higher station in the former Confederacy. Certainly, Charleston in the mid-1860s afforded ample evidence of the opportunities available to ambitious black men who dared to seize them.[58]

Nevertheless, White did not remain in Charleston for long, leaving the city sometime in 1866 or early 1867 without making his mark on the political landscape. However, he did leave with a wife. Anna, or Annie, was twenty-two or twenty-three when they married; she had probably been free before the war, like her mulatto sister Sarah, who had been born in 1824 and was now married to Robert, a carpenter. Sarah and Robert formed a household with White and his bride; other members included Harriet (born in 1852) and Gustave (1859), siblings of either Sarah or Robert.[59]

Soon after their marriage, Richard and Anna and their extended household moved to Savannah, a place with which he had some familiarity, based on his deployment there in early 1865. The city had a small black leadership class, but one fractured among many individuals with divergent political views. Representative of men native to the city were Charles DeLaMotta, before the war an enslaved ship carpenter; editor and activist James Simms, whose professorial air belied a fierce commitment to full civil rights for all black people; James Porter, a teacher and talented musician; the Reverend Ulysses L. Houston, a Baptist preacher with an established constituency, his home congregation of First Bryan Baptist Church; and John Deveaux, son of an iconic figure in the city, Jane Deveaux, longtime teacher of a clandestine antebellum school for black children. From the North came the Reverend Tunis G. Campbell, founder of self-sufficient black colonies along the coast in Liberty County (on Saint Catherine's Island) and McIntosh County (Belleville); and lawyer Aaron A. Bradley, a onetime fugitive slave from Georgia who had spent the last several years in the North reading law and earning a well-deserved reputation for his provocative language in the service of black rights.[60]

After the war many Savannah whites were disconcerted by the rise to political prominence of men who, by virtue of their appearance at least, were clearly more white than black. For example, the up-and-coming John Deveaux was a native of the city; only eighteen in 1865, he hailed from a well-established family, descendants of early-nineteenth-century immigrants from Antigua. Jackson Sheftall, a successful butcher who looked white, was the son of a prominent white man and an enslaved woman. Still, it was the interlopers who caused the most consternation because their lineage remained a mystery. With his flowing red hair and copper-colored skin, Aaron Bradley proved a real curiosity, and a frightening one, among the city's elites; they had never encountered a black man who had studied law and then put his legal knowledge to use with such a vengeance. Richard White threw them off as well; more subdued than Bradley, he had a low-key manner but cultivated potentially threatening political alliances with white Republicans.

And, indeed, White found allies among some of Savannah's white men who, for various reasons, were enemies of the postwar neo-Confederate project. Georgia natives included wealthy physician Dr. J. J. Waring, now held in contempt by his white neighbors for his antisecessionist stance (he would post bond for the newly elected Richard White in the spring of 1868). Some northern white men, such as brothers Walter and Dr. Joseph Clift (from Massachusetts), Isaac Seeley (New York), and Thomas P. Robb (Maine), had settled in or near Savannah after the war to pursue business interests and political careers in the heart of the former Confederacy. Savannah was also at least a temporary home to northern teachers and school superintendents sponsored by the American Missionary Association (AMA), officials of the Freedmen's Bureau, and, after the imposition of Radical Reconstruction in the spring of 1867, US military men assigned to oversee the process of bringing Georgia back into the Union.[61]

What united all these men (for they were all men, with the exception of AMA teachers) was membership in various Union Leagues composed of persons loyal to the United States and then, after the enfranchisement of southern black men in March 1867, the Republican Party. Once in Savannah, Richard White wasted no time joining the party. He wanted to help rebuild the South, and this path offered the possibility of a livelihood in the form of a patronage job or elective office. If he had any hope of becoming a teacher, conditions in Savannah quickly disabused him of that notion: the AMA was in the process of pushing all competitors from the field, and the association refused to hire black teachers or teachers' assistants. By early 1867 the AMA was operating eight schools with 950 pupils taught by eleven teachers working multiple shifts in day and night schools. The few black-run schools were small and ephemeral affairs, ill suited for any teacher who needed to support a family. It is unclear how White made a living before his election as clerk of the court; but because he spent his years in the army as a single man, he had probably saved enough of his initial bounty and his wartime pay to last several months.[62]

For almost a decade after his arrival in Savannah, White embraced the full range of rights and responsibilities available to conscientious citizens. He ran for and won public office and then mounted a spirited defense of his right to serve. He penned and circulated reasoned petitions protesting white men's efforts to bar all black men from power. He wrote letters to his representatives in Congress and to leading national public officials. He addressed mass meetings, urging black Savannahians to vote and to use their numbers to good advantage. He worked as a civil servant for the federal government. When all else failed, he engaged in direct action and risked his life in the process. Yet gradually White was forced to adjust to political realities, sacrificing his idealism for his need to provide for his growing household.

White's steadiness of character rendered him suspect in the eyes of at least one fellow black activist. After many years of exile in the Northeast, Aaron Bradley had returned to his home state in late 1865. In Savannah he quickly established himself as a force to be reckoned with on all sides, a man whose antiwhite rhetoric and swaggering demeanor placed him at odds with both black clergy and other political aspirants regardless of skin color. Speaking at the Second African Baptist Church soon after his arrival, Bradley ridiculed the advice given by another speaker, the Reverend Garrison Frazier, an elderly Baptist preacher. Frazier urged his listeners to ingratiate themselves with their former masters and mistresses and to refrain from stealing. Taking the pulpit after Frazier, Bradley retorted that when the former slaves appropriated the fruits of their own labor, they did not steal but rather claimed what was rightfully theirs after slaving their whole lives for white people. According to a breathless account provided by a local paper, he urged his listeners to "*resist, if necessary, at the point of the bayonet all attempts on the part of the agents of the Freedmen's Bureau to dispossess or remove them from the lands.*" Local whites began to denounce Bradley as the "Great Wahoo," an "incubus" of torture, and a "narrow-minded colored pettifogger."[63]

Beginning in March 1867, the new plan of Radical Reconstruction unleashed a wave of political organizing among blacks in anticipation of election of delegates to the upcoming state constitutional convention, a body mandated by Congress to purge Georgia of the residue of rebellion once and for all. A cross-section of the black community in Savannah and its environs eagerly embraced politicking, with men, women, and children turning out for rallies in the city's leafy squares and in the brush arbors dotting the surrounding countryside. Alexander Stephens, the former Confederate vice president, regarded the whole enterprise as inherently dangerous for whites. The *New York Times,* now elevating Stephens to the role of elder statesman, quoted him as saying, "The negroes are compactly organized, their 'leagues' reaching every corner of the State. They coerce and threaten any black man who does not join them." He concluded, "They are a unit politically." The *Daily News and Herald* promptly anointed the Republicans the "Mongrel Party," attesting to its support among a few whites in addition to many blacks.[64]

In October 1867 Richard White won election as a delegate to the Savannah Republican Party convention. The following April he rode a wave of support for black Republican candidates in the elections for national, state, and local offices and won for himself the Chatham County Superior Court clerkship. Savannah black voters outnumbered white ones by 3 to 2 (3,062 to 2,269), and helped send Dr. Joseph W. Clift to the US House of Representatives and, among other black candidates, James Porter and James Simms to the Georgia House and Aaron Bradley to the Georgia Senate. Tunis Campbell won a seat in the State Senate, his son and namesake a seat in the House. Campbell Senior was also elected a justice of the peace in Darien.[65]

Nevertheless, these impressive electoral results could not shake the iron hold that white men retained over the machinery of Georgia government at every level. In September 1868 enough whites in the state legislature overcame their partisan differences to join together and vote to expel all the black representatives and senators elected four months before. Anticipating *Clements v. White,* these white legislators claimed that the law forbade black men from running for or holding office. The Reverend Henry M. Turner, a Union wartime chaplain now turned politician, accused white Republicans of wanting "the black man to be a mere ass, upon whose back any white man may ride into office, and then sink him to eternal infamy by their votes on diabolical legislation." The Democrats used more direct means. Savannah authorities had managed to fend off attempts by blacks to gain some influence in the local government; during the general election in November, white authorities used a combination of poll taxes, violent intimidation, and legal maneuvering to deny an estimated 90 percent of all registered black voters the chance to cast a ballot. A police-led rout of would-be voters the first day of the election claimed the lives of three black men and three white policemen, wounded seventeen blacks—and gave local Democrats an over-whelming victory.[66]

The next month White, together with two other black leaders, sent a letter to Representative Clift in Washington summarizing resolutions passed at "a mass meeting of colored citizens" of Savannah on December 28. The intent of the meeting was to urge Congress "to secure to every citizen of this State the rights of citizens of the United States." Calling the expulsion of the black legislators "an unjust deprivation of our most sacred rights as citizens, a high-handed outrage," the meeting condemned "fraudulent" acts of the legislature and "the persecution we have suffered, the barbarities committed in the name of the law, and the defiance of all law." The letter, in White's handwriting and probably his words, denounced lawmakers' efforts to "de-clare a large number of its members, who were allowed to participate in said election, ineligible, and expel them therefrom, thereby with strange inconsis-tency and utter disregard of all principle vitiate and nullify its own action in the premises."[67]

Even though White could blame white lawmakers in Georgia for his po-litical troubles, in fact General Sherman had laid the foundation for Savan-nah's postwar reactionary government. In December 1864 he allowed the city council to remain in place and he declared that the need for public order trumped all other priorities, including the rights of newly freed slaves. Two postwar city elections returned to the council several familiar faces, includ-ing former slaveholders who had enjoyed an unbroken stint of power before, during, and now after the war. In March 1868 General George Meade, head of the Union occupying forces, suspended municipal elections for the fore-seeable future out of fear, or on the pretext, that balloting would call forth thousands of South Carolina rice hands who would inundate the city and dominate the balloting. In June 1868 Richard White organized a petition calling for the removal of city officers, an appeal that Meade ignored.[68]

Facing a solid wall of white opposition in Savannah, White used the occasion of his trial to begin reaching out to national Republicans. On Jan-uary 21, the day before Judge Schley ordered him to appear at the Savannah courthouse, White wrote to Senator Charles Sumner of Massachusetts, de-scribing his election and the subsequent travesty affecting the black legisla-tors. White warned Sumner that "the Georgia Legislature composed as it is of opponents of the reconstruction acts will deprive all Republican office holders of their positions should Congress not interpose its authority, or give us that protection which we unfortunately & Sadly need at present." White couched his appeal in terms of loyalty to the Republican Party rather than as a broader defense of black civil rights.[69]

The *Clements v. White* decision held that blacks could run for office in Georgia, but Savannah Democrats refused to cede control. In March 1869, in response to the threat posed by White and other would-be black office-holders, the city had instituted an additional poll tax for municipal elections (the state already imposed its own) and initiated a ward system for aldermen's races in order to limit the choices of white voters and eliminate the influence of black voters altogether. A city election held in October 1869, the first in two years, firmly reestablished the Democratic Party in Savannah. Its seventy-person "challenging committee" monitored the city's three polling sites. A local white judge ruled against adding a ballot box exclusively for black voters, a demand black leaders believed would minimize violence at the polls.[70]

On July 6, 1870, Richard White together with J. J. Waring and Isaac Seeley, a federal post office appointee, attended a city council meeting; the three men came armed with legal briefs protesting the use of a poll tax to suppress the black vote. The council adjourned without allowing them to speak. By this time the local Republican Party had lost whatever power it once had had and collapsed into bitter infighting. Aaron Bradley led the way in challenging the so-called Regulars, most of them white men who fervently believed that they were truly the best leaders of the party, as well as black men who were willing to accommodate themselves to a party that operated on this principle. Bradley had early called upon blacks to beware their professed white "friends," and he excoriated Union officers, federal appointees, bureau agents, and other so-called white allies of the freedpeople in equal measure. Bradley put the matter succinctly: "In places where the majority are colored, why should we seek to elevate a third-class white man over a *first-class* colored man?"[71]

To Bradley, Thomas P. Robb represented all that was reprehensible about the Republicans. In 1870 the fifty-year-old Maine native was serving as collector at the Savannah customs house, a federal position that paid exceedingly well and that allowed Robb to reward his friends with patronage jobs of their own. Yet in denouncing the so-called Customs House Ring, Bradley saved his most potent dose of vitriol for Richard White, whom he considered an enemy to his color. White had remained steadfast in his support for white

Republican Regulars such as Robb. Nevertheless, Bradley's harangues about white federal appointees could not help but resonate with other black leaders. The September 1868 expulsion of the black legislators had proved that "whiteness" could function as a powerful ideology and plan of action quite divorced from partisan or class divisions. At the same time, many would-be black politicians realized that their color worked against them, while at the same time uniting them in common cause in the face of white opposition.[72]

Meanwhile, Bradley took to carrying a Derringer pistol and a Bowie knife. City officials understood that they harassed him at the risk of angering his most vocal supporters: coastal rice workers. Bradley also used his connection to these laborers to heap contempt on other black politicians who had their own political agenda. Bradley saw White as an easy mark, focusing on his light skin color to call into question his commitment to the freedpeople toiling in the fields. White had worked closely with Waring and Seeley, and he was keen to make alliances with white Republicans generally. Even more damningly, according to Bradley, White, during his 1869 trial, had sought to deny that he was black at all. In December 1870 Bradley decided to run against White to fill a partial term representing Georgia's First Congressional District in the US House of Representatives.

On the campaign stump Bradley harkened back to what he considered White's subterfuge during the *Clements* trial, but then went further and charged that White had once told him that his home state was Ohio, not South Carolina, and that his mother was white and his father Indian. Bradley mocked White's claim to respectability by referring to him as "Saint Richard" and "this carpet-bag saint of Ohio," an apparent reference to White's cautious and ultimately conflict-averse demeanor. Warming to the fight, Bradley took to denouncing White as the "Big Injun," the "Red, White and Leopard colored clerk of the court, Richard W. White," a man who "betrayed the confidence of his fellow citizens." Should the "hybrid" white be elected, Bradley asked, "What color will he represent himself?" The answer was, "The greasy color." The *Morning News* gleefully reprinted Bradley's diatribe and opined "that a man who is an Indian today and a negro to-morrow is not the right sort of man to trust in politics or anything else. A color that won't stand won't do to rely on. What faith can they have in a man who, elected to day as a negro, turns out an Indian or a 'heathen Chinee' tomorrow?" The paper's editors also took to calling any appearance by White as a "pow-wow." With the black vote split between White and Bradley, the white Democratic candidate easily won the election for the district's representative.[73]

In March 1871 White's rocky tenure as Chatham County Superior Court clerk came to an end (it is unclear whether the court met at all from the summer of 1868 until none other than William P. Clements replaced White two and a half years later). Yet upon leaving office, White landed on his feet when Thomas Robb offered him a customs house clerk's job at the munificent salary of $1,500 year. By this time White had taken on heavy family responsibilities. He and Anna had two children: two-year-old Lillian and nine-month-old Richard. Living with them were Anna's sister Sarah; Sarah's brothers (or brothers-in-law) Charles, eleven, and Gaston (sometimes Gustave), ten; and Henry King, thirty-four, perhaps another relative, born in South Carolina. White's relatively comfortable status was evident from the fact that he headed a household of seven dependents, none of whom worked; Anna was "keeping house," and Sarah was "at home." Between August 1869 and November 1870, White made five Freedman's Bank deposits "in trust" for Anna. These deposits, combined with an insurance policy that listed Anna as its beneficiary (introduced into evidence in White's trial), suggest that the thirty-year-old husband and father possessed some discretionary income.[74]

Beginning in 1871 White made a career out of federal appointments. National presidential politics ruled the local patronage scene, and White had his best chance for a job during Republican administrations: Grant, Hayes, and Garfield (1869–1881); Harrison (1889–1893); and McKinley (1897–1901). In Savannah the two main sources of patronage were the federal customs house and the post office, with the former offering by far the greater variety and number of jobs; its employees were in charge of assessing tonnage dues, collecting tariffs, examining lading lists, checking for smugglers and illegal landings, maintaining the port, and fining shippers who had committed infractions. Employees included cashiers, clerks and auditors, night/day inspectors, deputy collectors, messengers, and an assortment of storekeepers, porters, surveyors, and assistant entry clerks. The highest officer, the port collector, made an annual salary of $4,000, a handsome sum and more than three times what White had earned as a clerk in the same building. The customs house itself, a massive gray granite structure of neoclassical Greek design, stood at the center of Savannah's business district; its hulking presence reminded all city residents of the continuity of federal authority in Savannah before and after the war.[75]

Another source of federal employment for White was the Southern Claims Commission, established in March 1871 to compensate southern Unionists whose property had been seized by federal troops during the war. In December 1864 Sherman's troops had swept through southeastern Georgia, and over the next month they had foraged throughout the countryside and appropriated lumber and livestock from blacks and whites in the city. Seven years later claimants came forward with lists of chickens, pigs, mules, horses, household goods, and farm tools taken by the federals. The process of filing an application was an arduous one; claimants needed a notary public to certify their signature and an attorney to guide them through the extensive paperwork. Together, Richard White and James M. Simms served these respective functions for a number of Georgia applicants. White earned a small fee for notarizing documents, but he required authorization from the man who succeeded him as clerk of the superior court, William Clements, in order to do his job. And so accompanying White's signature on applications was the statement by Clements that he certified White as a "duly qualified and commissioned Notary Public in and for the said County of Chatham." Over the next six or seven years, White would extract a modest income from the claims commission, swallowing his pride while seeking Clements's permission to do so. Of 764 Chatham County claims, the commission approved only 82.[76]

For thirty years White rotated in and out of various positions in the customs house and post office; the vagaries of politics and personalities meant that job security would always elude him. In 1872 he was demoted from a clerk in the customs house to an inspector, which paid $4 a day. Finding himself bound to the sordid world of patronage, he endured in a painfully personal way the clash between his lofty ideals and his need to support his family. Having served his country honorably, he believed he deserved the means to make a living. At the same time, he had to worry constantly about currying favor with any white man in a position to hire him. Nevertheless, for all black men who received such appointments, the jobs themselves represented a lifeline in a city where only black preachers could hope to work steadily throughout the year. A Georgia-born white Republican spoke for other white men regardless of political affiliation when he complained that patronage provided benefits for a select few black men "who are making money and buying lots" in a way they would not otherwise be able to do.[77]

Soon after starting his first customs house job, White wrote again to Senator Sumner, warning that "an effort is now being made to remove the Collector of Customs at this Port (Col. T. P. Robb) the Colored Man's friend And one in whom we all have the utmost confidence as a Republican." The effort to oust Robb amounted to (and here the handwriting is unclear) either an "iniquity" or an "inequity"—in any case both, in White's view. Responding to Aaron Bradley's call for Robb's ouster, White initiated an equally aggressive pro-Robb petition drive; by October 1871 the effort had netted a reported (but no doubt overstated) 3,000 signatures.[78]

On January 15, 1872, White wrote to Sumner again, this time expressing his support for the civil rights bill under consideration in the Senate. The passage of the bill, which would have outlawed discrimination in public transportation and lodging, "will effectually do away with the present Sistem of Social Ostricism which now prevails in this, and other Southern States," wrote White, "and place us in position to better enjoy as we should our political rights." Yet within a few days of writing Sumner, White sent a far more personal and revealing letter to Benjamin F. Butler, a former Union general now serving as a Republican representative of Massachusetts in the US House. White was contacting Butler "to secure your influence if possible, in my behalf for a position in the Boston Custom House. I would be willing to accept any position whereby I can earn a livelihood for myself and family." White continued: "My reason for wishing to leave this State is on account of my children, it being impossible to Educate them as I desire in Georgia, and if I could get a position in Boston I would then be able to accomplish my desire in that direction." By this time White knew that he would be nominated as a customs house inspector, but at the same time his friend John Deveaux was supplanting him in the clerkship, a job that paid much better. In February Robb bowed to pressure and resigned as collector. White must now ingratiate himself with yet another white man.[79]

Acknowledging to Butler the "great interest you have always taken in the welfare of the Col'd men, and particular those who were Soldiers in the late war," White recounted his own military service, including his promotion to second lieutenant and his job in the customs house. Because of his record as a war veteran and a federal appointee, White himself was, he wrote, "the object of great persecution." He was willing to take even a "minor position" as long as he could return to Massachusetts, his "adopted State (one I served as a soldier)." He concluded the letter by listing the names of men who could testify to his "past history and character," including four officers of the Fifty-fifth, Hartwell and Fox among them. Among his other references were Tunis Campbell, James Porter, James Simms, Thomas Robb, and John Mercer Langston (now teaching law at Howard University in Washington, DC). By this time White must have deeply regretted that he had not followed the example of his army comrade James Monroe Trotter, who after the war settled in Boston, where he and other black officers received federal post office appointments and their children received decent schooling.[80]

Georgia reentered the Union again in 1872. Outmaneuvered on every level by the state's Democrats, the Republicans there hardly functioned as a party at all. What newspapers they operated were sustained only by federal patronage. In Savannah both of the major papers were Democratic. The Republicans not only lacked any prospect of winning elections; they also remained splintered by skin color and political ideology. An increasingly large number of Savannah Republicans saw the party primarily as a vehicle for patronage appointments, some lucrative, most modest. For blacks, such positions would insulate them from the prejudice of private white employers. As long as a Republican president was in office, the party diehards in Savannah would jostle among themselves for jobs in the customs house, courthouse, and post office.[81]

On July 12, 1872, White sent a petition to President Ulysses S. Grant defending the recently departed Robb, whom critics had blamed for declining Republican fortunes in the southeastern part of Georgia. White and the other signatories maintained that Robb had been active in promoting the Republican cause not just in Savannah, but also throughout the First Congressional District, an area that included twenty-eight counties. At the same time it was true that the canvassers appointed by Robb in several instances "for their own personal safety were obliged to abandon their labours of love," thus hindering their usefulness to the party. Indeed, according to White, in some counties Republicans were kept "in such fear by the Rebel Democracy, they could not render assistance, and in counties with a large Republican population, we failed to poll a single vote, for the reason stated." Southern whites' reign of terror over blacks and their allies would not abate for more than a century—and then only under pressure from black activists backed by the federal government.[82]

A few days after White sent off this latest petition, Savannah Republicans—a group largely congruent with post office and customs house employees—orchestrated several acts of civil disobedience meant to challenge the recent segregation of the city's streetcars. The protests began on Saturday, July 27. The next evening at 6 Richard White boldly boarded a downtown "white" streetcar; immediately a group of men took hold of him and threw him off. Having been consigned to a desk job for so long, he must have felt the thrill of a righteous war wash over him once more. Over the next few days blacks and whites engaged in pitched battles that left five whites and five blacks wounded. Local papers condemned the city's "mulatto chiefs" for inciting the riot and then disappearing into the crowd once violence erupted. The *Savannah Daily Republican* asked its black readers, "Did you see Indian Dick? . . . Did you ever see any of those worthies, who support the Custom House steps or rest their lazy sides under the trees of the Bay to hatch their diabolical schemes for your destruction, in any place of danger in which they have thought you would earn the wreaths of victory? *No.*" (In this the paper was mistaken: Richard White had indeed placed himself in danger during this series of confrontations.) The *Daily Republican* speculated that White and other troublemakers intended to "raise such a difficulty as would give some grounds for the present [federal] Administration to declare martial law in this city or State, for the purpose of depriving the white population of the privilege of voting at the next Presidential election." A Savannah-based US commissioner assigned to the case ruled that segregation was legal and that the protesters had acted illegally in disregarding "the kindly relations, confidences, and friendships" between blacks and whites under slavery and since.[83]

Soon after the streetcar riots, the Savannah City Council voted to change municipal elections from annual to biennial affairs, to move city elections from October to January, and to ease registration rules. These latter two "reforms" made it easier for white seasonal migrants from the North to vote in city elections. Although Republicans now had virtually no chance of winning any elective office, that fact did not diminish Bradley's capacity to frighten whites. After one outdoor political rally, a local newspaper claimed that he had exhorted his supporters, 2,000 strong, to march to the polls with hatchets, not pistols, because "hatchets were better at close quarters." Bradley continued to posture on the stump, but Richard White quietly and gradually removed himself from the crosshairs of white newspaper editors. In 1873 he ran unsuccessfully for county sheriff. Around this time Deveaux and others began to initiate annual legal challenges charging Democratic officials with orchestrating fraudulent election returns.[84]

By the end of 1874 a critical chapter in the freedom struggle of Savannah blacks had come to a close. That year Richard White managed to convince the city's postmaster to discontinue a recent practice forcing blacks to drink from separate water fountains; this directive did not last long. In March Charles Sumner died, his death marked by 4,000 black men, women, and children mourners who gathered for an ecumenical service at Saint Philip African Methodist Episcopal Church and in the streets surrounding the church. On July 2 the Savannah branch of the Freedman's Bank closed its doors forever; questionable investments and bad bookkeeping practices had bankrupted the institution. Under pressure from local black preachers, the American Missionary Association ceded its schools to the city, which proceeded to starve black education of taxpayer funds.[85]

Republicans continued to suffer, in the words of one, "isolation, contempt, ostracism, & ignominy." Eventually, Thomas Robb picked up and headed to California, where he started a new life for himself and his family. Aaron Bradley abandoned Savannah for Kansas and then St. Louis, where he died, poverty stricken, in 1888. In contrast, Richard White remained loyal to the Republican Party, and he accepted whatever reward, no matter how modest, it could bestow upon him for enduring the contempt of white Savannahians.[86]

Ten years after moving to Savannah, Richard White had established himself as an active and respected leader in the black community. Strolling around his East Savannah neighborhood, he was a recognizable figure to all, thoroughly integrated into its vibrant associational life.

White's professional and personal partnership with Deveaux proved to be a lifelong connection. In 1875 the two men joined others to found the *Savannah Tribune* and in 1876 to organize the Forest City Benevolent Association in response to a yellow fever epidemic that fall. Throughout the last quarter of the nineteenth century, White served as an active member of the local Masonic chapter and the Republican Party. He and other public-spirited black men and women had to content themselves with the relatively limited sphere of Savannah's many church, charitable, and benevolent societies— Masonic Eureka Lodge No. 1 and Hilton Lodge No. 2 (both organized by James Simms in 1866), the American Union Ethiopian Association, Knights of Pythias and Knights of Damon, the Odd Fellows, Bible and literary clubs, and the Chatham Light Infantry. Yet what set White apart from the other leaders of Savannah's postwar political battles was his status as a war veteran. Though Simms, Porter, and others had kept alive the promise of emancipation in the darkest days of the conflict, they had never worn a Union uniform. White proudly took his place as an officer of the local Robert G. Shaw Post No. 8, Grand Army of the Republic.[87]

Black men dependent on the federal government for their jobs expended much time and energy fighting among themselves over whom to send as delegates to city, county, and state central committees. These fights took the form of disputes over credentials and procedures, and in this regard White held posts of considerable influence. On and off for two decades he represented Savannah at meetings of the state central committee of the Republican Party and headed the city's Republican Executive Committee. As chair of the local party's credentials committee, White found himself at the center of angry, long-winded debates over who should serve on various ultimately powerless committees or county or state delegations. Ever patient, White won plaudits for his "conciliatory" speeches and his heroic efforts to restore order to rowdy gatherings.[88]

In 1880 the White family was living on Duffy Street, next door to the Deveauxs. Anna was keeping house, and Richard was working as a postal route agent for the Atlantic and Gulf Railroad, a position that, alternating with an inspector's job at the customs house, provided him with steady work between 1877 and 1882. The three Deveaux children were about the same age as White's three; they were probably playmates. Yet since the census taker's last round, a dual tragedy had befallen the White household; baby Richard (nine months in 1870) and Lillian (two) had died. In June 1880 the household had a new baby, six months old, also named Richard. White and his wife had three other children: Marie, seven, Thaddeus four, and Ella, two. Bonnette, called Bonnie, would arrive in 1888.[89]

In March 1882 White once again found himself in the humiliating position of applying to the customs house; he had just lost his post office job. In his letter of application, he gave his birthplace as Sumter, South Carolina, and his level of education as "common school." He went over the details of his military service and appended a statement by a local white justice of the peace: "We hereby certify that R. W. White is of good moral character, of temperate and industrious habits, and faithful to the Union and Constitution." White again worked for the customs house from 1883 to 1887, but in 1888 he lost his job to Clement Saussy, a forty-two-year-old white grocer. In Boston a few years before, James Trotter had faced a similar predicament, displaced from his federal post by a white man. Yet unlike White, Trotter had quit the Republican Party to become one of Boston's leading black Democrats, claiming the Republicans should never take black voters for granted.[90]

White remained a Republican, but his precarious financial state forced him to work alternately as a porter for a white-owned business, C. M. Gilbert and Company, as an insurance agent, as a financial adviser, and even as a construction laborer and carpenter. Periodically, the *Savannah Tribune* ran this ad: "If you wish to make a beginning towards purchasing a home, you will find it to your interest to consult Capt. R. W. White before investing elsewhere. . . . If you want to have your property insured against lost [*sic*] by fire call on Capt. R. W. White." White had adopted the title of captain, as many veterans of public prominence did.[91]

In 1888 he was working as a porter and the following year, "being out of Government employ," as he put it, as a carpenter at a Waldburg Street construction site, a five-tenement building. In 1890 he fell from scaffolding and sprained his ankle. He hired a Washington lawyer, James Tanner, to file a claim with the US government for a veteran's pension. (Congress had passed pension legislation that summer.) In his initial application White described "a paralysis of the entire right side" exacerbated by general "ill Health incident to Army Service and a wound received from falling off a Building on or about April 10, 1889." His application was denied.[92]

In March 1892 White served on a panel of judges for exercises held at First African Baptist Church, which included singing, recitations, and a debate on the question "Which Produces Most Crime: Woman, Wealth or Poverty?" The winner had answered, "[Woman] inasmuch as she is the great source from which evil flowed she must naturally be the cause of most crimes." Of White's relation with his own "woman," Anna, we know little; she was absent from the society notices published by the *Tribune*. The loss of at least two of her children, combined perhaps with the domestic repercussions of her husband's thwarted ambitions, kept her out of the spotlight in the black community.[93]

In March 1893 White once again applied for a pension, and once again he was unsuccessful. The doctor who examined him did little to bolster his case when he wrote that White was a "tall, well nourished, bright mulatto of 54," and then continued, "I have known him many years and never have heard him complain about his foot; I have no doubt that he did have the accident he alleged but as far as the foot is concerned, I don't believe he would do manual work if he could. He always hunted the soft positions."[94]

Two years later White was the victim of a nasty effort by two white postal clerks to have him fired. The *Tribune* reported, "The plan of the conspiracy was to protect certain [white] men and to report all colored employees and Catholics in the office, and particularly to mix the letters of the general delivery, thus giving the post master grounds for finding fault with the clerk Mr. R. W. White." The conspirators suffered dismissal from their jobs.[95]

White held a post office job sporadically over the next nine years, working as a retail clerk in 1896 and a laborer two years later. By this time he was no longer head of his own household. Anna had died, and he was living with Gaston Lloyd (whom he identified as his brother-in-law), a bartender. Other members of the household included White's thirteen-year old daughter, Bonnette. Thaddeus, twenty-five, was serving in the army. White's difficult circumstances—his constant anxiety about his job, his need to ingratiate himself with white Republicans, the routine and even menial nature of his positions—must have taken a great emotional and physical toll on him.[96]

During the national presidential campaign of 1896, the emerging People's Party challenged Republicans and Democrats in a third-party bid to give voice to desperate industrial workers and farmers, black and white, all over the country. Republican William McKinley of Ohio ran on an unapologetic probusiness platform, portraying the Populist (and eventually also Democratic) candidate William Jennings Bryan as a wild-eyed fool. Deveaux and White were among McKinley's earliest and most steadfast Savannah supporters. While farmers and other debtors around the country were calling for an expansion of the currency and were creating black and white coalitions, Richard White and his fellow Republicans were resolving "to secure the election of our Matchless Standard Bearer, the champion of sound money and protection to American industry. . . . Major McKinley believes in an honest dollar and the privilege to earn it." McKinley's campaign talking points revealed a shift in the party's worldview from the moral fervor of Lincoln to a defense of entrenched business interests. The national party evinced no concern for black suffrage, leaving White and others to call in vain for "a free ballot and a fair count" in Savannah. Ironically, Bryan, the self-proclaimed candidate of the dispossessed, won the votes of whites in Georgia but lost the national election. Like their counterparts in Providence decades before, black men in Savannah found the two-party system a poor vehicle for pursuing the cause of justice.[97]

According to the *Savannah Tribune,* the Republican Party of Georgia was now "largely composed of colored men," and so perhaps it is not surprising that relations among the stalwarts remained fractious and annual conventions routinely descended into "ire and venom" spewed by feuding parties. Once again, the *Tribune* called for "all good Republicans to lay aside personalities and technicalities as to the past and unite for the general good of all," and once again, White stood at the forefront of such efforts. In late December 1897 he presided over a gathering of one thousand hoping to beat back city officials' efforts to eliminate all black patronage appointees. The tone of the meeting was accommodating: "We recognize and appreciate the good will and harmony existing between the two races, and have confidence in our white friends with whom we have so longed lived and with whom we expect longer to live, that the mere matter of appointing a competent colored man as collector of customs for this port will not in any way disturb the friendly relations that now exist." In a polite but indignant aside, the meeting also noted that black federal appointees were no longer an "experiment" but rather "a fact demonstrated by the proper and efficient manner in which they discharged their duties in the various offices held by the many of their race all over this country, and do not consider it an authority over the white man." President McKinley could choose either a white Democrat or a black Republican. Eventually, he chose the latter, solidifying his support among the "loyal colored Republicans of Georgia."[98]

White played no role in the national debate over black citizenship rights and the nature of increasingly destructive racial ideologies. Dependent on the goodwill of white Republicans, he devoted his energies to the cramped realm of securing patronage jobs and sorting out squabbles among party loyalists in Savannah. Perhaps, though, he took vicarious pleasure in the career of John Mercer Langston, who after the war emerged as an outspoken leader on the national stage; he traveled around the country to denounce the southern neo-Confederate project of disenfranchisement and segregation, a project touted as the New South. Langston condemned the belief among whites generally that the black man's "former condition of servitude, nationality, and color, make him a political nondescript, if not a political outcast, under our Constitutional and legal provisions." The Constitution, in fact, had nothing to say about either race or color. He ridiculed whites' obsession with skin color, a stigma associated with enslaved forebears, and the idea that the quality of a person's hair texture and the shape of his nose or lips disqualified him from citizenship. Was not such a view equivalent to the argument "'Your hair is very red, your face excessively freckled, your nose is crooked, and altogether you are a homely person'—*ergo* you cannot vote or serve on a jury?" No doubt he would have been disgusted with the proliferation of ads in the *Savannah Tribune* and other black papers around the country touting skin lighteners, like the "Black Skin Remover" that promised the buyer "a peach-like complexion," a black person turned "perfectly white." In any case, Richard White could have testified to the mistaken premise that white skin alone could turn anyone white.[99]

In 1901 the sixty-one-year old White consulted a new physician and reapplied for a veteran's pension. This doctor reported, "The soldier is feeble, ataxic and paralysed, is confined to his bed and requires the attention of an attendant. . . . He appears honest and intelligent, answering frankly all questions plyed." White also submitted an affidavit saying that "he has no income . . . no means of support these are the facts of the case." The pension board approved his application for $12 a month because of White's "inability to earn a support by manual labor," the standard criterion by which the vast majority of black veterans were judged.[100]

Around this time White moved in with his married daughter Ella Hackett, who told pension officials, "My father has been paralyzed for three years. He is a pensioner and lives with me." She continued: "He was born in Ohio, I think. He is entirely helpless and confined to his bed all the time. He has no wife." Ella kept track of all his paperwork, and whenever the pension was up for renewal, John Deveaux "comes here to the house and fixes the papers for my father. I handle the proceeds of the pension check and my father gets the full benefit of it. He is well cared for by me." In 1904 White managed briefly to go back to the federal post office, for the last time.[101]

His health failing, he had no choice but to retreat from the fray and depend on the tender mercies of his daughter. In 1905 it was Ella who wrote to pension officials and informed them of her father's death on March 3.[102]

A few years later the *Savannah Tribune* announced the return visit home of a young prodigal son after a sixteen-year absence: White's son Thaddeus. The thirty-five-year-old had for a while worked in Savannah as a hostler, groomsman, and stable keeper. Enlisting as a private in the army on June 28, 1898, in Chicago, he joined Company F of the Eighth Illinois Volunteer Infantry and gave the name of his sister Bonnette White, 309 Duffy Street, as the person to be notified in case of an emergency. Thaddeus served in the war against Spain, in Soriana de Cuba, and subsequently suffered from rheumatism in the back and shoulders; he claimed "disability caused by exposure to the elements." However, the examination board that processed his discharge in March 1899 disputed his claim and found that he had "no disability." He left the army with a favorable evaluation: "Character, Excellent." However, his second tour of duty, which began in San Francisco in 1905, ended with a dishonorable discharge two years later. In the service, he had been working as a cook.[103]

Returning to Savannah that Christmas, Thaddeus probably stayed with his sister Bonnie, twenty-two, a schoolteacher presiding over a boarding-house with three "inmates" and two servants. A high school graduate, she was teaching at Saint Anthony's, a Catholic school for black children spon-sored by a French order called the African Mission Society of Lyons.[104]

Both White's daughter and son, she a schoolteacher and he a soldier, fol-lowed in their father's footsteps—after a fashion. She avoided serving un-der the mean-spirited public education officials in Savannah by working for a school run by a Catholic order. There and throughout the country John Mercer Langston's vision of the schools as an instrument of equality and democracy remained an unfulfilled dream. As a young man still in his teens, Thaddeus had left home and joined the army, but no grand ideals animated the US projects in Cuba and the Philippines in 1898. Unlike his father, he saw the army not as an instrument of the country's moral regeneration, but as a source of a menial job. For neither Bonnie nor Thaddeus then was public employment the means to financial security or personal dignity. In this, perhaps, they had taken note of the example set by their father: he had had faith in—and placed his life on the line for—the United States, only to be let down again and again when the nation's white leaders refused to ac-knowledge his most basic rights.

Despite a lifetime of deep disappointments, Richard W. White left his mark on history through the public documents that reveal his remarkably robust citizenship: military service records; pension applications; transcripts and rulings in the 1869 *Clements* case; Freedman's Bank savings accounts; petitions of protest; letters to public figures such as Sumner, Butler, and Grant; Southern Claims Commission forms; and even his answers to census takers. Inscribed in those documents is one man's commitment to the idea of democracy, an idea that ultimately failed him and 4 million other Amer-icans of African descent after the Civil War.

FIVE

WILLIAM H. HOLTZCLAW

The "Black Man's Burden" in the Heart of Mississippi

In the autumn of 1908 black men, women, and children were toiling bare-foot and stooped over in Mississippi cotton fields, picking the fluffy fiber off the spindly plants and depositing it into tow sacks the workers dragged behind them. Methods of cotton-picking had remained essentially the same since the days of slavery. Indeed, although it had been more than forty years since human bondage was finally outlawed in the United States, the lives of early-twentieth-century black field laborers closely resembled those of their enslaved forebears, at least in material terms. Most still made their homes in cramped, smoke-filled cabins and spent their workdays toiling under the supervision of white landowners. Deprived of the right to vote, vulnerable to white-initiated violence, blacks inhabited a world apart from their white neighbors, no matter how poor. Struggling to get by in central Mississippi's Hinds County, one black farmer observed, "Times don't never get no different with a man that ain't got nothing."[1]

William H. Holtzclaw begged to differ. The twenty-eight-year-old had arrived in the county determined to found a black "industrial" school modeled after Alabama's Tuskegee Institute, his alma mater. Holtzclaw was a self-made man, and education had proved a certain, if rocky, path of upward mobility for him. Now the young teacher was convinced that by sheer willpower he could bring literacy and enlightenment to the blacks of Hinds County, where fully 40,000 of the county's total population of 52,000 were

FIGURE 5.1 This portrait of William H. Holtzclaw appears as the frontispiece of his autobiography, *The Black Man's Burden*, published in 1915. The principal of Utica Normal and Industrial Institute appears weary, no doubt because of his arduous and never-ending fund-raising efforts, which took him from his family and the school for weeks and months at a time throughout his adult life. Courtesy Schomburg Center for Research in Black Culture, New York Public Library.

former slaves; he would thereby disprove the farmer who believed that time stood still in the Black Belt.

On the surface at least, Holtzclaw provided a striking contrast to the parents of his pupils. By the time he arrived in the county, he had long abandoned the rough denim overalls of a field hand in favor of formal Victorian menswear and a professorial demeanor. Small and bookish, with an expansive vocabulary, he resembled a city-born clerk more than the country-bred son of former slaves. Unlike most men and women in Hinds County, who remained mired in everyday hardships, Holtzclaw possessed what he considered a clear vision of the means by which rural southern blacks might improve their lot in life—a program of action that demanded accountability from his pupils, their parents, and members of the general community, all acting in concert.

Educated black men like Holtzclaw were a rarity in Hinds County. Ideologies of race had reached a vicious intensity in Mississippi; there, in a bid for power, a new breed of white politicians set about demonizing black people regardless of class or skin color. State lawmakers had disenfranchised black men in 1890, and together with local sheriffs and judges, they remained complicit in promoting lynch mobs as agents of state-sanctioned terrorism. Such measures effectively relegated black families to poverty and the margins of politics, replicating in large measure slavery's consequences, if not its legal codification.

In 1902, when Holtzclaw had first arrived in the small town of Utica on the edge of the Mississippi Delta, thirty miles southwest of Jackson, he found "the Negroes groping in darkness and suffering on every hand as a result of that darkness," prompting him to carve from the region's hardwood forests what would become the Utica Normal and Industrial Institute. Later he would title his autobiography *The Black Man's Burden,* a nod to Rudyard Kipling's 1899 poem, which began with an exhortation for Europeans and white Americans to embrace the duties of empire: "Send for the best ye breed / Go bind your sons to exile / To serve your captives' need." In Utica Holtzclaw sought to serve the needs of the captives in the wilderness that was Mississippi, "the most benighted state in the Union for the black man." For one of so slight, even frail, a frame, the young man exuded an outsized missionary zeal. Warned by one of his Tuskegee Institute teachers, "You know there is no God in Mississippi," Holtzclaw nevertheless described himself as "possessed" with a need to start a school, a need "which I cannot rid myself of if I would."[2]

Holtzclaw oversaw the growth of Utica from a small open-air primary school that began under a tree in 1902 to an enduring institution of vocational training and higher learning. It was arguably the first school of its kind in Mississippi to be founded by a black educator on behalf of black people; other similar institutes and colleges owed their beginnings to a variety of church and missionary groups representing the (white) Methodists, Congregationalists, and Baptists. Just a few years after its founding, Utica consisted of a number of imposing frame structures—including a chapel, classroom buildings, and dormitories—built with the donations of prominent northern philanthropists. More than two dozen teachers, all black, instructed more than three hundred students, two-thirds of whom were girls and women. The school sponsored classes at the elementary and secondary levels during the day and at night and included training in agriculture and skilled crafts. Each student devoted a day and a half of each week to an "industrial" course, with the boys learning carpentry, blacksmithing, tailoring, shoemaking, and printing, and the girls learning sewing, millinery, housekeeping, cooking, mattress-making, and printing. The school was well on its way to boasting a physical plant worth $200,000. The fact that annual income equaled annual expenses testified to the daunting task that consumed its founder: without an endowment to draw upon for the future, Holtzclaw was forced to scramble each year to meet basic operating costs, including pay for the staff and room and board for the students, financial obligations not covered by tuition and fees alone.[3]

Some of Holtzclaw's most ambitious plans for Utica met with resistance—and not just from expected quarters. In September 1908 he had to acknowledge that his black neighbors were in a quiet state of panic, gripped with fear that the impending visit of a special guest whom the founder had invited to Utica would lead to strife and even bloodshed. Certainly, whites in the area had reacted violently to far lesser provocations in the past. And so now, together, local black leaders appealed to principal Holtzclaw to dissuade his guest—Booker T. Washington—from coming to the tiny Mississippi town.

Initially, the local trustees of Holtzclaw's school refused even to gather and discuss the prospect of meeting Washington. A famous educator, confidant of northern philanthropists, and adviser to and dining companion of a president, the head of Alabama's Tuskegee Institute nevertheless bore the label of a black man—and presumably his national reputation and well-known accomplishments would risk inciting the local white populace. Yet Holtzclaw had founded his own school precisely on Tuskegee principles; he considered Washington a mentor and a friend. To withdraw the invitation at this late date would mortify both men. The trustees finally met just a few days before the planned visit, and, according to Holtzclaw, "they promptly advised me that it would be a very unwise thing to have him come to Utica; in fact, they thought it would be a dangerous thing, that Dr. Washington could never pass safely through the streets of Utica." The consensus of the group was "that we ask Dr. Washington not to come to Utica—for his good and for ours."[4]

Holtzclaw understood these fears full well; Mississippi was rife with lawless brutality perpetrated by white people and aimed at blacks and whites alike. That fall the Jackson *Daily Clarion-Ledger* carried frequent stories about so-called Night Riders, poor white men threatening to destroy cotton gins and sawmills and to murder the men who owned them in order to protest the fact that modest farmers paid higher prices at these establishments while the great planters received discounts. The local Law Enforcement League, a group of vigilantes, was routinely destroying "blind tigers," purveyors of illegal alcohol. The torture of black men and women had become public spectacles attended by crowds of white parents and children, farmers and businessmen. The newspaper alerted its readers so that they could plan to attend and witness the horror: "Prospects Good for a Lynching, And the Indications are that when it Comes it Will be by Wholesale; Five Negro Men and Two Women."[5]

In the village of Utica memories of violence were still fresh: not too many years before, whites had terrorized local black families in a concerted campaign to drive them out of Mississippi altogether. In the early twentieth century, the heyday of these so-called White Caps, black landowners were waking up to find posters that read, "If you have not moved away from here by sundown tomorrow we will shoot you like rabbits." Holtzclaw himself had to contend with periodic rumors that unknown white men were plotting to kill him, and he had faced down young white toughs and a knife-wielding sheriff's deputy. As he put it delicately in his autobiography, his teachers and students, and black people generally in Hinds County, refrained from "moving to and fro among our white fellow-citizens in this section of the country."[6]

Alarmed but determined not to rescind the invitation to Washington, Holtzclaw consulted a local businessman, "one of my good white friends," who advised him not to have the educator come "if you have the least idea that there is any danger." This man, Holtzclaw remembered, speculated that "some crazy, drunken fellow, having heard so many things about Washington, might attempt to do violence to him; and that would disturb the friendly relations between the races here which everybody has been working so hard to cement." Moreover, the white man warned Holtzclaw, "Booker might say something in his address that would cause trouble for you after he is gone."[7]

Not everyone in Utica, however, was so apprehensive about Washington's visit. Unwilling to let the matter rest after his conversation with this white man, Holtzclaw approached a number of other leading whites, who assured him that Washington would meet with no harm in Utica, ridiculing the idea that there was "the slightest danger in the proposed trip."[8]

The visit took place according to plan, but during the twenty-four hours that Washington was in Utica, Holtzclaw "was careful to stay by his side, because I had said to the colored people when they were in their highest pitch of excitement that when he came I would be right by his side, and if any harm came, I would meet it first; I would see to that." Holtzclaw had also taken the precaution of hiring two detectives to "watch the younger, less inhibited white men that nothing untoward would happen."[9]

The throngs of black men and women who turned out to greet Washington early on the morning of October 7, 1908, were immediately reassured about his safety—and presumably their own. Washington was traveling with a most impressive entourage of thirty black men of refinement and distinction, including eight bankers, several college presidents and professors, representatives of the black Baptists and Knights of Pythias, newspaper editors and journalists, and a photographer. The group had chartered Pullman railroad cars that allowed them to travel and sleep undisturbed by the humiliation they would have endured in segregated transportation and lodging facilities. The train pulled over on a side track of the Jackson and Natchez branch of the Yazoo and Mississippi Valley Railroad, which had a station at the school. Many of the white onlookers were apparently drawn to see Washington out of curiosity, for it was exceedingly rare in Mississippi to see a black man wearing, as he was, a fashionable gray worsted suit with a four-button linen waistcoat, starched white shirt, high stiff collar, and silk bow tie.[10]

The group's stop at Utica was part of a five-day tour of the state sponsored by the Mississippi Negro Business League (MNBL), a branch of a national group Washington had founded in 1900. No one disputed the fact that he was venturing into hostile territory, though the frenetic pace of the tour ensured that he did not linger in any one place for long—and thus tempt fate, not to mention any number of angry white men who might have resented his presence. Washington's purposes in making the tour were to fact-find for his northern benefactors, including John D. Rockefeller and Andrew Carnegie; to provide some homespun advice to black farmers; and to live up to his name as the great "pacificator," calming whites who saw even modest signs of black well-being as profoundly threatening to their own interests. Yet he no doubt also took pleasure in forcing whites of all classes to acknowledge a group of black men who bore little resemblance to the illiterate field hands they claimed to know and understand so well. As Washington moved from place to place, Holtzclaw and his neighbors wondered, Would the Jackson newspaper cover the story? Refer to the visitor as "Mr. Washington"? The answers to these two questions were yes and no; the paper called him "Booker."[11]

The tour's itinerary yielded maximum symbolic value. The first stop had been Holly Springs, where several years before Governor James K. Vardaman had cut off state aid to a black vocational school and where a new one, funded by northern white donors and Mississippi blacks, had risen in its place. Declared Vardaman at the time, "I am not anxious even to see the Negro turned into a skilled mechanic. God Almighty intended him to till the soil under the direction of the white man." Utica was next, the site of Holtzclaw's impressive, relatively new school. After Utica the group would move on to Jackson, the state capital and home to ninety-three black businesses. The next stops, Natchez and Vicksburg, were legendary settlements of wealthy antebellum slave owners and cotton merchants. The visit to Greenville would include a side trip to the expansive land holdings of Alfred Holt Stone, author of a book on the so-called Negro problem lamenting the rapid annual turnover among black sharecroppers, a fact of rural southern life that Washington, too, deplored. On October 10 the tour would end in Mound Bayou, an all-black town where even the railroad stationmaster, telephone operators, and bank tellers were black. Charles Banks, the head of the MNBL and chief cashier of the Bank of Mound Bayou, had overseen the plans for Washington's visit to the state.[12]

In Utica Washington spoke in the chapel of Holtzclaw's institute while whites milled around outside. At this and other places on his tour, he gave a speech "boldly declaring" (in the words of one sympathetic black listener) the ambiguous proposition "that no power on earth could stop the Negro from acquiring an education of some kind, and it was to the interest of all classes to see that he secured a good one." Washington outlined the guiding principles of the school he had attended, Hampton Institute in Virginia; the school he had founded, Tuskegee; and the schools he had inspired, including Utica Institute. During his "cheerful journey" through Mississippi, he flattered whites by singling out a particular county, Marshall, where, he claimed, the absence of lynch mobs was a sure sign that blacks and whites were now living together "on such friendly terms."[13]

Washington offered nuanced bits of advice to blacks, challenging some aspects of the state's white power structure while seeming to accept—or at least abide by—others. He exhorted blacks to remain rooted in the southern soil and avoid the siren call of city living, to save their money and buy their own homes, and to teach their children personal hygiene and the difference between right and wrong. He stressed that black men should preside over modest but industrious rural households and add to the wealth of the region, all the while foregoing both formal political power and "modern" life in the form of urban wage work and consumerism. For whites, he made the case for black education in terms of their own self-interest: "In every Southern white home the food is prepared by Negro women. Your health, your very life, depends on their knowing how to prepare it." By way of summary he highlighted "those fundamental things" on which all Southerners could agree, including the "the dignity of labor" and the "importance of those simple, common, homely things which make the life of the common people sweet and wholesome and hopeful."[14]

Washington's departure from Utica, and from Mississippi, left Holtzclaw exhausted but exhilarated, convinced that his guest had impressed upon whites "that he is a wise, conservative, trust-worthy leader." And, in fact, "one of the foremost white men" of Utica agreed, telling Holtzclaw, "If we had enough men in this country like Booker Washington, we would be soon rid of the ills that beset us." Why then, given the nature of Washington's seemingly innocuous pronouncements, and his strenuous efforts to ingratiate himself among whites—hallmarks of his leadership style—had Utica blacks reacted so fearfully upon learning of the great man's proposed visit?[15]

The answer was as complicated as Washington himself. Although his call for sharecroppers to cultivate their own gardens and buy a piece of property may have seemed inoffensive, in fact it posed a potential threat to the South's political economy, which relied on the dependence of landless blacks (and, in certain areas, whites as well) upon a small group of white elites. Farm-labor contracts, which ran from January 1 to December 31, were inherently exploitative; many workers found it impossible to accumulate any cash, beholden as they were to landlords for advances of supplies and food. As the saying went of the sharecropper, "He is always twelve months from freedom." Schools such as Tuskegee and Hampton trumpeted the transformative power of vegetables—that is, if farmers grew their own and saved enough money to buy their own land, then (in the words of one Hampton student) "the mortgage system of the South would lose its binding and destructive power." Still, neither formal education nor landownership could guarantee black men and women a secure existence free from fear. In fact, Holtzclaw understood that "the more respectable Negroes" also faced threats of violence from whites of all classes and that many of them had "to abandon the homes they had paid for and leave the county without any compensation for their property or any protection for their lives."[16]

Washington's efforts to provide southern blacks with even a limited amount of formal instruction threatened the status quo in other ways as well. Governor Vardaman's distaste for black schooling had a self-contradictory, if familiar ring. As paraphrased by Holtzclaw, Vardaman believed that God had established the eternal "place" of blacks as menials; at the same time, "it was, therefore the duty of the white man to use every effort to keep him in his place." The governor certainly did his part: in 1904 Vardaman pardoned five whites convicted of killing a black landowner in Lincoln County. By that time, however, bankers and planters were complaining that vigilantism was depleting the local agricultural labor force. Vardaman eventually backed off his support for the White Caps, but he ramped up his rhetoric on the evils of black education, which, he charged, only "serves . . . to sharpen [a black person's] cunning, breeds hopes that cannot be gratified, creates an inclination to avoid honest labor." He went further and proclaimed lynching—the dismemberment, hanging, and burning alive of black men and women—to be a necessary weapon in the arsenal of white supremacists, who were, he said, the agents of "God Almighty" on earth.[17]

The rawness of the governor's language marked a new chapter in the history of racial mythologies in the United States. Confronted by black people recently released from the shackles of slavery and now fighting for legal rights and human dignity, Vardaman and others deployed the hangman's noose and the sheriff's shotgun as the ultimate arbiters of civil order in service of maintaining tenuous "racial" hierarchies. Remaking racial ideologies assumed an urgency as never before: the prospect of landless white farmers joining with their black counterparts in any kind of political organization accounted for the new and frightening images of black men, this time portrayed as beastlike sexual predators spawning children lacking in intelligence and moral sensibility. Long past was the postwar trope of the black man as unwitting dupe of white Republicans, for by 1900 southern white Democrats could locate precious few white Republicans to worry about. Instead, in the latter part of the nineteenth century, southern whites remade "race" to create a place-and time-specific narrative that featured aggressive black people and that criminalized the everyday behavior of those men and women who refused to act in a slavish way. Molded not by some abstract prejudice but by a southern-style competition for political influence, land, and other resources, this fiction resonated among whites as a group. Yet even stringent antiblack laws could not contain the yearnings of a still-unfree people—yearnings encapsulated in the life of William Holtzclaw.

————————

As whites shifted their depictions of blacks in the wake of Reconstruction, so, too, did black leaders remake their own political message. Vardaman's virulent antiblack rhetoric played well among poor white voters, whom he called the "good old-fashioned people—the hale, hard-working people." He precisely calculated this appeal to woo constituents who were not sharing in the putative New South prosperity enjoyed by textile mill owners, railroad operators, merchants, and lumbermen. Washington's appeal to his own supporters was calculated as well. This group included northern whites; a slice of the black middle class, North and South; and what he called the "better" white men of the South. Washington stressed the redemptive power of schooling to lead rural folk to fuller, more productive lives through a series of incremental steps designed to inculcate in pupils specific farm-management and artisanal skills.[18]

In fact, southern whites disagreed among themselves about the value of black schooling in its many forms, whether literacy instruction at the elementary level, "vocational" training in wheel-making and blacksmithing, the preparation of common-school teachers, or classical higher education. Vardaman condemned black instruction of any kind and argued that the money paid by black taxpayers into the state's educational fund could be better used staffing white schools. In contrast, some planters, such as Alfred Holt Stone, held that modest rural schools could keep sharecroppers rooted to one place and thus discourage annual turnover. Stone worried that if state authorities did not provide money for black schools, meddling Northerners would. Other whites promoted black "industrial" schools that trained cooks, laundresses, carpenters, and tinsmiths. Significantly, few argued that blacks had no ability or willingness to learn—just the opposite. One anxious southern politician noted that "it had come to his knowledge that Negroes would give the clothing off their backs to send their children to school, while too often the white man, secure in his supremacy, would be indifferent to his duty"—that is, to educate his own children. And indeed statistics confirmed rapidly declining illiteracy rates among the southern black population, from 44 percent in 1900 to 30 percent ten years later.[19]

Beginning in the 1890s, debates over the nature and capabilities of the "darker" or "subject" races took place in the halls of Congress, the classrooms of universities, and the pages of popular magazines and southern agricultural journals. These arguments encompassed peoples of all colors and ethnicities, not just those considered black. Controversies surrounding public education reflected larger domestic concerns about the fate of Native Americans, a so-called dying race, and recently arrived Eastern European immigrants and about the related dilemma of integrating Hawaiians, Cubans, Puerto Ricans, and Filipinos into an emerging American empire.[20]

As colonial powers sought out the raw materials that would fuel emerging industrial economies, the plight of rural southern blacks bore marked similarities to that of other oppressed laborers around the world. Millions of American field workers were part of a global labor force in agriculture, mining, and lumbering. Whether in the Belgian Congo, British Soudan, Nigeria, Rhodesia, Puerto Rico, Chile, India, Malaya, or the Mississippi Delta, these laborers lacked basic human rights, and they were integral to the extractive businesses that undergirded the rise of industrial capitalism. Political oppression of these discrete national, colonial, and regional workforces subverted the tenets of free-market ideology, for the greater the demand for labor, the more repressive the practices to control it. In the southern Black Belt, planters followed a corporate model and consolidated their landholdings in an effort to achieve factorylike efficiency; key to that efficiency was a black population that remained immobile, disenfranchised, and landless—a condition southern whites declared "natural." The logical incoherence of the system did little to halt its spread.[21]

In the United States politicians, academics, and policymakers expressed doubts about the capacity of darker-skinned peoples—"wards" of the country—for US citizenship. Assuming that full integration of these groups into the body politic was untenable, intellectual and political leaders conceived of halfway measures that would bring them under the protection of the state and at the same time prepare them for, and coerce them into, productive labor. In keeping with this worldwide project of colonial elites, subject peoples were now cast as objects of benevolence, ripe for religious proselytizing. This impulse toward missionary zeal faced some resistance among southern whites, who preferred to portray blacks in their own region as potentially dangerous subjects of New South "masters." At the same time, northern missionaries and philanthropists often spoke the same language of "civilization" as their European counterparts who sought to bring Christianity to the benighted masses of Africa or Asia. Indeed, southern planters enjoyed some success in convincing their white allies in the industrial North that the cultivation of cotton via the sharecropping system was part of an international, not just regional, effort that blended economic development with ministering to "uncivilized" peoples. Like their Revolutionary-era South Carolina forebears, late-nineteenth-century planters prided themselves on their cosmopolitan views that connected them to wealthy white landlords everywhere.[22]

Booker T. Washington's own life story challenged the ideologues who held that a person's race constituted an immutable condition—an identity written in the genes, rather than imposed. Within the space of a few decades, the educator himself had moved up and out of the "barbarity" of bondage and into the company of indisputably "civilized" men and women. The real and symbolic power of his visit to Mississippi, then, emanated from the way he presented himself—and here the stiff trappings of a Victorian suit were critical—and the way he surrounded himself with a large group of similarly educated and well-dressed men. (The party's travel arrangements, and its members' determination to attach a "manly" face to black progress, precluded the inclusion of any women, whether wives or teachers.) No one could argue that Washington had benefited from privileges of any sort: he had been born in slavery, and he had made his way in the world quickly by virtue of his ambition, intelligence, and political savvy. His words might prove soothing to whites, but his biography remained a powerful rebuke to currently fashionable views of biological determinism.

In establishing the school in Utica, Holtzclaw followed Washington's lead, though with more modest results. Utica Institute never became as well funded or as well known as Tuskegee. Washington, always territorial to a fault, preferred it that way; over time he even came to see Holtzclaw as a rival of sorts to his own fund-raising machine. At the same time, the broad outlines of their respective careers were remarkably similar. Both had been born in abject poverty and claimed inspiration from a hardworking mother who valued schooling. Both scrimped and sacrificed to attend an industrial institute. Imbued with an extraordinary work ethic enhanced by a sense of mission, each man oversaw the development of a substantial school, relying on his wife (or in Washington's case, a series of wives) to run the day-to-day operations of the institution while he was out frantically fund-raising. And each negotiated a white-dominated local rural economy in a bid to win a measure of security for staff and students.[23]

Holtzclaw's career brings into sharp focus all the ironies and contradictions of turn-of-the-century ideologies of racial difference. Ever the proper gentleman, he felt ambivalent toward the black masses, with their (in his view) superstitions and spendthrift ways. He joined with Washington in issuing dire warnings about black immorality. At the same time, even early in his career he boldly denounced disenfranchisement, lynching, and the diversion of black tax dollars to white schoolchildren. He was also receptive to the drive for civil rights represented by new organizations, such as the National Association for the Advancement of Colored People (NAACP), founded in New York in 1909, a political stance that Washington found personally threatening. Holtzclaw promoted the view that, even though blacks remained a separate race, they deserved full integration into American life and institutions.

The conviction on the part of both Washington and Holtzclaw that all men of goodwill might hammer out some mutually agreeable solution to what was generally referred to as the Negro problem flew in the face of the southern and national political economy. Throughout this period southern blacks were imprisoned in a legal system designed to relegate them exclusively to menial, task-oriented labor. Lawmakers deprived blacks of all semblance of formal political power, and employers enforced degrading living and working conditions among sharecroppers and domestics. Federal cover for the whole system came in the form of indifference or outright complicity among presidents and US congressmen. Every day ritualistic performances of violence, intimidation, and submission remained central to the white supremacist project; in the presence of whites, southern black people were expected to talk and even walk a certain way. The white South simultaneously embraced the trappings of modernity and created the myth of the Lost Cause, which glorified the antebellum slave plantation and the whites who had fought to defend it.[24]

The segregationist system amounted to a form of public humiliation for all black Southerners. The system allowed and even encouraged some forms of close black-white interaction—for example, when black women domestics daily entered the homes of white employers and attended to the intimate needs of the people who lived there. And in some cases white business owners and shopkeepers became dependent on blacks for their business, a dynamic of which both Washington and Holtzclaw were quite keenly aware. Settling in Utica, Holtzclaw operated on the principle that black people must prove themselves of value to all well-to-do whites, not just the planters, around them. He took his cue directly from Washington, who had written in his autobiography, "I think that the whole future of my race hinges on the question as to whether or not it can make itself of such indispensable value that the people in the town and state where we reside will feel that our presence is necessary to the happiness and well-being of the community."[25]

In the narrow world that Holtzclaw and Washington inhabited, black advancement and the status quo occasionally had a strangely symbiotic relationship. While Mississippi politicians were railing against black education, in Utica and its immediate vicinity white bankers, department store owners, and sellers of building materials were more than willing to reach a mutually advantageous relationship with the black school in their midst. If Holtzclaw accommodated himself to southern segregation, then the merchants of Utica accommodated themselves to the school. R. Fulton Holtzclaw, the principal's son, estimated that during his father's forty-year career, he brought in $2.4 million to Utica, most of it going to white merchants in the town. Away from the publicity surrounding Washington's visit, Holtzclaw navigated the fierce local racial politics that turned not at all on "scientific" theories but rather on questions of taxes, elections, labor demands, and the circulation of cash. The ideological was, in fact, subsumed into the practical mainly because the ideology itself was a creature of everyday realities shaping labor and political relations between blacks and whites.[26]

Later, recounting Washington's 1908 visit to Utica, particularly his breakfast at the family homestead the morning after his speech, Fulton Holtzclaw wrote, "This was the highlight of Father's forty years at Utica. Nothing that happened throughout his career ever pleased him as much as this visit by the man and teacher he admired more than any other." Yet for principal Holtzclaw, the visit amounted to but a fleeting respite from a seemingly endless round of fund-raising far from home. Utica Institute was the creature of its founder, and for forty years its very existence depended upon his own.[27]

William Henry Holtzclaw was born about 1874 in Randolph County, Alabama, on a cotton plantation near the village of Roanoke. At the time of his birth he had four half siblings; his mother, Adaline, would give birth to ten more children. His father, Jerry, sharecropped while Adaline worked as a cook and housekeeper for their white employer-landowner, a Mr. Yarbrough. Jerry and Adaline were former slaves, and their tiny dwelling, a fourteen- by sixteen-foot windowless split-pine cabin, had been part of the slave quarters on the plantation before the war. Looking back on his early childhood, Holtzclaw remembered most vividly the physical deprivation and the lifelong damage it inflicted on his health. Dressed in simple, one-piece shifts made out of burlap sacks, the children went barefoot year round and began work at an early age. For a few weeks each summer they enjoyed vegetables from a small kitchen garden, a rare privilege for croppers. Nevertheless, mostly they were dependent on Adaline to bring home food at night: the so-called service pan that domestics accepted as their due. Food was so scarce at times that they had to fight the scraggly family dog for sow-belly scraps. Remembered Holtzclaw, "I was hungry nearly all the time. . . . We were emaciated, underfed little creatures."[28]

Randolph County is located in the Piedmont, on the east-central edge of Alabama, just north of the sandhills. With its thin soil and hilly terrain, the county grew cotton but never partook of the antebellum boom in that staple. During the Civil War white residents came together to protest the economic policies of the Confederate government, which, they claimed, were worsening their already precarious situation. Just barely able to feed its own population in "ordinary times"; bereft of fully three-quarters of its white men, now serving in the army; and possessing relatively few slaves, the county could not pay the required tax-in-kind in corn, nor could it turn over the requisite number of enslaved laborers to military authorities. In 1864 "women riots" testified to the desperation of mothers and wives moved to raid local stores of wheat and corn. Fifteen years later yeoman farmers were falling from landownership into tenancy, caught up in a crop-lien system that mandated they grow cotton if they wanted a loan from a bank or a local planter-merchant. In Alabama as a whole the percentage of white farmers owning their land slipped from a majority in 1880 to a minority (42 percent) twenty years later.[29]

Like other sharecropping families, the Holtzclaws received monthly rations from the landowner: three pounds of flour, one pound of bacon or ham, a peck of cornmeal, plus a plug of tobacco and a box of snuff. For the privilege, they paid from 15 to 100 percent interest depending on the time of year. Meanwhile, Yarbrough claimed an extraordinary degree of authority over their comings and goings, day and night. In his autobiography Holtzclaw recounted how Jerry abided by a verbal annual contract that stipulated the landowner "was to furnish land, mules, feed, seed,—in fact, everything but labor,—and it further provided that he was to help do the work and receive as his share three-fourths of all that the land produced, while we were to receive the other one-fourth." Every December 31 family members watched as Yarbrough took three corncobs for every one cob he allowed them to keep and appropriated their whole cotton crop for himself. He "was at great pains to explain to my father that we ate ours during the year"—that is, they owed him more for supplies advanced to them than they had earned. For planters, cotton was the perfect crop because (unlike rice, for example) it could not be eaten by the people who grew it.[30]

One of the illiterate men working for Yarbrough—Holtzclaw's son Fulton later claimed it was Jerry himself—devised a system of keeping track of advances by notching a stick in a way that recorded rations, their cost, and the date "purchased" at the plantation store. His ingenuity allowed him to challenge Yarbrough successfully in court in a dispute over account-keeping. However, most sharecroppers were at the mercy of their landlords and had no say in the annual division of the crop. These conditions help to account for the high rates of annual labor turnover (called "shifting")—as high as 50 percent in certain areas of the postbellum Cotton South. Some workers left a landlord of their own accord at the end of the contract year, eager to try their luck down the road, perhaps closer to kin. Others were evicted by an owner who thought the parents were resistant to discipline, the children too slow in the fields. Hence, the local "labor market" in share-croppers was hardly "free"; all landowners expected compliance from their workers, and no shortage of workers would encourage them to revise their standards for the ideal family: two parents and many children all willing and able to pick cotton.[31]

Whites throughout the South, as well as federal officials and social scientists, equated end-of-the-year shifting with shiftlessness, a sign that black people lacked the personal responsibility to remain in one place for any length of time. Presumably, shiftlessness was to blame for many of the ills endured by blacks—from high mortality rates to lack of creditworthiness. Yet the resourcefulness of the Holtzclaws and other sharecropping families belied that indictment. During the winter and the lay-by season, Jerry scoured the countryside for wage work on railroad construction projects and in sawmills and coal mines. After several weeks' absence, he might bring home as much as $50, his savings from earning 60¢ cents to $1 a day, money that helped pay debts to the landlord. When William was born, Jerry was away, working on the Central of George Railroad; he borrowed a handcar to get home to see his new son.[32]

Labor contracts typically prohibited sharecroppers from keeping chickens, cows, or pigs or from engaging in virtually any activity that would divert them from the cotton crop or other demands imposed by the landlord. Still, to provide for themselves and the family, the Holtzclaw children foraged in swamps and forests for hog potatoes, berries, persimmons, muscadines, and nuts to supplement their meager diet. At the age of four William began to help out in the fields, and by the time he was a teenager he was hunting for possum, trapping or stoning other small animals for food, and earning 50¢ for every hundred rails he split. Yarbrough spent his own time giving orders to his croppers without ever picking up a hoe himself; he explained "that he was doing more work in a day without a tool in his hand than my father was doing in a month," a proposition that even the young Will found highly dubious.[33]

Jerry and Adaline were illiterate, but they were not ignorant, and they valued education for their offspring. She fashioned hats out of raccoon skins, and whole suits out of her only petticoat, so that the children could attend school. When the landlord arrived at their cabin early in the morning to send everyone into the fields, Holtzclaw recalled, she "used to outgeneral him by hiding me behind the skillets, ovens, and pots, throwing some old rags over me until he was gone. Then she would slip me off to school the back way." Around age nine Will became too big to hide, but his mother carried out a plan that allowed him to alternate at the plow with his brother Sidney. Whoever went to school that day taught the other one that night what he had learned: "In this way we each got a month of schooling during the year, and with that month of schooling we also acquired the habit of studying at home."[34]

In 1880 Jerry decided to try farming on his own. He was "encouraged," William would later remember, "by the success of other Negroes around him and urged on by the determination of my mother and the persistence of us children." He moved the family a few miles south, to Chambers County, where the census taker found them at home on July 12: Jerry, thirty-five, Adaline, twenty-nine, Susan, sixteen, Green, fourteen, Martha, twelve, Bud, ten, Sidney, eight, Will, six, and Effie, four. Securing a loan, Jerry rented a forty-acre farm and bought a mule, horse, and pair of oxen—"and so we started out for ourselves." The effort energized the whole family: "We all became better workers and for the first time began to take an interest in our work."[35]

Yet despite their newfound freedom from Yarbrough, the Holtzclaws continued to live on the thin edge of distress, and a number of misfortunes doomed their efforts at self-sufficiency. Many years later William Holtzclaw could still remember in vivid detail the ox that broke its neck caught in a fence; the mule so weak and ailing the children and a neighbor had to lift it up each morning; his father hobbled from stepping on a sharp sugarcane stub, rendering him "useless as a field-hand for the greater part of the year"; and the magnificent harvest of corn swept away by a flash flood. After four years of strenuous effort, the Holtzclaws were still in debt, and creditors arrived one day prepared to "clean them out"—to seize their small stores of corn, vegetables, chickens, and pigs. Tears streaming down her face, Adaline managed to talk them out of taking everything. Yet the family was "so completely broken" they had no choice but apply to Yarbrough for "a home under the old system."[36]

Like Elleanor Eldridge's memoir, Holtzclaw's *The Black Man's Burden* offered a pointed critique of contemporary stereotypes of black men and women. When he published the book in 1915, he was reacting to the invectives spewed by politicians like Vardaman—hence, the description of his long-suffering parents, especially his saintly mother, and the argument that even families living under the most oppressive conditions might show a remarkable degree of initiative. In recounting the story about his brief and youthful foray into stealing ("I was hungry and I wanted the eggs"), Holtzclaw noted that his mother's response, an injunction against all forms of theft, came with the warning "that 'white folks' thought all Negroes would steal, and that we must show them we would not." Later, he claimed that his hard childhood "strengthened my will and my body, and prepared me for more trying tests which were to come later."[37]

In describing Randolph County, Holtzclaw said virtually nothing about the three-quarters of the population who were white, many of them also sharecroppers. Fulton Holtzclaw's account of his father's life, *William Henry Holtzclaw: Scholar in Ebony,* included an evocative image of Jerry and an unnamed white man working together to bank and ditch a canal across a swamp. Still, William Holtzclaw's erasure of poor whites from his childhood omitted a critical piece of postwar political history. Poor whites had their own complaints about the high-handedness of the wealthy. Randolph County petitioners who expressed their grievances to Jefferson Davis in 1864 attacked the rich planters and their "large numbers of negroes about our towns & cities (used for the pleasure of their owners); or idling about; a curse to the community—*consumers not producers*." After the war some of these aggrieved whites joined the Republicans, a viable opposition party in Alabama from the end of the Civil War through the 1880s.[38]

During the penultimate decade of the nineteenth century, southern whites joined in a concerted backlash against Reconstruction efforts to advance the rights of black Americans. By that time Democrats were seeking to dismantle any black-white cooperation by encouraging the vicious raids of White Caps on black homesteaders and by appealing to white men's racial and masculine identities: one Democratic rallying cry went, "Come Sirs, you have fornicated with the Negroes until your liberties are endangered." Nevertheless, not until Alabama disenfranchised black voters in 1901 did Democrats enjoy the fruits of a true one-party system. State lawmakers argued for the measure by suggesting that bribing black men to vote Democratic—and here Randolph County was singled out—had become too expensive.[39]

In 1889 Will left home to make money on his own, and after six months he managed to save $40 by splitting logs for a white man for 25¢ a day. Around this time he happened across a pamphlet describing Tuskegee Institute, fifty miles to the south. Founded in 1881, the institute had already acquired a national reputation, but among Will's neighbors it was not necessarily a good one: "All the older neighbors counselled me not to go to Tuskegee. They said it was nothing but an old Baptist school where they fed you on bread,—corn bread,—and worked you to death. They said that boys who had no money and had to work their way through would be looked down on by the more fortunate; that Booker T. Washington was an infidel; and lastly, that I had enough education anyway." Will was no stranger to either hard work or a steady diet of cornbread. He sent off his application—"Der Book i wants to go to tuskee to get a ejercashuch can i come." He was accepted, and on October 1, 1890, he arrived at the school as a work-study student.[40]

When Holtzclaw first saw Tuskegee, the nine-year-old school was growing rapidly, its physical plant expanding to include classroom buildings, dormitories, and barns. Students tilled gardens, tended livestock, and made bricks on the one-hundred-acre parcel. For the youth from Randolph County, the school opened up a whole new world of sensations: the soft feel of bedsheets, the sight of a huge mule-drawn machine plow, the sound of a sawmill's "throbbing steam engine," the smell of flowers in the garden tended by the women students, the taste of a more varied diet. Will underwent a series of entrance tests under the sympathetic supervision of a young teacher named Margaret Murray. The results showed he could plow, feed hogs, and hay. Before long he had worked his way up to the "most coveted position on the farm—that of assistant manager." Recalled Holtzclaw, "I was dazed by the splendor of Tuskegee."[41]

Just as Hampton founder Samuel Armstrong had been impressed by the drive of the young Booker Washington, so Washington admired the eager brashness of Will Holtzclaw. Barging unannounced into the principal's office one day, Holtzclaw secured a job as his personal errand runner and wagon driver. The younger man took note of Washington's temperament and administrative abilities: his punctuality and rigid adherence to a daily schedule; his attention to small details, such as the amount of molasses a student had poured on his plate; his fastidious dress; and his powers of concentration, which at times produced a startling degree of absentmindedness. This management style partook of a kind of obsessiveness that made Washington admired by many of his students and staff but beloved by far fewer.[42]

Determined to follow Washington's example, Holtzclaw attacked his studies, carrying his books everywhere and even reading while driving a mule-pulled wagon loaded with wood. Such dedication did not escape the ever-alert gaze of the school principal, who took Will off the school farm and put him to learning the printer's trade. Still, Holtzclaw's early years at Tuskegee were difficult. His health suffered, and at one point he contracted spinal meningitis, a life-threatening illness that confined him to his bed for three months and left him owing $100 to the school's infirmary. He accounted for his overall poor health by noting, "This was the penalty that I had to pay for trying to make too rapidly the transit from a lower to a higher civilization." He believed he was ill equipped for this "transit" because of his thin clothing and lack of experience with "modern" living quarters featuring "glass windows and other comforts."[43]

Holtzclaw's poor health was only the first interruption to his studies. In June 1893 his father died, leaving Adaline with ten children to support and a large debt to repay to Yarbrough. To help his mother, Will returned to Randolph County to work in the fields and teach a small pay school held in a log cabin. He also visited his pupils' homes and "made [the parents] whitewash their fences and clean up their houses and premises generally, just as I had been taught to do at Tuskegee." They paid him whatever they could—a cat or a pair of scissors, but more often vegetables, meat, corn shucks, and cotton seeds, all of which he gave to his mother.[44]

Holtzclaw's time away from Tuskegee provided lessons in local politics. In the winter of 1893 Will set out for Whitesburg, Carroll County, Georgia (twenty-five miles southwest of Atlanta), where he taught for two school terms of four months each. There he encountered Richard W. White's ossified Republican Party, a largely powerless and uneasy coalition of many blacks and a few whites. By this time the cumulative poll tax had decimated black voting strength all over the state; this means of voter suppression required the voter to pay not only a tax to vote in the current election, but also all outstanding taxes for past elections in which he had not cast a ballot. Attaching himself to a local Republican political boss, Holtzclaw began a campaign to reclaim the party from its white leaders; he wrote a letter to the local newspaper in which he "appealed to the black Republicans to cut loose from the half-hearted white Republicans," for the "White Wing" of the party was actually "only a white feather in the wing of a Republican blackbird, as the party was nine-tenths black." This effort to purge the local party of whites was largely successful, and Holtzclaw found that he had become, as he put it, "popular, an honor to which I had never aspired." Besieged by offers to speak throughout the county, he seemed on the verge of pursuing a serious political career when he made a fateful decision to challenge the integrity of the local black teachers' Passing Club, which sold teaching licenses to anyone who could pay a fee. In the process he undermined the authority of some influential men, a move that made him distinctly less popular than he had been.[45]

Holtzclaw turned his back on whatever future Whitesburg might have offered him, resuming his Tuskegee studies in 1894. He later claimed he felt obliged to please his mother, who urged him to continue his schooling and take two of his siblings, Sidney, age twenty-two, and Effie, eighteen, with him. Indeed, his father had always discouraged Will from pursuing a career in politics and from becoming a lawyer or, in the older man's view, a "liar"; on his deathbed, Jerry implored Will to teach because "the people need your services." By exposing the Passing Club, Will had burned his bridges with Carroll County black leaders dependent on the operation as a source of scarce dollars in a largely cashless rural economy. At the same time, he was developing a deep commitment to working among black farmers.[46]

Back at Tuskegee, Holtzclaw received a warm welcome. Margaret Murray, now Mrs. Booker T. Washington, took a special interest in him and gave him a "Prince Albert" suit, a secondhand castoff that allowed him to continue his studies in some style. Always pressed for money, he worked as a substitute teacher in the institute's night school, earning $8 a month. In his senior year (1898) he prepared for a commencement oratorical contest. His mother, now fifty-two and remarried to a man ten years her senior,

Floyd Joiner, traveled from Randolph County to watch her son perform in May, but once she got to Tuskegee, she lacked the money to pay for her return trip, putting immense pressure on Will to win the prize money. He managed to place second in the contest and used the $25 award to get his mother back home. The trip must have thrilled her and freed her for a couple of days at least from her considerable domestic responsibilities. Living with her and her new husband, Floyd, were two of his children by a previous wife, one son they had together, four of her children by Jerry, and two grandchildren.[47]

Upon graduation, Holtzclaw turned down an offer to teach at Tuskegee and decided instead to "render service" in "one of these backwoods places," some remote rural area like the one where he had grown up. To prepare for such a strenuous undertaking, though, he accepted a job as a printer from another Tuskegee graduate, thirty-year-old William J. Edwards, who had founded his own industrial institute at Snow Hill, Wilcox County, forty-five miles southwest of Montgomery. The four years Holtzclaw worked on and off at Snow Hill helped prepare him in a number of ways for his own future as a school principal. First, he learned that a print shop could fulfill, and even create, a demand for its services among local whites. Ransom O. Simpson, "a southern planter of considerable means," gave Holtzclaw $10, which, with contributions from the school's teachers, he used to start a printing class. The students put out a weekly newspaper, and "nearly all the white merchants sent their work for the students to do." As a result, the print shop turned a profit. At Snow Hill Holtzclaw also established what he called the Black Belt Improvement Society to help local farmers market their crops without resorting to white middlemen. Yet this association had its limits and could only promote "co-operative buying and selling up to a point"—in Holtzclaw's words, "A complete co-operative would have antagonized those white merchants who were almost wholly dependent on the black farmers for their existence." Here then was the essence of the rural southern economy: because whites relied on the labor and patronage of blacks in order to profit, black self-sufficiency threatened the whole system.[48]

Holtzclaw remained restless at Snow Hill. In 1901 he ventured out from Alabama to the Mississippi Delta and for a few weeks picked up odd jobs near the town of Tunica—first as a laborer in a cotton warehouse, then as a hotel worker, and finally as a traveling clock repairer. Having no experience in this last trade, he had to admit that "the first two or three clocks that I attempted to fix were left not much better off than they were when I found them." Unable to locate a suitable place to start his own school, he was relieved when Edwards took pity on him and beckoned him back to Snow Hill and offered him the job of school treasurer.[49]

Soon after his return Will married the Snow Hill dean of girls, Mary Ella Patterson, a Tuscaloosa native and graduate of Tuskegee, class of 1895. Holtzclaw's son later wrote that his father "had married a beautiful Victorian-type woman as sincere and devoted to duty as he was. It was an ideal marriage, founded on true and abiding love." Within a year they had a son, William Sidney, but six months later the baby died of pneumonia.[50]

In the summer of 1901 Holtzclaw engaged in a decidedly un-Washingtonesque form of protest by registering his opposition to the deliberations of the Alabama State Constitutional Convention meeting in Montgomery. Among other tasks it set for itself, the convention sought to devise new ways to deny the state's black citizens the right to vote under the banner of establishing "white supremacy in this State," in the words of the body's president, John B. Knox. Approved measures included a $1.50 poll tax and a bar to illiterate voters. Writing from Snow Hill the day after the 4th of July, Holtzclaw condemned in particular the proposed grandfather clause, which would limit suffrage to those men whose male forebears had voted and fought for the Confederacy. Noted Holtzclaw, "I sincerely believe that if you lay down a law which will operate in favor of the white man because of his ancestry, and operate against the negro because of previous conditions over which he did not and could not have any control, it will be a great step backwards, for it seems to me that if we allow heredity to enter too largely into our politics we drift away from the basic principles of our institutions." Holtzclaw understood that "race" referred to blacks' unique historical circumstances—their ancestry—rather than to their biological makeup. The convention printed, but did not discuss or probably even read, his letter.[51]

Leaving Mary Ella behind grieving for their son, Holtzclaw soon struck out again for Mississippi. This time he headed to Mound Bayou, the all-black town whose mayor would later organize Booker T. Washington's whistle-stop tour of the state. Founded in 1887 on the edge of the Delta in Bolivar County, Mound Bayou was a political statement premised on, in the words of contemporary historian and booster Aurelius P. Hood, a "practical direction through which the satisfactory and amicable adjustment of an irritating race situation might be approached." Owners of the Louisiana, New Orleans, and Texas Railroad, the major line linking the Delta to Chicago, hoped to attract laborers to the booming lumbering industry. Believing that blacks would adapt well to the "semitropical" climate of the area, and needing a residential workforce, the railroad's owners appealed to a black businessman, Isaiah T. Montgomery, and offered him grants of land. He seized the opportunity to enable black people to "build a civilization of their own." Soon the town was attracting settlers, "pioneers" who set about chopping down the thick hardwoods and building houses. Within a few years they established a successful lumbering operation that produced staves, headings, and crossties for the railroad. Holtzclaw marveled at the bustling community—several churches, a normal and industrial institute, a fully functioning public school system, substantial homes, and a variety of small enterprises devoted to blacksmithing and shoemaking and dressmaking. Soon the town would have its own bank; under the direction of Charles Banks, the business boasted typewriters and adding machines, modern forms of technology reserved exclusively for use by white employees in other parts of the country. Mound Bayou suggested that in certain cases supply and demand could be a great moderating force. Of whites' tolerance for the community, Hood wrote, "They sell us their wares and buy our products."[52]

Holtzclaw, however, was unable to find a parcel of land in the area, and, dejected, he once more headed back to Snow Hill, where his unsuccessful forays into Mississippi were making him something of "a joke" among the other staff members. Then one day he picked up a book written by New Hampshire–born Orison Swett Marden, a hotel manager turned practical philosopher: *Pushing to the Front: Or, Success Under Difficulties, a Book of Inspiration and Encouragement to All who are Struggling for Self-Revelation Along the Paths of Knowledge and Duty*. Holtzclaw took heart from propositions such as these: "Your talent is your *call*. Your legitimate destiny speaks in your character. If you have found your place, your occupation has the consent of every faculty of your being." Later he said the book "not only aroused me, but seemed also to condemn me; every chapter I read seemed to say, 'You are a coward not to stick to what you know to be your duty.'"[53]

A coward Holtzclaw was not. Reinvigorated by Marden's book, he determined to set off once more for one of the South's many "backwoods places" where he might found a school. Unwilling to leave Snow Hill, Mary Ella remained behind. Will took her bicycle and boarded a train to Mississippi. This time he found his place and stayed—in a region many non-Southerners considered "foreign" in the extreme.

———

In 1902, around the time that Holtzclaw headed back to Mississippi, President Theodore Roosevelt made national headlines after his encounter with a small bear in rural Sunflower County, north of Hinds. The state's governor, Andrew L. Longino, had invited Roosevelt to join him to hunt for black bear and perhaps a wolf or panther or two in the Delta. Setting out in November, mounted on horseback, the party crashed through forests and canebrakes and sloshed through swamps. Presented with a wounded bear tied to a tree, Roosevelt refused to shoot it, prompting praise for his sportsmanship on safari, Mississippi style.[54]

With its forests and rich soil, the Delta offered a bounty ripe for economic development. The region resembled a European colony in Africa in terms of the eagerness of corporations, land speculators, and railroad companies to exploit its natural resources and the 907,630 black people (compared to 641,200 whites) who lived there in 1900. Debt peonage was rife throughout company lumber towns and large plantations. Most landless black farmers toiled as wage hands, their earnings penurious and their labor closely monitored by white "riders" akin to plantation overseers of old. Thirty-five years after the end of slavery, only 6 percent of black Delta farmers owned land. After the introduction of an all-white primary in 1902, the Democrats enjoyed unchecked power. Defeated by Longino in the 1899 governor's race, Vardaman was positioning himself for another run for the state's highest office with declarations such as, "The white man has no other use for the Negro than his labor . . . and when the Negro ceases to render that labor willingly, then the white man will get rid of him." The time and place hardly seemed propitious for a young black man on a mission.[55]

Holtzclaw pedaled around the dirt roads of what he termed the "wild and unfrequented part of Mississippi," taking time to survey the attitudes among well-to-do white men toward black education. His guiding principle was this: "You cannot build a school that will be useful unless the [white] people are in sympathy with your efforts." The results of his initial inquiries were not encouraging. Most of the whites he talked to believed that formal black schooling of any kind was not only a waste of time and money, but also a potential harm to the interests of all whites. Said one Minter City landlord who presided over holdings worked by several hundred blacks, "What I want here is Negroes who can make cotton, and they don't need education to make cotton." Regardless of their particular views, these men filtered the question of black education—and their understanding of the idea of race more generally—through the lens of the region's intense labor demand. Like the seventeenth-century Chesapeake, the Delta was of little economic value without large numbers of subordinate laborers to work it.[56]

Holtzclaw considered several factors in his decision to settle in the central prairie hill country just east of the Delta. He was convinced that the absence of corporate plantations there would moderate whites' views toward black education. He found the rolling hills more to his liking; they reminded him of his boyhood home in Alabama. And he early decided, "I am not going to antagonize any school or anybody." Absent from Hinds was a large class of sharecropping whites who might have posed a violent threat to any form of black schooling. Most of the county's whites lived in small towns or the state capital, Jackson, which sat in the county's northeastern corner. The black population (nearly one-third of whom were illiterate), meanwhile, was overwhelmingly rural. At the same time, regardless of race, rural families in Hinds County were organized along lines similar to those in Randolph County, Alabama, with large, two-parent families predominating. Thus, Holtzclaw found the local black community familiar, for it resembled the one he had grown up in and the ones in Whitesburg and Snow Hill where he had taught.[57]

Holtzclaw wasted no time in committing himself fully to his mission in Hinds County. Applying to the county school superintendent in Raymond, he secured an assignment teaching in the hamlet of Utica, southwest of Jackson on the boundary of Hinds and Copiah Counties. Because Utica had no schoolhouse for black children, Holtzclaw would essentially be starting its public education system from scratch.[58]

Arriving in the town, Holtzclaw sold his bicycle to a nineteen-year-old for $2 in cash and a watch. He then convinced the head of the Bank of Utica, W. J. Ferguson, to accept his $2 as a deposit. Over the next months the teacher gradually turned his tiny public school, held outside under an oak tree, into a permanent private institution. He focused his initial efforts on the white men of the town, seeking their approval for and "advice" on his venture, but also patronizing their businesses and paying for their professional services. He consulted J. B. Chapman, Utica's only attorney, as well as a young planter named Alexander Yates, the local postmaster and a father of mulatto children. Over the next few years Holtzclaw bought lumber from Curry Brothers Company and shopped at General Zachary Wardlaw and Company, Mimms and Newman, Kelley-Simmons and Company, and other merchants. He hired as the new school's lawyer a young white man, Paul D. Ratcliff. Holtzclaw soon learned that, whatever the misgivings of Hinds County planters toward his venture, for Utica's businessmen cash was a great force for moderation; even former Confederate generals had no problem pocketing the school's dollars.[59]

With a loan from Ferguson's bank, Holtzclaw managed to buy several dozen acres one mile south of town from a white woman. Then organizing and fund-raising within the black community commenced in earnest. He relied on Pleas McCadney, a respected black landowner in the area, as a go-between in negotiations with both blacks and whites, and he hired as a teacher Clara J. Lee, mother of one of his earliest supporters, Dan Lee. Isaiah Marshall, another landowner, and Aaron Caldwell, a white man raised by a black woman, also joined the board of trustees. Festivals and other entertainments to which the local black community contributed fried chicken and other tasty foods also brought in money. By Thanksgiving Holtzclaw had collected donations amounting to $37.50. In *Black Man's Burden* he quoted a note from a laundress, one of several mothers who "sent in their mites": "Dear fessor Please cept dis 18 cents it is all I has I saved it out n my washin dis week god will bless yo will send some more next week." Early on he made a tactical decision to insulate the school from either the state or a specific religious denomination. Repudiating the institution's public school origins, he ensured that Utica Institute remained nonsectarian and private, wholly reliant on donations and tuition—a financing strategy that over the years would leave the "fessor" perpetually in crisis mode, chasing donations.[60]

The school grew rapidly despite its modest financial foundations. Neighborhood men rolled up their sleeves and went to work felling trees when they ran out of funds to buy lumber for the institute's first building. By the spring of 1903 the schoolhouse was attracting new pupils—more than two hundred—from the area outside Utica. It was about this time that Mary Ella arrived from Snow Hill; as Holtzclaw recalled, she had written to him that "it did not matter what the conditions were, or what the hardships might be in the future, she preferred to come on and live with me and share them." Raised in Tuscaloosa and a real "city girl" (in William's words), she nevertheless set up housekeeping for the family in what he variously called "a little ramshackled log cabin" and "a hovel."[61]

With boarding students and a family to support (Fulton was born in 1904), Holtzclaw began seeking white patrons in the North. He embarked on fund-raising trips with letters of introduction from Washington of Tuskegee, Edwards of Snow Hill, and the mayor and other "leading whites" of Utica, who by now were convinced of the founder's benign intentions and the institute's potential economic benefits to the town. Perfecting his account of founding a school in the heart of the Mississippi wilderness, the earnest young man began to find success with donors. One of his earliest benefactors was Fidelia Jewett, a philanthropist and head of the Mathematics Department of the Girls' High School of San Francisco; in 1904 she had given him and his wife less than a day's notice before showing up with a traveling companion on the doorstep of their rude cabin. Will and Mary Ella put the two women up and fed them breakfast, surprised that "these highly cultured women could be satisfied with such humble fare." As word spread of the school, other wealthy people made gifts, including Boston publisher B. F. Ginn and New York banker Jacob Schiff. Holtzclaw began to spend the summer months in the parlors of Boston and New York City mansions and townhouses.[62]

In 1904 he launched an outreach effort to Hinds County farmers. A "Teachers' Extension Movement" sent instructors out of the classroom and into the community, where they were charged "to do all in their power to show the people in that locality how to better their condition." The staff might count as small victories the farmers and their wives who bought a few chickens for the first time or learned that fruits and berries were a nutritious dietary supplement. Holtzclaw also founded Utica's Black Belt Improvement Society, based on the Snow Hill effort. The society promoted a ten-stage process intended to take its members from "a *desire* to better their condition" all the way to owning one thousand acres of land. Incremental steps included owning a cow, mule, or horse; purchasing a small piece of land; building on the land "a neat and comfortable dwelling house"; and then adding to the acreage year by year. Soon the society had turned into a cooperative and had also founded a community court of justice. This court heard cases related to theft and domestic abuse, thereby bypassing the county's formal judicial system, dominated as it was by judges and juries looking for black men to send to the chain gang on virtually any pretext or no pretext at all.[63]

Holtzclaw also founded a related program, the annual Negro Farmers' Conference. Participants heard lectures on animal diseases, modern farming methods, and the eradication of hookworm. The conference was premised on the idea, according to Holtzclaw, that the black man "must follow the beaten path of history by making the soil the source of all prosperity, the basis of his temporal existence." He urged his listeners to renounce dependence on whites: success required blacks "to shoulder some of the responsibility, to carry some of the burdens of the world and not leave them all on the white man's shoulders." One of the highlights of the conference was the round of testimonials offered by men who could claim a radical improvement in their condition based on Tuskegee principles. Some men told of their childhoods in slavery times and their arduous ascent up a tenure ladder, from field hand to sharecropper, from cropper to renter to landowner.[64]

At one meeting Frank Wallace, whom Holtzclaw described as a slight, very black man "with every appearance of being of unalloyed African descent," told his own inspirational story, which highlighted a heroic level of struggle and self-denial. "I tell you," Wallace said to his listeners, "if you want anything you've got to work hard and let pleasure alone till you get it." Holtzclaw quoted at length another farmer, whom he did not identify, perhaps because of the grimness of his message: this man reported that it took him fifteen years to buy his own home, and in that time he had to work from dawn to dusk and eat cornbread and salt meat and forgo coffee, rice, biscuits, and other luxuries. Such effort, he said, "means you have to hide yourself on Sunday to keep folks from seeing your rags while they are going to church with their fine slick clothes on." He exclaimed, "Brethren, I am telling you what I knows, and if you ain't prepared to stand these thing, you better stay like you is." This startlingly frank assessment of the price of "striving" led one member of the audience to respond, "If that is the case, I believe I'll stay like I is."[65]

The speaker who described in such detail his own sacrifices also said that a man would face stiff resistance from the womenfolk of his household if he set his sights on landownership and insisted they shun new dresses and other presumably frivolous items. Yet the problem of consumerism, as represented by the desire for decent household furniture and nice clothes, transcended gender and went to the heart of the South's postbellum political economy. Utica was just a crossroads of 400 people, but Jackson, only thirty miles away and with a population of 31,000, offered whites and blacks alike a cornucopia of consumer goods: ready-made clothing at S. L. Johnson Company ("the Style Store"), shoes at Jones Kennington, chocolate bonbons at Lowney's, and "whisky at panic prices" at Harry Hoyle's liquor store.[66]

Out in the countryside, Hinds County croppers had little in the way of consumer choices; country merchants stocked trinkets but discouraged their workers from aspiring to buy things that required more cash than most would ever see in the course of a contract year. Still, some families scraped

FIGURE 5.2 The log cabin that served as Utica Institute's first dormitory, as well as the home of its founder, William H. Holtzclaw, and his family. By including this photo in *The Black Man's Burden,* the author hoped to highlight a favorite theme promoted by Booker T. Washington: the ability of a black person, or institution, to overcome humble beginnings and grow and develop. This notion of change over time for the better contradicted white supremacists' claims that blacks were incapable of intellectual or moral development. COURTESY SCHOMBURG CENTER FOR RESEARCH IN BLACK CULTURE, NEW YORK PUBLIC LIBRARY.

together enough money to buy a pump organ or to have their picture taken by a traveling salesman. Small circuses perambulated about the rural South these years, and they attracted large numbers of rural folk, black and white, young and old, drawn to the sight of a parade of elephants and scantily clad trapeze artists. In *Black Man's Burden,* Holtzclaw failed to mention whether any such shows appeared near Utica; but if they had, he would have surely disapproved of them. He also condemned many rural clergymen as akin to circus ringmasters—cynical men of questionable morals seeking to fleece the gullible with crass forms of entertainment, whether fiery sermons or dancing dogs. In Utica churches he found only ignorance, with the church offering plate a means for congregants to squander what little cash they had.[67]

In truth, Holtzclaw maintained an ambivalent attitude toward consumerism. Both he and Washington called for rural blacks to become dissatisfied with their lowly condition, and they were impatient with men and women who believed that they retained a certain amount of personal autonomy if they eschewed a desire for things of all kinds—in the words of one Alabama black man, when a person made up his mind "that he weren't goin to have anything and after that, why nothing could hurt him." Most blacks were aware of the families who had bought a small piece of land or opened a small grocery store only to find themselves the targets of White Caps or lynch mobs—yet fear of the price of prosperity was sure to limit blacks' opportunities, a danger to which Holtzclaw was sensitive. At the same time, he was contemptuous of spending that might waste a household's hard-earned money on nonessential luxuries. Nevertheless, to some rural folk, enjoying the instant gratification that came with the purchase of alcohol, candy, or tobacco seemed a safer and more pleasurable way to live life than saving and refusing modest pleasures in the hope of buying land someday. Predictably, Holtzclaw had no sympathy for men who dug themselves deeper into debt in order to buy "extra Sunday hats and fancy calicoes."[68]

A corollary of the anticonsumption ethos of Tuskegee and all the "mini-Tuskegees" that it spawned held that, no matter how difficult their lives, black people were better off in the rural South than in the cities, or even the small towns. Self-sufficiency was possible on a farm, whereas town dwellers were enmeshed in a consumption-oriented economy that might restrict their options even more. One of the functions of the schoolhouse was to provide an incentive for blacks to stay where they were; in this view, the school did not facilitate upward social mobility so much as geographical stability. Holtzclaw proclaimed his motto to be not "back to the farm" but "stay on the farm." Even as the boll weevil began to devastate cotton fields throughout Mississippi, he urged his students and their parents to resist the temptation to seek work elsewhere. Nevertheless, thousands of black families were deciding that in towns and cities they could earn cash, enjoy a more convivial social life, send their children to school, shop in well-stocked stores, and find refuge from abusive landlords. Many of these in-migrants were inclined toward industry and ambition: of his decision to leave Jackson for Chicago, writer Richard Wright noted, "Well, it's my life, I told myself. I'll see now what I can make of it."[69]

In extolling the virtues of the rural South, Holtzclaw was reacting to Vardaman's views of black crime—the idea that blacks who refused to stay in their appointed "place," the sharecropper's cabin, were by definition hardened criminals. Unlike the supposedly childlike slaves of the antebellum period, members of the new generation of blacks, the Mississippi governor charged, were vicious, promiscuous, and resistant to plantation discipline. Singled out for a special dose of vitriol were young black men, many of whom lacked the obsequious bearing expected of them. Reacting to statistics that showed blacks were disproportionately overrepresented among incarcerated men and women, both Holtzclaw and Washington accepted Vardaman's narrative to the extent that they warned blacks of the baneful effects of city life, with its crowded living conditions, irregular work patterns, and temptations of liquor, prostitution, and gambling. Faced with hostile state and local law enforcement and judicial systems, Holtzclaw exhorted all black men and women to refrain from criminal and immoral behavior, if for no other reason than that it brought disgrace upon the whole "race."[70]

Within four years of its founding, Utica was poised for a major expansion drive. With the help of lawyer Paul Ratcliff, Holtzclaw had secured a state charter for the Utica Normal and Industrial Institute of Colored Young Men and Women. He had assembled a distinguished board of trustees, including, among others, the Reverend Charles B. Galloway, bishop of the Methodist Episcopal Church of Mississippi; the Reverend Henry C. Cobb, pastor of the West End Collegiate Reformed Church of New York City; Mary Clement Leavitt, a Boston-based activist on behalf of the Women's Christian Temperance Union; W. J. Ferguson, president of the Bank of Utica; Emmett J. Scott, Booker T. Washington's personal secretary; W. J. Edwards of Snow Hill Institute; Ransom O. Simpson, Holtzclaw's early print shop patron at Snow Hill; E. H. Currie, a Utica merchant; and Dr. Sidney D. Redmond, an African American lawyer and activist living in Jackson. (Redmond stood out among this group; a businessman, he had pursued postgraduate studies at Harvard Medical School and the University of Michigan Law School, and he was an early leader of the NAACP.) The board set the principal's salary at $2,500 a year—a munificent sum for the time—but stipulated that he should not be paid the full amount until all other financial obligations of the school had been met. This condition was never achieved.[71]

Holtzclaw was quickly gaining a reputation as one of Washington's outstanding protégés, and his theme of "right living for Negroes" was receiving favorable attention in the local white press, with editors reassured by Utica's exhortations for students to work hard and adapt themselves to what

Washington called the "wholesome" pleasures of country life. Enlisting the help of Ratcliff and Ferguson, Holtzclaw determined to relocate his school from the original, modest one-hundred-acre lot to a considerably larger parcel in Copiah County that was closer to a better water supply. By the early summer he had initiated a drive to raise $25,000, winning a pledge from Andrew Carnegie for $5,000. Carnegie, who had also given a considerable amount of money to Washington's institution, was representative of wealthy northern donors who believed that "the southern Negro problem" could be solved with vocational training, which still left unchallenged black people's subordinate position in the region. Emmett Scott provided ongoing advice in the effort, gently chiding Holtzclaw to improve his handwriting (which prompted him to enlist the services of a scribe) and to always include the date on any letter to donors.[72]

Holtzclaw was not the only person who sacrificed for Utica so that the school could move to the larger parcel of land. The school's shadow board of local black trustees agreed to mortgage their farms, his teachers gave up their salaries for a month, the students each donated 25¢, and Ferguson promised him a $10,000 loan. Yet 150 white men, including abutters to the plantation Holtzclaw wished to purchase, signed a petition warning him not to build there; they had their eyes on the same land: "We, the undersigned, demand that you do not build a school or college near this community." Within a few months, however, an economic recession had set in, putting the land out of the reach of local white farmers. In September Holtzclaw announced to his staff that he planned to meet and discuss with his antagonists his intention to buy the land. The teachers were "all afraid" that the principal's boldness would stir up trouble, and "several of them had packed their trunks and were ready to go home, and one had actually bought a ticket." Leaving behind his terrified wife, Holtzclaw rode out to the plantation, secured assurances that he had no rivals for the land, and bought all 1,500 acres. During the last four months of 1907, he embarked on a frantic round of fund-raising, with pledges coming in via telegraph the day the bank loan from Ferguson was due.[73]

Dutifully, Holtzclaw wrote frequently to Washington, sending him copies of speeches and articles he had written, commencement programs, and publicity brochures. Usually, it was Scott who answered or acknowledged the materials. Holtzclaw accompanied Washington on some of his northern trips, and more than once he sat uncomfortably as the accolades and donations flowed to Washington, leaving him with nothing. Still, over time he gained substantially from his association with the head of Tuskegee, and his field of canvassing expanded from the Northeast to the Midwest. Besides Carnegie, other major Utica donors included William H. Baldwin, president of the Long Island Railroad. B. F. Ginn eventually endowed a building on the campus with a gift of $30,000. Fund-raising was never-ending, for almost every penny of the school's operating budget came from gifts, "all of which I must raise by direct effort," Holtzclaw noted.[74]

By the time of Washington's triumphant tour through Mississippi in October 1908, most white merchants in the area had a substantial economic stake in the school. Concerns about young inebriated whites notwithstanding, these businessmen were willing to tolerate Washington's visit. On one level perhaps they appreciated the peculiar choreography of the all-male entourage, the aspiring "manliness" of it all. Local blacks were impressed by Washington for other reasons. Pleas McCadney, one of the farmers fearful about Washington's visit, was surprised to see that the famous educator was "the most commonplace man on the platform," well versed in barnyard matters: "He uttered no high-sounding phrases that only the faculty could understand, but began by telling us farmers about raising hogs, chickens, and cows, and how to own our homes and farms."[75]

The fact that donors, most of them northern whites, were providing six-sevenths of the school's annual operating expenses—with the rest coming from boarding and tuition fees—indicated that the institution remained on less than solid financial footing. Meanwhile, Holtzclaw's family was growing. By the summer of 1910 Will and Mary Ella had four children: Robert Fulton (six), Jerry Herbert (four), Alice Marie (two), and infant Ella Adaline. Moses Joiner (eighteen), one of Adaline's sons by Floyd, was a Utica student. The school, too, was growing. Around this time Utica consisted of 1,500 acres, fourteen classroom buildings, a modern sawmill and cotton gin, brick yard, broom factory, printing office, "scientific training kitchen," laundry, and residences that included the large plantation house and thirty small bungalows for the students. Utica's steady growth over six years was a testament not only to Washington's willingness to lend the prestige of his name to the enterprise, but also to Holtzclaw's political savvy.

Not surprisingly, Holtzclaw took care to stage annual exhibits and commencement ceremonies that conformed to the expectations of whites, local and northern. The Jackson *Daily News* noted with approval Utica students' handicraft, gardening, and stock-raising talents on display at the State Fair during the two days of the ten set aside for "Negro days." The exhibits included immense quantities of fruits and vegetables (at one fair, 6,000 pounds of corn) and school-made brooms, shoes, beds, mattresses, and quilts, all "demonstrating to the students that they can make their things at home, if they desire." Also impressive were the institute's annual graduation exercises, which one northern black man considered "odd, but interesting." The program one year included the usual speeches, recitations, and songs, but also displays of the "manual arts" such as the preparation of a meal by a young girl who, in the words of the visitor from the North, "like a true farmer's wife, led the whole vast congregation in plantation songs while she worked." Such performances reified the notion of an independent black peasantry divorced from the modern world of buying things and working for wages. Critics estimated that not one in ten of industrial school graduates would find jobs in trades they had learned there and pointed out that the vast majority of Utica students, impoverished, never graduated at all.[76]

Though providing substantial entertainment value, commencement exercises were not necessarily an accurate reflection of the school's basic curriculum or even its larger enterprise. Course subjects included traditional academics, Bible study, and (at least by the teens) "office machines." The profile of staff members offered its own lessons: almost all of the school's teachers were black, many of them graduates of Hampton, Tuskegee, and Snow Hill as well as of universities, all black or otherwise, such as Howard and Atlanta. The head of the Academic Department was L. C. Jones, an alumnus of the University of Iowa. If white people looked at Utica and saw a place that offered instruction in twenty trades, black people could look at the school and see a group of well-dressed men and women adhering to a rigid schedule that began at 5:10 every morning and teaching both academic and vocational subjects. The inner workings of the school, then, refuted the fictional narrative of all black people as shiftless and inclined to crime and vice, but whites had no interest in a reality that challenged racial orthodoxy.[77]

Holtzclaw himself offered the students his own brand of moral instruction by example. In January 1910 he wrote an open letter to the Mississippi legislature protesting the fact that the state was taxing black people but funding only all-white agricultural high schools. He couched his argument in polite terms, noting with considerable understatement that "the Negroes in this state do not get a square deal from their white fellow-citizens." He continued, "That, being excluded from the ballot, and having no direct representation at the capital, and being therefore, compelled to take whatever is given them, they are, as a matter of fact, deprived of much that they by

right ought to have." Many blacks, he warned, saw the state's discriminatory policies as "an effort to re-enslave them." In essence, then, the process
of making laws was a farce, for "my race [has] absolutely no voice in either
the making or the administration of them." Holtzclaw noted with some
satisfaction that a few days after he sent his letter, the legislature authorized
separate high schools for blacks and whites alike, though five years later he
had to admit that "very little progress has been made toward establishing
such [black] schools."[78]

Around this time Holtzclaw also wrote to Governor Edmond F. Noel,
lamenting "these trying days for my race, when so many of them are being
put to death without the semblance of a trial and when our state is listed
so prominently among the states that have recently suffered from the evils
of lynch law." Holtzclaw condemned this "institution" as "absolutely unjus-
tifiable under all circumstances" and "a relic of barbarism"; he called upon
Noel to renounce lawlessness in all its forms and to reject the pretext of
black crime as a motive for lynch mobs. Noel responded, assuring Holtzclaw he was in agreement with him about the rule of law and commending
him for "the industrial work in which you are engaged."[79]

Threats to Utica's very existence remained outside Holtzclaw's control and
included forces other than the menace of racial ideologies. On the night of
June 9, 1910, a tornado swept through the campus and leveled several school
buildings, including the nearly completed Booker T. Washington Hall. This
structure would have been the largest to date on the campus. Holtzclaw
went out to survey the damage the next morning and immediately began to
formulate a plan for rebuilding. Over the next month and a half he called
upon "many of my friends both at home and in the East" and managed to
raise $14,000. The destruction of Washington Hall, though, coincided with
a shift in Holtzclaw's relationship with his mentor, as his outspokenness
and ever-more-impressive fund-raising prowess began to upset the affable
teacher-student connection that had prevailed for many years.[80]

Holtzclaw's search for donors had reached fever pitch by the second decade of the twentieth century. In late 1912 he supported an effort to form
the Association of Negro and Rural Industrial Schools (ANRIS). The purpose of the group was to systematize donor outreach among more than two
hundred privately supported small schools "patterned after Tuskegee and
Hampton" and to eliminate from competition for northern dollars those
institutions deemed unworthy of aid. In the contest for support, Holtzclaw
and others were finding the field increasingly crowded, with new schools

cropping up and their principals hastening to New York and Boston to solicit funds. Invited to a meeting scheduled for April, Washington begged off
because of his upcoming trip to the Pacific Northwest, where he would be
"seeking new friends" for Tuskegee.[81]

Washington did more than refuse to attend the ANRIS meeting; he had
his secretary advise Holtzclaw to stay away from the gathering, an outward
sign that the Tuskegee head would spare no effort in "throwing cold water
on the project," in the words of a northern donor. Washington argued that
a study currently in progress, a survey of black industrial schools in the
South, would provide all the necessary information on these smaller institutions; he considered ANRIS superfluous. Nevertheless, a meeting of the
new association took place at NAACP headquarters on April 17–18, with
one hundred people in attendance. The group elected Holtzclaw president
of the group, even though he was not present to accept the honor—perhaps
having heeded the words of his former mentor. Discussions centered on
dividing up the philanthropic community and assigning a particular school
to each section in order to avoid overlapping campaigns.[82]

Clearly, Washington had refused to give the group his blessing for a reason. A summary of the meeting indicated that "the need of good academic
training was strongly employed by the conference. It was argued that in his
zeal for industrial work, the principal must not forget the foundation of all
school work, the ability to read and write well, and to reason clearly and
intelligently." Washington saw the call for "good academic training" as an
implicit criticism of himself and his life work. And as a matter of his accom-
modationist principles and fund-raising politics, the Tuskegee head objected
to Holtzclaw's association with the NAACP.[83]

The relationship between Washington and Holtzclaw remained strained
in the years that followed. In January 1914 Washington summoned the
younger man to talk about unspecified matters, either at Tuskegee or in New
York City, but he declined because, he said, he was lobbying the state legislature on behalf of black schools. And then in mid-July Washington wrote
Holtzclaw a brief, cryptic letter that began "I am sure you will not misun-
derstand us when I say that I have heard from one or two important friendly
sources lately that things do not present so good and encouraging an appearance that they did some years ago." He continued, "One criticism is in
the direction that you do not give enough attention to the development of
your farming and other agricultural interests, that is, that matters have rather
gone backward in this and other directions during the last few years."[84]

Washington was probably referring to the preliminary findings of the study he cited as his reason for opposing ANRIS, a survey of black education sponsored by the Phelps-Stokes Fund in cooperation with the US Department of Education. Investigators praised Hampton and Tuskegee but implied that smaller, struggling schools did not deserve private support. Published in 1917, the final report described Utica, with 317 students, as "an elementary school with a few pupils in secondary subjects." The school's twenty-seven teachers were owed $3,051 in back pay. The report's author recommended "that the enlargement of the plant be not allowed to interfere with simple educational activities whether in books or industries," suggesting that Holtzclaw had mismanaged the school.[85]

Not everyone agreed. In 1912 William Pickens had visited Utica and later published a glowing account of the school in *The Independent*. The Yale-educated Pickens had been an active member of the NAACP since its founding, and in 1918 he would be named its director of branches. He was the northern observer who devoted part of his report to an account of what he had called the "odd, but interesting" commencement exercises at the school. And whereas Pickens rejected the obsequious tone of Washington's public pronouncements, he found much to commend in Holtzclaw's labors. The Utica principal had clearly reached a mutually advantageous accommodation with local well-to-do whites, especially the merchants of building materials and dry goods supplies. Pickens noted that one businessman donated a $65 watch each year as a prize to be awarded to "the most manly young man in the school"—this in a state "where the idea of the Negro's being a man has for a decade been most vigorously and eloquently attacked." Utica's "Christian white women" had adopted the school as an object of charity, contributing cash and household supplies. Pickens's visit convinced him that the students and teachers all "display an exhilarating freedom of body and soul." That Holtzclaw could win praise from an NAACP leader, and at the same time earn for the school a measure of tolerance from Utica whites, spoke to his powers of diplomacy leavened with his own principles.[86]

Booker T. Washington died at his home in Tuskegee on November 14, 1915. William Holtzclaw served as one of the pallbearers at his funeral. He was no doubt gratified that Washington had lived to see the publication of *Black Man's Burden*. The Tuskegee head had provided an introduction to the book—though it had taken him more than two years to do so, and he did not like the title, which he thought inadequately conveyed Holtzclaw's life and labors. In September of that year Holtzclaw had taken his sons

Fulton and Jerry to Boston, and together the three attended one of Washington's last lectures, at Symphony Hall. Fulton, eleven at the time, recalled many years later, "When the session was over, being a precocious child, I advanced to the platform and introduced myself to the great educator." His memory of this encounter, which clearly made a great impression on him, included no mention of a conversation between his father and "the great educator."[87]

———

By the time of Washington's death, Utica had become a Holtzclaw family affair, with William's mother, Adaline White Holtzclaw Joiner, the school's unlikely matriarch and his wife, Mary Ella, its de facto day-to-day manager.

Adaline had been living at Utica for nearly a decade, and no doubt she continued to marvel at her new surroundings, so dramatically different from those earlier in her life. She had her own "up from slavery" story to tell. Born in Georgia around 1850, she wed her first husband at age fifteen and then married Jerry Holtzclaw about 1873. She was the daughter of an enslaved woman and her master, and her half brother (the son of her master and his white wife) was her owner until 1864. Adaline came to Alabama either in a slave coffle or after 1865 with a man named George White; they had at least one child born during the war. When she married Jerry Holtzclaw, she was the mother of three daughters and a son.[88]

Adaline and Floyd Joiner wed soon after Jerry died in 1895, and they had a son together; Floyd was the father of at least two other sons born in the 1880s. In 1910 she and Floyd were still living in Randolph County, now with a single grandson, Sam Garfield, eight, in their household; the surrounding countryside was populated by her close kin, including a number of children with the names Addy, Jerry, and Floyd. In 1918 Floyd died, and Adaline moved to Utica Institute. There she joined the household of her youngest son by Jerry, Ernest Holtzclaw, thirty-four, who had graduated from the school and attended Tuskegee to become a veterinarian. Surrounded now by a number of her children and grandchildren, she kept herself busy running a successful chicken farm on the Utica campus, a small but profitable enterprise that helped defray the school's operating expenses. She also took classes at the institute and "graduated" from Utica three years before her death, at age ninety-seven. She had come a far way from her hard life with Jerry, when the children were young, and before that, her harder life in bondage.[89]

FIGURE 5.3 Mary Ella Holtzclaw, the principal's wife, had primary responsibility for the school and their growing family while her husband was away raising money. William H. Holtzclaw introduced *The Black Man's Burden* by expressing appreciation to her and his mother, Addie: "This volume is dedicated to my mother, Addie, whose affection and foresight inspired me in my youth with a desire to get an education, and to my wife, Mary Ella, whose patience and fidelity have supported me in my ambition to be of service to my race." Courtesy Schomburg Center for Research in Black Culture, New York Public Library.

Adaline's story contrasted mightily with that of her daughter-in-law Mary Ella, who had been raised in relative comfort in Tuscaloosa. Holtzclaw described his wife as his "deputy," for it was she who remained in charge of the institute while he was away from campus for as much as half of every year. By all accounts Mary Ella was just as devoted to the school as her husband was: "She murmured not for she knew she was helping to answer the cry of thousands of God's people who wanted the light but knew not where to turn." The Holtzclaws remained self-consciously formal in their interactions at home. Fulton wrote, "I never heard Father call Mother anything but 'Mrs. Holtzclaw,' and she always called him 'Mr. Holtzclaw.'" Outside the house, propriety could serve a larger purpose. When a white man "of less refinement" demanded to know why Will called his wife "Mrs. Holtzclaw," he replied, "If I don't call her Mrs. Holtzclaw, how are you to know what her name is?"[90]

Private correspondence between the couple reveals a more playful side to their relationship, with Will calling Mary Ella "My Very Dear Wife" and "My Dear Girl" and signing his letters, "Your lover William Henry." He missed his family when he was away and worried about the responsibilities he was placing on his wife, by 1920 the mother of five. From New York he wrote, "I have been thinking of you all the day, and wondering how you are faring. You must take plenty of rest, for it is two [*sic*] much for you to think that you can nurse a baby and be awake most of every night and then work in the day. A human frame has its limit." A woman of enormous energy, Mary Ella took correspondence courses from the American School of Home Economics in Chicago, writing papers on such topics as "Chemistry of the Household," and she served as postmistress of the school post office beginning in 1913. Holtzclaw described her in his autobiography as "the greatest and most lovable woman I ever saw" and "truly the power behind the throne, and sometimes all around the throne."[91]

All five of the Holtzclaw children attended college between 1925 and 1934—Fulton graduated from Howard, Jerry Herbert from Tuskegee, Alice Marie and Adaline from Talladega, and William Jr. from Hampton. By the middle of the Great Depression, all were back at Utica with their spouses, teaching pro bono to keep the institute going. Fulton served as dean and Jerry Herbert as head of the Applied Electricity Department, while Alice Marie and Adaline taught in the high school and William Jr. offered courses in agriculture. Members of the family presented a contrast to their students, many of whom were just as poor as Will had been when he started at Tuskegee.[92]

Despite Holtzclaw's superhuman exertions, Utica Institute existed hand to mouth from month to month. Most of the money he raised each year disappeared into annual operating expenses, which grew larger and larger with each passing year and new building project. Yet ominously, by the time the short-lived ANRIS was founded, white philanthropists' zeal for black education was waning: in 1915 annual donations to Utica slipped by 25 percent compared to the previous year.[93]

And then a series of disasters struck: between 1917 and 1930 Jewett Hall was the only campus class or dormitory building to escape a major fire. In the early 1920s a tornado leveled the school's infirmary and nurses' training hospital, as well as several faculty cottages. A rebuilt Booker T. Washington Hall was the target in 1926 of arsonists, three students who had been expelled the day before. More than buildings and stores of supplies were lost. The conflagration that consumed Ginn Memorial Hall in 1923 took the lives of two students, and the tornado killed Holtzclaw's granddaughter and maimed one of his sons-in-law. These tragedies shook Holtzclaw to the core. Fulton recalled that when his father returned home after Ginn Hall burned, his hair had turned white during his time away. In addition to the emotional toll, the serial destruction of the physical plant exacted more time and energy from the principal, now forced back on the road to plead for the large sums needed to rebuild.[94]

The death of Booker T. Washington and the publication of Holtzclaw's autobiography, both in 1915, marked a turning point in Holtzclaw's life and the end of an era in Mississippi. That year, 100,000 black men, women, and children from the state moved north, many to Chicago; gone forever were the days when raising vegetables and marketing eggs signaled "progress" for a black family. This "Great Migration" out of the South was marked by a series of global, national, and regional transformations that opened up the way out of peonage for many southern blacks, even as those transformations led to a more violent repression of those who remained behind. With the beginning of war in Europe, the international market for southern cotton collapsed, and in 1916 floods devastated parts of Alabama and Mississippi. World War I led to other dramatic developments for black workers, most notably the effects that conscription and an abrupt halt to foreign immigration had on the domestic labor market. For the first time in history, northern industrial employers were receptive to hiring black workers from the South.[95]

Northern labor agents recruited aggressively in Jackson and in surrounding cotton fields and labor camps. Many migrants left quickly, selling their furniture and other modest belongings at a loss, a decision that no doubt greatly disturbed Holtzclaw. Theoretically, a mass out-migration of workers should have tempered the exploitative conditions facing croppers as planters, contending with a labor shortage, improved the terms they offered their workers. Yet standard economic theories could rarely capture or account for the brutal political economy of the rural South. Some landlords sought to induce their croppers to remain in one place by installing screens and glass windows in their cabins, but in 1921 only 3 percent of black dwellings had such improvements. (When a sociologist asked one Black Belt tenant about her dilapidated house, the woman replied, "'Scuse me, but dis ain't no house.") Moreover, these incremental changes were overshadowed by larger, structural constraints on black laborers. In the name of "efficiency," investors continued to consolidate their holdings and model their plantations on corporations that controlled every stage of processing and marketing a product—in this case, cotton. These owners also ran their workers "through and through," disregarding family-based tenant holdings in favor of organizing laborers indiscriminately in work gangs.[96]

As most of the rest of the country embraced a national consumer economy built on automobiles and moving picture shows, the plight of an impoverished rural southern population came to resemble that of subjects living under colonial rule. In 1921 NAACP leader William Pickens coined the term "American Congo" to describe the Mississippi Delta; cotton, he observed, was the nation's equivalent of Congo's ivory and rubber, a valuable resource that propelled massive environmental degradation and human suffering. By this time lumber companies had destroyed many of Mississippi's hardwood forests, prompting landowners to hearken back to antebellum patterns of staple-crop agriculture. With its economy reverting to a reliance on cotton, the region staked its future on the fiber, despite the fact that the drop in wartime demand had driven cotton prices to historic lows. Soon a series of crop failures left the black population around Utica literally starving, the students unable to pay their tuition. Holtzclaw spent the summer of 1923 traveling from Maine to Colorado raising $15,000 toward the school's debt of $30,000. In his appeal to donors he solicited not only money but also used shoes and clothing. The Reverend Henry E. Cobb, a Utica trustee, wrote to the *New York Times* outlining the school's desperate situation: "Here is a 'Near East' condition within our own land in which great suffering can be relieved by immediate and generous donations."[97]

That same year, reacting to what his son Fulton described as "considerable apprehension" among blacks and whites throughout the state, Holtzclaw joined with other Mississippi black leaders, including officers of the state's Federation of Colored Women's Clubs, to form a civic association called the Committee of 100. According to Fulton, whites feared that black veterans returning to the South might become "unmanageable" and blacks feared that whites, "expecting the worst[,] . . . might become violent." Drawing one delegate from each of the state's eighty-two counties, and then eighteen at-large representatives, the organization tried to leverage black out-migration into better working and living conditions and increased funding for black education in Mississippi. Planters could secure a stable labor force, they argued, by embracing a more enlightened view of civil rights. Some members, such as Jackson's Sidney D. Redmond, belonged to both the committee and the NAACP, suggesting the former was a transition between the heyday of Washington in the past and the more militant activists of the late 1940s and beyond. Holtzclaw himself was using his school's annual Negro Farmers' Conference as an occasion to condemn lynching, which he called "America's shame." Nevertheless, when the Great Mississippi Flood of 1927 displaced thousands of croppers, white officials compelled black men at gunpoint to build and repair levees. The flood was a stark reminder of the way that natural disasters, combined with federal, state, and local policies, could reinforce insidious forms of discrimination.[98]

Throughout these years Holtzclaw managed to keep the school going by virtue of sheer willpower and the forbearance and generosity of his children and their spouses. Local families were no longer able to pay tuition for their children. New Deal programs in many instances intensified the immiseration of the southern poor, as planters cashed federal farm subsidy checks, evicted tenants, and invested in labor-saving machinery such as tractors. Throughout the South local administrators had free rein to shape federal initiatives to conform to white supremacist imperatives. One federal administrator admitted that his office had ceded administration of Deep South relief programs to local planter-politicians, who justified discriminating against black applicants: "The explanation is given that the negro is better adjusted to the open country environment than the poor white and hence is less in need of relief, or that the negro is better able than the poor white to shift for himself or to obtain aid from relatives and friends." Such was the bitter fruit of a peasant proprietorship that marked blacks as outside the boundaries of modern life and hence unworthy of federal aid.[99]

In the middle of the 1930s Holtzclaw reduced Utica's teaching staff from twenty-five to fifteen; fully two-thirds of those who remained were members of his extended family. He did manage to preserve his credit line among merchants in Utica and Jackson. Herman H. (Shine) Davis, the son of one of the institute's early white supporters, continued to supply the school. Fulton recalled, "He was the young man who, from his small grocery store, carried the school's unpaid account through the Great Depression." By this time the principal was looking and feeling "wan and tired," according to his son. At sixty-two Holtzclaw was still on the road, sleeping on park benches and eating only what he could buy from street peddlers. Of his begging life up North, he told his students, "If my body suffered, my soul was so aflame with the fire of enthusiasm that it never flagged nor held aught against my fellow men."[100]

During a fund-raising trip to Boston in the spring of 1943, Holtzclaw fell ill; admitted to the hospital, he lapsed into a coma. Respectful of her husband's long-held wish to die at home, as soon as he regained consciousness Mary Ella arranged for his travel from Boston to Utica by Pullman car. However, the refusal of the conductor to accept his first-class ticket forced him to make the journey slumped over in a seat in the coach car, an indignity and a source of physical discomfort he bore with characteristic stoicism. Arriving in Utica in early July, he seemed to rally, only to fail again. His mother managed to say good-bye to him; she died ten days after he came home from Boston. Five weeks later, on August 27, he, too, died.[101]

The funeral service for William Holtzclaw featured twenty-two honorary pallbearers and many speeches from luminaries in the field of southern black education. One of the school's earliest supporters, seventy-nine-year-old Pleas McCadney, spoke with great emotion; in a testimonial that Holtzclaw would have appreciated, McCadney noted that the principal "never got too busy to come to my house and go to the homes of the other lowly farmers of this community and break bread and discuss the problems confronting our people." Standing at their father's casket, blanketed with roses and ferns sent by his "white friends" in town, family members refrained from weeping, for, as Fulton put it, "We, his children, and Mother knew that Father would not have approved of our tears."[102]

———————————

In 1902, the year William Holtzclaw founded Utica Institute, a white man named Dunbar Rowland, director of the Mississippi Department of Archives and History, gave a speech to the Alumni Association of the University of Mississippi; his topic was "A Mississippi View of Race Relations in the South." In the talk he argued that "the common every day relations between the white man and the negro are sincere and kindly." Black men had been disenfranchised, and rightly so, according to Rowland, for they were ignorant and of a "defective moral nature." No doubt referring to Mississippi's counterparts to Richard W. White, active Republicans in the postbellum period, Rowland claimed, that their participation in the state's political life after the Civil War had led to "terrible results." In sum, Mississippi "race relations" were good to the extent that blacks had been expunged from the body politic. Of a black man such as Holtzclaw or Washington, Dunbar opined, "He will never be accepted as an equal no matter how great his future advancement. He may gain the culture of the schools and acquire something of the polish of polite society, but he can never beat down the barriers between black and white."[103]

In the early twentieth century many northern and southern men and women invoked the term *race relations* as part of a wider discussion of the so-called Negro problem. Rowland used the term *good race relations* to suggest that, after the disruption of Reconstruction, southern society and politics had finally reverted to traditional antebellum patterns of white power and black subordination. Washington and Holtzclaw also used the term, but to acknowledge what they believed was a futile quest for full equality, social, political, or otherwise. Washington believed that "intelligence and friendly race relations" would solve the race problem, and Holtzclaw condemned Vardaman and others for bringing about "strained relations between the races." Both black men held that good race relations were contingent on the absence of white-initiated violence and that, freed from white interference, blacks might live full and satisfying lives—hence Washington's view that the absence of lynch mobs in a particular region signified promising race relations and Holtzclaw's claim that the very existence of his school was proof of the friendly relations between the races.[104]

In promoting the idea that the southern soil was the fount of all that was good and virtuous, both educators tried to shield themselves and their students from the reality of an industrializing modern America and especially the appeal of city life. More to the point, perhaps, they continued to express optimism for the future of race relations despite overwhelming evidence that the fraught relationships between white and black Americans were in fact a function of labor and political dynamics, rather than some sort of primal prejudices on the part of whites. To fuel the South's extractive economy, whether based on lumber or cotton, southern planters required a cheap, vulnerable workforce—and the descendants of former slaves, already deprived of basic human rights, remained ripe for exploitation. By denying black men the right to vote, and by preventing black families from earning either cash or credit, these white elites ensured the continued dependence of the descendants of former slaves. The fiction that all blacks were capable only of mindless manual labor amounted to a vicious self-fulfilling prophecy, one that had great resonance throughout the nation as well as the South.

Yet the economic imperatives underpinning this new form of racial ideology were readily apparent even then. The year of Holtzclaw's death, the Mississippi Agricultural Experiment Station published a study of the plantation land tenure system in the state, where planters continued to seek out "a docile, low-status labor supply." The study concluded, "Elaborate codes, now largely receded from consciousness, have grown up to rule relations between the white and Negro races." Those "relations," though called "race," were contingent on white power and black powerlessness.[105]

After the death of its founder, Utica Normal and Industrial Institute lost its appeal to northern donors altogether. William Holtzclaw Jr. succeeded his father as head of the school, but World War II took a toll: teachers were leaving, contributions dwindling, and number of students declining. In 1946 the all-white County Board of Supervisors assumed control of the institute and renamed it the Hinds County Agricultural High School for Negroes. A board of trustees oversaw both this school and a local junior college that admitted whites exclusively. On June 8, 1954, the board changed the name again, to Utica Junior College, no doubt in an effort to suggest the school's parity with its white counterparts. The Supreme Court decision *Brown v. Board of Education,* declaring unconstitutional the "separate but equal" doctrine, had been announced three weeks before, on May 17. Mississippi officials intended that a change in the school's name would compensate for their generations-long neglect of black public education.[106]

As dramatic as legal milestones like the *Brown* decision were, such developments left intact the underlying racial rationales that had caused so much suffering for blacks throughout the nation's history. At the same time, the uniqueness of American racial ideologies could not mask the larger global forces that produced similarly impoverished populations around the world. The growing political activism among black Americans was crucial to obtaining basic but long-denied human rights and identifying the many political and economic channels by which their oppression continued. When as a group black Mississippians of the 1940s and 1950s organized and assumed the role of freedom fighters, their struggles mirrored those of contemporary colonial peoples elsewhere in the world seeking to dismantle empires based on the exploitation of natural resources and of the people who harvested, mined, and processed them. Yet the focus of the US civil rights movement on political rights—to vote, sit on juries—at times obscured the nation's persistent, fundamental inequalities in jobs and schools. Had William Holtzclaw been able to survey Mississippi in the early twenty-first century, he would have been amazed at the plethora of black mayors, state representatives, and congressmen and congresswomen. Yet he would have found distressingly familiar the segregated schools, the high rates of black poverty, and the overwhelming preponderance of black workers in service and manual labor jobs. Perhaps then he would have called not for better race relations, but for the elimination of race relations altogether.

SIX

SIMON P. OWENS

A Detroit Wildcatter at the Point of Production

Early in the morning of July 24, 1973, two spot welders at Chrysler's Jefferson Avenue auto plant in Detroit scaled a ten-foot wire fence and climbed down into a power cage that fed electricity to the metal-body shop where they worked. Locking the cage with heavy wire and shutting off the power, Isaac Shorter and Larry Carter brought production to a sudden halt.[1]

Shorter, twenty-six, and Carter, twenty-three, both black and southern born, were protesting the abuse meted out by their boss, Thomas Woolsey, who, they charged, routinely called the workers in his three-hundred-person department "black sons of bitches." The two men also issued a range of other complaints against Woolsey and union officials, tapping into a wellspring of anger among their assembly-line coworkers—black and white men and women who labored day in and day out, on mandatory overtime and then overtime on top of that, in shops with oil-slick floors, leaky roofs, and pieces of heavy metal dangling from the ceiling. Frustrated that their formal grievances had gone unheeded for months by local officials of the United Automobile Workers (UAW), Shorter and Carter had taken matters into their own hands. Now they declared that the strike would continue, and they would occupy the power cage, until management fired Woolsey and promised that the two of them would face no reprisals for their actions.[2]

Shorter and Carter's single act of protest immediately galvanized their coworkers. In a show of solidarity, a diverse group of them prevented plant

FIGURE 6.1 Isaac Shorter (left) and Larry Carter (right) exult in their "victory" over the Chrysler auto company on July 24, 1973. Leaders of the United Automobile Workers feared that the wildcat strike initiated that day by the two signaled a return to the late 1960s, when young, militant black men disrupted production and excoriated white union leaders and white workers in general. Shorter and Carter, however, were wildcatters who sought and claimed support from a wide variety of workers, including native-born whites and blacks, immigrants, and young and old men and women. COURTESY WALTER P. REUTHER LIBRARY, WAYNE STATE UNIVERSITY, DETROIT, MICHIGAN.

officials from dislodging Shorter and Carter from the cage and staged a day-long work stoppage that idled 5,000 employees plantwide, at a loss of 950 new cars worth $1 million. Chrysler officials, fearful of a delay in rolling out their 1974 models, negotiated directly with the two men and acceded to both demands. The next morning the two Detroit daily newspapers ran a photo of the men, Carter with an arm upraised and fist clenched, hoisted on the shoulders of their cheering coworkers. UAW officials, however, seethed at Chrysler's "capitulation," its "unconditional surrender to the strikers." The company's decision to bypass established grievance and disciplinary procedures promised to complicate upcoming contract talks between the 700,000-member union and the Big Three—Chrysler, Ford, and General

Motors. Shorter heaped scorn on the leaders of the UAW, who, he charged, cared more about maintaining a superficial peace on the shop floor than about promoting the safety and welfare of their own members: "They go behind closed doors and sell us out. They represent the interests of the corporation, not us."[3]

That summer a series of wildcat strikes—unauthorized labor demonstrations like the one Carter and Shorter had initiated—roiled the Detroit auto industry and proved that workers possessed the power, literally, to shut down any number of massive plants on a moment's notice. They could do so, moreover, without the endorsement of the powerful labor unions that typically orchestrated such actions. These wildcat strikers derived much of their explosive force from their ability to rally workers of all colors, ages, and backgrounds around a common cause, forming these disparate actors into coalitions capable of challenging the union leaders no less than the company managers.

On August 7 workers on the morning shift at Detroit's Dodge Forge plant refused to enter the fifty-year-old facility, a collection of antiquated buildings where more than half of the 1,400 workers had been forced for months by mandatory overtime rules to labor seven days a week. On three shifts running twenty-four hours a day, they had endured a brutal work pace and temperatures that reached into the triple digits, and they had suffered injuries from exposed electrical wires, broken assembly-line machinery, and a defective overhead crane. Of the bosses' verbal abuse and the constant threat of physical harm, one black worker (whose brother and father had lost fingers on the line) remarked, "It's like a cotton field in 1850." After a six-day strike, Chrysler fired eighteen of the leaders, and the UAW applauded the purge.[4]

A few days later, on August 14, William Gilbreth and Clinton Smith provoked a strike in the aging Chrysler Mack Avenue stamping plant run by 5,000 workers. The two had been fired from their jobs the week before when Gilbreth, a former college student turned autoworker, had led a work stoppage to demand a ventilator fan in the fume-saturated welding department. Now at 5 on a Tuesday morning the two men reentered the plant and sat down on the second-floor assembly conveyor belt, disabling it. When security guards Paul DeVito and Gene Prince tried to remove them, Gilbreth and Smith beat them bloody with metal pipes. (Prince required sixteen stitches in his head.)[5]

In the ensuing sitdown, strikers demanded that Douglas Fraser, head of the UAW's Chrysler Department, push for a shorter workweek and an end to mandatory overtime and hazardous work assignments. Gilbreth and Smith had acted as members of a group called Workers Action Movement (WAM), a small, New York–based splinter of the Communist Progressive Labor Party; WAM's slogan was "Shut the Big 3 in '73." Fraser charged that the strikes had been instigated by a few men "dedicated to the proposition of revolution and wildcat strikes. And they are being carried away by their own rhetoric." Some workers disputed that analysis. A machine repairman pointed out, "There are whites and blacks and young and old people out here and we aren't a bunch of radicals. This has been building up for the past three months and it just came to a head Tuesday night." Several dozen Detroit policemen armed with riot batons managed to evict the strikers, a task completed only after a brief but furious fistfight between cops and workers.[6]

The fight was but a prelude to a more coordinated, ominous attack directed toward the strikers, this one organized by UAW officials. To enable the next day's morning shift to report to work, union leaders assembled a force of an estimated 1,000 union officers from other Detroit area plants. Deputized as "Sergeants-at-Arms" and carrying baseball bats, walking sticks, and lead pipes, they positioned themselves in groups of 250 at each of four gates to the plant and beat any strikers they recognized, including Gilbreth.[7]

The assault on the Mack Avenue wildcatters by fellow autoworkers marked a widening rift in Detroit's labor front in the summer of 1973. Fraser justified what one UAW official called a "declaration of war against radicals" by asserting that he would not submit to "lawlessness" or to "blackmail." He and other high-ranking union officials were particularly alarmed at the prospect of a lethal shop-floor mix of radical college students, black nationalists, Communists, and socialists, all presumably contemptuous of the UAW and its proud history. Company executives expressed delight and amazement at this newfound alliance with the UAW leadership, their former antagonists, many of whom had been undisciplined wildcatters themselves in the 1930s when they birthed the Congress of Industrial Organizations (CIO).[8]

To one Mack Avenue worker in particular, the walkouts and sit-ins of the summer of 1973 possessed a revolutionary potential sufficient to vindicate his own thirty-year career advancing the cause of those "fighting the line." Simon P. Owens, a sixty-seven-year-old native of Lowndes County, Alabama, was a fervent believer in the transformative power of wildcats, labor actions that welled up spontaneously from the rank and file. A stamping machine operator, Owens believed that these actions represented in concentrated form the promise of a larger working-class revolt against inhuman factory working conditions. The white boss Thomas Woolsey at Chrysler's Jefferson Avenue plant personified the corrosive effects of antiblack ideas and actions. At the same time, black men such as the guard Gene Prince—described by Owens as "a Black with completely 'white' thinking"—offered living proof that neither skin color nor ancestry was a sure signifier of a person's politics or stance toward authority. For Owens, the white-black partnership of Gilbreth and Smith demonstrated the power of cooperation across races. And it occurred at the point of production where friendships were forged and workers educated, radicalized, and mobilized in resistance to bosses and machines.[9]

The disruptions to the US auto industry that summer revealed the contradictions at the heart of mass consumerism, the engine of twentieth-century American prosperity. By 1970 foreign imports accounted for 15 percent of the domestic car market. In response, the Big Three pursued a marketing strategy of hyperdifferentiation among their own models; this strategy necessitated the annual restructuring and accelerating of the production line, leading to an ever-more-specialized division of labor to account for minor variations in design from year to year. To reach daily quotas, some workers had to perform the same operation eight hundred times and stay overtime to do it—all so that the company would not have to hire, train, and pay benefits for new employees. Owens pointed out that these assembly-liners labored such long hours at such breakneck speed they had no time or energy to partake of the culture of consumer gratification that they were creating; after an eighty-four-hour workweek, they were too tired to shop for anything, to enjoy their families, or even to have sex with their spouses.[10]

Though particularly attuned to upheavals in the auto industry, Owens took a longer view of historic transformations in industrial capitalism, in the process highlighting the way his own externally imposed racial identity had shaped his place in the labor market. As a member of a Detroit-based democratic, anti-Stalinist Marxist collective called News & Letters Committees (NLC), he held that African Americans were in a unique position to act as a vanguard capable of challenging the onslaught of an inherently coercive economic system. Black men and women alone had carried the burden of oppression from slavery through the racial caste system of the mid-twentieth century, and now they accounted for increasing numbers of the industrial proletariat in essential enterprises such as autos, mining, and steel. Through wildcat strikes, they could express their centuries-long, deep-seated grievances and unite workers wracked by religious, ethnic, age, gender, and, above all, racial animosities.

Owens was a close observer and himself a victim of technological innovation. During his career he operated a series of different machines that made auto parts from steel; he strained to meet an hourly quota, feeding the parts into an assembly line. Eventually, he came to link the fortunes of southern sharecroppers—many of whom technology had displaced by the 1940s and 1950s—with those of coal miners and autoworkers like himself. By the mid-1950s laborers in the agricultural, extractive, and manufacturing sectors had all registered the effects of chronic unemployment caused by sophisticated, labor-saving machinery: the farm tractor and mechanical cotton picker, the continuous miner, the automated assembly line. Nevertheless, officials in the United Mine Workers (UMW) and the UAW heralded the inexorable advance of mind-numbing, soul-deadening technologies as "progress." Owens wrote, "To me, progress is when people live better lives, and there was nobody who could see these people [autoworkers and coal miners] and say that was progress."[11]

Owens was an eloquent chronicler of varied forms of workers' resistance in the North and South, in factories and fields. He understood that the forces of discipline, whether human or mechanical, were not all-powerful. The wildcats in Detroit and elsewhere arose out of everyday acts of sabotage that included breaking machinery and producing defective parts. Old-timers reined in newcomers who pushed too hard in a misguided effort to please the boss. Workers punched in late, left early, and absented themselves on a regular basis. They drank, smoked dope, gambled on the shop floor, and pulled out their pistols in a show of bravado. If the heat or fumes got too bad, they conducted "the Big Walkout." Or they snapped. In early July 1970 a worker at the Chrysler Eldon Avenue plant, thirty-five-year-old James Johnson Jr., was suddenly and arbitrarily demoted to an assignment that required him to stand less than a dozen feet from a 380-degree furnace. He came to work on the 15th of that month and shot dead two foremen and a coworker. (A jury of his peers judged him not guilty by reason of insanity.) The shop-floor pressure cooker could unleash deadly acts of rage, but it could also inspire remarkable forms of collective action. Said one autoworker, "You see when you have to work with people all day inside a common area, you really learn about them, and you find out they're not so bad."[12]

Exulting in the strike of his Mack Avenue coworkers, Simon Owens exclaimed, "This morning, Tuesday, August 14th at 6:30, I witnessed the most beautiful revolutionary action by some production workers that was ever demonstrated in the thirty years that I have worked in this plant." Not long after, however, he acknowledged that the victory had been fleeting. UAW officials approved Chrysler's firing of the wildcat's "masterminds" and their supporters. Owens himself disapproved of what he considered the irresponsibility of some of the strikers, a betrayal of the trust of comrades on the line. William Gilbreth, one of the two men who started the Mack plant strike, confessed to reporters that his sit-down was no spontaneous takeover by the masses, but the result of a plan he had concocted at a meeting of a handful of WAM members, only a couple of them workers, a few days before. "We did plan it out," Gilbreth admitted. "We got to be honest with the working class."[13]

Unlike Gilbreth, most workers struck only for better conditions on the job floor, not out of ideological fervor. (One countered Fraser's public pronouncements by declaring, "I wouldn't make a good Communist anyway. I don't even make a good Democrat because I don't vote all the time.") Owens, while a committed Marxist, was himself a pragmatist. Though he appreciated the scale and intensity of the strikes that summer, he concluded that they nonetheless revealed a lamentable, historic pattern of revolt, reaction, retreat: "The workers exploding into action, the company and union trying to get them back to work but failing, the radicals rushing in and giving the company and union the excuse to accuse outsiders for the problems and turning attention away from the workers' grievances." Owens and other long-term Detroit labor activists ridiculed outside groups inclined toward "stunts" in the plants. The interlopers were "American Airlines Revolutionaries—Fly in, make trouble, fly out." The head of Michigan's Communist Party (CP) derided Gilbreth and his ilk as college "kooks" who "grab their father's credit cards and hop on an airplane and rush all over the country to 'save' the working class."[14]

Owens feared that the greatest impediment to revolutionary transformation remained not well-meaning middle-class provocateurs, however, but those workers who insisted on identifying themselves as white in opposition to their black coworkers. He reluctantly identified himself as black or Negro, but only because he had no other choice: these terms had been "hurting us for three hundred years in this country. I wasn't the first to use the word [Negro]. Since I can remember it has been hurting me." Couched in the language of workplace democracy, antiblack prejudice befouled all Detroit factories, constantly thwarting those workers who wanted to create a unified coalition of the wounded and aggrieved. Hate strikes in response to the hiring or promotion of black workers also took the form of wildcats. In and of themselves, then, unauthorized job actions possessed no specific politics. And if the close quarters of the assembly line forged close friendships among coworkers, that intimate setting also unleashed brutal efforts on the part of white men to maintain their own prerogatives and punish what those whites considered the transgressive behavior of black men. Throughout his life Owens would take as the true measure of any community—a workplace, a union, a city, a nation—whites' willingness to accept the freely expressed erotic impulses among all women and men. In the urban North as in the rural South, an injunction against "social equality between the races" was the last refuge of whites, whether members of the Ku Klux Klan or the Democratic or Communist Party.[15]

The wildcats that summer took place against a backdrop of local and national unrest, much of it revolving around the ongoing struggle of blacks to obtain the same job opportunities that whites enjoyed. In Detroit blacks constituted one-quarter of all autoworkers; most were concentrated in jobs prone to punishing speedups and chronic layoffs. Young black men, facing an unemployment rate three times that of their white counterparts, surveyed their grim prospects and concluded that the major civil rights legislation of the previous decade was a sham, an excuse for cynical white politicians to proclaim the dawning of a new "color-blind" society. Structural unemployment—joblessness caused by mechanization and other shifts in various sectors of the economy—hit black men particularly hard, in turn leading to a declining number of male breadwinners and rising rates of impoverished, female-headed households in their communities.

These developments, generations in the making, spurred among whites the mistaken conviction that all blacks were poor and that all poor people were black. Some white politicians hearkened back to the contradictory ideologies of the antebellum North and charged that blacks as a group were simultaneously lazy welfare recipients and aggressive job-seekers intent on depriving whites of their livelihoods. These politicians spoke not in the raw language of Mississippi's James Vardaman, but in code, denouncing welfare recipients as parasites on hardworking taxpayers, and school busing as an attack on the "freedom" of white people. Although the legal trappings of state-sponsored prejudice had receded (if not disappeared), discriminatory policies and laws had so corrupted the housing and labor markets that gross inequalities persisted. Crowded into inner-city neighborhoods, deprived of decent schools and health care, black Detroiters formed a distinct subset of workers trapped by technological change and an emerging global economy.[16]

Nevertheless, in the early 1970s Detroit was not only a distressed community with a shrinking tax base, but also a vibrant place where fiercely divided groups of people battled within workplaces, neighborhoods, and civic institutions to make real their respective ideals of the good and just society. Black people targeted segregation and persistent barriers to job equality, pressing their increasing numerical advantage as jurors, voters, union leaders, cultural nationalists, and members of groups that ranged from the radical to the reformist. In November 1973, together with progressive whites they would elect Detroit's first black mayor, Coleman Young. By this time black men were well integrated into Detroit's industrial economy, which exploited working-class people regardless of skin color.[17]

Simon Owens's lifetime spanned a goodly part of the twentieth century, from 1906 to 1983, and in his writings he made connections between exploited workers in the rural South and in postindustrial Detroit. Growing up among sharecroppers, he became an inveterate wildcatter as a matter of principle and practice. From 1955 until 1983 he used his position as a regular columnist for his collective's monthly publication, *News & Letters* (*N&L*), to make the point that, as one of his headlines put it, "A Good Wildcat Strike Is [the] Best Weapon Workers Have," a way to defy indifferent union officials in the service of a truly egalitarian industrial democracy. At the same time, Owens advocated, above all, the merging of philosophy and activism. It was not enough for workers to rebel; they must understand the underlying causes of their grievances and possess a bold plan to build a new society on the remnants of the old. Revolt for its own sake was little more than a self-indulgent rant producing nothing of lasting value.[18]

Owens argued that labor concerns underlay so-called racial ones, and—fittingly—he was joined in his efforts by a small group of like-minded activist-philosophers who themselves transcended racial categories. In his middle age Owens formed an unlikely ideological-political partnership with theorists C. L. R. James, a Trinidadian philosopher and writer, and Raya Dunayevskaya, a Russian-born theoretician of Marx and Hegel. Breaking with other radical groups that held that black laborers could lay claim to no special historic or political uniqueness compared to their white counterparts, these thinker-activists wrestled with a central paradox of the twentieth century: while the forces of industrial capitalism favored labor-saving machines, which in turn led to job deskilling and high rates of unemployment for all kinds of production workers, stubborn ideas of racial difference kept workers from joining together and countering these assaults on their collective humanity. Surveying American history, Dunayevskaya insightfully concluded, "There is no such supra-historical abstraction as racism. In each historical period it was something different. It was one thing during slavery, another during Reconstruction, and quite something else today." In other words, racial ideologies were ever-shifting, contingent ideas serving various political purposes depending on the dynamics of power relations in any particular time and place.[19]

Owens's autobiography, *Indignant Heart,* first published in 1952 and later revised in 1978, made him a celebrity of sorts within leftist circles, though many admirers knew him not as Simon P. Owens but as Mathew Ward, his pen name for the first edition, or as Charles Denby, his pen name for the second edition and as editor and columnist of *News & Letters*. Whether living in the feudal South, the "Arsenal of Democracy" of World War II–era Detroit, or a postindustrial society, he never wavered in his commitment to the ideal of a unified working class challenging the degradation of industrial and extractive work and condemning the hollowness of progress.

Owens saw scant lasting evidence of true labor solidarity over his lifetime. Although the idea of race, as Dunayevskaya observed, had changed substantively from one era of American history to the next, its divisive power remained potent. Owens's experiences in 1970s Detroit, and in his earlier years in the Deep South, testified to the harsh reality of modern racial myths in their most cruel and adaptable forms. He and his comrades fervently believed that the modern, technologically driven workplace would expose to all men and women of goodwill the falsity of race. In fact, though, as the auto workforce shrank, whites scrambled to maintain privileges that only race could provide.

———

From an early age Simon Peter Owens identified and rejected the white supremacist strictures prevailing in rural Alabama. His persistent questioning of things that, in his words, "couldn't fit in" his mind made him "a very difficult boy for anybody in that community or around that country." Owens was a contemporary of William Holtzclaw's children, who in the early decades of the twentieth century were living in relative comfort on the campus of Utica Institute, but his own upbringing evoked conditions in Jerry and Adaline Holtzclaw's household of the 1870s. Owens's enslaved paternal grandparents had been forcibly brought to Alabama from the Eastern Seaboard. Together his parents William Owens (born in 1875) and his wife, Patti (1878), had four children: Buddy, Simon Paul, Mary Frances, and Hilliard. When Simon was born in 1906, the family was living on Section Place near the county seat of Hayneville, part of the expansive Lowndes County plantation holdings where hundreds of sharecroppers toiled for a wealthy white family, the Rudolphs.[20]

In Lowndes County the slave past was a palpable feature of the present, especially after the optimism of Radical Reconstruction politicking had faded. At the time of Owens's birth, the county had only 57 black registered voters, down from 5,000 in 1900, the result of a vigorous state disenfranchisement effort that combined a $1.50 poll tax—then an exorbitant fee for many poor rural blacks—with nonsensical literacy and "good morals" tests. In the 1890s blacks in the county had armed themselves for self-protection and had joined the Populist Party. By the end of the decade that effort had been supplanted by a Democratic one-party system akin to martial law. As William Holtzclaw had learned all too well, the "solid" South recapitulated in tangible ways ancient forms of oppression on the countryside. White men "were the law of their land," Owens noted. "It was slavery and it was true."[21]

Like Jerry Holtzclaw, Simon's father, William, was determined to escape from under the oppressive tenant system. In 1917, by working in a sawmill and profiting from the high wartime price of cotton, he was able to buy forty acres of his own. His son recalled him declaring, "I worked for the farm so we could live free as anybody should." Owens's mother insisted her children attend school for at least a few years, but by their early teens all of them were working in the fields full-time. Though neighbors expressed envy that William was an owner—"You're in the boat [and] you can sail," they would say—the family's ragged clothing and exhausting work routine meant that they could claim few advantages compared to their cropper neighbors.[22]

In describing life in Lowndes County through the early 1920s, Owens cataloged a striking variety of strategies used by black men and women, individually and collectively, to resist the demands of landlords and bosses. If they were able, croppers played planters against each other, finding that, in Owens's words, "moving back and forth" was "the only way out of their slavery." Rather than allow the landlord to market their cotton, they would "steal" some of what they grew and sell it directly to another buyer in a secret transaction called "night communications." Whole barns of Rudolph's cotton went up in smoke, with the cause of the fire never discovered. In the fields, hands would purposely overwork mules, or even "kill out" the animals, to win a respite, "a chance to rest and play around until they [the owners] brought out new mules" from the plantation's stock.[23]

Owens's independent-mindedness often put him at odds with his fellow black Americans, and he had no patience for the Washington-Holtzclaw glorification of rural life. He briefly attended Tuskegee Institute in the hope of learning mechanical skills that would enable him to avoid a lifetime of sharecropping, but he left after a year, expelled, he said, for resisting the rigid strictures imposed on all students there. At the age of seventeen he got a job in the industrial city of Anniston serving as an assistant to a crane repairer. To the rhetorical question posed by another southern black man—"*What men in their right minds would leave off tending green growing things to tend iron monsters?*"—Owens had a quick and easy answer: the kind of men who would flee from the plantation South in the hope of a better life.[24]

In 1925 Owens moved to Detroit, joining the wave of 1.2 million blacks leaving the South between 1916 and 1927. He later mocked his own high expectations for the North and the biblical metaphors of his fellow migrants: the idea that "when I get to heaven I [will] have milk and honey and pearly gates." Still, he marveled at Detroit, a city of 1 million with a black population of 80,000 and that number growing every day. Whites and blacks might sit next to each other on a streetcar, and black migrants and Polish immigrants might carouse together after work and then repair to the same boardinghouse in the Black Bottom neighborhood—a level of intermingling that Owens would never have seen in the South. Yet poverty remained a harsh fact of life for Detroit's blacks. Hiring officials enforced a strict social division of labor that relegated black men to the worst jobs the city had to offer. Like most newcomers, Owens found a room in a crowded private home. Though blacks represented 7 percent of the population, they occupied only 1 percent of the housing stock.[25]

During this period the more radical a black worker's politics, the less likely he or she was to support a labor union. Almost all unions discriminated against blacks, prompting John P. Davis, a black Communist, to declare, "And I urge all Negro laborers to adopt as their motto: 'Hurrah for the Scab and Open Shop and to Hell with the Unions.'" By the mid-1920s technological innovation had transformed many industrial work processes, elevating foreign immigrants and their children to semiskilled machine work; in contrast, as the most recent arrivals in the North, blacks found themselves confined to unskilled labor. High rates of turnover among low-paid black foundry workers and domestic servants quickly earned black migrants in general an unfounded reputation as inherently unreliable workers.[26]

At his first job, in a Dodge car foundry, Owens took home the seemingly munificent sum of $5 a day (more than he could make in a week in an Anniston plant), but the work left him dirty, greasy, and suffering from heat prostration at the end of his shift. Men routinely took hot blasts of molten iron to the skin and fainted from the searing temperatures. Owens recalled, "We had to work just like a machine. Take a mold, knock it out, set it back. Over and over for nine hours." After four months he was laid off—thankfully, he recalled—and he and a friend went to Pittsburgh and found work in a steel foundry, another blistering job. However, he soon returned to Detroit, taking a job as a street cleaner and working off and on again at Dodge. By this time 80 percent of all employed black men in Detroit were in manufacturing jobs, proportionately four times as many as in New York and twice as many as in Chicago. The local chapter of the National Urban League celebrated when black "pioneers" escaped this sort of menial labor and got jobs at gas stations and in grocery stores and breweries.[27]

Owens was proud that he never earned a paycheck at Ford, which he termed "a man-killing place . . . the house of murder," where 10,000 black men, fully half of all black autoworkers, were employed. Henry Ford hired more blacks than any other auto manufacturer, using local churches as recruiting grounds, because these workers had little choice but to tolerate harsh working conditions. Ford labeled this form of personal and collective desperation "loyalty" to him and his company. Concentrated in the foundry, the most disagreeable of the plant's many work sites, black workers endured such an inhuman pace that, according to Owens, the men "were all so worked down that they couldn't have sexual relations." Each night he witnessed the crushing effects of the job when his landlord, a Ford employee, came home and his wife "had to help him up the steps, bathe him and feed him in bed. . . . He laid on a sheet at night, and he didn't move from that spot."[28]

A year into the Great Depression, jobs were so scarce in Detroit that Owens reluctantly moved back to Lowndes County. His mother wept when, arriving on her doorstep, he told her, "I'd rather be in prison in Detroit than to be free in the South"—but the terrible state of the economy had left him no other choice. For a while he tried farming a three-acre plot that his father had given him, but he soon clashed with local white men over the ginning and selling of his cotton.[29]

Owens's troubles back home coincided with the growth of an organization intended to help southern famers like him. Around this time the Communist-backed, Alabama-based Share Croppers Union (SCU) was formally welcoming all agricultural workers regardless of skin color and advocating landownership among the rural dispossessed. The group, which by 1934 had established a local branch in Lowndes County, was attracting evicted sharecroppers and tenants, who were the victims of federal policies providing large landowners with subsidies if they promised to limit their production of cotton to increase its price. SCU members distributed what the authorities called "night mail"—handbills and leaflets delivered surreptitiously to announce upcoming strikes and mass meetings. Organizers also collected the stories of ordinary workers and sent them to Communist Party publications. This so-called workers' correspondence allowed the poor to speak for themselves and also provided party members all over the country with firsthand accounts of the ongoing class struggle in the South. In the early 1950s Owens, too, would become a regular producer of workers' correspondence detailing his life in an auto factory.[30]

The SCU appeared to falter in Lowndes and the surrounding counties of Montgomery and Dallas. A cotton choppers' strike, called for May 1, 1935, and intended to win $1 a day for the pickers, provoked an angry backlash among white vigilantes and their abettors, law enforcement agents. Police arrested three SCU organizers, and mobs beat several others. That August, however, the SCU led another strike; during it, one leader died at the hands of a posse. Dozens of strikers were thrown in the Hayneville jail, and other members of the community endured indiscriminate assaults—for example, black women were attacked while attending a missionary meeting. Lowndes County members of the SCU expressed their outrage in a letter to the governor demanding the freedom "of the Negro share Croppers that was shot and arrested for union activities and carried to Hayesville [sic] Alabama to jail." They continued, "We are holding you [responsible] for all this and are demanding justice for these two croppers!" The strike ended with the SCU admitting defeat and accepting a rate of only 40¢ per one hundred pounds of cotton picked.[31]

Owens apparently had no involvement with the Alabama SCU. He married about the time he set out to farm on his own, and within three or four years he and his wife, Effie, would have a young son, Simon Jr. Effie, twenty-three in 1935, had grown up near the Owens family; her father had inherited 150 acres from his father, a farmer and—rare for a black farmer in those days—the owner of a cotton gin, peanut thresher, and hay baler. One of eleven children, Effie worked in the fields, but she also graduated from high school. The planter who owned land next to theirs called her father (she recalled) a "biggity-nigger" because "if a white man can't work you like a dog, like slavery time, he hates you." Of her girlhood she noted, "Whites wouldn't let a colored person drive a Dodge or Oldsmobile," both considered "a white man's car."[32]

Effie and Simon had known each other for many years, but it was not until he returned from his nine-year absence in Detroit that the two began their romance. When they married, Owens had two other sons, Sam and Henry, born in the early 1930s, presumably in Lowndes County. In 1935 Effie and Simon moved to the state capital, Montgomery, though whether or not the two older children accompanied them is unknown. She took a job as a pocket setter at a shirt factory, where she learned that the white boss expected black employees to be sexually compliant as well as fast at sewing. Advised a coworker, "Honey, you got to do some work to stay here." Rejecting the boss's advances, she was then fired from that job; Effie worked for a while as a cook for a white family, but quit when she was daily required to clean eight bedrooms, wash diapers, and cook two meals for the family—all for $7 a week.[33]

Simon began work at a Montgomery foundry, laboring for eleven hours a day six days a week, an arduous regimen even for the large, broad-shouldered man he had become. He was shocked when he found that the white foreman was extorting 25 percent of each worker's paycheck at the end of every week. Recalled Owens, "That made me sick. I never thought I'd have to pay anybody to keep my job." Yet such schemes were not uncommon in southern industrial workplaces. With a regional labor surplus, bosses could count on an unlimited supply of hungry men willing to tolerate a systemic garnisheeing of their wages. During the Depression these jobs routinely paid black men less than promised for a seventy-two-hour week; kept them as "helpers" without any chance for promotion; barred them from supervisory positions; and excluded them from machine work, which was invariably higher paying than manual labor.[34]

One day, after long hours of unloading steel had left him "just beat," Owens boarded a bus to go home. According to a ritual of segregation, white passengers were supposed to move toward the front of the bus as it emptied, allowing the black people standing at the back of the bus a place to sit down. When a white woman failed to join her husband near the front, Owens took the seat in front of her. "Her husband jumped up and said, 'Nigger, get up. You're sitting in front of my wife.' The husband said he would knock hell out of me." Owens stood up and yelled, "Come on—knock hell out of me. Your damn wife had every chance to move up there with you. If you come back here I'll cut your damn throat."[35]

The white woman became increasingly agitated and her husband increasingly threatening. Yet a middle-aged black woman flashed a razor blade and shouted encouragement to Owens and her fellow black bus riders: "I'll cut everyone in two as fast as they come. They won't come at you in a gang. I'll send everyone of them to hell. I carry this razor every day and I'll keep on carrying it. No one is going to mess with me." Shaken, the white bus driver pulled over and scribbled down an account of Owens's troublemaking and asked the other passengers to sign. One nervous elderly black man—"a kind of Uncle Tom," in Owens's words—signed the piece of paper. However, a white woman called out to the driver that if forced to testify about the incident, she would "tell the truth. I'm going to tell the truth. That [white] woman should have moved." Hoping to defuse the situation, the driver stopped at a gas station and went inside. When he came out, he looked around and asked hopefully, "Did that fellow run who was making trouble?" Owens was still on the bus, and the woman with the razor shot back, "There are no damn rabbits on this bus." By this time the remaining black passengers were vowing to "teach this guy [the driver] a lesson. Let's beat him and half kill him." Owens remained in his seat—his own version of a sit-down strike—and declared, "I don't care what happens or what is done. I'm riding this bus home." Fearing for his life, the driver finished his route.[36]

The story of the clash on the bus served as a parable of sorts for Owens's politics, undermining conventional wisdom about white power and black subordination (and this two decades before Rosa Parks's famous ride on another Montgomery bus). The battle lines did not divide neatly along racial lines. The black woman who vowed to "cut everyone in two" possessed a strength that the driver clearly respected as much resented. Yet not all the other black passengers were willing to back up Owens. Ultimately, the principles of justice and fair play counted for more than some kind of essentialist politics based on skin color. Here on this Montgomery bus, then, was compressed a world of hierarchical relations—the driver lording over the passengers, some whites lording over the blacks—and the drama played out according to the immediacy of the situation shaped by weapons and threatening words, not some foreordained racial politics.

In 1936 Owens went to work as a chauffeur and personal assistant for Thomas Bowen Hill Jr., age thirty-three, a member of a prominent Montgomery "family of lawyers" and a partner in a law firm there. The job paid $7.50 a week, considerably less than the $11.25 Owens had made in the foundry, but the work was not hard, and Hill was a relatively benevolent employer. The black custodian in Hill's office told Owens, "These people [the lawyers] are hell, but you're working for the best one." Within two months Hill had given Owens a $1 a week raise and the keys to his office. Allowed to come and go on his own, Owens appreciated the respite from backbreaking labor.[37]

In Montgomery Owens honed his critique of two foundational American institutions: the courts and the military. He sat in on two murder trials involving black men where prosecutors ignored the men's alibis, relied on faulty eyewitness accounts, and, in one case, consulted a black fortune teller (dismissed by Owens as a "hoodoo woman" and "crystal gazer"). Both defendants were found guilty. Owens also recounted a pitched battle between Montgomery police and black GIs during the early years of World War II. If southern blacks were "the most hated of any people," then "the Negro G.I. was hated worse." One night a white cop provoked a melee outside a nightclub when he hit a black soldier and also a woman bystander who protested, "What in hell did you hit him for?" Together with other black men Owens went to the barracks at Maxwell field and retrieved twenty pistols, armed themselves, and lay in wait, in vain, for the city police to arrive. The show of force had cowed the authorities—"I never thought these white police would be scared." Meanwhile, the increasing assertiveness of blacks, especially black soldiers and veterans, had whites lamenting "deteriorating race relations."[38]

In the North the war was forcing a radical shift in the social division of labor. By 1943 Detroit defense plants had started to hire black men, and Owens made the decision to move back to the city after a two decades' absence; in the process, he joined the 500,000 black job-seekers moving north between 1942 and 1945. He left Effie and Simon Jr. (now five) behind in Montgomery because Detroit offered virtually no factory jobs for black women at this time. Owens arrived in the city one morning in April, found a place to live with one of his relatives, and started work at Briggs Manufacturing Company the same day.

The Second Great Migration that brought Owens and thousands like him to the North also incited the jealous ire of the city's largely white workforce, which was composed of second-generation immigrants and recent rural southern in-migrants. In the spring of 1943, white hate-strikers protested both the hiring and upgrading of blacks, framing their protest as a means of protecting their "right" to certain jobs. Likewise, whites who participated in a citywide Chrysler walkout on May 20 declared their "right" to a workplace where they alone determined the skin color of their coworkers—a prerogative they equated with American freedom, self-determination, and democracy: Declared a group of white workers, "Our rights are something the boys coming home from the battlefronts of the world expect to find intact." On June 3, 25,000 of Detroit's Packard workers, 90 percent of that company's labor force, walked off the job in a weeklong strike to protest the integration of three black drill-press operators into all-white departments.[39]

Just over two weeks after the Packard walkout, on June 20, a citywide riot broke out between blacks and whites. Provoked by the rumor that a black man had insulted a white woman, the violence claimed thirty-four lives— nine whites and twenty-five blacks (seventeen of the latter group killed by police). The wounded numbered more than four hundred. The death and destruction in Detroit that summer revealed a larger, nationwide wave of aggression against black soldiers, war workers, southern in-migrants, and seekers of decent housing. All over the country an intense labor demand, combined with overcrowded living conditions and a breakdown in white privilege on the job, sparked a violent backlash against black men, women, and children. Owens saw Detroit's three-day conflagration as a bid for black self-defense. The grandson of his former landlady declared that because black men were still marching off to war, now "they were going to accept their equality before going and not after they might all be dead." Owens watched as one man died trying to protect his sister from a beating by the police: "He rushed up and knocked the police down and took his revolver from him. Two other policemen came up and shot him through the head. The blood was very fresh on the sidewalk." At one point Owens found himself fired upon by a group of police patrolling the streets and shooting randomly at blacks from the top of a riot wagon. "In a few seconds I was out. I thought I was killed. I began to move like I was trying to wake up in a very bad dream." When Michigan state troopers arrived in the city, Owens was prepared to use his pistol.[40]

Yet black-white distinctions blurred the lines of combat in the streets. Of a friend's mother-in-law visiting from Alabama, Owens reported, "She was a mulatto and very white." In the heat of a battle she was killed by blacks because "she didn't live in the neighborhood long enough for the people to know her." Her assailants saw only the color of her skin. In another case police urged a white person to seek refuge inside: "The niggers will kill you sure as they see you." Seeing was misleading here, too, for the man the officers were trying to protect was actually "an albino Negro" well known in the community. He responded, "I'm a Negro myself. I'm not worried. They all know me." So traumatized were the city's blacks, who had seen women as well as men, children as well as adults, shot point-blank, that Owens wondered "if this was like the war."[41]

The pitched battles in Detroit reflected the gradual, hard-won inroads that black men and women were making into white workplaces. In that and other cities, the local "Double V for Victory" campaign waged by black newspapers and civil rights organizations pressed for victory over fascism at home as well as abroad and pressured employers to dispense with all-white job classifications. Still, as late as 1942, 119 of 197 Detroit manufacturers had no black workers. Employers persisted in posting job ads stating that no Negroes need apply. When forced to defend their hiring policies, personnel officers claimed that black people had no mechanical aptitude, that blacks and whites were incapable of working together, that blacks spread disease in the workplace, and that employers must respect white sensitivities. (These rationalizations also shaped segregated patterns of military deployment overseen by Secretary of War Henry Stimson, who declared that black men, by virtue of their lesser intelligence, "have been unable to master efficiently the techniques of modern weapons.") Company officials claimed that they could not be expected "to adopt a missionary attitude" or "buck the whole system" by hiring or upgrading blacks.[42]

In 1943 a critical labor shortage finally opened the factory gates to black men. Owens's own encounter with hiring officials suggested the difficulties in getting a white job. When he applied at the Briggs Mack Avenue plant, he learned that the whites there had recently conducted a hate strike to protest the hiring of blacks. By this time the plant had the reputation as having, in the words of one white radical, "one of the toughest and most hardnosed managements in the industry." Standing in line at the employment office, Owens struck up a conversation with a white man from Tennessee and mentioned he had heard that riveting jobs paid a decent wage. When Owens got to the front of the line, the personnel officer asked if had had ever riveted before. "'I said yes, in Mobile on bridges and in shipyards.' I was lying to him but I wanted to get the job." The officer replied that "this was an altogether different kind of riveting and that my experience wouldn't apply." Owens was offered a job that would pay 60¢ an hour while he learned riveting, or he could go directly to the "dope room" and make 87¢. He chose the dope room. Meeting up later with the Tennessean, Owens told him he had not been able to get a riveting job "because I had the wrong experience." The white man said that he was now riveting, though he had never used a rivet gun before, "and I just come in from the fields."[43]

In the stifling dope room saturated with the fumes of fuselage glue, workers suffered from nausea and lack of appetite. Gradually, the white men were transferred out of the room, leaving black men and women behind. Most white workers had no interest in challenging persistent segregation of this sort. One white coworker told Owens, "Simon, I like Negroes as well as anybody but I think they should stay in their own backyard." A UAW steward ignored Owens's complaint that the newest white women hires were sitting at tables in the clean and fume-free "lily-white" sewing room while the black women stood and worked in the dope room. To protest the UAW's complacency, Owens and other black men halted production, at that point not knowing "the difference between a strike and a wildcat strike," although certainly aware that they were breaking ranks with the union. The UAW steward ordered them back to work.[44]

The dope-room action was Owens's first taste of a wildcat, and he understood immediately the need for an alternative form of collective action separate from the dictates of the UAW. In the ensuing negotiations with four different officials, one from the company and three from the union, Owens and his coworkers extracted a promise that within a week the black women would be transferred to the sewing room. One of the stewards gave Owens a UAW button, which, she told him, required him to obey union procedures from now on. The next week the transfers still had not taken place. In response, Owens pointed out that "we had relatives dying for rights the same as the whites were." Finally, a black committeeman named Bill Oliver arrived. Recalled Owens, "We thought it would be solved fairly here now because he was a Negro," but instead Oliver talked the women into accepting transfers to another plant. There they were assigned to machine work, not the sewing room. Owens blamed Oliver for the segregated workplaces: "All of us dislike him. Some guys said he ought to be killed."[45]

Oliver's ostensible betrayal of his own "race" spoke to the complexities of forming a meaningful labor coalition in America's wartime economy. In the cauldron of World War II labor politics, and throughout his life, Owens searched for fellow workers and union leaders who shared his commitment to a humane workplace. He had mixed success—the war years radicalized some while turning others into establishment-minded conservatives. Owens believed that Oliver, for instance, routinely ingratiated himself with higher-ups and shied away from conflicts arising from prejudice. Lillian Hatcher, one of Owens's fellow autoworkers, born in Alabama in 1915, proved to be an outspoken advocate of women in testosterone-laden defense and, later, auto plants. Owens nevertheless remained suspicious of her embrace of UAW president Walter Reuther and the Democratic Party. Reuther considered himself a socialist during the 1930s, but the war and his own ambitions had moderated his politics until, according to Owens, they had become indistinguishable from those of auto executives. Steadier allies were to be found further out on the political spectrum. Leftists whom Owens worked with in some capacity included Sam Sage, at one point president of the Wayne County CIO Council, a militant labor organization; Genora Johnson Dollinger, founder of the Women's Emergency Brigade during the famous Flint sitdown of 1937; and James Boggs, Martin Glaberman, and Johnny Zupan, members of the Socialist Workers Party (SWP), a Trotskyist group.[46]

Owens's leftist allies and inclinations put him at odds with the UAW's core policies, which had grown increasingly cautious and even reactionary over the course of the war. His litmus test of true radicalism was a worker's willingness to wildcat on behalf of a more just shop floor for all. In contrast, the UAW considered any unauthorized job actions a dangerous threat to its own authority. As early as 1939, when the UAW had achieved a modicum of stability, Reuther declared that established grievance procedures represented the only legitimate means of redressing workers' demands: "We must demonstrate that we are a disciplined, responsible organization, that we not only have the power, but that we have *power under control*." Soon after the bombing of Pearl Harbor in December 1941, the UAW embraced a no-strike pledge as a patriotic duty, leaving workers no recourse when the union acquiesced in speedups and policies that included forgoing overtime pay. Under the "Victory Through Equality of Sacrifice" program, union officials at all levels spent much of the war tamping down spontaneous strikes. In 1943 one-quarter of all autoworkers took part in some kind of wildcat, and the following year the proportion was one-half, dividing not only the UAW leadership from the rank and file, but also radical groups from each other. Communists supported the no-strike ban; they were eager to see the United States and its allies defeat Nazi Germany, even at the cost of collective bargaining and workers' control over production standards and health and safety issues. In contrast, the Socialist Workers Party insisted that strikes, whether authorized or not, remained a critical means of radicalizing the shop floor. Most workers, however, eschewed politics altogether and sought only to protect traditional customs governing assembly-line pace, not to mention their own self-interest.[47]

Effie and Simon Jr. eventually arrived in Detroit (probably sometime in 1944), and she soon got a job in a Chevrolet plant, where she worked a drill press. (As late as April 1943, only 74 out of 280 plants organized by the UAW were hiring black women, and in Detroit black women held only 1 percent of the 96,000 jobs held by women in general.) Effie described a workplace riven by tensions that crosscut black and white, men and women, Northerners and Southerners. The plant employed few blacks, and the white women, noted Effie, "had the light work." One black woman named Eve confronted a Tennessee man who complained about "these old colored girls." She threatened to hit him with an iron pipe: "She was going to whip him." Managers transferred him the next day.[48]

UAW officials saw in this upstart Simon Owens a natural leader; he had shown a remarkable ability to push shop-floor bosses as far as he could without getting fired. Yet he remained firmly opposed to the UAW's no-strike pledge and ridiculed the union's self-proclaimed "culture of unity": white members continued to exclude blacks not only from their workplaces but also from their neighborhoods, restaurants, and bowling alleys. (Blacks could not join the UAW bowling leagues because the American Bowling Company franchised only those alleys that prohibited blacks from playing.) The last months of the war provided Owens with "the best time of my life in the shop." This was not because of his involvement in the union, but because of the lessening of production quotas: "We had a regular routine on the line like it was organized. A husband would punch in for his wife and she would stay home all day. Workers would go home early in the day and stay out altogether the next."[49]

The decrease in wartime labor demand also eliminated the pressure on employers to hire black women factory workers. Later Owens recalled, "The end of the war was in sight and they began firing Negroes every day." In fact, Effie lost her job at Chevrolet right after VJ Day in the late summer of 1945. That winter, when she inquired about an opening at Chrysler, the personnel official looked at her and said, "Not for you." The strategies of exclusion were varied: employment offices dismissed all women applicants but then hired white women the next day or required black women to file their applications at a plant across town or refused to hand out any applications at all. When black women stopped trying, the auto companies claimed they could not hire anyone who did not apply, prompting Effie to jump on a bus one day and go down to the Briggs plant. However, she was told, "I couldn't have an application blank." Other black women launched grievances with the UAW's Fair Practices Committee, only to win their case and find themselves harassed on the job by hostile coworkers and foremen alike.[50]

Despite these egregious forms of discrimination, the UAW refused to acknowledge the particularly vulnerable status of black workers. Reuther objected to any black advocacy groups in the plants on the theory that, Owens observed contemptuously, "Negroes shouldn't raise any problems about Negroes as Negroes. He says they should raise questions about workers in general." Reutherites discouraged use of the word *Negro* in the course of conducting union business. Owens pointed out that as long as unionists refused to acknowledge the current and historic liabilities of blacks, the word would remain relevant to their struggle. At one meeting he stood, identified himself as a "plain factory worker," and denounced the auto companies' preference for newly arrived southern white workers over blacks who already lived in Detroit. Officials remained unmoved. The reason, Owens believed, was clear: "If there is any issue raised by Negroes as Negroes we are told by the union leaders that this is the most damaging thing a Negro can do to himself. They say don't raise the question of Negroes." The UAW was not alone in this view: the Communists joined with the Socialist Workers Party in urging blacks to downplay their unique grievances and defer to white leaders.[51]

In Detroit the process of demobilization revealed that white public officials, employers, union members, and home owners were determined to enforce prewar patterns of segregation, even though the city's black population had swollen in numbers and grown in militancy. The City Council voted down public housing projects for black families, and whites invoked their "rights" as property owners to justify their violent opposition to residential integration. In the 1950s whole black neighborhoods were razed, their residents displaced, to make way for a new interstate highway system. Many places remained off-limits to blacks despite the 1947 Diggs Act, which theoretically guaranteed all people the opportunity to eat in any restaurant and stay in any hotel. Unions continued to confine black members to separate locals or to exclude blacks altogether through bylaws or the tacit consent of

white members. Black high school graduates who passed civil service exam-
inations could look forward only to working as kitchen or cafeteria employees. Noted one man, "What I am talking about is living a very narrow life in
a large, dynamic city with a host of opportunities but for 'whites only.'" And
UAW higher-ups failed to protest as black men were either laid off or sent
back to the foundry. James Boggs startled whites when he bitterly claimed
that "Hitler and Tojo, by creating the war that made the Americans give
them [blacks] jobs in industry, had done more for them in four years than
Uncle Sam had done in three hundred years."[52]

Disillusioned with mainline liberal and progressive institutions, Owens
nevertheless remained an active leader in the fight for civil rights and workers'
rights. As a board member of the local NAACP, he protested discrimination
in restaurants, and he was elected a delegate to the Communist-controlled
Wayne County CIO board. Yet his most satisfying moments in struggle
came at times and in places where no institutional rules applied. In 1945 he
joined black and white men and women picketing an appearance by fascist
reverend Gerald L. K. Smith in downtown Detroit. When the police started
to attack the protesters, Owens jumped into the melee—"We started to
fight"—and felt an exhilaration borne of common cause with like-minded
people. "I felt good," he recalled later. "This was a new feeling and situation
for me. It was the closest feeling I ever had to whites." When the police
swung their clubs and cursed, "a wave of happiness went through me."[53]

Within the UAW Owens remained ever the principled critic even
among the most radical whites. Pressured by black members to put forth
black candidates for leadership positions, "the C.P. got very mad with us,"
he noted. To protest the party leaders' indifference, Owens delivered angry,
"rough speeches." He also hosted meetings of "all the leading Negroes" at
his house. Nevertheless, blacks composed only 20 percent of the Communist caucus, and so the candidates they supported, including Owens, con-
sistently lost elections. Nevertheless, he persisted, serving on the General
Council of UAW Local 212 from 1947 to 1951, even though the Reutherites left the workers "so whipped and crushed down they say 'The hell with
the union.'" And rank-and-file whites were becoming even more intolerant
of any black-white fraternization: "We'll defend our American way of life,"
they said, meaning they would defend segregation. Increasingly, some white
workers were equating the civil rights movement with communism, a political ideology foreign to most Americans. The UAW seemed to be lapsing
into its former ways, relegating black members to the sidelines and perpet-

uating a discriminatory division of labor on the shop floor and at social gatherings. Seeing black waiters serve at union functions, Owens believed the North was "just like the South."[54]

Disillusioned with the CP as well as the UAW, Simon and Effie Owens joined the Socialist Workers Party. They were recruited by Genora Johnson Dollinger, who one day was delighted to overhear Owens arguing with a shop steward. (A pivotal player in the violent Flint sit-ins of 1937, a decade later she was nevertheless deemed by union officials to be a "very dangerous" woman because of her radical ideas.) Soon, however, Owens concluded that SWP leaders valued him and other black members chiefly for their ability to sell the party's paper. Outside of meetings these same leaders discouraged black men from socializing with white women, and in fact the white female SWP members were more fearful of being seen in the company of black men by members of their own party than by the general public. Gradually, blacks began to stay away from party meetings because, according to Owens, "they wanted to do something big and they wanted a political education. . . . They didn't mind selling papers but they wanted something else."[55]

By early 1948 the Detroit chapter of the SWP included only three black members. Disgusted, Effie would no longer have anything to do with the group, but Simon continued to attend monthly meetings even though he resented whites' conviction that blacks had never "done anything progressive." Stymied by the party's refusal to address what he was calling "the Negro question," Owens pushed back against the notion that the party had interests distinct from those of its black members. So in December when he headed off to the annual SWP convention in New York, his expectations were decidedly low, his feelings toward the party angry and resentful.[56]

In New York Owens found himself reevaluating the SWP and his role in it, all because of one speech: "I never was so shocked and so happy in all my life." Trinidadian social theorist C. L. R. James had delivered the keynote address, titled "The Revolutionary Answer to the Negro Problem in the United States." In his talk James deplored the fashionable leftist idea that blacks must subordinate their own interests to those of the working class generally. In fact, James argued, "the Negro struggle, the independent Negro struggle, has a vitality and a validity of its own; [and] it has deep historic roots in the past of America and in present struggle." He proposed "that this independent Negro movement has got a great contribution to make to the development of the proletariat in the United Sates, and that it is in itself a constituent part of the struggle for socialism." James also argued that black churches and newspapers were critical forces for radical change. These words of affirmation thrilled Owens and left him "floating someplace," he wrote. "That was complete for me. I couldn't see how I could even think of leaving the party after hearing him. I was tied and wedged deep into the party."[57]

James was a former member of the Workers Party (WP), a splinter group that broke from the SWP in 1940. In 1941 he and another WP member, Raya Dunayevskaya, a Russian-born economist and political philosopher, had formed what they called the "Johnson-Forest Tendency (J-FT)" (Johnson was James's pseudonym; Forest was Dunayevskaya's). The J-FT, a faction within the WP, believed that because Trotskyists insisted that collective ownership of property was the one true answer to the needs of the proletariat, they were incapable of grasping the revolutionary potential of African Americans. As a result, according to the J-FT, Trotsky's followers saw discrimination against blacks as a decidedly low-level issue. Hoping to make inroads among black workers, the SWP had welcomed James and Dunayevskaya back into the fold in the fall of 1947 and allowed them to keep the J-FT intact. James's convention speech the following year, intended to bolster the black membership of the SWP, was the occasion for the first meeting between the two New York–based Marxists and the forty-two-year-old Owens.[58]

The J-FT was an eclectic group. James wrote widely on topics such as pan-Africanism, literature, film, and sports. Dunayevskaya had served as Leon Trotsky's translator and secretary when he was in exile in Mexico in the late 1930s. Trained as an economist and drawn particularly to Karl Marx and G. W. F. Hegel, she later broke from Trotsky because of his continued defense of Soviet totalitarianism, which she labeled "state capitalism." Chinese American Grace Lee, another member of the J-FT, had earned a PhD in philosophy at Bryn Mawr and had recently worked in a factory in New York. She remained convinced that Marx's predictions in *Capital* were now coming true: out of the upheavals of worldwide conflict, especially as revealed in the wave of domestic wildcat strikes, was emerging "a class always increasing in numbers and disciplined, united and organized by the very mechanism of the process of production itself." Lee noted that as a matter of principle "we Johnsonites [after James's pseudonym] hailed the wildcats." Another member, Constance Webb, a twice-divorced model and actress whom James married in 1948, had an abiding interest in black history and culture; later she would write a biography of Richard Wright.[59]

The J-FT applied Marxist theories of class struggle to American history, charting what it considered the inexorable rise of a revolutionary black-white proletariat through various opposition movements, including abolitionism, Populism, and a still-nascent industrial unionism. Faction members believed that a primary means of organizing was to allow workers to speak for themselves, a practice used by the CP in organizing the landless poor in Lowndes County and other parts of the Depression-era South. In 1942 James had reported on a recent southeastern Missouri sharecroppers' strike in the WP paper, *Labor Action*. The story consisted of statements from the strikers themselves, such as "We have to change these conditions and we can only change them through struggle." James and the J-FT elevated this kind of transcribing to a political art: it was the intellectual's task to record and publicize the stories and insights of workers.[60]

Owens returned to Detroit energized by James's ideas, but his newfound enthusiasm for the SWP quickly dissipated when he heard white members still insisting that "the Negroes will have to forget they are Negroes and be Marxists." Yet he continued to commit his time and energy to shop-floor organizing. A 1949 flyer identified him as a member of Local 212's General Council for three years and an "independent" candidate for committeeman in the body shop of the Briggs Mack Avenue plant. The committeeman's role was to represent his department in dealings with the company, and Owens's campaign literature promised that he would "fight to wipe out favoritism and the daily violation of the anti-discrimination provision of the contract. He will fight to guarantee that all job openings, whether involving more money, the same money, or less money, are filled according to seniority if the senior worker so desires." Owens and James Boggs served as captains in the NAACP membership drive within the UAW in the late 1940s, though Owens believed that the NAACP would remain marginal as long as it was dependent on the UAW for funding. Of the need for a revolutionary organization, he later said, "I understood as a Negro. I understood as a Negro first, in the South, the North, in the union, in the NAACP, in the C.P. and in the S.W.P." Because generations of white people had defined him and all other blacks first and foremost as "Negroes," he had no alternative but to acknowledge—or, rather, react to—that spurious identity.[61]

In 1949 a massive coal miners' wildcat prompted the J-FT to act—and philosophize. That year 400,000 coal miners in West Virginia, western

Support An Independent Candidate For Shop Committee

Elect . . .

SIMON P.

OWENS

Mack Plant Shop Committee

Brother Owens has been a Briggs worker for 7 years — a spotwelder in Department 23. He is serving his third term as delegate to the General Council. He is a former active member of the Local 212 FEPC Committee. He is a sincere and unflinching union fighter!

A VOTE FOR SIMON P. OWENS IS A VOTE TO

MAKE SENIORITY COUNT!

Simon P. Owens if elected will fight to wipe out favoritism and the daily violation of the anti-discrimination provision of the contract.

He will fight to guarantee that all job openings, whether involving more money, the same money, or less money, are filled according to seniority if the senior worker so desires.

The experience of the body shop Dept. 377 demonstrates that aggressive unionism can enforce such a policy even under the provisions of the present contract. The same can be done for all Briggs workers with the backing of an aggressive shop committee.

LET'S NAIL IT DOWN!

To make these rights more secure for all Briggs workers Brother Owens pledges to fight for the inclusion of the following clause in our next contract: "When new jobs are created or vacancies occur within a department, the oldest employees in point of seniority in that department shall be given preference in filling such new jobs or vacancies as may be desirable to them. Senior employees shall be given at least a three day trial on the job in question."

VOTE FOR A MILITANT UNION MEMBER
WHO WILL TAKE SERIOUSLY THE FIGHT TO

WIPE OUT FAVORITISM

Elect No. 4   Simon P. Owens

*Independent Committee to Elect
Simon P. Owens to Mack Shop Committee*

VOTE!   VOTE!

FIGURE 6.2 A shop leaflet distributed on behalf of "independent candidate" Simon P. Owens, running for shop committeeman at Chrysler's Briggs auto plant in 1949. The leaflet highlights Owens's record as a current delegate to the UAW General Council and a former member of his local's Fair Employment Practices Committee. Owens pledges to eliminate an antiblack bias in promotion policies, promising to support a clause in the next contract that will guarantee workers with the most seniority preference for new jobs or vacancies. COURTESY WAYNE STATE UNIVERSITY PRESS.

Pennsylvania, and Ohio protested the layoffs and increasing health hazards caused by the continuous miner machine. Wrote Dunayevskaya, "All theory you know to Marxists is but the conscious expression of the 'instinctive strivings of the proletariat to reconstruct society on Communist beginnings,' as Trotsky pointedly put it." Here the instinctive strivings of the miners produced huge wildcats. Owens drew upon these strikes to highlight the similar plight of autoworkers and miners, evidence of a major restructuring of the American workplace. Like the UAW's Reuther, the president of the United Mine Workers, John L. Lewis, applauded new forms of labor-saving technology, which supposedly guaranteed higher wages and better benefits. Still, miners paid a price in working conditions even more hazardous than before. More generally, neither the UAW nor the UMW challenged a discriminatory division of labor that relegated black workers to unskilled jobs and rendered them particularly vulnerable to layoff. Both Reuther and Lewis spoke out boldly in favor of civil rights on the national stage, while allowing local bosses to preserve all-white job classifications and turn a blind eye to everyday forms of hate.[62]

Members of the J-FT saw the miners' strike of 1949–1950 as brimming with radical potential, with the workers defying the machine, the UMW, and the Taft-Hartley Act, which forbade strikes "that imperil national health or safety." In Detroit Owens helped spearhead an effort among members of Ford Local 600 to coordinate a citywide food and clothing drive on behalf of the miners, yielding $1,000 in cash and twelve tons of food packed into seven trailer trucks. The J-FT hoped the aid would help gain the miners' trust and also arouse the interest of autoworkers, many of whom hailed from coal country. The strike ultimately failed, and over the next ten years the number of coal miners would decline from 450,000 to 175,000. According to the J-FT, in political fact and in Marxist theory the job action had highlighted the toll the industrial machine took on ordinary workers throughout the economy.[63]

In late 1951 the J-FT withdrew from the SWP. The faction had arrived at a point where its members rejected the party's founding principles, particularly Trotsky's view that the Soviet Union was a true socialist state. They also objected to his support for a vanguard party—rather than a grassroots movement among blacks and whites—as the catalyst for revolution. Dunayevskaya and her allies condemned what they called the SWP's "plodding, pretentious attitudes" on display in the midst of the recent dramatic miners' strike. The J-FT formed a new group, the Correspondence Publishing Committee, named after the Correspondence Committees of the American Revolution. Correspondence identified three "layers" of political actors—the intelligentsia, union leaders, and the rank and file—a means of categorizing members at times at odds with the group's professed egalitarian impulses.[64]

Under the Correspondence Publishing Committee, Owens would finally come into his own—and receive national recognition—as a principled labor activist and theorist. In 1951 James visited Detroit and met with Owens. When James returned to New York, he reportedly told his wife, Constance Webb, that she must "strike a blow for the revolution" and "take notes about a black comrade's [i.e., Owens's] life." Webb and Owens had met before on several occasions at SWP conferences. Now for two weeks she took up residence in the front room of a Detroit couple who were J-FT members. Each morning for three to four hours, Owens—"Si," as she and his friends called him—would talk and she would take notes in longhand and then spend the rest of the day typing her notes. He also provided her with his own handwritten reminiscences. When she had a complete manuscript of his ghostwritten autobiography, she moved to California and began to edit chapters and send them back to Detroit for Owens's approval.[65]

Webb's efforts to tell Owens's story were complicated from the beginning by tensions within Correspondence. According to Webb, James had assured her that "I would be in charge and only Si and I would be responsible." However, she had started with an outline that James had to approve. Then James passed the outline on to Dunayevskaya, who at one point contacted Webb directly and insisted that she add a chapter about the formation of the CIO. Webb balked: "Since Si had never had any experiences with the formation of the CIO, I refused." Webb also objected to Dunayevskaya's choice of a title for the book. Webb and Owens had already agreed on one that they both "felt reflected his character and accomplishments." However, "Raya intervened" and picked the phrase *indignant heart* from an 1850 quotation by Massachusetts abolitionist Wendell Phillips: "So no indignant heart is beating anywhere whose pulses are not felt on the walls of our American Bastille." (Dunayevskaya often used the phrase in her writings on the French Revolution: "And the people, the san-cullotes, the enrages, the indignant hearts—they had something to say about things.") Apparently, Owens felt that "that word in no way described his feelings. Although there had been serious difficulties in his life, he had been astute enough to overcome them." "If anything," Webb thought, "the title needed to express the character of a strong man, confident of himself and beyond a feeling of indignation." In the end, though, "Si and I lost, of course, and Raya had her way."[66]

For the published version, Owens chose the pseudonym Mathew Ward because, in Webb's words, he feared "that he could lose his job and lose the support of the UAW" if he used his real name. Around this time he began to write a column, "The Worker's Journal," for *Correspondence* (a semi-weekly first published in October 1953) under the name Charles Denby. It was no wonder he concealed his identity: in early February 1952 the House Un-American Activities Committee opened hearings in Detroit targeting UAW Local 600 (and especially its black leaders) at Ford's River Rouge plant. Conservatives conflated civil rights activists with Communists, and Walter Reuther used the hearings as an excuse to purge the local of its top left-leaning leaders. In fact, members of the J-FT changed their pen names frequently—"to the point," noted Grace Lee, "where we ourselves could not identify who was in our letters and minutes."[67]

While Webb was in California editing the Owens manuscript, James indulged in a series of extramarital affairs, and soon after he joined his wife on the West Coast, their marriage fell apart. In 1952 he was incarcerated on Rikers Island in New York for passport violations; released the following year, he returned to England, where he had lived for five years before entering the United States. Dunayevskaya moved to Detroit in 1953, along with Grace Lee, who would soon marry James Boggs. The J-FT split into two groups, with Grace Lee and James Boggs and about half of J-FT's fifty to seventy-five Detroit members remaining with James and Correspondence, at least for the time being. The causes of the split were ideological, practical, and personal: the role of philosophy in guiding workers to self-understanding, as opposed to simply collecting workers' stories and letting those stories point the way toward the revolution; the viability of local partisan politics; whether to go underground in the face of McCarthy repression. In 1955, in what James termed an act of "shameful apostasy," Dunayevskaya formed a new group, News & Letters Committees, and expressed her relief to be rid of James and "the rottenness" that was "Johnsonism"; he always thought, she said, that he "was the measure of all things."[68]

NLC was dedicated to what Dunayevskaya called "Marxist Humanism"—an idea encapsulated in her conviction that workers, leading the fight against bosses and machines, must take as their motto "The Root of Mankind Is Man." Overlapping groups of blacks, workers, women, and young people all chafed under unbridled authority, members of the NLC asserted, and thus held promise as revolutionary actors, but only if they became philosophers as well; to be productive, laborers must merge mental with manual activity. In 1955 NLC began publication of a periodical of the same name, intended to engage the nation's diverse constituency of workers. That Owens's *Indignant Heart* quickly became a "proletarian classic," combined with his dozen years in auto production, made him a logical editor and columnist. On virtually every issue from the first, on June 24, 1955, until shortly before his death twenty-eight years later, Owens's "Worker's Journal" maintained pride of place on the left-hand column of the first page. For many years Effie, too, wrote a regular column, using the pen name Ethel Dunbar. Originally titled "We Are Somebody," it was renamed "Way of the World" to reflect the fact that she commented not only on domestic and international news, but also on the media: radio, TV, and print. Within a few years Si Junior (as he was called) would also begin to write for *N&L;* a longtime worker at GM's Fleetwood plant, he signed his name "Department 21 Worker."[69]

Owens, for his part, used his platform to blast the self-satisfied officials of the UAW, what he considered the lazy bureaucrats presiding over the lily-white departments they protected. For him, politics was always not just "a question of labor . . . it was a question of the labor*er*." On the front lines at the Mack Avenue plant, he covered the convulsions of the auto industry— from 1953 to 1961, the "heat strikes" (wildcats to protest the unbearable heat of the summer workplace) and the plant closings, layoffs, and 80,000 jobs lost to new machines. And he remained attentive to Detroit's advocacy groups, including the city's Wayne County CIO, the National Negro Labor Council (founded in 1950), the Trade Union Leadership Council (1957), and the Negro American Labor Council (1960), all of which condemned separate seniority lines for blacks and whites, lack of black representation in the UAW hierarchy, and relegation of blacks to unskilled jobs.[70]

In 1960 NLC published a pamphlet, "Workers Battle Automation," that Owens wrote, compiled, and introduced. In it he recounted his own time on the line, when bosses would not let him take a short break to get a drink of water. Though not an assembly-line worker, he had labored under the pressure of piece-rate quotas, his pace dictated by hectoring bosses and made more difficult by the challenge of adjusting to a succession of new stamping machines. He also included firsthand accounts from other workers in auto shops, steel mines, coal mines, and business offices testifying to the physical and emotional price exacted from men and women not working with, but rather being worked over by, machines and toxic chemicals. In his introduction Owens seemed to anticipate the negative reaction of company engineers and chief executives to his analysis, but also the skepticism of those scholars who held that labor-saving technology would ultimately bring respite to harried and overworked employees. He wrote, "Not being in a factory, the intellectual may think that the worker in Automation is being turned into a technician." In fact, however, men and women on the assembly line actually lost control of the production process and found themselves, in Owens's words, "subjected to the inhuman speed of the machine." He was convinced that manual laborers understood larger truths about economic structures in a way that people with more formal education did not.[71]

When "Workers Battle Automation" came out, Effie and Simon Owens were in the midst of chronicling the emerging civil rights movement, what he called a genuine "Revolution." Their first columns in the summer of 1955 appeared two months before Emmett Till was murdered in Mississippi and six months before boycotters stayed off buses in Montgomery. Over the years Simon followed the integration of Little Rock Central High School, freedom rides and sit-ins, the protests in Birmingham and Selma. Here was a challenge posed by ordinary black students, domestic servants, sharecroppers, all people of courage in the forefront of a struggle organized and led by black people alone. At the same time, Owens detected glimmerings of white allies, especially during workers' strikes in southern cities. As for lynch mobs and trigger-happy sheriffs, he remained defiant: "If violence comes, we're not running away."[72]

At least initially, the movement was notable for its lack of formalized leadership. Owens was overjoyed at Rosa Parks's spontaneous sit-down strike on a bus in Montgomery the first day of December 1955 and the boycott that arose in response. The Reverend Martin Luther King Jr. followed, rather than presuming to lead, the black masses. Owens lambasted individuals, groups, and institutions that showed outright opposition to, or tepid or belated support for, this grassroots uprising. He singled out for blame Presidents Dwight Eisenhower, John F. Kennedy, and Lyndon B. Johnson; the NAACP; Representative Charles Diggs of Michigan; the US Supreme Court and Congress; middle-class blacks; the FBI; and Walter Reuther and other hypocritical labor bosses of the UAW. He believed that Communists, too, lagged behind, claiming the movement was but one of many fights. And so, he wrote, "it is the Negro people themselves," without "so-called" leaders, making history.[73]

Effie Owens used her "Way of the World" column to comment on conditions in the South as she and her husband witnessed them on their frequent trips back to Lowndes County. At the same time, her pronouncements revealed some differences—perhaps more of style than substance—with her husband. For example, she invoked the Bible generally as a source of inspiration ("The good book, the Bible, says God made all of us in his own image"), whereas her husband did not; he was a nonbeliever and had been since his youth in Lowndes County. Simon still held out hope for black-white cooperation on the shop floor and beyond, but Effie remained suspicious of the motives of most white people, noting, "I have always had my doubts about whites, except those I know personally." Still, she was open to white support; a conspicuous white presence at a huge civil rights protest in Detroit led her to exclaim, "I was never so happy in my life."[74]

Simon Owens helped to organize that march, held on June 23, 1963, in response to the murder of Mississippi civil rights activist Medgar Evers eleven days before. The protest, one of the largest in the history of Detroit, drew 125,000 marchers and featured King two months before the preacher's more famous rally for jobs and justice in Washington. In Detroit some progressive whites joined with blacks, leading Owens to agree with his wife that "the feeling and morale was so high that I felt as though I could almost touch freedom, and that nothing could stop this powerful force from winning." The march reflected Detroit's shifting coalitions of blacks and whites who supported a concerted government effort to combat discrimination, an effort that provoked a violent backlash among conservative whites. These intense forms of political strife coexisted with the city's iconic dual image as the Motor City, engine of American consumerism, and as Motown, the home of the soul and rhythm-and-blues commercial music complex. Voters had elected a liberal white mayor, Jerome Cavanaugh, in 1962. Nevertheless, white property owners and workers were becoming simultaneously more defensive and aggressive, seeking to prevent the "invasion" and "penetration" by black people of all-white residential and working spaces.[75]

In Alabama's Lowndes County, little had changed since Owens had left for Detroit in 1943: though blacks represented 81 percent of the total population of 15,000, they had no right to vote and they held no public offices. However, in March 1965 the civil rights movement came to Simon and Effie's birthplace. The historic march from Selma to Montgomery, begun on March 21 to draw national attention to the police clubbing of peaceful demonstrators two weeks before, passed through the county. When protesters pitched their tents overnight, the local sheriff warned, "We have been getting along fine here, and we will continue to unless they come in here with a lot of this unlawful stuff and this provocation." These threats led county residents such as John Hulett, as well as Owens's usually acquiescent kin, to embrace civil rights activism for the first time.[76]

In the meantime, members of the Student Non-Violent Coordinating Committee (SNCC) found irresistible the idea of organizing in a county variously described as a "totalitarian" or "feudal" place, "an insulated police state," and "the very heart of darkness." The murders of a thirty-nine-year-old mother of five, Viola Gregg Liuzzo (wife of a Detroit teamster), on March 25, 1965, and Jonathan Daniels, a white seminary student killed outside a store in Hayneville on August 13, brought not only college student activists but also national attention to Lowndes. Hulett helped to found the Lowndes County Christian Movement for Human Rights (LCCMHR), which mobilized local people to join forces with SNCC. The Lowndes County Freedom Organization (LCFO) formed to register voters. On primary day, May 3, 1966, 1,000 black men and women chose black candidates for office. By the November 8 election, 2,758 black voters were on the rolls.[77]

Seeking to counter the all-white Democratic Party logo of the white rooster, with its motto "For White Supremacy," LCFO chose as its symbol a black panther. In Hulett's words, when backed into a corner, the black panther "comes out to destroy everything that's before him." SNCC leader Stokely Carmichael (a native of Trinidad and graduate of Howard University) called it "a bold, beautiful animal, representing the strength and dignity of black demands today." White officials retaliated by raising filing fees for would-be office-seekers and warning all blacks that their votes would not count if cast for any candidate other than a Democrat. Vigilantes armed with wrenches and tire irons and led by county politicians beat SNCC workers and local activists. Black schoolteachers and NAACP leaders began to fear for their lives. One landowner remarked, "The Snick workers will leave after the election, and the rest of us will have to stay. Now, I don't believe in going the third-party route."[78]

The Lowndes County movement drew on its ties with Detroit for money and moral support. The father of Diane Nash, an active SNCC member, was a dentist in that city, and many natives of the county lived there. Reprising his role as liaison between southern and northern workers, Simon helped to found the Detroit-LCCMHR in June 1965. The group collected clothing and books and bought tents. Annual fund-raisers attracted as many as 2,000 former residents of Lowndes now living in the Motor City. Some of the money went to buy land so that evicted tenants could eventually find refuge in tents pitched in a field near Lowndesboro. Among the displaced workers was fifty-year-old Amanda Glover, who up to that time had been living on the same plantation since January 1931. She had registered to vote, but, she noted, "my husband didn't. He was scared of losing his job [as a sharecropper] but he could have went on and registered for all the good it did him." Owens helped to organize a rally featuring the Reverend King at Detroit's Cobo Hall on June 19, 1966, with part of the proceeds going to the tent city. A story in *Jet* magazine lauded Owens as Lowndes's "Northern guardian angel." Meanwhile, unbeknown to him, the Mississippi Sovereignty Commission, a secretive state agency, was gathering information about his role in LCCMHR.[79]

Even as he became more active in the Deep South freedom struggle, Owens made clear his conviction that race was a historical but ultimately useless classification, one that must inevitably give way to the truer divisions of labor against capital. Deeply committed to black-white cooperation, he was appalled that Stokely Carmichael and other members of SNCC seemed bent on turning LFCO into not just an all-black but also an antiwhite organization. In his March 1965 "Worker's Journal" column, Owens quoted Lowndes resident Lillian McGill in response to news reports that residents embracing the black panther symbol were black nationalists: "We are not. We would have been glad to listen to any whites that cared to come and work with us. None did. That is why all our candidates are black. . . . We want to have a free hand in determining the future course of Lowndes County, not all black or all white, but all free." Owens warned, "The Negro Nationalists are called radical today. But I think they are conservative because their action will inevitably take them into an unconscious coalition with the politics of the extremist whites." Predictably, Carmichael and SNCC left Lowndes County in the winter of 1966 after all the LCFO candidates lost their election bids. A persistent minority among registered voters, blacks had been subjected to threats, beatings, evictions, and electoral fraud. Some stayed away from the polls, and others cast their ballots for white Democrats. Owens criticized Carmichael, who "made a big name for himself in Lowndes County—that's where he got the most publicity. I felt he was just using people."[80]

The Civil Rights Acts of 1964 (passed July 2) and 1965 (August 6) ended legal sanction for discrimination in hiring and for the disenfranchisement of blacks. Owens, however, saw these twin pieces of landmark legislation as similar to Walter Reuther's attention-grabbing pronouncements in support of civil rights—hollow gestures without the muscle on the ground to make much of a difference. Only ordinary men and women, Owens believed, blacks and whites working together, could bring about the meaningful transformations that were at the heart of a real political movement.

In the spring of 1967 Owens returned to Lowndes and assured readers of *News & Letters* that "the Negro Revolution in the South has not stopped." Rather, the situation was "in action," marked by the people's quiet determination. Still, conditions were dispiriting. In the world's richest country, with millions of dollars going to support the war in Vietnam, "there they are, Negro Americans, cast out of society and living like animals in a jungle for committing the crime of crimes, registering to vote!" Working-class people had to contend with, in Owens's words, "the distortions and attacks on us by Uncle Toms in the county, teachers and other middle-class blacks who feared for their jobs and could be pressured by the white racists to oppose our work." He urged readers to send donations to Amanda Glover of Hayneville, evicted cropper turned activist, and added these hopeful words: "The movement in the South—and in the North as well—cannot stand still. It must either go forward or it will go backward. And it has proved that it does not intend to go backward." Later that summer he wrote, "It hasn't been a real revolution. But I think if we don't recognize the changes that have been made through the struggle of Blacks and the whites who supported them five or six years ago, we're missing something."[81]

Owens realized that any putative coalition among northern blacks and whites seemed to be faltering. Alabama's segregationist governor, George Wallace, was running for president on his new American Party ticket and making inroads among midwestern white workers. Meanwhile, the failure of national civil rights legislation to reduce black unemployment, combined with ongoing police brutality and stubborn unemployment rates at least double those of whites, left inner-city residents seething. On July 27, 1967, Detroit exploded, the city ignited by a police raid on an unlicensed bar in a black neighborhood. The ensuing rebellion claimed the lives of 43 people, with 467 others injured and 7,200 arrested. The riot left 5,000 people homeless and leveled 1,300 buildings. Owens saw in the carnage the desperation of an impoverished people fighting back against trigger-happy cops and greedy white store owners. Calls for "law and order," he wrote, served to exonerate the "power structure," which emerged intact after the violence.[82]

To Owens and his NLC comrades, the Detroit rebellion of 1967 was of a piece with concurrent uprisings among oppressed peoples throughout the

United States and the world. The pages of *News & Letters* documented the strikes and demonstrations of multiple groups in revolt—miners and autoworkers, migrant grape pickers, public school teachers, welfare recipients, high school and college students, antiwar protesters and draft resisters, and women's rights activists, among others. Their protests took place against the backdrop of resistance on the part of men and women living under totalitarian regimes in Eastern Europe, the Soviet Union, Latin America, Africa, the Middle East, and China. At home, Owens saw Detroit's distress as emblematic of a broader crisis of capitalism, for nowhere else was "the concentration of dead capital over living labor greater." As auto plants moved from automation to cybernation and robotics, the demand for factory workers diminished and unemployment rose accordingly.[83]

The promise of the 1960s, encapsulated in the apparently radical ferment of the decade, soon gave way to a reactionary current of thought according to which African Americans were claiming undue privileges in what had become a color-blind society. Title VII of the Civil Rights Act of 1964 produced only uneven gains for black job-seekers. Women cracked the barrier to clerical work, and southern blacks got jobs as textile-machine operatives, but some industries, such as construction, persisted in excluding black workers at all levels. A new enforcement agency, the Economic Employment Opportunity Commission (EEOC), proved unequal to investigating cases of employer discrimination; eight years after the creation of the EEOC, it had a backlog of 53,000 cases.[84]

Owens continued to devote many of his monthly "Worker's Journal" columns to new and long-standing hazards faced by autoworkers on the shop floor, regardless of race. By the late 1960s demographic changes in the labor force in favor of young men, Middle Eastern immigrants, and African Americans had led to new challenges to foremen and to company-imposed quotas on minorities appointed to be bosses on the shop floor. Newcomers found novel ways to resist the speedups and mandatory overtime necessary to produce 370 different car models, each one with a wide range of options that served to complicate assembly-line configurations. Wildcat strikes, workplace drug and alcohol use and abuse, increased absenteeism, and high rates of job turnover testified to a new generation of workers unwilling to tolerate the indignities of the line in return for a relatively generous paycheck. The introduction of robotics heralded what Owens called "the last step of the capitalist's dream"—namely, replacing "the refractory hand of the laborer" with a machine.[85]

Yet where Owens expected solidarity in opposition to shared hardship on the shop floor, he found instead a raw fissure created by rank-and-file whites who believed that any gains blacks made in terms of jobs or civil rights must come at whites' expense. In this respect, the efforts of whites to retain their hold on privileges in the rapidly changing economy of 1960s Detroit echoed 1830s Providence, Rhode Island. New national political leaders emerged to stoke the fires of fear and resentment against black men and women. In 1968 presidential candidate George Wallace rallied his white working-class supporters at Detroit's Cobo Hall and, according to Owens, "yelled about law and order and never used the word freedom or justice." Finding himself the lone black person among cheering whites, Owens feared, "This is fascism."[86]

One of the responses to the 1967 summer insurrection was a job-creation program sponsored jointly by Chrysler and the US Department of Labor. The program aimed to get angry young black men off the streets and put them to work—as it turned out, in plants that were dirty and deteriorating, on assembly lines that were operating at breakneck speed, under the supervision of bosses determined to meet their own quotas and harass those workers seemingly impervious to discipline. Although in theory the program conformed to Owens's hopes for increased economic opportunities for blacks, he had become thoroughly disgusted with the industrial system that had sponsored it. He might well have asked himself, Was the program a recipe for revolution or for disaster?

The young black men recruited for the auto industry's new jobs showed little inclination to accommodate themselves to the inhuman conditions in the factories. At the Dodge Main plant, where 60 percent of all workers were black, tensions boiled over on May 2, 1968, when 4,000 workers walked out to protest a new speedup and a recent firing of black workers. It was a familiar story: UAW officials had persistently ignored workers' escalating grievances over the weeks, months, and years.[87]

Yet this time the response from black workers would be a new one, drawing upon the exclusionary tactics of Stokely Carmichael's SNCC—much to the frustration of organizers, who, like Owens, strove for a broad and diverse labor movement in terms of age, gender, and ethnicity. A group of Detroit's radical organizations, including some based at Wayne State University, had the previous autumn begun publication of a black Marxist newspaper, *Inner City Voice* (*ICV*), that now served as an organ for a new group called the Dodge Revolutionary Union Movement, or DRUM. Over the next two years DRUM would spawn RUMs in other plants and in other industries throughout Detroit, culminating in the formation of the League of Revolutionary Black Workers (LRBW), founded in June 1969. DRUM made no apologies for promoting the interests of black workers exclusively.[88]

Describing themselves as black nationalist Marxists, DRUM members used words and images that seemed calculated to shock and drive away older workers, women, whites, and potential middle-class allies outside the plant. *ICV* featured a "Tom of the Month" (such as Bayard Rustin in June 1968) and took as its motto "I have a gun" in place of Martin Luther King's "I have a dream." Fund-raisers included the raffling of an M1 rifle. Photos of autoworkers came with captions such as "Capitalism is a vulturistic beastly system which creates winners and losers. Here are the losers leaving their exploitative grind" and "The Union lackeys are shown here sitting around the table bullshitting." Though DRUM and LRBW served as advocates for welfare recipients and victims of police abuse, they focused primarily on the UAW (for "U-Ain't-White) led by Reuther and others they considered big-shot bigots, with racism as their "calling card." Picketers carried signs that read "Be-Head the Redhead," a reference to Reuther.[89]

Appropriating DRUM's militant rhetoric, the CP USA, the Black Panther Party, the SWP, and Students for a Democratic Society, among others, were leafleting the plants at this time. One short-lived mimeographed sheet, the "Mack Stinger," produced at the Chrysler Mack Stamping plant, assumed a decidedly different tone compared to the rest of the ephemera published, posted, and handed out in the plants. The editor/writer of "Stinger" was Simon P. Owens. In the first (April 1969) issue, Owens offered a paean to Martin Luther King Jr., reminding his readers that "it is not only black workers who have a good reason to honor the memory of Dr. King, but white workers too." Owens recapitulated long-standing grievances related to barriers to blacks in the skilled trades, the lack of black leadership in the higher reaches of the UAW, and the indifference of union officials to health and safety issues. Claiming that "very seldom does violence come from workers," Owens chided UAW officials for sending threatening messages to the rank and file: "This letter sounds like it came from the police department."[90]

Although DRUM pinpointed many of the issues that Owens had been writing about for years, he blasted its young, so-called radical leaders, who thought that by looking sloppy and disheveled they could better connect with workers. He also ridiculed DRUM's raw rhetoric: workers wanted to "tell their stories loud and clear. They want them to ring with the sound of freedom, not 'dirty words.'" And he considered counterproductive the "vulgar name calling" and invocations of Mao Zedong's Little Red Book at DRUM meetings. At a gathering of five hundred or six hundred people, he agreed with the worker sitting next to him, "an Old Communist," who reflected on the likely impact of a speaker calling Mao "our closest ally": "Man, this guy has just sounded the tocsin for the death of this movement, because this is all that Reuther has been waiting to hear. Now watch him move to break it up." Added Owens, "And I knew it was true."[91]

UAW officials excoriated the DRUM activists, who "specialize in obscene language and the vilest type of name calling." A drop in auto sales in July 1969 gave the union and the Big Three reason to lay off recent hires in the hope of also ridding themselves of the troublemakers. In a ruthless attempt to suppress the militants, the UAW broke wildcat picket lines and enlisted retirees to vote in union elections where DRUM candidates were running for office. By the spring of 1970, DRUM was all but dead, a victim of its lack of support among workers who were not young black men, as well as of its own inconsistencies—was it a workers' group or a black group? Still, DRUM's furious denunciation of the existing options for black laborers would endure in other forms. Soon after the demise of the organization, a new black caucus movement arose to proclaim, "Unions have become pimps of labor, with a history of collaborating with owners." Unrest would continue on the shop floor as long as workers suffered "from speed-ups, dangerous life-taking 'jobs,' discriminatory hiring practices, [and] harassment from white racists in both the unions and management." Predictably, the fierce pronouncements of the black caucuses did nothing to soften the opposition of white factory managers or union leaders. Walter Reuther died in May 1970, but his successor, Leonard Woodcock, inherited the former leader's abiding fear of young black men in the plants.[92]

Throughout these tumultuous times Owens maintained a busy speaking and organizing schedule. He had charge of NLC finances, "concretizing" the group's often dire straits with projections of funds needed for the year to come. He enjoyed talking to college students, appearing regularly at Wayne State. He spoke at Pittsburgh's Carnegie Mellon University as, he noted proudly, "the first black production worker with less than a high school education" to address an all-white "audience of higher learning." In January 1969 he helped organize the Black-Red Conference in Detroit, telling the sixty participants that it was "the first time that such a conference of black youth, black workers, black women, and black intellectuals will have a chance to discuss with each other as well as with Marxist-Humanists, who lend the red coloration not only for the sake of color, but for the sake of philosophy, a philosophy of liberation." Owens and his comrades singled out for ridicule the considerably diminished Black Panther Party, indicting its leaders Eldridge Cleaver and Huey Newton for the "international follies [they] staged for the press, radio, and television. . . . [These two] were a bunch of clowns, playing fast and easy with the Black Revolution, as they handspring politically around the twin capitals of State-Capitalism, Moscow and Peking."[93]

Owens's particular animus toward SNCC and the Oakland, California–based Black Panther Party derived at least in part from the stalled revolution in Lowndes. When Carmichael and other black nationalists abandoned the county, they left behind what Owens saw as a nasty legacy of separatism—"with Negroes over here and whites over there," as he put it. Still, some dramatic gains were in evidence: John Hulett had been elected the county's first black sheriff in 1970, a cause for rejoicing, according to Owens. Hulett halted the routine practice of whipping black men and women who had been incarcerated in the county jail, and whites who killed or assaulted blacks were no long automatically exonerated. At least in terms of wanton violence against blacks, the bad old days were coming to an end—the days when, according to one black physician, "white coroners used to rule as suicide the death of blacks tied in chains and found in rivers. The story goes that one coroner said that the black had no business stealing more chain than he could swim with."[94]

The overall gains in Lowndes were limited, however. Although some middle-class blacks felt moved to participate in politics for the first time, young people tended to stay away from the polls. In late 1972, dismayed at splits within the ranks of the Lowndes County Freedom Party, Hulett joined the white Democratic Party and endorsed George Wallace for reelection in 1972. Hulett later told Owens that Nixon-initiated cuts in social welfare funding for Lowndes forced him to join the Democrats to secure any aid, federal or otherwise, for local programs. Owens explained what he considered the sheriff's descent into crass opportunism this way: "It is a question of losing faith in the masses in action as Force and Reason. Once you have lost your philosophy of liberation—which is based on that— you automatically end up wheeling and dealing." Meanwhile, most of the county's white children were attending private academies and black farmers were disappearing amid suburban-sprawl encroachment. In 1975 the county was still among the poorest in the nation, with a black population of 80 percent and a median annual income of $1,600.[95]

In contrast to the lassitude of the young blacks of Lowndes, the Detroit wildcatters of the summer of 1973 ignited a rebellion. Certainly, the time seemed propitious: in 1972 major strikes by workers at brand-new General Motors plants in Lordstown and Norwood, Ohio, had captured national headlines and led to congressional hearings on automation and worker alienation. The Lordstown strikers were mostly young and white; they had engaged in spectacular instances of sabotage and slowdowns to counter what critics called the "paramilitary management" of assembly lines operated by workers toiling eleven hours a day seven days a week. The company's strategy to decentralize production and locate plants in rural white areas of the Midwest and South could not lessen the demoralizing physical and emotional effects of speedups. In June 1973 a small team of Lordstown picketers was able to thwart production among 1,200 morning-shift workers, a sign that discontent still simmered there.[96]

To UAW chiefs Leonard Woodcock and Douglas Fraser, though, the wildcat strikes on July 24 at Chrysler's Jefferson Avenue plant, and on August 18 at the Mack stamping plant where Owens worked, signified not workers' understandable discontent over shop-floor conditions, but rather the frightening resurrection of DRUM. Certainly, the front-page newspaper photo of wildcatters Shorter and Carter, defiant, Black Power style, and the widespread publicity accorded to William Gilbreth's Workers Action Movement, suggested a revival of radicalism that had lain dormant for three years. It was within this context that UAW officials condemned the company's decision not to fire Shorter and Carter and then proceeded to assemble an unprecedented level of manpower to physically beat back the strikers on August 15.[97]

That fall, after three decades spent working in the auto industry, Owens retired, taking advantage of a new "30 and out" retirement plan. The agreement liberated him and others from work, but for those who continued to toil in the plants, it did not address safety and health concerns, the focus of the summertime strikes. Exactly thirty years had passed since Owens entered the Briggs factory and staged a wildcat on behalf of the black women in the dope room there, but conditions in many of Detroit's factories had actually deteriorated for workers on the assembly line. Although he bade

FIGURE 6.3 This photo of Simon P. Owens, c. 1975, was taken by acclaimed independent documentary filmmaker Allen Willis; it appeared on the cover of the German edition of *Indignant Heart*. Willis (1916–2011) met Raya Dunayevskaya in the 1930s and wrote for *News & Letters* under the pseudonym John Alan. WITH SPECIAL THANKS TO FRANKLIN DMITRYEV, NEWS & LETTERS COMMITTEES.

good riddance to Chrysler Mack, Owens continued to write his "Worker's Journal" column for *N&L* with unflagging regularity, targeting what he considered the venality of the UAW hierarchy.[98]

Both Owens and Effie held out hope that Detroit's new mayor, Coleman Young, would usher in an egalitarian form of city politics. Noting that her husband had worked on Young's campaign, Effie wrote a month after the election in her pungent style, "Black people have always had the job of cleaning out white folks' messes. We started by cleaning and straightening out their messy homes in the South many years ago. So I do believe this Black mayor here might straighten out the mess the whites have made running Detroit." Si Junior remained a worker-activist, continuing to write for *N&L* about conditions in the plants and editing a newsletter, "Fleetwood Workers Speak," focused on conditions at GM's Fleetwood Fisher Body plant, where he had worked for many years. The February 1974 issue exposed injuries suffered by workers on the job and the unseemly rush to get those injured workers back on the line: "If we stick together, we can come out ahead. The union was built by the workers, not by lazy union officials. WE ARE THE UNION." All the writings by father and son seemed to describe a city and an industry stuck in a time warp, where dangerous conditions on the shop floor had prevailed since the early 1950s, and where black workers continued to bear the brunt of the drawdown of human involvement in a rapidly changing auto industry.[99]

The disastrous effects of automation in a global marketplace would only worsen in the years after Owens retired. In his newsletter, Si Junior highlighted the new round of auto layoffs following the oil embargo imposed by the Organization of Petroleum Exporting Countries in 1973. When Coleman Young took office in early 1974, he found that the city's shrinking tax base deprived him of any meaningful leverage in addressing high black unemployment. His decision to turn his back on striking sanitation workers prompted Owens to write, "You can have a Black man as head of the city but as long as he represents the interests of the capitalists he is not different from the man with a white face, and in many instances, worse." And, indeed, for a variety of reasons Young's tenure as mayor saw a precipitous decline of Detroit's working class, black and white alike. By the end of the decade Detroit's car production had plummeted to the lowest levels since the early 1950s and 250,000 autoworkers had lost their jobs, together with nearly twice that many in related industries. An estimated 25 percent of black autoworkers were jobless (and more than 80 percent of black youths), leading to rising rates of female-headed black households, homelessness and drug addiction among black men and women, and incarceration among black men. Only time would tell the story of the late 1970s as the end of the "Great Prosperity" and the beginning of the "Great Regression"—the period when the working and middle classes lost ground to the wealthy, who benefited the most from rising productivity. In 1976 the richest 1 percent owned 9 percent of the country's wealth; thirty years later that group owned 25 percent.[100]

In the summer of 1977 Owens began to revise the original edition of *Indignant Heart,* bringing his life story up to date from 1952. Part 2 opened with the Montgomery bus boycott of 1955; proceeded through the civil rights movement, DRUM, and the wildcats of 1973; and ended with warnings about industrial robots. He included excerpts from his 1960 pamphlet,

"Workers Battle Automation," which now seemed all the more prophetic. Whereas the original edition of the memoir had focused on Owens's coming of intellectual age through 1952, the revised version offered Owens's close reading of class and racial ideologies as they affected both auto work and the black freedom struggle in the South. Published by South End Press in 1978, the book was offered in paperback for $4 and hardback for $12. Owens began a new round of speaking engagements to promote it.[101]

The new edition of the book told a story of Owens's encounters with, and ultimate rejection of, a variety of political theories and organizations, culminating in his membership in NLC. Thus, the book was not only a narrative but also a lesson in method, process, pathways—how an individual came to see his own life experiences through the prism of Marxist humanism and thereby weld theory to practice. The book garnered reviews in leftist publications all over the world and in scholarly journals by historians. Members of NLC used it as a recruiting device, inviting members of the public to meet and talk with "Charles Denby" face to face. Owens's byline on his monthly column now included under his name "Author of *Indignant Heart: A Black Worker's Journal.*"[102]

The year 1980 proved a turning point in labor history, and in the life of Simon Owens. In 1979 Chrysler had closed its sixty-three-year-old Mack Avenue stamping plant; in the coming years the abandoned site would become an environmental hazard, polluted by a poisonous mix of crushed concrete, asbestos, and polychlorinated biphenyl spilling from the rotting factory's transformers, a fitting symbol of the end of an era of US auto manufacturing. Japanese carmakers Toyota, Honda, Mazda, and Nissan were building assembly plants in the rural North and South, thereby seeking to avoid both import duties on their cars and what they feared were the added expense and aggravation of union labor. The post–World War II gains enjoyed by workers, and won by a strong union movement and federal regulation of the financial sector, eroded in the face of policies promoted by newly elected president Ronald Reagan, the genial former governor of California. Owens lamented what he saw as Reagan's attacks on working people, minorities, retirees, unionists, and the poor. In his columns he drew attention to the president's material support for repressive regimes around the world, especially in Latin America: "Reagan's smile never fooled blacks," he wrote.[103]

That year Owens had received a diagnosis of prostate cancer. Failing in health, he kept up the "Worker's Journal" until late 1982, when he began to turn the column over to other NLC comrades. He continued to travel regularly to Lowndes County, where he found scant evidence of the civil rights movement that had seemed to hold such promise two decades before. By the 1980s the county was but one of many impoverished communities throughout the nation, all with similar characteristics: a lack of decent, well-paying jobs for workers without much in the way of skills or formal education; underfunded public schools; high rates of unemployment; and large numbers of people without adequate medical care or health insurance.

If nothing else, the plight of the working-class men and women Owens saw in Lowndes reinforced his long-held conviction that economic transformations—not meaningless racial factors—were the forces that truly united and divided Americans and other peoples around the world. Over his career Owens had documented the origins and advance of this phenomenon of postindustrial capitalism—the horrible synchronicity among the dispossessed in mining towns of West Virginia, inner-city Detroit, and rural Lowndes County. Throughout the country runaway shops, technology, anti-union policies, and other strategies to cut labor costs had taken their toll on a workforce now defined less by skin color and history than by shared powerlessness within a global economy. A group of radicals had indeed restructured American industry, but they were the corporate heads, the financiers, and the assembly-line engineers.[104]

In the late summer of 1982, when Owens was in the last months of writing his "Worker's Journal" column, he and NLC comrade Michael Flug went back to Lowndes County. The challenges there, Owens reported, were not only "about racism and employment or about the loss of Black-owned land. They are also about the loss of a direction for the movement." With old battles won—the fight against disenfranchisement, for example—future battlefields seemed amorphous, elusive. Now the dispossession of black farmers was a process borne of their poverty, not their race, and new sources of employment in the county, open to blacks as well as whites, barely paid a living wage. Among black men and women supposedly well integrated into the country's politics and economy, what were the appropriate targets for change, the appropriate strategies for action? A quote from Italian political theorist Antonio Gramsci, one favored by *N&L* writers, seemed apt: "The crisis consists precisely in the fact that the old is dying and the new cannot be born; in this interregnum a great variety of morbid symptoms appear."[105]

Lowndes exhibited more than its share of "morbid symptoms." The leading paper of the area, the *Montgomery Advertiser,* was giving voice to old ideas repackaged for the times, editorializing that slavery was "'an idea ahead of its time,' because it showed 'genetic screening' of workers, since Blacks could stand work in the hot sun in the fields better than whites." Owens found young black men and women "hanging around without a job" and taking drugs; they had no incentive to move north or to Montgomery or Selma because jobs were scarce everywhere. Like their Detroit counterparts, Lowndes black elected officials had little money to spend now that federal funds for social welfare programs were drying up. Meanwhile, corporations were enjoying generous tax breaks and banks refused loans to people they considered poor credit risks. The new Dan River textile mill received relocation-inducement tax breaks from the county, but its state-of-the-art fully automated operations provided few jobs for local men and women.[106]

When Owens spoke to a group of young black leaders, he was astounded to learn that they had never heard of SNCC or its work in Lowndes sixteen years before. He told them, "I was a Marxist-Humanist, and I am one today; I am for revolution then and now. But I know the preparation for it has to be carefully worked out, in thought and in action. It has to come from the masses of people and not out of your head." He urged his young listeners to resist becoming "a people waiting for Moses to lead them out of the wilderness." Still, he saw some promising signs. A young black man from Marion Junction had gotten his hands on a copy of *Indignant Heart,* and when he went with his friends to a disco hall, he stayed outside "reading the book for nearly an hour under the street lights because it was too dark and noisy to read inside," Owens remembered. Some women in Macon County were meeting openly, and one was considering running for sheriff there. During the trip Owens and Flug sold $65 worth of NLC literature, including fifteen subscriptions to *N&L.* Owens was heartened that some people at least found much of interest in the paper and that they wanted "revolutionary ideas." These developments boded well. He wrote, ever hopeful, "So I feel that the relationships can begin on a new level, a total level."[107]

During that trip to Alabama Owens realized that this would be the last time he visited Lowndes. One day, while he and Flug were driving around the county's back roads, he decided he wanted a picture of himself picking cotton. He got out of the car and waded into the field, stopping to stoop over the way he his forebears had done for generations. Flug followed with the camera. Because it was too early to harvest the crop, however, Owens had trouble extracting the white fiber from the brown boll. After the two got back in the car and resumed their journey, Owens remained silent for a long time. The photo, included in the 1989 Wayne State University Press edition of *Indignant Heart,* shows Owens standing in the field, a wan smile on his face.[108]

Simon P. Owens died on October 10, 1983, in Harper Hospital in Detroit. *N&L* gave over its full first page of the November issue to him, publishing his "last statement" to the 1983 News & Letters Convention: "And we won't stop until we have a human society in this country and in the whole world. That is what we are all living for." An obituary written by Dunayevskaya quoted one of Owens's favorite lines from her book *Marxism and Freedom:* "There is nothing in thought—not even in the thought of a genius—that has not previously been in the activity of the common man." It was perhaps predictable that his old comrade, whose egotism and strong opinions had defined much of her working relationship with other members of the NLC, would single out as Owens's defining quotation her own words, despite the fact he had written so many himself.[109]

On November 6 the First Unitarian Church of Detroit hosted a memorial service for "Charles Denby," indicating the role of the NLC in organizing it. A rendition of the Wendell Phillips quote appeared on the front page of the program: "So no *Indignant Heart* is beating anywhere whose pulses are not felt on the walls of our American bastille." Ten men and women, including Rosa Parks, gave "remembrances," and another fifteen read selections from *Indignant Heart* and "Worker's Journal" columns. The program also included the last sentence from the most recent edition of Owens's autobiography: "I'm looking forward to that new world [of freedom], and I firmly believe it is within reach, because so many others all over the world are reaching so hard with me."[110]

Neither of Owens's immediately family members would live to see that new world. Simon Junior suffered an untimely death, from liver failure, just two years after his father. Effie died in 1993.[111]

Owens had spent his lifetime fighting against the forces of injustice, in the process offering his comrade-readers a powerful assessment of the damage inflicted upon all working men and women in the name of twentieth-century progress, too often measured in purely technological terms. Especially compelling in his life and thought was the insistence that the idea of race was simply a smokescreen—one that clouded the efforts of all people to secure justice and equality for themselves and their fellow sufferers regardless of where they lived. For any people to continue to identify themselves in racial terms ignored the lessons of history and foreclosed a just world in the future, he argued. The fates of all members of the laboring classes in the United States and abroad continued to be inextricably linked with one another. Employers persisted in their quest for cheap, compliant labor, and that quest abided no arbitrary distinctions based on skin color, ethnic background, or even regional or national boundaries. So-called white and black laborers would suffer equally, but they would do so apart from each other so long as they allowed myopic racial politics to distract them from the deeper economic forces that shaped their lives and opportunities. Of his own racial identity, Owens had said, "Since I can remember it has been hurting me." All his life he had looked forward to the day when prejudice based on skin color or heritage dissolved—that is, the day when race disappeared.

EPILOGUE

In 2008 the United States elected its first black president. That same year the black middle class began to suffer a precipitous decline in terms of rates of employment and home ownership, and the plight of impoverished black men, women, and children worsened. Even as an individual black man had reached the pinnacle of political accomplishment in the United States, black people as a group watched their economic fortunes enter a downward spiral.

Simon P. Owens would have understood and appreciated the apparent paradox: by the dawn of the new millennium, although explicit mythologies of racial difference had largely receded from public discourse, centuries of violent discrimination against people of African descent had deeply scarred and twisted fundamental structures of American life. Even in the absence of widespread, derogatory stereotyping, these structures—segregated housing, workplaces, and schools—perpetuated forms of inequality that no civil rights legislation, or enlightened rhetoric for that matter, could erode or erase.

Yet poverty is not—nor has it ever been—an exclusively "black" phenomenon. The postindustrial economy produces ever more multiethnic distressed communities around the country, in rural as well as urban areas. Running for president in 1988, the Reverend Jesse Jackson observed that the new global economy was blind to differences of ancestry or skin color when he declared, "When the plant lights go out, we all look the same in the dark." Still, there is no denying that blacks as a group in the United States have suffered disproportionately deep wounds in the body politic and in local communities.

These enduring wounds, inflicted by generations of people who promoted race as a social category, have festered year after year and generation after generation.[1]

The devastating impact of the Great Recession of 2008 on black Americans reflects their unique, historic vulnerabilities. Between June 2009 and June 2012, median annual black household income fell 11 percent, compared to 5.2 percent for white households and 4.1 percent for Hispanic households. These patterns derived in part from a social division of labor that concentrated black men and women in public employment, manufacturing, and low-wage service jobs. Like Richard W. White, many blacks after 1865 found public-sector employers more open in their hiring practices than private employers. At the beginning of the second decade of the twenty-first century, black men and women were about 33 percent more likely than the general workforce to have jobs with the federal government or with state or local governments. They worked as bus drivers, postal workers, teachers, firefighters, police officers, social workers, secretaries, and office administrators. Beginning in 2009, drastic cutbacks in public services and wholesale layoffs of public employees took a particularly high toll on these workers.[2]

Upheavals in the economy's private sector also continue to have disastrous effects for black Americans. As part of a decades-long slide toward deindustrialization, some American manufacturers closed their doors during the Great Recession and others either shipped jobs overseas or installed labor-saving technology at home. A 2009 government bailout of Chrysler and Ford rescued the domestic auto industry within a few years, but those companies, together with General Motors, continued a steady process of replacing people with robots on assembly lines and laying off or offering retirement incentives to plant workers. Although increasingly hamstrung by antilabor legislation some four decades after Simon Owens and his compatriots clashed with union leaders in the 1970s, the UAW acquiesced in a two-tier wage system that paid new, younger workers just half of what older workers were making. In Detroit the consequent lack of well-paying auto jobs, combined with a shrinking local tax base, had a particularly destructive effect on black families. In 2012 the city, with an 83 percent black population, had the highest poverty rate in the nation—37.6 percent, a figure that nevertheless underestimated the widespread misery borne of industrial change and shrinking government services. Valerie Kindle, a black Michigan state government employee laid off in April 2011, told a reporter later that year, "There hasn't been one family member who hasn't been touched by a layoff. We are losing the bulk of our middle class. I was much better off than my parents, and I'm feeling my children will not be as well off as I was. There's not as much government work and not as many manufacturing jobs. It's just going down so wrong for us." Around this time Simon Owens's successors, the editors of *News & Letters,* warned that Detroit had become an encampment of "the permanent army of the unemployed [which] Marx analyzed as a consistent feature of capitalism." The national unemployment rate for blacks stood at 15.8 percent; for Hispanics, 13 percent; and for whites, 8.5 percent.[3]

In certain professions even highly educated African American men and women saw their prospects diminish in the aftermath of the 2008 economic crisis. Some elite law firms, for example, deemed their own affirmative-action programs a luxury borne of more prosperous times, one their firms could now ill afford to support. Yet in law and other fields, these programs remained a critical necessity because social connections played such a large part in hiring and promotion decisions. For example, in many cases white applicants who had grown up in the same neighborhood or vacationed in the same place or attended the same college or professional school as their potential employer retained a critical advantage in the hiring process. Historic patterns of segregation thus contributed to the maintenance of all-white law offices and corporate boardrooms. Noted Gerald Roberts, a black lawyer, of his years working for a large, venerable Houston law firm, "For the most part they [blacks and whites at the firm] don't go to church together on Sunday enough, they don't have dinner together enough, and they don't play enough golf together to develop sufficiently strong relationships of trust and confidence." Without specific programs in place to redress this historic imbalance in job opportunities, employers in the professions would find it tempting to revert to custom—that is, to hire and promote those people in whom they had trust and confidence by virtue of their shared college fraternities, neighborhoods, and church pews.[4]

In time-honored and in new ways, bankers and other economic and political elites continue to exploit blacks' economic liabilities and aspirations for a better life. In the late twentieth and early twentieth-first centuries, predatory lenders sought to make money via a perverse reversal of earlier "redlining" efforts. Now, instead of denying mortgages to black credit-seekers whether or not they were qualified, banks aggressively marketed toxic financial products to blacks regardless of their financial condition. Elleanor Eldridge would have been chagrined, but not surprised, to learn that some banks considered the ideal mark to be an older, single black woman. Overall, black communities were five times as likely as white communities to be targeted by these lenders, even when class factors were held constant. Indeed, middle-class blacks received subprime loans at a rate three times higher than their white counterparts; such loans forced borrowers to pay exorbitantly high fees, interest rates, and hidden and deferred costs. Stable, gainfully employed black applicants for mortgages became caught up in predatory lending schemes when they lived in vulnerable neighborhoods (those with primarily black and older residents) and when they had fewer financial assets compared to their white counterparts. Because of the relative lack of equity accumulated over the generations by black families, deceptive lending practices had a crippling effect on the viability of the black middle class. Meanwhile, despite their illegality, the age-old discriminatory practices of real estate agents and landlords persisted; in some areas of the country, blacks looking to buy homes or rent apartments faced greater financial hurdles than their white counterparts and could not qualify for housing regardless of their income or assets.[5]

Local lenders also engaged in practices called "equity stripping" or "equity skimming"; in these cases a lender offered to buy a foreclosed property and then lease it back to the former owner. Many minority residents did not understand that they were essentially signing away all their rights to the property in question. The disproportionate number of black households affected by foreclosures after 2008 suggests a dramatic loss of the hard-won gains of the post-1965 generations: between 2005 and 2009 black households' median net worth—an indication of capital accumulation through the generations—declined from $13,124 to $5,677 (53 percent), while the decline for white households was from $134,992 to $113,149 (15 percent). Many black families saw their credit scores and retirement accounts plummet, their modest savings disappear, and their homes foreclosed, losses from which they would find it difficult, if not impossible to recover. The gap in average household wealth (based on assets, not income) between blacks and whites remained dramatic: in 2010 the average household wealth for blacks was less than $100,000, but for whites it was more than $600,000. The difference between these two numbers amounted to a harbinger of hardship among younger generations of blacks, who would not be able to count on substantial gifts or loans from their parents to start a business, pay for college, or buy a house.[6]

Unlike other minority groups, such as Hispanics or Asians, the country's black population has suffered from hypersegregation, with more than four out of ten black people nationwide living in neighborhoods characterized by concentrated poverty in 2010. Various means of exploiting the young black men who live there echo in modern ways both the greed and the fear of whites past. Like the lenders preying on black families who aspire to become home owners, the National Collegiate Athletic Association (NCAA) makes millions of dollars each year from young black men looking for a way out of the ghetto. An estimated 90 percent of NCAA revenue comes from just 1 percent of the "stars," 90 percent of whom are black. These players forfeit their constitutional rights of due process and give over their bodies, and images of their likeness, to college coaches in the unrealistic hope of a future in the National Basketball Association or the National Football League—a modern iteration of the "plantation mentality" among colleges and universities. Like other athletes within the NCAA system, blacks face severe repercussions if they or their family members accept even modest financial or material assistance from agents or sports fans; unlike white players, however, blacks are more likely to be from homes of modest means, unable to afford travel or living expenses on their own. The same dynamic applies to for-profit college recruiters who take advantage of black students' desire for higher education, promising them good jobs at decent pay but actually leaving them heavily in debt and without prospects.[7]

Another indicator of the dire circumstances of impoverished young black men is their high rate of incarceration. In 2010 black men were incarcerated at a rate of 3,074 per 100,000 in the population; the figures for Latinos and whites were 1,258 and 459, respectively. Almost 40 percent of all black male high school dropouts were in jail. A whole host of prejudgments based on ancestry have shaped America's criminal justice system, determining whom the police stop and then among those stopped, who is arrested. Many judicial officials hold that black youths brought before the criminal justice system are culpable as individuals, whereas white youths supposedly have mitigating factors of family dysfunction and mental illness. Moreover, many of these youthful offenders had been arrested for drug use. A report released by the American Civil Liberties Union in 2013 found that blacks were nearly four times as likely as whites to be arrested for possession of marijuana. Some observers charged that local police departments sought to boost their drug-arrest statistics by targeting poor or minority communities. Blacks thus became victims of law enforcement agents' attempts "to meet numerical arrest goals instead of public safety goals," in the words of one critic of such policies.[8]

The widespread practice among law enforcement officials of associating young black men with criminality remains in force in the twenty-first century. This is the same kind of association that animated lynching and other forms of domestic terrorism with which William H. Holtzclaw and his students had to contend in the segregationist South. In the antebellum period slaveholders sought to contain young black men by harnessing their labor within the system of bondage; now modern law enforcement agents reflect a general (white) anxiety toward the same demographic and, on the pretext of drug use in many cases, seek to remove men of this age from the general population altogether by confining them within the penal system. In 2010 nearly seven out of ten black male high school dropouts thirty-five years and younger had prison records.[9]

This "carceral state," in which black men are jailed in wildly disproportionate numbers and the owners of for-profit prisons prosper, can be viewed as a modern response to an oversupply of black labor, especially now that workers are no longer needed in the fields or mines. Such high rates of incarceration have also fueled the nonsensical myth that the victims of these historical forces are members of a distinct race of people. Like Antonio and the eighteenth-century South Carolina black rebels and runaways, young black men in the modern era remain stigmatized as inherently dangerous to whites. Now, though, whites "racialize" a threat that is in fact a function of historical developments: the physical concentration of impoverished people, setting them apart from other domestic populations. More generally, local and state authorities continue to subject jobless and homeless applicants for basic kinds of public aid to humiliating conditions, such as drug tests, reams of paperwork, and stringent work requirements imposed without providing child-care assistance or even reasonable compensation. Thus does a whole segment of the US population, imprisoned and "free," suffer from state-sanctioned forms of monitoring and control.[10]

The crosscurrents of history both mitigate and exacerbate the legal and political vulnerability of American blacks. In the early twenty-first century, to a large extent place—not race or skin color—is destiny. Poor neighborhoods perpetuate gross inequalities regardless of the ethnic or cultural makeup of their residents. Together with refugees from Central America and Southeast Asia, black men and women remain overrepresented in low-wage service jobs that lack benefits such as health insurance. Most children growing up in poor communities have no access to quality public schooling, and as a result few have opportunities to pursue higher education. In these and other ways discriminatory patterns of employment, housing, and education are inscribed in twenty-first-century American life. At the same time, employers, college coaches, public officials, police officers, and bank officers have no need to resort to historic mythologies of race in perpetuating such patterns. In fact, "place" has now become a signifier of "race," with whites making a whole host of assumptions about the character and abilities of men, women, and children confined to all-black neighborhoods.

The idea of race itself has emerged and then undergone dramatic transformations over the last four hundred years of American history. In the seventeenth-century Chesapeake, slave owners exploited a group of people uniquely vulnerable within the Atlantic world without needing to invoke racial reasons for doing so. Likewise, in the early twenty-first century, employers, bankers, politicians, and policymakers can boast of their color-blindness while remaining willfully ignorant of, or indifferent to, the history that produced concentrated populations of impoverished black people. Therefore, these elites—and the managers and technocrats who do their bidding—take advantage of those who are poor or those plagued by job insecurity, not because these people belong to a specific race, but because they are easy targets for fraud and exploitation. All this is to say that in certain times and places race has a raison d'être; but at other times structures of power carry their own logic, and their defenders believe these structures need no explaining.

Still, the use of race as a partisan political strategy endures, albeit in slightly altered form. The runup to the 2012 presidential election saw a multipronged effort by Republican state legislators to suppress the vote of minorities and the poor in general, and blacks in particular, in ways reminiscent of the segregationist South. Just as delegates to late-nineteenth-century disenfranchisement conventions showed great ingenuity in preventing blacks from voting, so, too, have modern officials devised a range of measures to diminish the black vote, all in the name of eliminating the nonexistent, so-called scourge of "voter fraud." These measures include requiring would-be voters to obtain specific kinds of official personal identification, curtailing early voting, disenfranchising felons who have served their time, and intimidating voter registration groups. The requirement that voter registrants who lack a driver's license present a birth certificate (available only for a fee) at the polls has prompted critics to claim that the new regulations are poll taxes only thinly disguised.[11]

Periodically, a party official will drop the pretense of protecting the integrity of the political process and acknowledge that the aim is to prevent blacks from voting. Doug Priesse, the Republican Party chairman of Franklin County, Ohio, complained in August 2012 that extending voting hours, especially on the weekends, would amount to a "contortion" of "the voting process": "I guess I really actually feel we shouldn't contort the voting process to accommodate the urban—read African-American—voter turnout machine." He and other Republicans objected to the practice of transporting black voters to the polls after Sunday services—a practice known as "souls to the polls," common in urban areas. Complementing these efforts to restrict minority voting were aggressive measures by some southern legislatures to gerrymander representative districts to concentrate blacks in the smallest number of districts possible and thereby dilute their voting strength in mixed or swing districts. Taken together, disenfranchisement measures gave new expression to the antebellum Rhode Island legislator's response to debates surrounding black suffrage: "Shall a nigger be allowed to go to the polls and tie my vote? No, Mr., Speaker, it can't be."[12]

Although that derogatory term (a form of outmoded racism) is rarely invoked anymore by politicians or mainstream media commentators, it continues to lead a lively life, as revealed by Google searches, if not by material published, broadcast, or otherwise disseminated to a large audience. And the emotions and prejudices evoked by the word have not gone away. The presidential campaign of 2012 suggested that, to a certain segment of the population, Barack Obama represented a threatening combination of the exotic "other" and an enduring figment of "racial" mythologists. Some of these fears were expressed in coded language—the conviction of "birthers" that the president was not in fact a US citizen, the demand that he "learn how to be an American" (John Sununu), and the claim that he was an agent of global socialists. With his Ivy League credentials and professorial air, Obama confounded the purveyors of black stereotypes, but antagonists linked him to those stereotypes nonetheless. Denouncing "moochers" and "freeloaders" feeding at the public trough at taxpayers' expense, rivals portrayed him as the "food stamp president" (Newt Gingrich) and as a chief executive determined to dismantle work requirements for welfare recipients (Mitt Romney). Glenn Beck, a right-wing entertainer, claimed that Obama had a "deep-seated hatred for white people." In an effort to dodge stereotypes of both style and substance, Obama projected an almost preternatural calm in public (he was obviously not "an angry black man") and avoided prolonged disputations on "racialized" subjects such as poverty, affirmative action, and the depredations of the ghetto.[13]

The results of the 2012 presidential election indicate that history mattered: Republican nominee Mitt Romney won all but two of the former Confederate states (Virginia and Florida were the exceptions), and an estimated 93 percent of black voters cast their votes for Obama. Nevertheless, some black men and women considered Obama perversely inattentive to the plight of descendants of America's slaves, and in the process they suggested the perils faced by any group that found itself taken for granted by one of the two major parties. Richard W. White discovered that, despite his lifelong allegiance to the Republicans, most whites in the party of Lincoln felt no compunction to address deep forms of inequality. In the early twenty-first century, the two-party system remains stubbornly unresponsive to the proliferation of distressed communities, whether inner-city neighborhoods or faltering coal and steel towns.[14]

The son of a Kenyan father and a Kansas mother, Obama embraced America's unique construction of "blackness" by marrying a woman descended from South Carolina Lowcountry slaves and by joining a black church. In answer to critics that he himself was not "authentic" because he did not have the blood of American slaves coursing through his veins, he pointed out that he was authentic enough to have trouble hailing a cab driven by a white driver. Nevertheless, in the way pinpointed by Simon Owens, Obama had little choice in identifying himself as a black man because that identification derived from the color of his skin.[15]

The destructive legacies of various racial mythologies continue to ravage American society. And the word *race* itself remains ubiquitous, reinforcing the destructive consequences of those mythologies. Pollsters and social scientists reify race when they ask respondents to describe black people as friendly and intelligent, or violent and complaining, and to associate black or white faces with words such as *hurt* and *failure* or *joy* and *love*. Physicians and journalists continue to write about racial disparities in health when the factors at work are products of class-based inequalities. For example, a 2012 study summarized in the *New York Times* purporting to show that "How Well You Sleep May Hinge on Race" pinpointed a range of factors affecting black people's sleep patterns, including their residence in high-crime, noisy neighborhoods and their chronic health problems, such as hypertension and diabetes. The article blatantly conflated socioeconomic status with the idea of race. Contrary to the headline, sleep problems afflict poor and stressed people rather than a particular race.[16]

The attempt to portray all American descendants of Africans as inferior to all whites in intelligence and moral sensibility remains a component of modern pseudo-scientific racial inquiry. More often today, though, race is invoked to allude to divisions in American society flowing from the institution of slavery. If in fact the word has evolved as a kind of shorthand to distinguish descendants of enslaved Americans from descendants of people who were not enslaved, what is the harm in that? The harm is that problems labeled racial are in fact historical and that persistent use of the word keeps the fiction of race alive in all its adaptable destructiveness. Moreover, it is doubtful that those who use the word know much about its specific historical dimensions, the many ways it was deployed to justify a whole range of legal restrictions and violent attacks upon people defined as black.[17]

And so the powerful legacies flowing from the myth of race appear to be facts best forgotten, as when widely read commentators and public intellectuals recycle the claim that a foundational "American creed" consisted of "liberty, individualism, [and] equal opportunity," thereby deftly eliminating slavery from the nation's past altogether. Such pronouncements ignore the fact that the country's longtime defense of human bondage mocks its presumed timeless commitment to the principles of this creed.[18]

Most disturbingly, our continued fixation on race distracts us from multiple forms of injustice in twenty-first-century America, not just those that affect so-called black people. Arguably, the most vulnerable people—those most likely to suffer from rampant labor exploitation, wage theft, and lack of basic legal protections—are undocumented foreign immigrants, demonized as criminals who drain the public coffers. In the Great Recession of 2008 and beyond, indicators of widespread economic distress did not hew neatly to racial categories; rather, the increased demand for food stamps, housing vouchers, aid for the disabled, and other forms of assistance registered hard times among various segments of the US population. Thus, dependence on the government-sponsored free lunch program remained high in predictable places such as Newark, Chicago, and the Mississippi Delta, but spiked among families whose living depended upon industries and enterprises hit by the recession: lumber and paper mills in North Carolina; high-tech firms in Rochester, New York; the construction industry in Las Vegas; and various businesses throughout the country that closed their doors, shipped their operations overseas, or downsized their workforces. In the twenty-first century, then, the success of the American democratic project depends upon public policies that take into account two distinct but interrelated aspects of the nation's political economy: first, the enduring institutional structures produced by narratives of race, and second, the recent economic transformations that reach deep into the lives of many Americans regardless of their skin color or heritage.[19]

Ultimately, the myth of race can be best understood through an examination of the lives that have been defined by it. Whether an enslaved laborer in colonial America, a freedperson in the Reconstruction South, or a worker on a modern assembly line, people labeled "black" have been affected in various ways by the term. At some points in American history whites did not feel the need to invoke race, but at other times they did. Exploring race as a political strategy peculiar to a particular time and place offers an alternative history of the evolution of this insidious notion.

For Symon Overzee, race had no practical meaning in his decision to put to work enslaved Africans in the seventeenth-century Chesapeake; Overzee chose his field hands on the basis of a precise calculation he made about various groups and their viability within an immediate and long-term labor force. Antonio's plight stemmed from his extreme vulnerability as an individual wrenched from his homeland, without a tribe or a nation-state to protect and defend him in the Atlantic world. Subsequent laws decreeing that the offspring of an enslaved woman would remain enslaved signaled that bondage was never a "race-based" labor system; for over the generations, many white owners and overseers fathered children by black women, meaning that an indeterminate number of slaves would be as white as black or, in some cases, *more* white than black. Similarly, Revolutionary-era South Carolinians felt no need to justify human bondage by invoking race-based differences; they framed the issue of slavery as a matter of their own self-interest, one they could defend by force without bothering to explain themselves. In his search for a transcendent identity based on religious faith, Boston King countered this crass politics of self-interest among whites, a politics that informed the military strategies of patriots and British alike.

The subjugation of free, native-born citizens in the antebellum North did require a robust justification, however; here the persistent legal vulnerability of people of African descent fueled new notions about their "natural" inferiority to whites. Elleanor Eldridge surprised her antagonists when she refused to play the part of the helpless woman of African and Narragansett heritage, but she was savvy enough to understand that she would need the patronage of powerful whites to overcome the obstruction of race. More generally, ideas of racial difference prevented blacks from gaining access to public education, the ballot box, and better jobs, thus cementing the privileges of whites, no matter how poor. White political leaders eagerly promoted the project of discrimination, which bolstered the fortunes of their own constituents. A similar dynamic pertained after the Civil War in the South, where white Democrats and Republicans either crafted or acquiesced in legal mechanisms that ensured black people as a group would remain landless and powerless. Despite his willingness to die for the Union, Richard White could not overcome the limitations of race, which trumped his education, military service, and even skin color.

William Holtzclaw contended with a particularly pernicious form of racial ideology: ideas according to which the inherent inferiority of blacks naturally inclined them toward criminality and shiftlessness. And the late-nineteenth-century southern segregationist imperative gave license to lynch mobs, officials enforcing barbaric convict-lease laws, duplicitous landlords, and murderous whites generally. The fact that Holtzclaw and Booker T. Washington demonstrated extraordinary personal ambition, and that many ordinary black men and women aspired to a better life for themselves and their families, exposed the myth of race, but whites remained unmoved because they believed they gained much by invoking the myth and lost much by acknowledging it as a fiction. By this time generations-long structures of inequality had produced a largely poor and disenfranchised black population, thus perpetuating the stereotypes that produced it.

Simon Owens understood that the power of race could withstand the everyday realities that refuted its lies. On the front lines of the Detroit labor wars of the mid-twentieth century, Owens saw white and black workers laboring under the same debilitating conditions in the plant, victims of the same forces of inexorable technological change on the line. Nevertheless, members of the white working classes persisted in paying obeisance to race, a tactic they hoped would insulate them against the vagaries of a new, postindustrial world. In all these stories resources—land, labor, public tax dollars—were at stake, and in all these stories whites used the idea of race to advance their own interests on the assumption that the more rights and property blacks gained, the less whites themselves would possess. The American creation myth, then, has sprung not from misguided but ultimately corrected notions of social difference, but from the calculations and recalibrations of specific groups who sought to protect what they had, or go after what they wanted, at all costs.

The stories of this book's subjects have a striking relevance to modern America. Together these biographical accounts do more than illuminate the past. They point the way to a more humane future arising out of the need to challenge in a robust way those who cravenly worship *the market,* a catchall term used to rationalize slavery and other injustices in the name of individual "self-interest"; the need to dismantle a white supremacist culture that continues to feed off historic forms of discrimination and state-sponsored terrorism; the need to make equal opportunity a reality—not just a tired slogan—through a collective commitment to public education and job-training programs, residential integration, a living wage, and universal health care; and the need to promote strong labor unions as a counter to the overweening power of big businesses and transnational corporations. Thus, these stories continue to resonate: Antonio's ongoing, desperate resistance to enslavement; Boston King's quest for a universal community of men and women; Elleanor Eldridge's determination to follow her entrepreneurial impulses as far as they would take her; Richard W. White's challenge to the mythology that skin color denoted identity; William Holtzclaw's defiance of the generations-old injunction that black people were incapable of learning and hence that they should be prevented from learning; and Simon Owens's prescient critique of technological change and the attendant costs borne by workers in all sectors of the economy.

These stories, and their continued resonance, stand as a warning. Racial mythologies as a rationale for injustice are not necessarily just America's history. Preserved in the ongoing use of the word "race" itself, they could be America's future as well.

ACKNOWLEDGMENTS

I am grateful to my friends and colleagues who read this book in draft form and gave me the benefit of their wise counsel, to the many archivists and reference librarians who facilitated the retrieval and use of document collections and images, to a number of research assistants who helped locate material and compile data, and to the colleagues and staff in the University of Texas (UT) History Department who have made my teaching and writing in Austin so rewarding.

I owe a special debt of thanks to several individuals who went out of their way to help me reconstruct the lives of individuals featured in this book. Dr. Henry Miller, Director of Research and Maryland Heritage Scholar at Historic St. Mary's City, Maryland, shared with me information about Symon Overzee's grand house, now recreated at Historic St. Mary's City, and about the earliest settlers of Maryland generally. Dr. Jane Lancaster of Providence sent me her essay on Elleanor Eldridge before it was published in *Rhode Island History*. Michael Flug, formerly of the Vivian G. Harsh Research Collection at the Chicago Public Library and close friend and comrade to Simon P. Owens, reminisced about Owens and his work in a lengthy interview and in numerous e-mails to me. Michael also provided me with a copy of *Indignant Heart* in typescript, a document that includes the original names and places later excised or changed in the published version. Olga Domanski of *News & Letters* kindly sent me a disc containing all of the back issues of the periodical of that name and shared information with me about Simon and Effie Owens and their deep commitment to the collective.

I particularly want to acknowledge the following archivists, librarians, and local historians: Lia A. Kerwin, Library of Congress, Washington, DC; Janet Bloom, William L. Clements Library, University of Michigan, Ann Arbor; Robert Barnes, Maryland State Archives, Annapolis; Andrew Smith, Rhode Island Judicial Records Center, Pawtucket; Lee Teverow, Rhode Island Historical Society Library, Providence; Jean B. Greene, Hinds Community College, Raymond, Mississippi; Charles Gehring, New Netherland Project, New York State Library, Albany; Christopher E. Haley, Study of the Legacy of Slavery in Maryland, Maryland State Archives, Annapolis; William W. LeFevre, Reference Archivist, Walter P. Reuther Library, Wayne State University, Detroit; Beth M. Howse, John Hope and Aurelia E. Franklin Library Special Collections, Fisk University, Nashville; Derol Martin, Smithfield Friends Church, Smithfield, Ohio; Ken Grossi, Oberlin College Archives, Oberlin, Ohio; and Pamela Madsen, Houghton Library, Harvard University, Cambridge.

Research assistants who located information, compiled data, drew up lists, provided translations, and made copies of material include Regina Boot, Christine Lamar, Sarah Shoenfeld, Anita Sower, Rob Heinrich, Melinda Ward, Cameron Strang, Kyle Shelton, Stephen Dove, Peter Weiss, Sarah Steinbock-Pratt, Jessica Luther, Chloe Ireton, Henry Wiencek, and Bradley Boovy.

I prevailed upon several friends and colleagues to read all or parts of this book while it was still in draft form: Michael Flug, Henry Miller, Olga Domanski, Elaine Tyler May, Ellen Fitzpatrick, Tiffany M. Gill, Bill Harris, Mark Smith, Tim Borstelmann, Daina Ramey Berry, Gabe Loiacono, Neil Kamil, Jim Sidbury, and Bob Olwell.

I wish also to acknowledge the help of individuals who provided me with images, crucial information, suggestions for sources, and the names of other people to contact: my colleagues Laurie Green and James Vaughn, as well as William Cheek, Kevin Anderson, Franklin Dmitryev, Lou Turner, Nettie Kravitz, Rachel Peterson, Grace Lee Boggs, Stephen Ward, Christopher Phelps, Dianne Feeley, Scott Kurashige, Alan Wald, Franklin Dmitryev, and Nelson Lichtenstein. Frances Gouda, University of Amsterdam, and Dick van Lente, Erasmus University, Rotterdam, helped me locate my terrific research assistant and translator in Rotterdam, Regina Boot. The University of Sydney's Cassandra Pybus, whose own scholarship related to the "Book of Negroes" has been an inspiration to me, suggested I consider Boston King as part of my study of Revolutionary War slave runaways.

Under the admirable leadership of Alan Tully, the UT History Department staff provided me with various kinds of technical, logistical, and emotional support: Marilyn Lehman, Tatiana Calliham, Laura Flack, Art Flores, Martha Gonzalez, Judy Hogan, Jackie Llado, and Courtney Meador. Released time from teaching in the fall of 2008 and a college research fellowship in the fall of 2009 allowed me to concentrate on research and writing during those months.

My agent, Geri Thoma, has offered much support and assistance along the way. Lara Heimert, publisher of Basic Books, believed in this project and provided both encouragement and hands-on guidance, hallmarks of an excellent editor. I have benefited greatly from her good judgment. Alex Littlefield, editor, did a brilliant job of getting the final manuscript in shape. I also want to acknowledge at Basic Books Katy O'Donnell, assistant editor and multitasker par excellence; Jan Krisriansson, my meticulous copyeditor; and Michelle Welsh-Horst, the efficient project editor, who remained attentive to all details related to production.

A number of family members, friends, and colleagues in Boston and Austin helped smooth my transition from one city to the other. In Boston and other points on the East Coast, via new and old-fashioned technologies, Kent Jones and Tonya Price, Randy and Barb Jones, Karin and John Lifter, Ellen Fitzpatrick, Nina Tumarkin and Harvey Cox, Robin and Chris Miller, and Fran and John Whyman especially have kept in close touch over the miles that now separate us. In Austin, the entire UT Department of History and our neighbor Wayne Whistler offered a particularly warm welcome.

I am fortunate to be a member of two wonderful, vibrant extended families, the Joneses and the Abramsons, and I want to single out in particular Anna Jones Abramson, Ashley Hanson, Sarah Jones Abramson and Steven John Halloran, and, of course, Jeffrey Abramson, my life-partner and love.

This book is dedicated to the youngest member of the Jones-Abramson family, Amelia Esther Abramson Halloran, age two, in the hope that someday she will live in a world without race.

Austin, 2013

ABBREVIATIONS USED IN THE NOTES

AAAPSS	*Annals of the American Academy of Political and Social Science*
AER	*American Economic Review*
AH	*Agricultural History*
AHQ	*Alabama Historical Quarterly*
AHR	*American Historical Review*
AJLH	*American Journal of Legal History*
AM	*Alexander's Magazine*
AMD	*Archives of Maryland*
AQ	*American Quarterly*
AWJ	*Aframerican Woman's Journal*
BCTWLJ	*Boston College Third World Law Journal*
BDA	*Boston Daily Advertiser*
BMB	*The Black Man's Burden*
BPRO/SC	*Records in the British Public Records Office Relating to South Carolina*
BS	*Black Scholar*
BTW	Booker T. Washington
BTW Papers	*The Booker T. Washington Papers*
CAM	*Colored American Magazine*
CMHT	*Contributions from the Museum of History and Technology*
CR	*Christian Recorder*
CT	Charles Town
DCL	*Daily Clarion-Ledger*
DFP	*Detroit Free Press*
DN	*Detroit News*
DNH	*Daily News and Herald*
EEH	*Explorations in Economic History*
FMC	Federal Manuscript Census
GHQ	*Georgia Historical Quarterly*

GPO	Government Printing Office
HQPBAA	*Head Quarters Papers of the British Army in America*
ICV	*Inner City Voice*
"IH"	"Indignant Heart"
IH	*Indignant Heart*
JAfH	*Journal of African History*
JAH	*Journal of American History*
JBS	*Journal of Black Studies*
JEH	*Journal of Economic History*
JEL	*Journal of Economic Literature*
JIR	*Journal of Intergroup Relations*
JNH	*Journal of Negro History*
JRC	Judicial Records Center
JSF	*Journal of Social Forces*
JSH	*Journal of Southern History*
LAT	*Los Angeles Times*
MA	*Military Affairs*
MHM	*Maryland Historical Magazine*
MP	*Marxist Perspectives*
MR	*Monthly Review*
MVHR	*Mississippi Valley Historical Review*
MWT	*Macon Weekly Telegraph*
N&L	*News & Letters*
NAR	*North American Review*
NAR	Notarial Archive of Rotterdam
NARA	National Archives and Records Administration
NBM	*New Bedford Mercury*
NCHR	*North Carolina Historical Review*
NEHGR	*New England Historical and Genealogical Registry*
NYGWM	*New York Gazette and Weekly Mercury*
NYH	*New-York History*
NYRG	*New York Royal Gazette*
NYT	*New York Times*
OSUB	*Ohio State University Bulletin*
PG	*Providence Gazette*
PHL	*Papers of Henry Laurens*
PMHB	*Pennsylvania Magazine of History and Biography*
PP/CP	*Providence Patriot/Columbian Phoenix*
PSR	*Palestinian Solidarity Review*
QJE	*Quarterly Journal of Economics*
RAM	*Report on American Manuscripts in the Royal Institution of Great Britain*
RD Papers	Raya Dunayevskaya Papers
RG	Record Group
RIA	*Rhode-Island American*
RIH	*Rhode Island History*

SAQ	*South Atlantic Quarterly*
SCAGG	*South Carolina and American General Gazette*
SCGGA	*South Carolina Gazette and General Advertiser*
SCHM	*South Carolina Historical Magazine*
SCRG	*South Carolina Royal Gazette*
SDH	*Savannah Daily Herald*
SDR	*Savannah Daily Republican*
SE	*Scholar in Ebony*
SF	*Social Forces*
SMN	*Savannah Morning News*
SQ	*Southern Quarterly*
SR	*Savannah Republican*
SST	*Studies in Soviet Thought*
ST	*Savannah Tribune*
SW	*Southern Workman*
USDA	US Department of Agriculture
USCT	United States Colored Troops
VMHM	*Virginia Magazine of History and Biography*
VSL	Virginia State Library
WF	*Western Folklore*
WHH	William H. Holtzclaw
"WJ"	"Worker's Journal"
WMQ	*William and Mary Quarterly*
WP	*Winterthur Portfolio*
WW	*World's Work*

NOTES

INTRODUCTION

1. In shaping this project, I drew inspiration from the work of many scholars, including, among the most significant of those works, Edmund Morgan, *American Slavery, American Freedom: The Ordeal of Colonial Virginia* (New York: Norton, 1975); Herbert Hill, "The AFL-CIO and the Black Worker: Twenty-Five Years After the Merger," *Journal of Intergroup Relations* 10 (Spring 1982): 5–78; Alexander Saxton, *The Indispensable Enemy: Labor and the Anti-Chinese Movement in California* (Berkeley: University of California Press, 1971); Karen E. Fields and Barbara J. Fields, *Racecraft: The Soul of Inequality in American Life* (London: Verso Books, 2012); and Joanne Pope Melish, *Disowning Slavery: Gradual Emancipation and "Race" in New England, 1780– 1860* (Ithaca, NY: Cornell University Press, 2000),

2. David Walker, *Walker's Appeal, in Four Articles, Together with a Preamble, to the Coloured Citizens of the World, but in Particular, and Very Expressly, to Those of the United States of America, Written in Boston, State of Massachusetts, September 28, 1829* (Boston: self-published, 1829). The quotations are on 9, 14, 78, 12, 68, and 22. See also Peter P. Hinks, *To Awaken My Afflicted Brethren: David Walker and the Problem of Antebellum Slave Resistance* (University Park: Penn State University Press, 1996).

3. Walker, *Walker's Appeal,* 33, 56, 61.

CHAPTER 1 ANTONIO

1. *Archives of Maryland,* Vol. 41: *Proceedings of the Provincial Court, 1658–1662* (1922), 205. Hereinafter citations will include *AMD,* with volume number followed by page number.

2. The Trans-Atlantic Slave Trade Database, Voyage 11295, http://www.slavevoyages .org/tast/database/search.faces (accessed June 20, 2013); Lorena S. Walsh, *Motives of*

Honor, Pleasure, and Profit: Plantation Management in the Colonial Chesapeake, 1607–1763 (Chapel Hill: University of North Carolina Press, 2010), 94–95, 155–157.

3. "Nonsense, stuff": Ebenezer Cook, "The Sot-Weed Factor" (London, 1708), 13; "inform[d]": *AMD,* 41:90; "correction": ibid., 190; Lois Green Carr, "Sources of Political Stability and Upheaval in Seventeenth-Century Maryland," *MHM* 79 (Spring 1984): 44–70.

4. Lorena S. Walsh, "Community Networks in the Early Chesapeake," in Lois Green Carr, Philip D. Morgan, and Jean B. Russo, eds., *Colonial Chesapeake Society* (Chapel Hill: University of North Carolina Press, 1988), 202; "commonly . . . back": *AMD,* 41:190.

5. "Still remayned . . . the negro was dying": *AMD,* 41:190–191. Dr. Henry M. Miller, director of research and Maryland heritage scholar, Historic St. Mary's City, notes that the medical evidence related to Antonio's death indicates that he suffocated.

6. *AMD,* 41:191.

7. Ibid., 190–191.

8. Ibid., 205.

9. Ibid.

10. Ibid., 205–206.

11. Ibid., 206.

12. Jonathan L. Alpert, "The Origin of Slavery in the U.S.: The Maryland Precedent," *AJLH* 14 (July 1970): 189–221.

13. I am grateful to my colleague Neil Kamil for drawing my attention to the "wild man" in European folklore, mythology, and literature. See Neil Kamil, *Fortress of the Soul: Violence, Metaphysics, and Material Life in the Huguenots' New World, 1517–1751* (Baltimore, MD: Johns Hopkins University Press, 2005), 230–233.

14. Lois Green Carr, Russell R. Menard, and Louis Peddicord, "Maryland . . . at the Beginning" (n.p.: Hall of Records Commission of the State of Maryland, 1984); J. Frederick Fausz, "Merging and Emerging Worlds: Anglo-Indian Interest Groups and the Development of the Seventeenth-Century Chesapeake," in Carr, Morgan, and Russo, eds., *Colonial Chesapeake Society,* 47–98; John D. Krugler, *English and Catholic: The Lords Baltimore in the Seventeenth Century* (Baltimore, MD: Johns Hopkins University Press, 2004), 129–151.

15. Fausz, "Merging"; "this emperour": James H. Merrell, "Cultural Continuity Among the Piscataway Indians of Colonial Maryland," *WMQ,* 3rd series, 36 (October 1979): 555.

16. Merrell, "Cultural Continuity," 567; Carl Bridenbaugh, "The Old and New Societies of the Delaware Valley in the Seventeenth Century," *PMHB* 100 (April 1976): 143–172; John R. Pagan, "Dutch Maritime and Commercial Activity in Mid-Seventeenth-Century Virginia," *VMHB* 90 (October 1982): 485–501.

17. Antoinette P. Sutto, "Built upon Smoke: Politics and Political Culture in Maryland, 1630–1690" (PhD diss., Princeton University, 2008), 13–16; Michael Zuckerman, "Identity in British America: Unease in Eden," in Nicholas Canny and Anthony Padgen, eds., *Colonial Identity in the Atlantic World, 1500–1800* (Princeton, NJ: Princeton University Press, 1987), 116; April Hatfield, *Atlantic Virginia: Intercolonial Relations in the Seventeenth Century* (Philadelphia: University of Pennsylvania Press, 2004); "Lower Norfolk County Records," *VMHB* 39 (April 1931): 124.

18. Fausz, "Merging," 72–73; William L. Shea, "Virginians at War, 1644–1646," *MA* 41 (October 1977): 142–147; Walsh, *Motives,* 76–79.

19. "Furnished": Edward D. Neill, "Thomas Cornwallis and the Early Maryland Colonists," *NEHGR* 43 (1889): 137; Eric E. Bowne, *The Westo Indians: Slave Traders of the Early Colonial South* (Tuscaloosa: University of Alabama Press, 2005), 46; Regina Combs Hammett, *History of St. Mary's County, Maryland, 1634–1990* (self-published, 1994), 25.

20. Quoted in Neill, "Thomas Cornwallis," 138.

21. Edward D. Neill, *The Founders of Maryland* (Albany, NY: John Munsell, 1876), 73; Robert Brenner, *Merchants and Revolution: Commercial Change, Political Conflict, and London's Overseas Traders, 1550–1653* (Princeton, NJ: Princeton University Press, 1993), 167; Timothy B. Riordan, *The Plundering Time: Maryland and the English Civil War, 1645–46* (Annapolis: Maryland Historical Society, 2003); Arthur Pierce Middleton and Henry M. Miller, "John Lewger and the St. John's Site: The Story of Their Role in Creating the Colony of Maryland," *MHM* 103 (2008): 154; "the Money": quoted in Henry Hartwell, James Blair, and Edward Chilton, *The Present State of Virginia, and the College* (Williamsburg, VA: Colonial Williamsburg, [1697] 1940), 8; Fausz, "Merging," 74; Carr, "Sources"; Bowne, *Westo Indians.*

22. Carr, "Sources," 56; Hammett, *History of St. Mary's County,* 39; Sutto, "Built upon Smoke," 140–154.

23. "Notes and Queries: Thoroughgood and Chandler Families," *VMHB* 3 (January 1896): 321–324; John Frederick Dorman, comp. and ed., *Adventurers of Purse and Person, Virginia 1607–1624/5,* 4th ed. (Baltimore, MD: Genealogical Publishing), 3:328; Brenner, *Merchants,* 167, 195; Bernard Christian Steiner, *Maryland Under the Commonwealth: A Chronicle of the Years 1649–1658* (Baltimore, MD: Johns Hopkins University Press, 1911), 47, 57, 66, 99, 107, 132, 161–162; *AMD,* Vol. 10: *Judicial and Testamentary Business of the Provincial Court, 1649/50–1657* (1891), 428; "Immigration Between Virginia and Maryland in the Seventeenth Century," *WMQ,* 2nd series, 18 (October 1938): 441.

24. Dorman, *Adventurers,* 328; *AMD,* 10:247; Christian J. Koot, "In Pursuit of Profit: Persistent Dutch Influence on the Inter-Imperial Trade of New York and the English Leeward Islands, 1621–1689" (PhD diss., University of Delaware, 2005); Pagan, "Dutch Maritime," 486; Thomas C. Parramore, Peter C. Stewart, and Tommy L. Bogger, eds., *Norfolk: The First Four Centuries* (Charlottesville: University Press of Virginia, 1994), 38, 47; "Calendar to Amsterdam and Rotterdam Notarial: Acts Relating to the Virginia Tobacco Trade," http://library.uvic.ca/site/spcoll/book/Kupp_calendar.pdf (accessed June 25, 2013); "Thoroughgood and Chandler Families," 323; "Lower Norfolk County Records," *VMHB* 39 (January 1931): 9. Information on the Overzee family comes from *Notariel Archief Rotterdam, 1645–1668* (Notarial Archive of Rotterdam), including microfilm 499:857, 858, 859; microfilm 668:7; and microfilm 338:825 (hereinafter NAR).

25. Pagan, "Dutch Maritime," 489; *AMD,* 41:147; Lois Green Carr and Lorena S. Walsh, "The Planter's Wife: The Experience of White Women in Seventeenth-Century Maryland," *WMQ,* 3rd series, 34 (October 1977): 542, 552; "Lower Norfolk County Records," *VMHB* 40 (April 1932): 135; Martha W. McCartney, *Virginia Immigrants and Adventurers, 1607–1635: A Biographical Dictionary* (Baltimore, MD: Genealogical Publishing, 2007), 771–774; Dorman, *Adventurers,* 328; Walsh, *Motives,* 41.

26. *AMD*, Vol. 51: *Proceedings of the Court of Chancery of Maryland, 1669–1679* (1934), 12, 369; Michael Graham, "Meetinghouse and Chapel: Religion and Community in Seventeenth-Century Virginia," in Carr, Morgan, and Russo, eds., *Colonial Chesapeake Society*, 257; *AMD*, Vol. 4: *Judicial and Testamentary Business of the Provincial Court, 1637–1650* (1887), 35; "Thoroughgood and Chandler Families," 321; Lois Green Carr, Biographical Card #3133, Maryland Historical Society, http://www.msa .md.gov/msa/speccol/html/carr.html (accessed June 20, 2013); Gust Skordas, *The Early Settlers of Maryland* (Baltimore, MD: Genealogical Publishing, 1968), 344; Carson Gibb, *A Supplement to the Early Settlers of Maryland* (Annapolis: Maryland State Archives, 1997), 165–166.

27. "Our trusty . . . Merchant": *AMD*, Vol. 3: *Proceedings of the Council of Maryland, 1636–1667* (1885), 263; "special trust": ibid.; John Langford, "Refutation of Babylon's Fall," in Clayton Colman Hall, ed., *Narratives of Early Maryland, 1633–1684* (New York: Charles Scribner's Sons, 1910), 257; Donnell M. Owings, *His Lordship's Patronage: Offices of Profit in Colonial Maryland* (Baltimore: Maryland Historical Society, 1953), 77–79, 166.

28. "Hardly": quoted in Hammett, *History of St. Mary's County,* 28, 24; Walsh, *Motives,* 120–130; Middleton and Miller, "John Lewger." For a sense of what Overzee left behind in the Netherlands, see Simon Schama, *The Embarrassment of Riches: An Interpretation of Dutch Culture in the Golden Age* (New York: Vintage Books, 1987).

29. Parramore et al., *Norfolk,* 39; W. G. Stannard, "Lancaster County Book: Estates, Deeds, &c, 1654–1702," *WMQ* 2 (April 1894): 268; McCartney, *Virginia Immigrants*, 775; microfilmed Lower Norfolk County Records, reel 44B: Wills and Deeds, 1646– 1651, reel 44C: 1651–1656, Library of Virginia, Richmond, Virginia; Pagan, "Dutch Maritime," 490; NAR, microfilm 502:197; Survey Report No. 11335 (Depository: Public Records Office, Class HCA 13/253, Part I), "High Court of Admiralty Examination on Commission, 1652," Examination Taken at Plymouth, October 5, 1652, Library of Virginia online catalog, http://image.lva.virginia.gov/VTLS/CR/11335/index .html (accessed June 25, 2013).

30. "Emperors . . . Virginia's honor": "Francis Yeardley's Narrative of Excursions into Carolina, 1654," http://mith2.umd.edu/eada/html/display.php?docs=yeardley_narrative .xml (accessed June 20, 2013); Walsh, *Motives,* 41.

31. Pagan, "Dutch Maritime," 493; "Letters Extracted from the County Record Books," *WMQ* 4 (January 1896): 169–171; Hatfield, *Atlantic Virginia,* 101–102, 114; Schama, *Embarrassment,* 8, 28–33.

32. Langford, "Refutation," 256; *AMD,* 10:293, 354.

33. *AMD,* 3:276–277.

34. Berkeley quoted in Pagan, "Dutch Maritime," 494.

35. "Mateship": Carr, Menard, and Peddicord, "Maryland," 31; *AMD,* 41:72, 77, 88–89, 615–616; Walsh, *Motives,* 87.

36. "To uphold": Langford, "Refutation," 256; *AMD*, Vol. 1: Proceedings *and Acts of the General Assembly of Maryland* (1883), 340.

37. "By the Petitions": "Letter of Verlinda Stone," in Langford, "Refutation," 266; *AMD,* 10:428; Fausz, "Merging," 84–85; Carr, "Sources," 56.

38. *AMD,* 51:66, 120–121, 333; Cary Carson, Norman F. Barka, William Kelso, Garry Wheeler Stone, and Dell Upton, "Impermanent Architecture in the Southern

American Colonies," *WP* 16 (Summer–Autumn 1981): 185–187; Garry Wheeler Stone, "St. John's: Archaeological Questions and Answers," *MHM* 69 (1974): 146–168.

39. *AMD,* 1:356, 10:437; inventory of Overzee's estate from Northumberland County, Virginia, record book, 1658–1666, fols. 84, fol. 107, photostat and microfilm, VSL, transcribed by Lois Green Carr. I wish to acknowledge Dr. Henry M. Miller for providing me with copies of these two inventories.

40. *AMD,* 41:186–188; "to be bred . . . become": "Francis Yeardley's Narrative"; Parramore et al., *Norfolk,* 36–40.

41. *AMD,* 10:343, 346; Sutto, "Built upon Smoke," 170.

42. *AMD,* 41:187.

43. Trans-Atlantic Slave Database, Voyage 11295; John Thornton, *Africa and Africans in the Making of the Atlantic World, 1400–1800* (Cambridge: Cambridge University Press, 1998), 161; Ira Berlin, *Many Thousands Gone: The First Two Centuries of Slavery in America* (Cambridge, MA: Harvard University Press, 2000), 104; Marcus Rediker, *The Slave Ship: A Human History* (New York: Penguin, 2008). For permission granted by Dutch officials in Amsterdam to the *Wittepaart,* see New York State Archives online, http://iarchives .nysed.gov/PubImageWeb/viewImageData.jsp?id=176889 (accessed June 19, 2013).

44. "Been . . . Slaves": "Ordinance Imposing a Duty on Exported Slaves," http:// people.hofstra.edu/alan_j_singer/Gateway%20Slavery%20Guide%20PDF%20Files/2 .%20Dutch%20New%20York,%201600-1664/5.%20Documents/1629-1655.%20N .Amst.&Slave%20Trade.pdf (accessed June 20, 2013); W. E. B. DuBois, *Suppression of the African Slave-Trade to the United States of America, 1638–1870,* Harvard Historical Studies No. 1 (New York: Longmans, Green, 1896), 289; Linda Heywood and John Kelly Thornton, *Central African Atlantic Creoles and the Foundation of the Americas, 1585–1860* (Cambridge: Cambridge University Press, 2007), 191, 276; Elizabeth Donnan, ed., *Documents Illustrative of the History of the Slave Trade* (Washington, DC: Carnegie Institution, 1935), 3:405, 410–411, 416–417; Joyce D. Goodfriend, "Burghers and Blacks: The Evolution of a Slave Society at New Amsterdam," *NYH* 59 (April 1976): 128–129, 132; Leslie M. Harris, *In the Shadow of Slavery: African-Americans in New York City, 1626–1863* (Chicago: University of Chicago Press, 2003), 15.

45. Ralph T. Whitelaw, *Virginia's Eastern Shore: A History of Northampton and Accomack Counties,* vols. 1, 2 (Richmond: Virginia Historical Society, 1951); Hatfield, *Atlantic Virginia,* 56–57, 225; Koot, "In Pursuit of Profit," 101; T. H. Breen and Stephen Innes, *"Myne Owne Ground": Race and Freedom on Virginia's Eastern Shore, 1640–1676* (New York: Oxford University Press, 1980), 50; McCartney, *Virginia Immigrants,* 626; Goodfriend, "Burghers and Blacks," 143–144; James R. Perry, *The Formation of Society on Virginia's Eastern Shore, 1615–1655* (Chapel Hill: University of North Carolina Press, 1990), 211.

46. April Lee Hatfield, "Dutch and New Netherland Merchants in Seventeenth-Century English Chesapeake," in Peter Coclanis, ed., *The Atlantic Economy During the Seventeenth and Eighteenth Centuries: Organization, Operation, Practice, and Personnel* (Columbia: University of South Carolina Press, 2005), 210; Thornton, *Africa and Africans,* 276; Edmund Scarborough, http://freepages.genealogy.rootsweb.ancestry.com/~candice /np43.htm (accessed June 20, 2013); E. B. O'Callaghan, comp. and trans., *Laws and Ordinances of New Netherland, 1638–1674* (Albany, NY: Weed, Parsons, and Co., 1868), 12:93–94; Perry, *Formation,* 55, 159.

47. Rediker, *Slave Ship,* 94–99; Johannes Postma, "The Dimension of the Dutch Slave Trade from Western Africa," *JAfH* 13 (1972): 237–248; Sylvia R. Frey and Betty Wood, *Come Shouting to Zion: African-American Protestantism in the American South and British Caribbean to 1830* (Chapel Hill: University of North Carolina Press, 1998), 8; Gwendolyn Midlo Hall, *Slavery and African Ethnicities in the Americas: Restoring the Links* (Chapel Hill: University of North Carolina Press, 2005), 144–154, 164.

48. Stephanie Smallwood, *Saltwater Slavery: A Middle Passage from Africa to the American Diaspora* (Cambridge, MA: Harvard University Press, 2008), 19, 104–105; Rediker, *Slave Ship.*

49. Rediker, *Slave Ship,* 94, 120–128; Vincent Brown, "Social Death and Political Life in the Study of Slavery," *AHR* 114 (December 2009): 1231–1249; Orlando Patterson, *Slavery and Social Death: A Comparative Study* (Cambridge, MA: Harvard University Press, 1982).

50. Jacqueline Jones, *American Work: Four Centuries of Black and White Labor* (New York: Norton, 1998), 23–80.

51. Berlin, *Many Thousands Gone,* 38; Breen and Innes, *"Myne Owne Ground,"* 40, 70; Thornton, *Africa and Africans;* Charles Boxer, *The Portuguese Seaborne Empire, 1415–1825* (New York: Random House, 1969), 96–103; Northumberland County inventories, VSL.

52. "A moore": *AMD,* Vol. 53: *Proceedings of the County Court of Charles County, 1658–1666* (1936), 74, and *AMD,* 41: 499; Gloria Main, *Tobacco Colony: Life in Early Maryland, 1650–1720* (Princeton, NJ: Princeton University Press, 1983), 123; *AMD,* 41:485; Theodore W. Allen, *The Invention of the White Race: The Origin of Racial Oppression in Anglo-America* (New York: Verso Books, 1997), 189; Whittington B. Johnson, "The Origin and Nature of African Slavery in Seventeenth-Century Maryland," *MHM* 73 (September 1978): 239. In a Rotterdam notarial document dated April 11, 1650, Cornelis Syomonsen Overzee commissions a third party to demand payment from Jan Baptista [*sic*] for a certain amount of wholesale linen he sold Baptista in July 1649, NAR, microfilm 502:142.

53. *AMD,* 10:560; Bowne, *Westo Indians;* Alan Gallay, *The Indian Slave Trade: The Rise of the English Empire in the American South, 1670–1717* (New Haven, CT: Yale University Press, 2003); Robbie Ethridge and Sheri M. Shuck-Hall, eds., *Mapping the Mississippi Shatter Zone: The Colonial Indian Slave Trade and Regional Instability in the American South* (Lincoln: University of Nebraska Press, 2009); Jennifer L. Morgan, *Laboring Women: Reproduction and Gender in New World Slavery* (Philadelphia: University of Pennsylvania Press, 2004).

54. "Courteous": Cook, "Sot-Weed Factor," 9; *AMD,* 4:177, 1:346; "black . . . behold": George Alsop, "A Character of the Province of Maryland" in Hall, ed., *Narratives of Early Maryland,* 367; Kathleen Brown, "Native Americans and Early Modern Concepts of Race," in Martin J. Daunton and Rick Halpern, eds., *Empire and Others: British Encounters with Indigenous Peoples, 1600–1850* (Philadelphia: University of Pennsylvania Press, 1999), 82, 90.

55. "Where": Alsop, "Character," 353, 365; "judged . . . Mariland": quoted in Neill, *Founders of Maryland,* 131; Philip D. Morgan, "Encounters Between British and 'Indigenous' Peoples, c. 1500–c. 1800," in Daunton and Halpern, eds., *Empire and Others,* 47.

56. *AMD,* 10:352–353; *AMD,* Vol. 2: *Proceedings and Acts of the General Assembly, April 1666–June 1676* (1883), 523–525; *AMD,* 1:346–340; Merrell, "Cultural Continuity," 551–560; Bowne, *Westo Indians.*

57. Helen T. Catterall, ed., *Judicial Cases Concerning Slavery,* Vol. 4: *Maryland* (Washington, DC: Carnegie Institution, 1926), 13, 41, 231, 499; Walsh, *Motives;* Christine Daniels, "'Getting His [Or Her] Livelyhood': Free Workers in Slave Anglo-America, 1675–1810," *AH* 71 (Spring 1997): 150.

58. Hartwell et al., *Present State of Virginia,* 9; Jones, *American Work,* 64–76; Lois Green Carr, Russell R. Menard, and Lorena S. Walsh, *Robert Cole's World: Agriculture and Society in Early Maryland* (Chapel Hill: University of North Carolina Press, 1991); *AMD,* Vol. 5: *Proceedings of the Council of Maryland, 1667–1687/8* (1887), 53, 626.

59. "Wenches": James Hammond, *Leah and Rachel, or the Two Fruitfull Sisters, Virginia and Mary-Land* (London: T. Mabb, 1656), 290; "a Rude . . . Servant": *AMD,* 5:1, 465; Kathleen Brown, *Good Wives, Nasty Wenches, and Anxious Patriarchs: Gender, Race, and Power in Colonial Virginia* (Chapel Hill: University of North Carolina Press, 1996).

60. "The voyce": *AMD,* 5:53, 410.

61. "Letters Extracted from the County Record Books," *WMQ* 4 (January 1896): 174; *AMD,* 1:353, 496; Main, *Tobacco Colony,* 97–139; Karen Ordahl Kupperman, "Fear of Hot Climates in the Anglo-American Colonial Experience," *WMQ,* 3rd series, 41 (April 1984): 213–240.

62. Walsh, *Motives,* 20–23, 112–114, 131–141.

63. Russell R. Menard, "From Servant to Freeholder: Status Mobility and Property Accumulation in Seventeenth-Century Maryland," *WMQ,* 3rd series, 30 (January 1973): 37–64.

64. Susan Wilkinson, "Good Neighbor Clocker," http://www.stmaryscity.org/History/Good%20Neighbor%20Clocker.html (accessed June 20, 2013); Edmund Morgan, *American Slavery, American Freedom: The Ordeal of Colonial Virginia* (New York: Norton, 1976).

65. Thoroughgood genealogy: http://www.esva.net/ghotes/thorowgd/d0/i0011734.htm; and http://www.esva.net/ghotes/thorowgd/d0/i0017455.htm (accessed July 31, 2013).

66. "Sooner condemn": *AMD,* 5:324; Sutto, "Built upon Smoke," 251–275.

67. *AMD,* 10:535, 538, 540, 541, 559.

68. "Sir . . . avoid it": *AMD,* 41:41–42; SR reel 2284-1-2 (MSA SM 23–2), 1658–1669, Maryland State Archives, Annapolis, Maryland.

69. *AMD,* 41:82, 254.

70. Ibid., 89.

71. Ibid., 139, 354.

72. Ibid., 141, 147, 174–175; Ralph Semmes, *Crime and Punishment in Early Maryland* (Baltimore, MD: Johns Hopkins University Press, 1938); Stone, "St. John's," 158. For testimony given in the trial of Clocker and Williams, see *AMD,* 41:212–213.

73. *AMD,* 41:186–188.

74. Ibid., 190.

75. Walsh, "Community Networks," 202–209; Carr et al., *Robert Cole's World,* 242; Sutto, "Built upon Smoke," 256.

76. *AMD,* 41:206.

77. Ibid., 210–211.

78. Ibid., 235–236, 245.

79. Ibid., 245–246.

80. Ibid., 244, 254; Wilkinson, "Good Neighbor Clocker."

81. *AMD,* 41:284, 289, 327, 335.

82. "Brother": ibid., 312; *AMD,* 53:175–176, 460; "Thoroughgood and Chandler Families," 322.

83. "Strange": Augustine Herman, "Journal of the Dutch Embassy to Maryland," in Hall, ed., *Narratives of Early Maryland,* 319; J. Thomas Scharf, *History of Maryland, from the Earliest Period to the Present Day* (Baltimore, MD: J. B. Piet, 1879), 1:244–249, 251.

84. Herman, "Journal," 330; George Johnston, *History of Cecil County, Maryland* (Baltimore, MD: Regional Publishing, 1967), 20–47.

85. Alsop, "Character," 379.

86. Lorena S. Walsh, *From Calabar to Carter's Grove: The History of a Virginia Slave Community* (Charlottesville: University of Virginia Press, 1990), 31, 85–86; Karen E. Fields and Barbara J. Fields, *Racecraft: The Soul of Inequality in American Life* (London: Verso Books, 2012), 124.

87. Merrell, "Cultural Continuity," 559.

88. Philip D. Morgan, *Slave Counterpoint: Black Culture in the Eighteenth-Century Chesapeake and Lowcountry* (Chapel Hill: University of North Carolina Press, 1998), 262.

89. "Loathsome": *AMD,* 41:273–274; Alpert, "Origin of Slavery," 216; Johnson, "Origin and Nature," 239.

90. "Both": Ralph Hamor, *A True Discourse of the Present State of Virginia, and the Success of the Affaires there Till the 18 of June 1614* (New York: DaCapo Press, [1615] 1971), 44; Johnson, "Origin and Nature"; Walsh, *Motives,* 115–116; Carl H. Nightingale, "Before Race Mattered: Geographies of the Color Line in Early Colonial Madras and New York," *AHR* 113 (February 2008): 62–65.

91. *AMD,* 41:366.

92. Overzee's burial place is not revealed in extant historical records related to deaths or cemetery indices.

93. *AMD,* Vol. 662: *His Lordship's Patronage, Offices of Profit in Colonial Maryland* (1953), 166; "Thoroughgood and Chandler Families," 322; *AMD,* 41:306, 335, 500, 53:175.

CHAPTER 2 BOSTON KING

1. Boston King, "Memoirs of the Life of Boston King, a Black Preacher, Written by Himself, during his Residence at Kingswood School." This work was serialized in *Methodist Magazine* for March 1798 (105–110); April 1798 (157–161); May 1798 (209–213); and June 1798 (261–265). The quotations here are from March, 106–107. Available online at http://antislavery.eserver.org/narratives/boston_king/bostonking proof.pdf/ (accessed June 20, 2013).

2. For an overview, see Sylvia R. Frey, *Water from the Rock: Black Resistance in a Revolutionary Age* (Princeton, NJ: Princeton University Press, 1991).

3. Robert Olwell, *Masters, Slaves, and Subjects: South Carolina Low Country, 1740–1790* (Ithaca, NY: Cornell University Press, 1998), 8; J. William Harris, *The Hanging of Thomas Jeremiah: A Free Black Man's Encounter with Liberty* (New Haven, CT: Yale University Press, 2009), 160. Here the Lowcountry is defined as the following districts bordering the coast: Horry, Georgetown, Berkeley, Charles Town, Beaufort, and Colleton. For an overview, see Philip D. Morgan, *Slave Counterpoint: Black Culture in the Eighteenth-Century Chesapeake and the Lowcountry* (Chapel Hill: University of North Carolina Press, 1998).

4. S. Max Edelson, *Plantation Enterprise in Colonial South Carolina* (Cambridge, MA: Harvard University Press, 2006), 166–199; Jack P. Greene, "'Slavery or Independence': Some Reflections on the Relationship Among Liberty, Black Bondage, and Equality in Revolutionary South Carolina," *SCHM* 80 (July 1979): 193–214; Rebecca Starr, ed., *Articulating America: Fashioning a National Political Culture in Early America* (Lanham, MD: Rowman & Littlefield, 2000), 237–256; Karen E. Fields and Barbara J. Fields, *Racecraft: The Soul of Inequality in American Life* (London: Verso Books, 2012), 141.

5. Morgan, *Slave Counterpoint*, 62; Frey, *Water from the Rock*, 117.

6. Daniel Stevens to John Wendell, February 20, 1782, Massachusetts Historical Society *Proceedings,* Series 3, 48 (June 1915): 342–343. See also Olwell, *Masters, Slaves,* 255–256; Betty Wood, "'High Notions of Their Liberty': Women of Color and the American Revolution in Lowcountry Georgia and South Carolina, 1765–1783," in Philip D. Morgan, ed., *African American Life in the Georgia Lowcountry: The Atlantic World and the Gullah Geechee* (Athens: University of Georgia Press, 2010), 64–65.

7. "Ethiopian . . . them"; "state": Stevens to Wendell, 342–343; "peculiarity . . . gentlemen": H. Roy Merrens, ed., "A View of Coastal South Carolina in 1778: The Journal of Ebenezer Hazard," *SCHM* 73 (October 1972): 190; Wood, "'High Notions,'" 64; Robert Stansbury Lambert, *South Carolina Loyalists in the American Revolution* (Columbia: University of South Carolina Press, 1987), 289.

8. These examples of consumer items stocked on the shelves of Charles Town shops are taken from the *South Carolina Royal Gazette,* especially the issues for January and February 1782. See also Lambert, *South Carolina Loyalists,* 185–197.

9. Leslie to Clinton, near Charles Town (hereinafter CT), January 29, 1782, *Report on American Manuscripts in the Royal Institution of Great Britain* (Dublin: John Falconer, 1906), 2:388 (hereinafter *RAM*).

10. "Their misery" Leslie to Sir, CT, January 29, 1783, *Head Quarters Papers of the British Army in America,* vol. 35, reel 12 (hereinafter *HQPBAA*); Leslie to Sir, CT, December 27, 1781, *HQPBAA,* vol. 34, reel 11; "sudden": Franklin Benjamin Hough, *The Siege of Charleston, by the British Fleet and Army Under the Command of Admiral Arbuthnot* (Albany, NY: John Munsell, 1867), 148; "my houses": *RAM,* 2:150.

11. "Too many": Leslie to Clinton, Camp, Davis's House, March 12, 1782, *RAM,* 2:418; "and send": Andrew Cowie, Savannah, April and May 1780, *RAM,* 2:127, and 13 (nos. 149 and 151); Jim Piecuch, *Three Peoples, One King: Loyalists, Indians, and Slaves in the Revolutionary South, 1775–1782* (Columbia: University of South Carolina Press, 2008), 299; Philip G. Swan, "'The Present Defenceless State of the Country': Gunpowder Plots in Revolutionary South Carolina," *SCHM* 108 (October 2007): 297–315.

12. Leslie to Clinton, Camp near CT, February 18, 1782, *RAM*, 2:400; Moncrief to Clinton, CT, March 13, 1782, ibid., 419; "excellent": Leslie to Sir, camp near CT, January 29, 1782, *HQPBAA*, vol. 35, reel 12.

13. Benjamin Quarles, *The Negro in the American Revolution* (Chapel Hill: University of North Carolina Press, [1961] 1996), 137–140; Simon Schama, *Rough Crossings: Britain, the Slaves, and the American Revolution* (New York: HarperCollins, 2006), 86, 136, 321; George S. McCowen, *British Occupation of Charleston, 1780–1782* (Columbia: University of South Carolina Press, 1972), 135–136; Aedanus Burke to Arthur Middleton, Jacksonborough, January 25, 1782, "Correspondence of Hon. Arthur Middleton, Signer of the Declaration of Independence," *SCHM* 26 (October 1925): 192–193; Barbara Doyle, Mary Edna Sullivan, and Tracey Todd, *Beyond the Fields: Slavery at Middleton Place* (Charleston, SC: Middleton Place Foundation, 2008).

14. Quarles, *Negro*, 66, 125; William Edwin Hemphill, Wylma Anne Wates, and R. Nicholas Olsberg, eds., *Journals of the General Assembly and House of Representatives, 1776–1780*, State Records of South Carolina (Columbia: University of South Carolina Press, 1970), 253–278; Gen. Marion to Col. Peter Horry, March 29, 1782, in R. W. Gibbes, ed., *Documentary History of the American Revolution Consisting of Letters and Papers . . . in 1781 and 1782* (New York: Appleton, 1855), 280. Note that Gibbes's documentaries are published in three separate volumes—one dealing with 1764–1776, one with 1776–1782, and the other with 1781–1782.

15. "Totally unfit": Greene to George Washington, January 13, 1781, in Richard K. Showman, ed., *The Papers of General Nathanael Greene* (Chapel Hill: University of North Carolina Press, 1994), 7:11–12; Charles Cotesworth Pinckney to Arthur Middleton, Camp near Bacon's Bridge, April 24, 1782, "Correspondence of Middleton," *SCHM* 27 (April 1926): 61–62; "all the": North Carolina Delegates to South Carolina Delegates, Philadelphia, April 2, 1779, in Philip M. Hamer, ed., *Papers of Henry Laurens* (December 11, 1778–August 31, 1782) (Columbia: University of South Carolina Press, 1999), 15:74–75 (hereinafter *PHL*); Jerome J. Nadelhaft, *The Disorders of War: The Revolution in South Carolina* (Orono: University of Maine Press, 1981), 61; David Duncan Wallace, *The History of South Carolina* (New York: American Historical Society, 1934), 2:297.

16. Quarles, *Negro*; Frey, *Water from the Rock*.

17. The following account draws primarily from these sources: William Moultrie, *Memoirs of the American Revolution*, vol. 2 (New York: David Longworth, 1802); Johann Ewald, *Diary of the American War: A Hessian Journal*, ed. by Joseph P. Tustin (New Haven, CT: Yale University Press, 1979); Hough, *Siege of Charleston*; [Peter Russell,] "The Siege of Charleston: Journal of Captain Peter Russell, December 25, 1779, to May 2, 1780," *AHR* 4 (April 1899): 478–501; and George Fenwick Jones, ed., "The 1780 Siege of Charleston as Experienced by a Hessian Officer," Parts 1 and 2, *SCHM* 88 (January and April 1978): 23–33, 63–75, respectively.

18. "Raising . . . mariners": Hemphill et al., eds., *Journals, 1776–1780,* 277; *PHL*, 15:234–235n4; Quarles, *Negro*, 52; "no Rum": quoted in Thomas J. Kirkland and Robert M. Kennedy, *Historic Camden: Part One: Colonial and Revolutionary* (Columbia: The State Company, 1905), 126; J. Rutledge to Col. Garden, CT, March 2, 1780, in R. W. Gibbes, ed., *Documentary History, 1776–1782* (New York: D. Appleton, 1857), 129; John C. Cavanagh, "American Military Leadership in the Southern

Campaign: Benjamin Lincoln," in John Richard Alden and W. Robert Higgins, eds., *The Revolutionary War in the South: Power, Conflict, and Leadership* (Durham, NC: Duke University Press, 1979), 122–131; David Ramsay, *Ramsay's History of South Carolina* (Newberry, SC: W. J. Duffie, 1858), 1:182–183.

19. "Our long": *NYGWM,* April 26, 1780; "full Security": ibid., January 29, 1780 (a reprinting of Clinton's Philippsburgh Proclamation of June 30, 1779).

20. Ewald, *Diary,* 197, 202; Quarles, *Negro,* 152; [Russell,] "Siege of Charleston," 484–487; Doyle et al., *Beyond the Fields,* 21.

21. "English . . . ornament ": Ewald, *Diary,* 231–232; [Russell], "Siege of Charleston," 498.

22. Ewald, *Diary,* 203–205; Ramsay, *Ramsay's History,* 1:183–184; [Russell,] "Siege of Charleston," 494; Jones, ed., "1780 Siege of Charleston," Part 2, 64.

23. "Accident": John Lewis Gervais to Henry Laurens, George Town, April 17, 1780, *PHL,* 15:277; Cavanagh, "American Military Leadership," 127; Ewald, *Diary,* 236–238; [Russell,] "Siege of Charleston," 294.

24. King, "Memoirs" (March 1798), 106–107.

25. "Some": J. Simpson to Clinton, CT, August 13, 1780, *RAM,* vol. 23, reel 8; "compelled": Hough, *Siege of Charleston,* 205; "protection": McCowen, *British Occupation,* 59–60, 70 (the term was Edward Rutledge's); "several": Ramsay, *Ramsay's History,* 1:197.

26. "Negroes . . . Cloathing": Leslie to Clinton, June 3, 1780, *RAM,* vol. 23, reel 8; "go about": *SCRG,* December 19–22, 1781.

27. "Which sweeps": James Simpson to Sir, CT, July 16, 1780, *RAM,* vol. 23, reel 8; "distribute": Leslie quoted in Quarles, *Negro,* 142; King, "Memoirs" (March 1798), 107.

28. George Fenwick Jones, "The Black Hessians: Negroes Recruited by the Hessians in South Carolina and Other Colonies," *SCHM* 83 (October 1982): 287–302; Ira Berlin, *Many Thousands Gone: The First Two Centuries of Slavery in North America* (Cambridge, MA: Harvard University Press, 1998), 297–298; McCowen, *British Occupation,* 58; "compelled": John Cruden, *Report on the Management of the Estates Sequestered in South Carolina by Order of Lord Cornwallis, in 1780–1782,* ed. by Paul Leicester Ford (Brooklyn, NY: Historical Printing Club, 1890); Cassandra Pybus, "Jefferson's Faulty Math: The Question of Slave Defections in the American Revolution," *WMQ,* 3rd series, 62 (April 2005): 254. See also "The Journal of Alexander Chesney: A South Carolina Loyalist in the Revolution and After," *OSUB* 26 (October 1921): 23.

29. "He . . . forgiven": *SCRG,* January 10–13, 1781; ibid., March 10–14, 1781; "He may": ibid., June 20–23, 178; ibid., December 6, 1780; ibid., December 2, 1780.

30. Ibid., March 21–24, 1781; Berlin, *Many Thousands Gone,* 296; *SCRG,* May 19–23, 1781; Kinloch Bull Jr., *The Oligarchs in Colonial and Revolutionary Charleston: Lieutenant Governor William Bull II and His Family* (Columbia: University of South Carolina Press, 1991), 298; Wood, "'High Notions,'" 59.

31. "So necessary": William Bull to My Lord, CT, March 22, 1781, *Records in the British Public Records Office Relating to South Carolina,* vol. 36, reel 6 (hereinafter *BPRO/SC*); Wood, "'High Notions,'" 65; Quarles, *Negro,* 139; McCowen, *British Occupation,* 31; Lambert, *South Carolina Loyalists,* 192. See the March 1781 issues of the *SCRG;* and "Employment Lists from the Royal Artillery Department, CT," in the George Wray Papers, William L. Clements Library, University of Michigan, Ann Arbor, Michigan.

32. See the reports signed by Moncrief in the Clinton/MacKenzie Papers, William L. Clements Library, University of Michigan: Report 80 (December 31, 1780), 21/80; Reports 110 and 111 (June 30, 1781), 27/110 and 27/111; Report 172 (June 30, 1782), 3/172; and the James Moncrief Letter Book, 1780–1782. See also Quarles, *Negro,* 138.

33. Wood, "'High Notions,'" 60; Berlin, *Many Thousands Gone,* 295; "found . . . us": David George, "An Account of the Life of David George, from Sierra Leone in Africa," *The Baptist Annual Register for 1790, 1791, 1792, and Part of 1793,* 473–484, http://www.blackloyalist.com/canadiandigitalcollection/documents/diaries/george_a_life.htm (accessed June 20, 2013).

34. *SCAGG,* February 10, 1781; Leila Sellers, *Charleston Business on the Eve of the American Revolution* (Chapel Hill: University of North Carolina Press, 1934), 106–108; Robert Olwell, "'Loose, Idle, and Disorderly': Slave Women in the Eighteenth-Century Charleston Marketplace," in Barry Gaspar and Darlene Clark Hine, eds., *More Than Chattel: Black Women and Slavery in the Americas* (Bloomington: Indiana University Press, 1996), 97–110; "small": *SCRG,* January 30–February 2, 1782; "Rates . . . engrossing": *SCAGG,* February 10, 1781.

35. "I do hereby": *SCAGG,* March 28, 1782; Berlin, *Many Thousands Gone,* 295.

36. "Deranged": William Bull to My Lord, CT, June 28, 1781, *BPRO/SC,* 1776–1782, reel 6; "tak[e]": Francis Marion to Gov. Matthews, Watbo, September 24, 1782, in Gibbes, ed., *Documentary History, 1776–1782,* 232.

37. "Shameful . . . want": Gov. Matthews to Marion, Uxbridge, September 29, 1782, in Gibbes, ed., *Documentary History, 1776–1782,* 215; Governor Rutledge to General Marion, September 2, 1781, in Gibbes, ed., *Documentary History, 1781–1782,* 131.

38. "Steal": Greene to Marion, Dorchester, April 8, 1782, in Gibbes, ed., *Documentary History, 1776–1782,* 246; "flog out . . . plunder": A. R. Newsome, ed., "A British Orderly Book, 1780–1781," Part 3, *NCHR* 9 (July 1932): 276–278; "taken . . . effect": Matthews to Marion, Uxbridge, October 6, 1782, in Gibbes, ed., *Documentary History, 1776–1782,* 232–233.

39. King, "Memoirs" (March 1798), 108–109.

40. "They . . . orders": Harriott Horry Ravenel, *Eliza Pinckney* (New York: Charles Scribner's Sons, 1896), 277–278; James Custer to Henry Laurens, CT, June 1780, *PHL,* 15:303–304.

41. "The natural": Greene to John Rutledge, December 9, 1781, in Dennis M. Conrad, ed., *The Papers of General Nathanael Greene* (Chapel Hill: University of North Carolina Press, 1998), 10:22; "well known": "Reminiscences of Dr. William Read, Arranged from His Notes and Papers," in Gibbes, ed., *Documentary History, 1776–1782,* 267; "one negro": receipt signed by Thomas Sumter, in ibid., 138; Ewald, *Diary,* 305–306; A. S. Salley Jr., ed., *Journal of the Commissioners of the Navy of South Carolina, July 22, 1779–March 23, 1780* (Columbia: Historical Commission of South Carolina, 1912), 23–24; Hemphill et al., eds., *Journals,* 250, 253, 257.

42. "A negro bounty": Dr. Ramsay to William Henry Drayton, CT, September 1, 1779, in Gibbes, ed., *Documentary History, 1776–1782,* 121–122; "to receive": Col. Richard Hampton to Maj. John Hampton, April 2, 1781, in Gibbes, ed., *Documentary History, 1781–1782,* 48; "whether": Matthews to Marion, Cave Okre, May 21, 1782, in Gibbes, ed., *Documentary History, 1776–1782,* 121–122, 176; Quarles, *Negro,* 108–109.

43. Drayton to the Council of Safety, Lawson's Fork, August 21, 1775, in Gibbes, ed., *Documentary History, 1764–1776,* 150; William M. Dabney and Marion Dargan, *William Henry Drayton and the American Revolution* (Albuquerque: University of New Mexico Press, 1962), 89–90; Nadelhaft, *Disorders of War,* 20.

44. "Our brothers": Council of Safety quoted in Kirkland and Kennedy, *Historic Camden,* 111, 12; "word . . . public": Drayton to Francis Salvador, CT, July 24, 1776, in Gibbes, ed., *Documentary History, 1776–1782,* 29; Ramsay, *Ramsay's History,* 2:112.

45. Major Warley to Marion, Camp Congaree, August 11, 1782, in Gibbes, ed., *Documentary History, 1776–1782,* 206; "perpetrated": Lamb Benton to Matthews, St. David's, August 20, 1782, in ibid., 208; "fierce . . . Murderers": Aedanus Burke to Arthur Middleton, May 14, 1782, "Correspondence of Middleton," *SCHM* 26 (October 1925): 201; Kirkland and Kennedy, *Historic Camden,* 212.

46. "Excited . . . Children": Henry Laurens to William McCulloch, Westminster (England), March 9, 1782, *PHL,* 15:471; "Donations . . . Trade," July 26, 1776 (notes of debates on the Articles of Confederation, continued), in L. H. Butterfield, ed., *The Adams Papers,* Series 1: *Diary and Autobiography of John Adams* (Cambridge, MA: Belknap Press, 1961), 243–244; "with such a": Gibbes, ed., *Documentary History, 1764–1776,* 211.

47. "Brigade": Leslie to Clinton, Camp near CT, March 12, 1782, *RAM,* 2:417; "the many": Moncrief to Clinton, CT, March 13, 1782, ibid., 419; "as it appears": Leslie to Clinton, CT, March 1782, ibid., 438; "a very proper": Leslie to Clinton, CT, March 30, 1782, ibid., 435; Moncrief to Sir, CT, March 13, 1782, Moncrief Letter Book, Clements Library; Quarles, *Negro,* 65.

48. "Necessary": quoted in Benjamin Quarles, "The Colonial Militia and Negro Manpower," *MVHR* 45 (March 1959): 643–652; "as a corps": Hemphill et al., eds., *Journals,* 262; Matthews to Marion, Uxbridge, October 6, 1783, in Gibbes, ed., *Documentary History, 1776–1782,* 232; "all subordination": Ramsay, *Ramsay's History,* 1:178.

49. "The number . . . them ": Greene to John Rutledge, December 9, 1781, in Conrad, ed., *Papers of Nathanael Greene,* 10:22; "interest . . . army": ibid., 356; Greene to John Rutledge, Headquarters, February 11, 1782, in Gibbes., ed. *Documentary History, 1781–1782,* 250; "but from": Greene to George Washington, March 9, 1782, in Showman, ed., *Papers of Nathanael Greene,* 7:472; Piecuch, *Three Peoples,* 311–315; Frey, *Water from the Rock,* 78.

50. "An Account of the Negroe Insurrection in South Carolina," in Allen D. Candler, comp., *The Colonial Records of the State of Georgia* (Original Papers, Correspondence, Trustees, General Oglethorpe, and Others, 1737–1740) (Atlanta: Chas. F. Byrd, 1913), 22(pt. 2):232–236.

51. "Several": J. H. Easterby, ed., *The Colonial Records of South Carolina: The Journal of the Commons House of Assembly,* May 18, 1741–July 10, 1742 (Columbia: Historical Commission of South Carolina, 1953), 315; "notwithstanding": "Account of the Negroe Insurrection," 235–236.

52. "Domestic . . . nights": "Governor William Bull's Representation of the Colony, 1770," in H. Roy Merrens, ed., *The Colonial South Carolina Scene: Contemporary Views, 1697–1774* (Columbia: University of South Carolina Press, 1977), 261; William S. Pollitzer, *The Gullah People and Their African Heritage* (Athens: University of Georgia Press, 1999), 43; John K. Thornton, *The Kongolese Saint Anthony: Dona Beatriz Kimpa*

Vita and the Antonian Movement, 1684–1706 (Cambridge: Cambridge University Press, 1998), 113–115; Mark M. Smith, "Remembering Mary, Shaping Revolt: Considering the Stono Rebellion," *JSH* 67 (August 2001): 513–534. Joel S. Berson, "How the Stono Rebels Learned of Britain's War with Spain," *SCHM* 110 (January–April 2009): 53–68. On ethnic dimensions of eighteenth-century slavery, see Michael A. Gomez, *Exchanging Our Country Marks: The Transformation of African Identities in the Colonial and Antebellum South* (Chapel Hill: University of North Carolina Press, 1998); and Gwendolyn Midlo Hall, *Slavery and African Ethnicities in the Americas: Restoring the Links* (Chapel Hill: University of North Carolina Press, 2005).

53. Betty Wood, *Slavery in Colonial America, 1619–1776* (Lanham, MD: Rowman & Littlefield, 2005), 88; John Donald Duncan, "Servitude and Slavery in Colonial South Carolina, 1670–1776" (PhD diss., Emory University, 1992), 587–602; "Our Negroes": Edward A. Pearson, "'A Countryside Full of Flames': A Reconsideration of the Stono Rebellion and Slave Rebelliousness in the Early-Eighteenth-Century South Carolina Lowcountry," *Slavery and Abolition* 17 (August 1996): 37. For discussions of the imbalance in foreign trade, see the correspondence (especially from Henry Laurens) in Elizabeth Donnan, ed., *Documents Illustrative of the History of the Slave Trade to America,* Vol. 4: *The Border Colonies and the Southern Colonies* (Washington, DC: Carnegie Institution, 1935), 235–570.

54. "On this . . . Fortunes": Easterby, ed., *Colonial Records,* 84; Olwell, *Masters, Slaves,* 64–65.

55. W. Robert Higgins, "Ambivalence of Freedom," in Alden and Higgins, eds., *Revolutionary War,* 43–63; Pollitzer, *Gullah People,* 41; Duncan, "Servitude and Slavery," 460–462; Daniel E. Mcaders, "South Carolina Fugitives as Viewed Through Local Colonial Newspapers with an Emphasis on Runaway Notices, 1732–1801," *JNH* 60 (April 1975): 288–319.

56. "A Nation": quoted in Michael Mullin, "British Caribbean and North American Slaves in an Era of War and Revolution," in Jeffrey J. Crow and Larry E. Tise, eds., *The Southern Experience in the American Revolution* (Chapel Hill: University of North Carolina Press, 1978), 254; Gomez, *Exchanging;* Margaret Washington Creel, *"A Peculiar People": Slave Religion and Community-Culture Among the Gullahs* (New York: New York University Press, 1988); Philip D. Morgan, "Work and Culture: The Task System and the World of Lowcountry Blacks, 1700 to 1880," *WMQ,* 3rd series, 39 (October 1982): 573; Sharla M. Fett, *Working Cures: Healing, Health, and Power on Southern Slave Plantations* (Chapel Hill: University of North Carolina Press, 2002); Lorenzo Dow Turner, *Africanisms in the Gullah Dialect* (Chicago: University of Chicago Press, 1949).

57. "Of a barbarous": quoted in Olwell, *Masters, Slaves,* 64–65; Peter Wood, *Black Majority: Negroes in Colonial South Carolina from 1670 Through the Stono Rebellion* (New York: Knopf, 1974), 308–330; Marcus Rediker, *The Slave Ship: A Human History* (New York: Penguin Books, 2007), 36, 367n18; Daniel C. Littlefield, "The Slave Trade to Colonial South Carolina: A Profile," *SCHM* 91 (April 1990): 68–99; Jennifer L. Morgan, *Laboring Women: Reproduction and Gender in New World Slavery* (Philadelphia: University of Pennsylvania Press, 2004); Edmund Morgan, *American Slavery, American Freedom: The Ordeal of Colonial Virginia* (New York: Norton, 1975).

58. "Blow up . . . blood": Marion Tinling, ed., *The Correspondence of Three William Byrds of Westover, Virginia, 1684–1776* (Charlottesville: University of Virginia Press, 1977), 2:487–488; "Impossibility": quoted in Betty Wood, *Slavery in Colonial Georgia, 1730–1775* (Athens: University of Georgia Press, 1984), 42.

59. "Golden": "Account of the Situation, Air, Weather, and Diseases of South Carolina," in B. R. Carroll, comp., *Historical Collections of South Carolina* (New York: Harper & Bros., 1836), 2:468; "*A killing*": Ramsay, *Ramsay's History,* 2:288–289; Stephanie Smallwood, *Saltwater Slavery: A Middle Passage from African to American Diaspora* (Cambridge, MA: Harvard University Press, 2008), 193–197; Leigh Ann Pruneau, "All the Time Is Work Time: Gender and the Task System on Antebellum Lowcountry Plantations" (PhD diss., University of Arizona, 1997); Pollitzer, *Gullah People,* 18; Cheryll Ann Cody, "Cycles of Work and of Childbearing: Seasonality in Women's Lives on Low Country Plantations," in Gaspar and Hine., eds., *More Than Chattel,* 61–78; H. Roy Merrens and George D. Terry, "Dying in Paradise: Malaria, Mortality, and the Perceptual Environment in Colonial South Carolina," *JSH* 50 (November 1984): 533–550.

60. Philip D. Morgan and George D. Terry, "Slavery in Microcosm: A Conspiracy Scare in Colonial South Carolina," *Southern Studies* 21 (1982): 121–145; Olwell, *Masters, Slaves,* 46–47; 213–214; Olwell, "'Loose, Idle, and Disorderly'"; Robert Olwell, "A Reckoning of Accounts: Patriarchy, Market Relations, and Control on Henry Laurens's Lowcountry Plantations, 1762–1785," in Larry E. Hudson Jr., ed., *Working Toward Freedom: Slave Society and Domestic Economy in the American South* (Rochester, NY: University of Rochester Press, 1994); Sellers, *Charleston Business,* 97–108, 178–202.

61. "I . . . mercy": George, "Life of David George"; Creel, *"A Peculiar People,"* 73–74; Olwell, *Masters, Slaves,* 128, 134; Faith Vibert, "The Society for the Propagation of the Gospel in Foreign Parts: Its Work for the Negroes in North America Before 1783," *JNH* 18 (April 1933): 182–205.

62. Sylviane A. Diouf, *Servants of Allah: African Muslims Enslaved in the Americas* (New York: New York University Press, 1998); Michael A. Gomez, *Black Crescent: The Experience and Legacy of African Muslims in the Americas* (Cambridge: Cambridge University Press, 2005); Sylvia Frey and Betty Wood, *Come Shouting to Zion: African American Protestantism in the American South and British Caribbean to 1830* (Chapel Hill: University of North Carolina Press, 1998), 8, 82; Smallwood, *Saltwater Slavery,* 186, 201; Pollitzer, *Gullah People,* 140–143; "the sea": quoted in ibid., 184.

63. "Strainge": Thomas Griffiths, "A Journal of the Voyage to South Carolina in the Year 1767," in Merrens, ed., *Colonial South Carolina,* 242; T. H. Breen, *The Marketplace of Revolution: How Consumer Politics Shaped American Independence* (New York: Oxford University Press, 2004), 56–57.

64. Olwell, *Masters, Slaves,* 224; "Journal of Josiah Quincy, Jr., 1773," *Historical Society Proceedings* 49 (June 1916): 424–481; Wallace, *History of South Carolina,* 1:394; Richard Waterhouse, *A New World Gentry: The Making of a Merchant and Planter Class in South Carolina, 1670–1770* (New York: Garland, 1989); Rodis Roth, "Tea Drinking in 18th-Century America: Its Etiquette and Equipage," *CMHT,* Bulletin 225, Paper 14 (1961).

65. "Opulent": "Journal of Josiah Quincy," 454; "Journal of an Officer who Travelled in America and the West Indies in 1764 and 1765," in Newton D. Mereness, ed., *Travels in the American Colonies* (New York: Macmillan, 1916), 399; Waterhouse, *New World Gentry,* 92, 103; A. S. Salley, ed., "Diary of William Dillwyn During a Visit to Charles Town in 1772," *SCHM* 36 (July 1935): 73; Ellen Hartigan-O'Connor, *The Ties That Buy: Women and Commerce in Revolutionary America* (Philadelphia: University of Pennsylvania Press, 2011).

66. Hartigan-O'Connor, *Ties That Buy;* "Journal of Josiah Quincy," 443; A. S. Salley, ed., "Diary of William Dillwyn During a Visit to Charles Town in 1772," *SCHM* 36 (April 1935): 31, 34.

67. "Their darling": Tennent quoted in Hartigan-O'Connor, *Ties That Buy,* 162; "it is": Christopher Gadsden to General Marion, in John Bennett, ed., "Marion-Gadsden Correspondence," *SCHM* 41 (April 1940): 53; "if there": Gadsden to Marion, in ibid., 57; "The luxury": "Journal of Josiah Quincy," 453; "haughty . . . else": "View of Coastal South Carolina," 186.

68. Hartigan O'Connor, *Ties That Buy,* 22; "Negroes": Philip D. Morgan, "Black Life in Eighteenth-Century Charleston," *Perspectives in American History* 1 (1984): 198–199, 208–215; Duncan, "Servitude and Slavery," 499–504; Walter J. Fraser Jr., "The City Elite, 'Disorder,' and Poor Children of Pre-Revolutionary Charleston," *SCHM* 84 (July 1983): 167–179.

69. "Mimick'd": *PHL,* 5:53–54; "through": quoted in Peter H. Wood, "'Liberty Is Sweet': African-American Freedom Struggles in the Years Before White Independence," in Alfred Young, ed., *Beyond the American Revolution: Explorations in the History of American Radicalism* (DeKalb: Northern Illinois University Press, 1993), 155; "that God": quoted in Olwell, *Masters, Slaves,* 132.

70. "The cause": Wood, "'Liberty Is Sweet,'" 159; "burned . . . justice": quoted in William R. Ryan, *The World of Thomas Jeremiah: Charles Town on the Eve of the American Revolution* (New York: Oxford University Press, 2010), 67.

71. *SCAGG,* July 30, 1778.

72. "The men": "Regimental Orders by Lieut.-Col. Marion," in Gibbes, ed., *Documentary History, 1776–1782,* 61; "oblige . . . citizens": C. Pinckney Jun. to Mrs. C. Pinckney, CT, February 24, 1779, in ibid., 106–108.

73. Exchange recorded in George Livermore, "Historical Research Respecting the Opinions of the Founders of the Republic on Negroes—as Slaves, as Citizens, and as Soldiers" (Boston: John Wilson and Son, 1862), 69–70. For Rutledge's leading role in the debate, see David Waldstreicher, *Slavery's Constitution* (New York: Hill and Wang, 2009), 78, 90–99.

74. "No man . . . freedom": "The President's Speech to Both Houses, April 11, 1776," in Gibbes, ed., *Documentary History, 1764–1776,* 275; "We rather": Camden District Grand Jury quoted in Kirkland and Kennedy, *Historic Camden,* 107; Frey, *Water from the Rock,* 78. For a discussion of the use of slavery as a metaphor for the plight of the colonies vis-à-vis England, see Bernard Bailyn, *Ideological Origins of the American Revolution* (Cambridge, MA: Harvard University Press, 1992), 233–246.

75. Greene, "'Slavery or Independence,'" 23–24; Thomas Jefferson, *Notes on the State of Virginia,* ed. by David Waldstreicher (Boston: Bedford/St. Martin's Press, 2002), 29–32; Peter S. Onuf, *Jefferson's Empire: The Language of American Nationhood* (Char-

lottesville: University of Virginia Press, 2000); "A Circular Letter to the Committees in the Several Districts and Parishes of South Carolina, CT, June 30, 1775," in Gibbes, ed., *Documentary History, 1764–1776,* 111.

76. "British . . . mankind": "The First Remonstrance from South Carolina Against the Stamp Act," September 4, 1764, CT, in Gibbes, ed., *Documentary History, 1764–1776,* 3; "the fundamental . . . possess": "A Letter from 'Freeman' of South Carolina to the Deputies of North America, Assembled in the High Court of Congress at Philadelphia," in ibid., 34. See also Harris, *Hanging of Thomas Jeremiah,* 63; Olwell, *Masters, Slaves*; T. H. Breen, "Ideology and Nationalism on the Eve of the American Revolution: Revisions Once More in Need of Revising," *JAH* 84 (June 1997): 13–29; and James Haw, *John and Edward Rutledge of South Carolina* (Athens: University of Georgia Press, 1997).

77. "I . . . estate": Henry Laurens to John Laurens, August 14, 1776, *PHL,* 11:224–225; Gregory Massey, *John Laurens and the American Revolution* (Columbia: University of South Carolina Press, 2000); Robert J. Hargrove, "Portrait of a Southern Patriot: The Life and Death of John Laurens," in Alden and Higgins, eds., *Revolutionary War,* 182–202.

78. "Cede . . . soldiers": John Laurens to Henry Laurens, January 14, 1778, Hdqtrs, in William G. Simms, ed., *The Army Correspondence of Colonel John Laurens, in the Years 1777–8* (New York: Bradford Club, 1867), 7:108–109; "capable . . . tyrants": in ibid., February 2, 1778, 115–117.

79. "That monstrous": John Laurens to Henry Laurens, Hdqtrs, February 2, 1778, *PHL,* 12:115; "black Air": Henry Laurens to John Laurens, Philadelphia, September 27, 1779, *PHL,* 15:177; Quarles, *Negro,* 66; "very dangerous": Gadsden quoted in *PHL,* 15:65; "received": David Ramsay to William Henry Drayton, September 1, 1779, CT, in Gibbes, ed., *Documentary History, 1776–1782,* 121; "very much . . . Argument": E. Rutledge to Arthur Middleton, Jacksonborough, February 8, 1782, "Correspondence of Middleton," *SCHM* 27 (January 1926): 4.

80. Jefferson, *Notes,* 31–32, 35, 67–70.

81. "Politic": "A Description of Carolina," *Historical Collections of South Carolina,* 2:531; Ramsay, *Ramsay's History,* 1:65; ibid., 2:205, 216–217, 445–459, 540; "horse thieves": Aedanus Burke to Arthur Middleton, May 14, 1782, "Correspondence of Middleton," *SCHM* 26 (October 1925): 204; "scum": S. F. Warren, St. James Santee, January 22, 1766, in Merrens, ed., *Colonial South Carolina,* 234; "a Shame": George Milligen-Johnston, "A Description of South Carolina," in ibid., 187; "a pack": Rutledge quoted in Dabney and Dargan, *William Henry Drayton,* 89; "When a solider . . . duty": Extract from the Orderly Book of Charles Lining, December 28, 1775, in Gibbes, ed., *Documentary History, 1764–1776,* 244–245; "relaxness": Matthews to Middleton, "Correspondence of Middleton (Con't)," *SCHM* 27 (April 1926): 69; "refus[ing] . . . collectively": Col. Davis to Gen. Marion, Prince Williams' Parish, August 24, 1782, in Gibbes, ed., *Documentary History, 1776–1782,* 212.

82. "Every . . . custody": Bennett, ed., "Marion-Gadsden Correspondence," 49; "told": ibid., 54; Frey, *Water from the Rock,* 178.

83. "Sequestered . . . dispose": Leslie to Sir Guy Carleton, October 3, 1782, CT, *RAM,* 3:150; Pybus, "Jefferson's Faulty Math"; Edward McCrady, *The History of South Carolina in the Revolution, 1780–1783* (New York: Macmillan, 1902), 660–661; Eldon

Jones, "The British Withdrawal from the South," in Alden and Higgins, eds., *Revolutionary War,* 260; Lambert, *South Carolina Loyalists,* 227–256; McCowen, *British Occupation,* 131–150.

84. "Officers": Leslie to Sir Guy Carleton, October 18, 1782, *RAM,* 3:175–176; Pybus, "Jefferson's Faulty Math"; Carole Watterson Troxler, "Re-Enslavement of Black Loyalists: Mary Postell in South Carolina, East Florida, and Nova Scotia," *Acadiensis* 37 (Summer–Autumn 2008): 74; Joseph W. Barnwell, "The Evacuation of Charleston by the British in 1782," *SCHM* 11 (January 1910): 9, 22–24.

85. Barnwell, "Evacuation of Charleston," 26; Doyle et al., *Beyond the Fields,* 45.

86. Graham Russell Hodges, *Slavery, Freedom, and Culture Among Early American Workers* (Armonk, NY: M. E. Sharpe, 1998), 65–86; Graham Russell Hodges, ed., *The Black Loyalist Directory: African Americans in Exile After the American Revolution* (New York: Garland, 1996), xvii; Cassandra Pybus, *Epic Journeys of Freedom: Runaway Slaves of the American Revolution and Their Global Quest for Liberty* (Boston: Beacon Press, 2006), 26–32; Wilbur C. Abbott, *New York in the American Revolution* (New York: Charles Scribner's Sons, 1929), 229.

87. King, "Memoirs" (March 1798), 109–110, (April 1798), 157.

88. "This dreadful": ibid. (April 1798), 157; "had raised": Rawlins Lowndes to Sir Guy Carleton, August 8, 1782, CT, *RAM,* 3:60; "materially": Mackenzie to Lowndes, September 9, 1782, ibid., 111; Quarles, *Negro,* 164; Peggy Gwynn, negro, to Sir Guy Carleton, "Petition," no date, *RAM,* 4:465; *NYRG,* August 21, 1782, October 22, 1783.

89. King, "Memoirs" (April 1798), 157. See also the "Book of Negroes," http://www.blackloyalist.com/canadiandigitalcollection/documents/official/black_loyalist_directory_book_two.htm (accessed June 20, 2013). Based on their names, of the 133 blacks on board *L'Abondance,* 36 sailed as individuals, 38 in pairs, 27 in groups of three, and 32 in groups of four. Their origins included Pennsylvania, New York, Virginia, New Jersey, Maryland, North Carolina, Massachusetts, South Carolina, and Barbados.

90. See "Book of Negroes"; Lambert, *South Carolina Loyalists,* 242; Abbott, *New York,* 267–271, 281; Pybus, *Epic Journeys;* and Mary Beth Norton, "The Fate of Some Black Loyalists of the American Revolution," *JNH* 58 (October 1973): 402–426.

91. Many of the officers were listed as belonging to KAD, presumably King's American Division. Descriptions culled from the "Book of Negroes," *L'Abondance* passengers.

92. Pybus, *Epic Journeys,* 144–148; Ellen Gibson Wilson, *The Loyal Blacks* (New York: Capricorn, 1976), 62–131; Troxler, "Re-Enslavement," 82; John W. Pulis, ed., *Moving On: Black Loyalists in the Afro-Atlantic World* (New York: Garland, 1999); Neil MacKinnon, *This Unfriendly Soil: The Loyalist Experience in Nova Scotia, 1783–1791* (Kingston, ONT: McGill-Queen's University Press, 1986); John N. Grant, "Black Immigrants into Nova Scotia, 1776–1814," *JNH* 58 (July 1973): 253–270. Several scholars have pointed out that blacks who worked for the British, or evacuated of their own free will with the British, cannot be called "loyalists," which implies political or ideological support for the Crown's position in the war. See Barry Cahill, "The Black Loyalist Myth in Atlantic Canada," *Acadiensis* 29 (Autumn 1999): 76–87.

93. "Set . . . Lord": King, "Memoirs" (April 1798), 158; "killed": ibid. (May 1798), 209.

94. George, "Life of David George."

95. "Contributing": King, "Memoirs" (June 1798), 261; Schama, *Rough Crossings,* 321–322; James Sidbury, *Becoming African in America: Race and Nation in the Early Black Atlantic* (New York: Oxford University Press, 2007); Hodges, ed., *Black Loyalist Directory,* xxxv; Pybus, *Epic Journeys,* 169–202.

96. "Uneasy": King, "Memoirs" (June 1798), 264; Berlin, *Many Thousands Gone,* 305–324.

97. See, for example, G. J. Barker-Benfield, *Abigail and John Adams: The Americanization of Sensibility* (Chicago: University of Chicago Press, 2010).

98. Rachel Klein, *Unification of a Slave State: The Rise of the Planter Class in the South Carolina Backcountry, 1760–1808* (Chapel Hill: University of North Carolina Press, 1990).

99. "An Ordinance . . . and night": *SCGGA,* November 22, 1783.

CHAPTER 3 ELLEANOR ELDRIDGE

1. "Hard-Scrabble Calendar: Report of the Trials of Oliver Cummins, Nathaniel G. Metcalf, Gilbert Humes, and Arthur Farrier: Who Were Indicted . . . " (Providence, RI: For the Purchaser, 1824); "badly shattered": ibid.,10; "It was . . . hard": ibid., 23; "made himself": ibid., 7; "he had": ibid., 13; "the proceedings . . . ruins": ibid., 12. For accounts of the riot, see Joanne Pope Melish, *Disowning Slavery: Gradual Emancipation and Race in New England, 1780–1860* (Ithaca, NY: Cornell University Press, 1998), 204–205; Howard Chudacoff and Theodore C. Hirt, "Social Turmoil and Governmental Reform in Providence, 1820–1832," *RIH* 31 (February 1972): 21–33; Gabriel J. Loiacono, "Poverty and Citizenship in Rhode Island, 1780–1870" (PhD diss., Brandeis University, 2008), 113–119; John Wood Sweet, *Bodies Politic: Negotiating Race in the American North, 1730–1830* (Baltimore, MD: Johns Hopkins University Press, 2003), 353–597; and Jacqueline Jones, *American Work: Four Centuries of Black and White Labor* (New York: Norton, 1998), 246–248.

2. "Hard-Scrabble Calendar," 13, 18, 23.

3. Ibid., 16, 18.

4. Ibid., 26.

5. Jeffrey Bolster, *Black Jacks: African American Seamen in the Age of Sail* (Cambridge, MA: Harvard University Press, 1998), 184–185; *PG,* March 17, 1824; Sweet, *Bodies Politic,* 353–397.

6. *PG,* July 28, 1824.

7. "Determined . . . labour": "Our Black Population," *Beacon* (Providence), October 16, 1824. See also Dallett C. Hemphill, *Bowing to Necessities: A History of Manners in America, 1620–1860* (New York: Oxford University Press, 1999), 143; and Welcome Arnold Greene, *The Providence Plantations for Two Hundred and Fifty Years* (Providence, RI: J. A. and R. A. Reid, 1886), 74.

8. "A pious man": William J. Brown, *The Life of William J. Brown of Providence, R. I., With Personal Recollections of Incidents in Rhode Island,* with Foreword by Rosalind C. Wiggins and Introduction by Joanne Pope Melish (Durham: University of New Hampshire Press, [1883] 2006), 50; James Sidbury, *Becoming African in America: Race and Nation in the Early Black Atlantic* (New York: Oxford University Press, 2007), 13, 166–177, 181–193.

9. Sweet, *Bodies Politic,* 363; "taxation . . . 'can't be'": Brown, *Life of William J. Brown,* 48; Melish, *Disowning Slavery,* 84–188; Robert J. Cottrol, *The Afro-Yankees: Providence's Black Community in the Antebellum Era* (Westport, CT: Greenwood Press, 1982), 8, 42–43, 69; Irene Burnham, Linda Coleman, Rhett Jones, and Jay Coughtry, *Creative Survival: The Providence Black Community in the Nineteenth Century* (Providence, RI: Black Heritage Society, 1984). The other states were New Jersey (1807), Connecticut (1818), New York (1821), and Pennsylvania (1838).

10. "Had little": Brown, *Life of William J. Brown,* 73; "the order": ibid., 50; ibid., 63; Jones, *American Work,* 258–270; Lorenzo Johnston Greene, *The Negro in Colonial New England* (New York: Athenaeum, [1942] 1968); Joseph W. Sullivan, "Reconstructing the Olney's Lane Riot: Another Look at Race and Class in Jacksonian Rhode Island," *RIH* 65 (Summer 2007): 55; Burnham et al., *Creative Survival,* 43–46, 55.

11. Gary Kulik, "Factory Discipline in the New Nation: Almy, Brown & Slater and the First Cotton-Mill Workers, 1790–1808," *Massachusetts Review* 1 (Spring 1987): 164–184; Jones, *American Work,* 157–160; Barbara M. Tucker, *Samuel Slater and the Origins of the American Textile Industry, 1790–1860* (Ithaca, NY: Cornell University Press, 1984); Morton Keller, *America's Three Regimes: A New Political History* (New York: Oxford University Press, 2007), 67–132.

12. James L. Marsis, "Agrarian Politics in Rhode Island, 1800–1860," *RIH* 34 (February 1975): 13–21.

13. Karen E. Fields and Barbara J. Fields, *Racecraft: The Soul of Inequality in American Life* (London: Verso Books, 2012), 17–23.

14. "Brothers": Peter P. Hinks, *To Awaken My Afflicted Brethren: David Walker and the Problem of Antebellum Slave Resistance* (University Park: Penn State University Press, 1996), 71–73; Stephen Kantrowitz, "'Intended for the Better Government of Man': The Political History of African American Freemasonry in the Era of Emancipation," *JAH* 96 (March 2010): 1001–1026; Corey D. B. Walker, *A Noble Fight: African American Freemasonry and the Struggle for Democracy in America* (Urbana: University of Illinois Press, 2008); Patrick Rael, *Black Identity and Black Protest in the Antebellum North* (Chapel Hill: University of North Carolina Press, 2002); Robert Glenn Sherer Jr., "Negro Churches in Providence Before 1860," *RIH* 25 (January 1966): 9–25.

15. "It is . . . above you": Hosea Easton, "An Address," in George R. Price and James Brewer Stewart, eds., *To Heal the Scourge of Prejudice: The Life and Writings of Hosea Easton* (Amherst: University of Massachusetts Press, 1999), 62.

16. David Walker, *Walker's Appeal, in Four Articles; Together with a Preamble, to the Coloured Citizens of the World, but in Particular, and Very Expressly, to Those of the United States of America, Written in Boston, State of Massachusetts, September 28, 1829* (Boston: self-published, 1829), 2, 4, http://docsouth.unc.edu/nc/walker/walker.html (accessed June 20, 2013).

17. Walker, *Walker's Appeal,* 23, 24, 34, 68. See also Bruce R. Dain, *A Hideous Monster of the Mind: American Race Theory in the Early Republic* (Cambridge, MA: Harvard University Press, 2002); Hinks, *To Awaken My Afflicted Brethren*; Sidbury, *Becoming African,* 203–204; Joanne Pope Melish review of Dain, *Hideous Monster, WMQ,* 3rd series, 60 (October 2003): 895–899.

18. "To the savage": "Insurrection of the Blacks," *PP/CP,* August 31, 1831; "Insurrection of the Blacks in Virginia," *RIA,* August 30, 1831; Larry Tise, *Proslavery: A*

History of the Defense of Slavery in America, 1701–1840 (Athens: University of Georgia Press, 1987); Michael T. Gilmore, "Free Speech and the American Renaissance," *Raritan* (Fall 2006): 90–113. See also the following *RIA* issues for 1831: September 16, September 20, and September 30.

19. "History of the Providence Riots, from Sept. 21 to Sept. 24, 1831" (Providence, RI: H. H. Brown, 1831), 7, 8, 9. See also Sullivan, "Reconstructing"; and "Riot and Murder," *RIA,* September 23, 1831.

20. "History of the Providence Riots," 13, 14, 15. See also "Riot," *RIA,* September 27, 1831.

21. "Disorderly . . . authorities": "History of the Providence Riots," 5; "It was": "Town Meeting on Sunday," *PP/CP,* September 28, 1831; "City Charter," *RIA,* October 4, 1831.

22. Tise, *Proslavery,* 275–285; Emma Jones Lapsansky, "'Since They Got Those Separate Churches': Afro-Americans and Racism in Jacksonian Philadelphia," *AQ* 32 (Spring 1980): 54–78; Leonard L. Richards, *Gentlemen of Property and Standing: Anti-Abolition Mobs in Jacksonian America* (New York: Oxford University Press, 1970); Paul A. Gilje, *The Road to Mobocracy: Popular Disorder in New York City, 1763–1834* (Chapel Hill: University of North Carolina Press, 1987), 145–165; David Grimsted, "Rioting in Its Jacksonian Setting," *AHR* (April 1972): 361–397; "self-preservation": *The Liberator,* February 15, 1834.

23. *PG,* October 23, 1824.

24. Walker, *Walker's Appeal,* 11–12.

25. [Frances Whipple,] *Memoirs of Elleanor Eldridge* (Providence, RI: B. T. Albro, 1838).

26. Sarah C. O'Dowd, *Rhode Island Original: Frances Harriet Whipple Green McDougall* (Lebanon, NH: University Press of New England, 2004); "souls": Louisa May Alcott, *Work* (New York: Penguin Books, [1873] 1994), 9, 13.

27. *NBM,* January 11, 1839. See also Loiacono, "Poverty and Citizenship," 197–205.

28. "Indigent and obscure": [Whipple,] *Memoirs,* 11, http://docsouth.unc.edu/neh/eldridge/eldridge.html (accessed June 20, 2013); O'Dowd, *Rhode Island Original,* 1–31.

29. William Shakespeare, *Merchant of Venice,* Act 2, scene 9.

30. "Elleanor's documents": [Whipple,] *Memoirs,* 36; Sweet, *Bodies Politic,* 79–82. I am grateful to Jane Lancaster, who has done extensive research in court records, for providing a copy of her essay "A Web of Iniquity? Race, Gender, Class, and Respectability in Antebellum Rhode Island" before it was published (*RIH* 69 [Summer–Fall 2011]: 72–92). Census information from the author's review of the FMC for 1790–1860, Rhode Island.

31. Lancaster, "Web," 76–77; "Elleanor Eldridge": [Whipple,] *Memoirs,* 11–12; Jennifer D. Brody and Sharon P. Holland, "An/Other Case of New England Underwriting: Negotiating Race and Property in the *Memoirs of Elleanor Eldridge,*" in Tiya Miles and Sharon Patricia Holland, eds., *Crossing Waters, Crossing Worlds: The African Diaspora in Indian Country* (Durham, NC: Duke University Press, 2006), 31–56.

32. [Whipple,] *Memoirs,* 12, 16.

33. Jay Coughtry, *The Notorious Triangle: Rhode Island and the African Slave Trade, 1700–1807* (Philadelphia: Temple University Press, 1981); J. Stanley Lemons, "Rhode

Island and the Slave Trade," *RIH* 60 (Fall 2002): 95–104; Christy Millard Nadalin, "The Last Years of the Rhode Island Slave Trade," *RIH* 54 (May 1996): 35–49.

34. Sweet, *Bodies Politic,* 4; Daniel R. Mandell, *Tribe, Race, History: Native Americans in Southern New England, 1780–1880* (Baltimore, MD: Johns Hopkins University Press, 2008); Louis P. Masur, "Slavery in Eighteenth-Century Rhode Island: Evidence from the Census of 1774," *Slavery and Abolition* 6 (September 1985): 139–150.

35. "Presented . . . fathers": [Whipple,] *Memoirs,* 17, 19; Lorenzo Johnston Greene, "Some Observations on the Black Regiment of Rhode Island in the American Revolution," *JNH* 37 (April 1952): 142–172; Sidney S. Rider, *An Historical Inquiry Concerning the Attempt to Raise a Regiment of Slaves by Rhode Island During the War of the Revolution . . .* (Providence, RI: S. S. Rider, 1880); William C. Nell, *The Colored Patriots of the American Revolution* (Boston: Wallcut, 1855), chap. 4.

36. Rider, *Historical Inquiry,* 63; Sweet, *Bodies Politic,* 223; "literally": [Whipple,] *Memoirs,* 18; "that such faithful": quoted in Greene, "Some Observations," 171. On the New York land grants, see Anthony F. Gero, *Black Soldiers of New York State: A Proud Legacy* (Albany: State University of New York Press, 2009), 8–9; and Lloyd DeWitt Bockstruck, *Revolutionary War Bounty Land Grants: Awarded by State Governments* (Baltimore, MD: Genealogical Publishing, 2006).

37. "Oh LIBERTY": [Whipple,] *Memoirs,* 18; "the sole . . . world": "American Colonization Society," *New-England Magazine* (January 1832): 16.

38. "Where": [Whipple,] *Memoirs,* 19–20; Lancaster, "Web," 75–77; Warwick (Rhode Island) Town Council Records, MSS 221, box no. 2, folder no. 2, Rhode Island Historical Society Library, Providence, Rhode Island; Mandell, *Tribe, Race, History,* 16–19, xxii, 30–36; Brown, *Life of William J. Brown,* 4; Sweet, *Bodies Politic,* 26–33, 45, 52; Paul R. Campbell and Glenn W. LaFantasie, "Scattered to the Winds of Heaven: Narragansett Indians, 1676–1880," *RIH* 37 (August 1978): 67–69; Ann Marie Plane, *Colonial Intimacies: Indian Marriage in Early New England* (Ithaca, NY: Cornell University Press, 2002), 148; Ruth Wallis Herndon and Ella Wilcox Sekatu, "The Right to a Name: The Narragansett People and Rhode Island Officials in the Revolutionary Era," and Jean M. O'Brien, "'Divorced from the Land: Resistance and Survival of Indian Women in Eighteenth-Century New England," both in Colin G. Colloway, ed., *After King Philip's War: Presence and Persistence in Indian New England* (Hanover, NH: University Press of New England, 1997), 114–157.

39. Brody and Holland, "An/Other Case," 41.

40. FMC for 1790, Rhode Island, Kent County, Warwick; Lancaster, "Web," 76–77.

41. [Whipple,] *Memoirs,* 21, 22, 24. On child labor during this period, see Ruth Wallis Herndon, *Bound to Labor: Pauper Apprenticeship in Early America* (Ithaca, NY: Cornell University Press, 2009); and Brown, *Life of William J. Brown,* 32–42.

42. "Servant problem": a generic nineteenth-century term; "kind . . . them": [Whipple,] *Memoirs,* 26–27; Faye E. Dudden, *Serving Women: Household Service in Nineteenth-Century America* (Middletown, CT: Wesleyan University Press, 1985).

43. "All the . . . developed": [Whipple,] *Memoirs,* 29–30; Lancaster, "Web," 77.

44. Laurel Thatcher Ulrich, "Wheels, Looms, and the Gender Division of Labor in Eighteenth-Century New England," *WMQ,* 3rd series, 55 (January 1998): 3–38; Claudia Goldin and Kenneth Sokoloff, "Women, Children, and Industrialization in

the Early Republic: Evidence from the Manufacturing Censuses," *JEH* 42 (December 1982): 741–774; Jones, *American Work,* 258–270.

45. "From four . . . subject": [Whipple,] *Memoirs,* 31; Albert E. Lownes, "Cheese-Making in Old South County," *Rhode Island Historical Society Collections* 28 (January 1935): 21–24; Lancaster, "Web," 77.

46. FMC for 1800, Rhode Island, Kent County, Warwick; Masur, "Slavery"; "quite a belle": [Whipple,] *Memoirs,* 31; Greene, *Negro,* 249–254; Shane White, "'It Was a Proud Day': African Americans, Festivals, and Parades in the North, 1741–1834," *JAH* 81 (June 1994): 13–50; Joseph P. Reidy, "Negro Election Day and Black Community Life in New England, 1750–1860," *MP* 1 (Fall 1978): 102–117; William D. Johnston, *Slavery in Rhode Island* (Providence: Rhode Island Historical Society, 1894), 31–32.

47. "The very . . . &c-": [Whipple,] *Memoirs,* 33; Melish, *Disowning Slavery,* 45; "shining": Melvin Wade, "'Shining in Borrowed Plumage': Affirmation of Community in the Black Coronation Festivals in New England (c. 1750–1850)," *WF* 40 (July 1981): 211–231.

48. "No fair . . . lassie": [Whipple,] *Memoirs,* 33, 36; Brody and Holland, "An/Other Case," 44.

49. "There was . . . so": [Whipple,] *Memoirs,* 38–39; Lancaster, "Web," 78; O'Dowd, *Rhode Island Original,* 105–117; [Whipple,] *Memoirs,* 40–41, 52, 58–59; Martha S. Putney, "Black Merchant Seamen of Newport, 1803–1865: A Case Study in Foreign Commerce," *JNH* 57 (April 1972): 156–168.

50. "Robin . . . Adams": [Whipple,] *Memoirs,* 42–43, 51; Mandell, *Tribe, Race, History,* 41.

51. "There was . . . heart": [Whipple,] *Memoirs,* 61; Lee Virginia Chambers-Schiller, *Liberty a Better Husband—Single Women in America: The Generations of 1780–1840* (New Haven, CT: Yale University Press, 1984).

52. [Whipple,] *Memoirs,* 100.

53. "Alterations . . . business": ibid., 62; Burnham et al., *Creative Survival,* 40–45; Xiomara Santamarina, *Belabored Professions: Narratives of African-American Working Womanhood* (Chapel Hill: University of North Carolina Press, 2009), 12, 104; Juliet E. K. Walker, *The History of Black Business in America: Capitalism, Race, and Entrepreneurship,* 2nd ed. (Chapel Hill: University of North Carolina Press, 2009), 1:164–193, 201–206.

54. [Whipple,] *Memoirs,* 62–63.

55. John S. Gilkeson Jr., *Middle-Class Providence, 1820–1940* (Princeton, NJ: Princeton University Press, 1986), 18; Greene, *Providence Plantations,* 70–75; Paul G. Bourcier, "Prosperity at the Wharves: Providence Shipping, 1780–1850," *RIH* 48 (May 1990): 35–49.

56. Melish, *Disowning Slavery,* 127; Burnham et al., *Creative Survival,* 39; Robert P. Emlen, "The Great Gale of 1815: Artifactual Evidence of Rhode Island's First Hurricane," *RIH* 48 (May 1990): 51–61; O'Dowd, *Rhode Island Original,* 9–10.

57. "Vicious . . . *inhabitant*": "To the Editor of the Journal," *PG,* September 5, 1821; Sweet, *Bodies Politic,* 308–309.

58. "Commenced": [Whipple,] *Memoirs,* 63. For ads for fancy wallpapers, see *PP/CP,* September 16, 1817, July 7, September 28, and October 29, 1824.

59. [Whipple,] *Memoirs,* 64; Lancaster, "Web," 82. Biographical information on Eldridge's employers and the sponsors of the *Memoirs* has been gleaned from city directories, birth and death records, census data, tax records, local newspapers, and other material contained on ancestry.com, a searchable Web site of biographical and genealogical information.

60. "Occasioned . . . divinity": [Whipple,] *Memoirs,* 64–66; FMC for 1820, Rhode Island, Kent County, Warwick; Warwick, Rhode Island, Town Council Records and Meeting Records, MSS 221, series 1, subseries 2 and 3, 1790–1820 ("Colored People"), Rhode Island Historical Society Library.

61. "Public . . . them": "Public Notice," *PP/CP,* July 26, 1820; Dudden, *Serving Women,* 34.

62. Sidney S. Rider, "Bibliographical Memoir of Frances H. McDougall born Whipple," *Rhode Island Historical Tracts* No. 11 (1880): 35.

63. "Single . . . House": Deed ("William C. Clarke to Eleanor Eldridge") for $320, signed May 18, 1826, Court Records from the State of Rhode Island and Providence Plantations, Supreme Court, Judicial Records Center, Pawtucket, Rhode Island (hereinafter JRC); Lancaster, "Web," 82; "with its . . . aspect": [Whipple,] *Memoirs,* 69; "a fine . . . garden-spot": [Frances Harriet Green,] *Elleanor's Second Book* (Providence, RI: B. T. Albro, 1842), 5; Brown, *Life of William J. Brown,* 91–3. See Eldridge's tenants in the FMC for 1850, Rhode Island, Providence County, Providence.

64. Lancaster, "Web," 82; Cottrol, *Afro-Yankees,* 120–126.

65. [Whipple,] *Memoirs,* 68; "notice," *PP/CP,* October 20, 1830; FMC for 1830, Rhode Island, Providence County, Providence; Lancaster, "Web," 82. On Carder, see *PP/CP,* March 31, 1819; and *RIA,* February 21, 1831, March 19, 1824, February 21, 1832.

66. "Again seized": [Whipple,] *Memoirs,* 71; Lancaster, "Web," 84.

67. [Whipple,] *Memoirs,* 72, 75.

68. Ibid., 76–84; Lancaster, "Web," 84–85.

69. *RIA,* October 6 and October 8, 1824; [Whipple,] *Memoirs,* 77; Lancaster, "Web," 84.

70. "Having horse-whipped": [Whipple,] *Memoirs,* 97; "with force . . . murder": "Indictment: The State v. George Eldridge," August term, 1835 (defendant pleads not guilty), JRC; "in a state": [Whipple,] *Memoirs,* 98; "was there . . . trouble": ibid., 99; Lancaster, "Web," 85; "Recognizance State v. George Eldridge," at East Greenwich, RI, May 17, 1832, JRC.

71. Elleanor Eldridge to Albert C. Greene, Esquire, Providence, February 18, 1838, Albert C. Greene Papers, MSS 452, box 2, folder 9, Rhode Island Historical Society Library.

72. Lancaster, "Web," 85; FMC for 1830 and 1850, Rhode Island, Kent County, Warwick; summonses for witnesses to appear in *The State v. George Eldredge,* August 25, 1832, E. Burke, deputy sheriff (includes statements from witnesses re: travel expenses, length of time they spent in court, and related financial accounts), August terms, 1832 and 1833, JRC.

73. Promissory note for $376, Elleanor Eldridge to George Carder, February 20, 1834, Warren Arnold, witness, JRC; "wanton . . . woods": [Whipple,] *Memoirs,* 81–83. See copy of writ, *John Carder v. Elenor Eldridge,* January 20, 1835, signed by W. Bray-

ton Mann, deputy sheriff, and Charles F. Tillinghast (Carder's lawyer and a distant kinsman to Joseph), JRC. See also Court of Common Pleas Declaration, *John Carder vs. Ellnor Eldridge,* May term, 1835 (he was suing her for $800), January 25, 1835, JRC; and [Whipple,] *Memoirs,* 85–86. The deed reads "William B. Mann [sheriff] to Benjamin Balch, Sept. 16, 1835," JRC.

74. Rider, "Bibliographical Memoir," 37. Joseph L. Tillinghast is listed as Eldridge's attorney in the case *Elleanor Eldridge v. Benjamin Balch,* signed by J. L. Tillinghast, plaintiff's attorney, May term, 1836, Providence Court of Common Pleas, JRC; Lancaster, "Web," 86. For examples of estates owned by deceased women of color announced under "Public Notices" in the local paper, see *PP/CP,* June 5, 1822 (Comfort Ephraim), and March 22, 1826 (Lucy Brown).

75. "With force and arms": *Elleanor Eldridge v. Benjamin Balch;* "it was found": [Whipple,] *Memoirs,* 88. For various "notices" announcing sales of estates belonging to deceased women of color, see *PP/CP,* April 12, 1826, April 29, 1826, and May 17, 1826.

76. "Fee'd . . . weak": [Whipple,] *Memoirs,* 88–92; Lancaster, "Web," 88.

77. [Green,] *Second Book,* 2.

78. [Whipple,] *Memoirs,* 91.

79. "The colored": [Whipple,] *Memoirs,* 3; "If you were . . . them": Brown, *Life of William J. Brown,* 73; Leon Litwack, *North of Slavery: The Negro in the Free States, 1790–1860* (Chicago: University of Chicago Press, 1965), 103, 170; Lancaster, "Web," 73, 87.

80. [Green,] *Second Book,* 6; O'Dowd, *Rhode Island Original,* 19, 30; Lancaster, "Web," 73. Estimates of sales amounting to 30,000 books are no doubt wildly off the mark.

81. Biographical information has been gathered from the FMC, Providence city directories, and local newspapers. See also Lancaster, "Web," 74–75.

82. Lancaster, "Web."

83. Ibid., 90n12; poem and Garrison testimonial in *The Liberator,* November 30, 1838.

84. *The Liberator,* November 30, 1838; "had . . . now": *NBM,* January 11, 1839.

85. William Lloyd Garrison, *The Letters of William Lloyd Garrison,* Vol. 2: *A House Dividing Against Itself, 1836–1840* (Cambridge, MA: Harvard University Press, 1971), 408–410.

86. "Friends": Frederick Douglass in Philip S. Foner, ed., *The Life and Writings of Frederick Douglass,* Vol. 2: *Pre–Civil War Decade* (New York: International Publishers, 1950), 32.

87. "Our dark friend": [Green,] *Second Book,* 13; "Declaration: Elleanor Eldridge v. Benjamin Balch," G. L. Dwight, plaintiff's attorney, May 7, 1839 (list of articles he took from the house), JRC; "I": [Green,] *Second Book,* 6; "Declaration," n105. On Gamaliel Lyman Dwight, Esq., see *Report of Cases Argued and Determined in the Supreme Court of Rhode Island* (March term, 1858) (Boston: Little, Brown), 5:150.

88. O'Dowd, *Rhode Island Original,* 59–60.

89. "We know": Cottrol, *Afro-Yankees,* 72; Marvin E. Gettelman and Noel P. Conlon, "Responses to the Rhode Island Workingmen's Reform Agitation of 1833," *RIH* 28 (August 1969): 75–96.

90. "To pair . . . voters": Crummell quoted in Cottrol, *Afro-Yankees,* 73–74; Eric J. Chaput and Russell DeSimone, "Strange Bedfellows: The Politics of Race in Antebellum

Rhode Island," *Common-Place* 10 (January 2010), http://www.common-place.org/vol-10/no-02/chaput-desimone/ (accessed July 31, 2013).

91. Quoted in Chaput and DeSimone, "Strange Bedfellows." See also Loiacono, "Poverty and Citizenship," chap. 4.

92. Quoted in O'Dowd, *Rhode Island Original,* 75; Ronald P. Formisano, "The Role of Women in the Dorr Rebellion," *RIH* 51 (August 1993): 95–98.

93. "I have yet": *Might and Right by a Rhode Islander* (Providence, RI: A. H. Stillwell, 1844), 287; "They made . . . DUPE": ibid., 291; Formisano, "Role of Women."

94. Brown, *Life of William J. Brown,* xxxiii; Cottrol, *Afro-Yankees,* 89; J. Stanley Lemons and Michael A. McKenna, "Re-Enfranchisement of Rhode Island Negroes," *RIH* 30 (February 1971): 3–13.

95. "Acts": quoted in O'Dowd, *Rhode Island Original,* 79; Frances Harriet Whipple Green, "The Donner Tragedy: A Thrilling Chapter in Our Pioneer History," *Pacific Rural Press* (San Francisco), January 21, 1871.

96. "We acknowledge": "Mechanics Meeting," *PP/CP,* October 15, 1831; "Meeting of Mechanics," *Literary Subaltern,* October 13, 1831.

97. Editha Hadcock, "Labor Problems in the Rhode Island Cotton Mills, 1790–1840," *RIH* 14 (July 1955): 82–93; Jonathan Prude, *Coming of the Industrial Order: Town and Factory Life in Rural Massachusetts, 1810–1860* (Amherst: University of Massachusetts Press, 1999); David Zonderman, *Aspirations and Anxieties: New England Workers and the Mechanized Factory System, 1815–1850* (New York: Oxford University Press, 1992). Other New England states and the passage of ten-hour-workday laws: Vermont, 1867; New Hampshire, 1871; Connecticut, 1872; Massachusetts, 1874; Maine, 1875.

98. Martha S. Jones, *All Bound Up Together: The Woman Question in African American Public Culture, 1830–1900* (Chapel Hill: University of North Carolina Press, 2007), 34–35; "Address": *The Liberator,* August 10, 1833.

99. "The colored": Judson quoted in G. Smith Wormley, "Prudence Crandall," *JNH* 8 (January 1923): 74; "attacking . . . them": James Freeman Clarke, "Present Condition of the Free Colored People of the United States" (New York: Anti-Slavery Society, 1859), 5, 7; Hilary J. Moss, *Schooling Citizens: The Struggle for African American Education in Antebellum America* (Chicago: University of Chicago Press, 2009); Fields and Fields, *Racecraft,* 128.

100. "Set us . . . patriotism": "Will the General Assembly Put Down Caste Schools?" quoted in Cottrol, *Afro-Yankees,* 96; ibid., 95, 119; "To drive": Brown, *Life of William J. Brown,* 60; *PG,* July 30, 1791.

101. Cottrol, *Afro-Yankees,* 137; FMC for 1850 and 1860, Rhode Island, Providence County, Providence; Lancaster, "Web."

102. Lancaster, "Web," 88; Rhode Island Deaths, 1630–1930, www.ancestry.com (accessed June 20, 2013); Cottrol, *Afro-Yankees,* 31; "lived to": Rider, "Bibliographical Memoir," 37; Providence, Rhode Island, City Hall Deed Books for May 6, 7, 15, and July 14 and 21, 1863; FMC for 1860, Providence; Rhode Island Deaths, 1630–1930.

103. Cottrol, *Afro-Yankees,* 109, 114, 147; Burnham et al., *Creative Survival,* 44–47; Robert A. Wheeler, "Fifth Ward Irish: Immigrant Mobility in Providence, 1850–1870," *RIH* 32 (May 1973): 53–61.

104. "Five . . . and civilization": "Smellie's Philosophy of Natural History," *RIA,* October 19, 1824.

105. George Henry, *Life of George Henry, Together with a Brief History of the Colored People of America* (Providence, RI: H. I. Gould, 1895), 95; Melish, *Disowning Slavery,* 238–285.

CHAPTER 4 RICHARD W. WHITE

1. *SMN,* January 16, 1869.

2. Ibid.

3. *SMN,* January 21, 1869. See also "Lawless Negroes," *NYT,* January 4, 1869; Karen B. Bell, "'The Ogeechee Troubles': Federal Land Restoration Policies and the 'Lived Realities' of Temporary Proprietors, 1865–1868," *GHQ* 85 (Fall 2001): 375–397; and Jacqueline Jones, *Saving Savannah: The City and the Civil War* (New York: Knopf, 2008), 322–329, 335.

4. "Can a Negro Hold Office in Georgia?": Decided in Supreme Court of Georgia, June term, 1869, http://www.archive.org/details/cannegroholdoffi00geor (accessed June 20, 2013).

5. *DNH,* April 29, 1868; *SMN,* January 27, 1869; *MWT,* May 22, 1868; "Can a Negro Hold Office?"

6. "Negro melodies": *SMN,* January 28, 1869; "cotton mad": ibid., January 23, 1869.

7. "Can a Negro Hold Office?" 9.

8. "As Southerners": [Editor's note] *DeBow's Review* (May 1847): 421: "anatomical . . . races": *American Cotton Planter and Soil of the South* (November 1858): 366–368; Larry E. Tise, *Proslavery: A History of the Defense of Slavery in America, 1701–1840* (Athens: University of Georgia Press, 2004), 97–182, 323–346; Drew Gilpin Faust, ed., *The Ideology of Slavery: Proslavery Thought in the Antebellum South, 1830–1860* (Baton Rouge: Louisiana State University Press, 1981).

9. "Intelligent . . . enemy": Transcript of court-martial trial in Ira Berlin, Barbara J. Fields, Thavolia Glymph, Joseph P. Reidy, and Leslie S. Rowland, eds., *Freedom: A Documentary History of Emancipation, 1861–1867,* Series 1, Vol. 1: *The Destruction of Slavery* (Cambridge: Cambridge University Press, 1985), 785; "traitors . . . *labor*": Petition of Robert Q. Mallard et al. on behalf of Liberty County, Georgia, slaveholders, in ibid., 795–798.

10. *DNH,* July 6, 1866.

11. "Can a Negro Hold Office?" 33, 25, 34.

12. Ibid., 33.

13. Ibid., 22.

14. Ibid., 24, 29, 43.

15. Ibid., 19, 49.

16. Edmund L. Drago, *Black Politicians and Reconstruction in Georgia: A Splendid Failure* (Athens: University of Georgia Press, 1992), 53; Alan Conway, *The Reconstruction of Georgia* (Minneapolis: University of Minnesota Press, 1996), 166–167.

17. "Can a Negro Hold Office?" 102.

18. Eric Foner, *Reconstruction: America's Unfinished Revolution, 1863–1877* (New York: Harper & Row, 1988), 228–345; "morally delinquent . . . thieving": *Testimony Taken by the Joint Select Committee to Inquire into the Condition of Affairs in the Late Insurrectionary States: Georgia* (Washington, DC: GPO, 1872), 2:816 (vol. 2 of the two Georgia volumes, vol. 7 of the series).

19. "Can a Negro Hold Office?" 107–109, 122.

20. FMC for 1850, Ohio, Jefferson County, Smithfield; Account No. 2124, August 16, 1869, Savannah Branch of the Freedman's Savings and Trust Company, Registers of Signatures of Depositors, 1865–1874 (hereinafter Freedman's Bank), RG 101, Records of the Comptroller of the Currency, NARA (available on microfilm and on ancestry.com).

21. FMC for 1850, Smithfield; William Henry Siebert, *The Mysteries of Ohio's Underground Railroads* (Columbus, OH: Long's College Book, 1951), 128–130, 276.

22. "That old": quoted in Siebert, *Mysteries,* 263; William Cheek and Aimee Lee Cheek, *John Mercer Langston and the Fight for Black Freedom, 1829–65* (Urbana: University of Illinois Press, 1989), 282; John Mercer Langston, *From the Virginia Plantation to the National Capitol, Or the First and Only Negro Representative in Congress from the Old Dominion* (New York: Arno Press, [1894] 1969). For evidence of White's attendance at Oberlin, see record no. 52561 (fall semester) and Treasurer's Journal, November 2, 1858, Oberlin College Archives, Oberlin, Ohio.

23. Statistical compilation based on FMC for 1860, Ohio, Columbiana County, Salem; Cheek and Cheek, *John Mercer Langston,* 286; Harrold, *Border War,* 24–29, 89, 105–106.

24. Cheek and Cheek, *John Mercer Langston,* 297; Treasurer's Journal, Oberlin College Archives; Daniel J. Sharfstein, *The Invisible Line: Three American Families and the Secret Journey from Black to White* (New York: Penguin, 2011).

25. "Consisting": J. L. Stevens to Secretary of War, Cincinnati, August 10, 1861, in Ira Berlin, Joseph P. Reidy, and Leslie Rowland, eds., *Freedom: A Documentary History of Emancipation, 1861–1867,* Series 2: *The Black Military Experience* (Cambridge: Cambridge University Press, 1982), 78; "it was": quoted in Cheek and Cheek, *John Mercer Langston,* 383; Langston, *Virginia Plantation,* 202–205.

26. "The pay": Governor David Tod to Langston, Columbus, Ohio, May 16, 1863, in Berlin et al., eds., *Black Military Experience,* 92, 74–75; Charles Barnard Fox, *Record of the Service of the Fifty-Fifth Regiment of Massachusetts Volunteer Infantry* (Cambridge, MA: John Wilson and Son, 1868), 86; Langston, *Virginia Plantation,* 204.

27. Compiled Military Service Records of Volunteer Union Soldiers who served in the US Colored Troops, 55th MA Infantry, microfilm reel 15, Records of the Adjutant General's Office, 1780s–1917, RG 94, NARA, Washington, DC; FMC for 1850 and 1860, Ohio, Jefferson County, Smithfield.

28. Fox, *Record,* 4–5; Wilbert H. Luck, *Journey to Honey Hill: The Fifty-Fifth Massachusetts Regiment's (Colored) Journey South to Fight the Civil War That Toppled the Institution of Slavery* (Washington, DC: Wiluk Press, 1976), 49–52; "These negroes": Richard M. Reid, ed., *Practicing Medicine in a Black Regiment: The Civil War Diary of Burt G. Wilder, 55th Massachusetts* (Amherst: University of Massachusetts Press, 2010), 4–5n19.

29. "We have buried": quoted in Luis F. Emilio, *A Brave Black Regiment: History of the Fifty-Fourth Regiment of Massachusetts Volunteer Infantry, 1863–1865* (New York: Arno Press, [1894] 1969), 102–103; Russell Duncan, *Where Death and Glory Meet:*

Colonel Robert Gould Shaw and the 54th Massachusetts Infantry (Athens: University of Georgia Press, 1999); "thoroughly drilled": Fox, *Record,* 7; Luck, *Journey,* 52; Iver Bernstein, *The New York City Draft Riots: Their Significance for American Society and Politics in the Age of the Civil War* (New York: Oxford University Press, 1991).

30. "Worked almost to death": Letter dated January 27, 1864, Folly Island, South Carolina, to *CR* (pub. February 4, 1864) and reprinted in Noah Andre Trudeau, ed., *Voices of the 55th: Letters from the 55th Massachusetts Volunteers, 1861–1865* (Dayton, OH: Morningside Press, 1996), 64; "excessive": Fox, *Record,* 15, 11; Luck, *Journey,* 56; Berlin et al., eds., *Black Military Experience,* 24; Keith P. Wilson, *Campfires of Freedom: The Camp Life of Black Soldiers During the Civil War* (Kent, OH: Kent State University Press, 2002), 7.

31. "Deep-voiced . . . sermons": Letter dated March 14, 1864, Palatka, Florida, to *CR* (pub. April 2, 1864) and reprinted in Trudeau, ed., *Voices,* 75; Fox, *Record,* 25; Wilson, *Campfires,* 9.

32. Luck, *Journey,* 42; Fox, *Record,* 25, 83; Berlin et al., eds., *Black Military Experience,* 25.

33. Reid, ed., *Practicing Medicine,* 103; Wilson, *Campfires,* 71–74, 82, 97–104; Fox, *Record,* 20.

34. Wilson, *Campfires,* 97; Rayford W. Logan and Michael R. Winston, eds., *Dictionary of American Negro Biography* (New York: Norton, 1983), 602–603; Compiled Military Service Record for Richard W. White, reel 15, RG 94, NARA.

35. Trudeau, ed., *Voices,* 64–65.

36. "I suppose": ibid.; "No chance": soldier quoted in Reid, ed., *Practicing Medicine,* 27; Berlin et al., eds., *Black Military Experience,* 362–405.

37. Wilson, *Campfires,* 48–50; Berlin et al., eds., *Black Military Experience,* 366–367.

38. "On the same . . . Show": Letter dated July 16, 1864, Folly Island, South Carolina, in Berlin et al., eds., *Black Military Experience,* 401–402; Luck, *Journey,* 61–70; Reid, ed., *Practicing Medicine,* 177.

39. "We left": Soldiers of a Black Regiment to the President, Folly Island, South Carolina, July 16, 1864, in Berlin et al., eds., *Black Military Experience,* 401; "Mr President . . . 16 dollars?": Rachel Ann Wicker, September 12, 1864, to the Governor of Massachusetts, in ibid., 402; Reid, ed., *Practicing Medicine,* 131.

40. Letter dated March 14, 1864, Palatka, Florida, to *CR* (pub. April 2, 1864) and reprinted in Trudeau, ed., *Voices,* 75.

41. Letter dated May 1, 1864, Folly Island, South Carolina, to *Anglo African* (pub. June 4, 1864) and reprinted in ibid., 101–103. Dedicated to history, culture, and politics, the *Anglo-African* was a weekly published in New York from 1859 to 1865.

42. "Battery . . . do so": White to Maj. Gen. Curtis, Folly Island, South Carolina, July 28, 1864, Military Service Record for White; "Judging" [Hunt], ibid.

43. "Sergt. White": Trudeau, ed., *Voices,* 152; Reid, ed., *Practicing Medicine,* 187–189.

44. Luck, *Journey,* 79–90; Fox, *Record,* 41–45; "for the purpose . . . indulgence": Letter from George F. McKay, Headquarters, 55th Regiment, Folly Island, South Carolina, October 20, 1864, Military Service Record for White; FMC for 1880, Ohio, Jefferson County, Smithfield.

45. "Gen. Sherman . . . alone": Jenkins letter, in Trudeau, ed., *Voices,* 178; "Ours is": Trotter letter, in ibid., 180; Reid, ed., *Practicing Medicine,* 218.

46. "Cheers . . . at last": Fox, *Record,* 56; ibid., 57–58; "They had": "From Charleston: Condition of the City," *NYT,* March 9, 1865; "Good News," *NYT,* February 21, 1865; "Abandoned by Rebels," *NYT,* February 18, 1865.

47. "New and old": Fox, *Record,* 67; Reid, ed., *Practicing Medicine,* 235, 226–229.

48. Fox, *Record,* 74; Foner, *Reconstruction,* 72.

49. For a brief biography of Soule, see Fox, *Record,* 102.

50. Letter from Soule to "General," Orangeburg, South Carolina, June 12, 1865, http:// 153.9.241.55/atlanticworld/afterslavery/Unit%20One.pdf (document 4) (accessed June 20, 2013).

51. Ibid.

52. Reid, ed., *Practicing Medicine,* 20–21, 241, 246, 261.

53. "The Negroes on St. Helena," *NYT,* August 6, 1865; "Our Charleston Correspondent," *NYT,* May 22, 1865

54. *BDA,* October 9, 1865; Berlin et al., eds., *Black Military Experience,* 303–312; Thomas Holt, *Black and White: Negro Political Leadership in South Carolina During Reconstruction* (Urbana: University of Illinois Press, 1979), 14. See also USCT and Commissioned Officers of African-American Descent, http://home.usmo.com/~momollus /USCT.HTM (accessed June 20, 2013).

55. "Bring": Letter from Soule to "General"; "Do not": White's letter dated May 1, 1864, in Trudeau, ed., *Voices,* 103.

56. Foner, *Reconstruction,* 125.

57. "Affairs in the South," *NYT,* May 20, 1866; Foner, *Reconstruction,* 112; Freedman's Bank Account No. 141, Charleston, May 30, 1866, Freedman's Bank Branch Records, NARA.

58. John Ogden to John M. Langston, Fisk University, Nashville, June 8, 1868, box 1, folder 2, John Mercer Langston Papers, Fisk University Franklin Library Special Collections–Archives, Nashville, Tennessee.

59. FMC for 1860, South Carolina, District of Charleston, Charleston, Ward 6; "You will": Ogden to Langston, June 8, 1868.

60. For more about these men, see Drago, *Black Politicians;* Russell Duncan, *Freedom's Shore: Tunis Campbell and the Georgia Freedmen* (Athens: University of Georgia Press, 1986); and Jones, *Saving Savannah.*

61. Ibid.

62. *SDH,* October 21, 1867; "Georgia," *NYT,* February 10, 1867; "The Recent Trouble with the Freedmen on the Sea Islands of South Carolina," *NYT,* January 27, 1867; Jacqueline Jones, *Soldiers of Light and Love: Northern Teachers and Georgia Blacks, 1865–1873* (Chapel Hill: University of North Carolina Press, 1980).

63. "Resist": *SR,* December 12, 1865; Jones, *Saving Savannah,* 356; "Great Wahoo . . . pettifogger": *DNH,* July 6, 1867; *SDR,* January 27, 1867; Joseph P. Reidy, "Aaron A. Bradley: Voice of Black Labor in the Georgia Lowcountry," in Howard N. Rabinowitz, ed., *Southern Black Leaders of the Reconstruction Era* (Urbana: University of Illinois Press), 281–308.

64. "The negroes . . . politically": "Alexander H. Stephens of Georgia on Public Affairs," *NYT,* February 23, 1868; "Mongrel": *DNH,* December 21, 1867.

65. "Registration Closed at Savannah, Georgia," *NYT,* August 4, 1867; "Southern Elections," *NYT,* April 28, 1868; Drago, *Black Politicians,* 171–181; *DNH,* April 29, 1868.

66. "The black man": Turner quoted in Richard H. Abbott, "The Republican Party Press in Reconstruction Georgia, 1867–1874," *JSH* 61 (November 1995): 748; *Condition of Affairs,* 8, 55, 179, 228; Drago, *Black Politicians,* 76–77; *SMN,* November 4, 1868; ibid., November 8, 1868.

67. Letter signed by White, Moses Bentley, and Frederick Allen "per R. W. White" in *The Condition of Affairs in Georgia: Statement of Hon. Nelson Tift . . .* (Freeport, NY: Books for Libraries Press, [1869] 1971), 89–90.

68. Jones, *Saving Savannah,* 302–320.

69. Richard W. White to Charles H. Sumner, Savannah, January 21, 1869, Charles Sumner Papers, Houghton Library, Harvard University, Cambridge, Massachusetts. See also Stephen W. Angell, "A Black Minister Befriends the 'Unquestioned Father of Civil Rights': Henry McNeal Turner, Charles Sumner, and the African-American Quest for Freedom," *GHQ* 85 (Spring 2001): 27–58.

70. Jones, *Saving Savannah,* 339.

71. City Council Minutes of Savannah, July 7, 1870, Chatham County Records, Georgia Department of Archives and History, Atlanta, Georgia (available on microfilm); "In places": *SMN,* December 5, 1870.

72. Reidy, "Aaron A. Bradley," 297; E. Merton Coulter, *Negro Legislators in Georgia During the Reconstruction Period* (Athens: Georgia Historical Society, 1968), 95–105.

73. *SMN,* October 5, 1870; Coulter, *Negro Legislators,* 95–96; "Saint . . . Ohio": *SMN,* October 29, 1870; "Big Injun . . . color": ibid., December 5, 1870; "that a man": ibid., December 13, 1870; "pow-wow": ibid., December 14, 1870.

74. *Georgia Weekly Telegraph and Georgia Journal and Messenger* (Macon), February 21, 1871. For the deposits, see Savannah Branch, Freedman's Bank, Nos. 2124 (August 16, 1869), 2365 (October 7, 1869), 2710 (December 24, 1869), 3066 (February 25, 1870), and 4721 (November 22, 1870).

75. Information culled from General Records of the Department of the Treasury, Records of the Division of Appointments, Lists of Subordinate Officers, Vols. 1–10, Department of the Treasury, RG 56, NARA, College Park, Maryland.

76. John Hammond Moore, "Sherman's 'Fifth Column': A Guide to Unionist Activity in Georgia," *GHQ* 68 (Fall 1984): 382–409; United States Southern Claims Commission Disallowed and Barred Claims, 1871–1880, Records of the US House of Representatives, 1871–1880, RG 233, NARA. Records of claims allowed and disallowed are available on ancestry.com.

77. T. P. Robb, Customs House, Savannah, January 27, 1872, Records of the Division of Appointments, Records Relating to Customs House Nominations, 1849–1910, Savannah, June 1871 to October 1877, box 83, RG 56, NARA; "who are": George Washington Wilson to Colonel James Atkins, *SMN,* August 8, 1872.

78. "An effort . . . inequity": R. W. White to Charles Sumner, Savannah, March 20, 1871, Sumner Papers; Reidy, "Aaron A. Bradley," 298.

79. "Will effectually . . . rights": R. White to Charles Sumner, Savannah, January 15, 1872, Sumner Papers; "to secure . . . direction": R. W. White to Benjamin F. Butler,

Savannah, January 24, 1872, Benjamin F. Butler Papers, Manuscript Division, Library of Congress, Washington, DC; T. P. Robb, January 27, 1872.

80. "Great interest . . . character": White to Butler, January 24, 1872.

81. Abbott, "Republican Party Press."

82. Petition printed in John Y. Simon, ed., *The Papers of Ulysses S. Grant* (February 1–December 31, 1872) (Carbondale: Southern Illinois University Press, 1967), 23:25.

83. Jones, *Saving Savannah,* 378–380; "mulatto . . . No": *SDR,* July 31, 1872; "raise such": *SMN,* August 8, 1872; "the kindly relations": *SMN,* August 5, 1872.

84. *SDR,* September 25, 1872.

85. Eric Foner, *Freedom's Lawmakers: A Directory of Black Officeholders During Reconstruction* (New York: Oxford University Press, 1993), 228–229; "Memorial Services: Tribute to Hon. Charles Sumner, held in St. Phillip's A. M. E. Church, Savannah, Georgia, March 18th, 1874" (Savannah: D. G. Patton, 1874); Carl R. Osthaus, *Freedom, Philanthropy, and Fraud: A History of the Freedman's Savings Bank* (Urbana: University of Illinois Press, 1976).

86. Simon, ed., *Papers of Grant* (November 1, 1869–October 31, 1870), 20:437.

87. *ST,* September 16, 1876, December 30, 1876, December 10, 1892, July 2, 1898. See "A Letter from Lewis Hayden of Boston, Massachusetts, to Hon. Judge Simms, of Savannah, Georgia" (Boston: Committee on Masonic Jurisprudence, Prince Hall Grand Lodge, 1874).

88. See, for example, *ST,* April 2, 1897, October 22, 1898, May 20, 1876, August 5, 1876, January 1, 1892, March 26, 1892, September 10, 1892, and March 21, 1886.

89. FMC for 1880, Georgia, Chatham County, Savannah.

90. "Common . . . Constitution": White to Chas. J. Folger, Secretary of the Treasury, Savannah, March 13, 1882, box 84, entry 246, General Records, Records of the Division of Appointments, Records Relating to Customs House Appointments, Savannah, Georgia, RG 56, NARA; *Columbus Daily Enquirer,* October 2, 1886; Logan and Winston, eds., *American Negro Biography,* 603.

91. "If you wish": *ST,* December 5, 1891.

92. *ST,* May 4, 1889; Declaration for Invalid Pension, July 21, 1890, R. W. White Civil War Pension File, NARA (hereinafter Civil War Pension File).

93. "Which . . . crimes": *ST,* March 26, 1892; ibid., August 26, 1892.

94. E. H. Nichols, M.D., "Surgeon's Certificate," March 21, 1893, Civil War Pension File.

95. "The plan": *ST,* March 30, 1895.

96. FMC for 1900, Georgia, Chatham County, Savannah. White's on-again, off-again employment in the post office and customs house are recorded on an annual basis in Savannah city directories from 1877 to 1906.

97. *ST,* April 6, 1895; "to secure . . . a fair count": ibid., October 31, 1896.

98. "Largely": *ST,* January 4, 1896; "ire": ibid., April 11, 1896; "all good": ibid., August 22, 1896; "we recognize . . . white man": ibid., December 25, 1897; "loyal": ibid., October 22, 1898.

99. "Black . . . white": *ST,* April 14, 1900; Cheek and Cheek, *John Mercer Langston;* J. Mercer Langston, "Equality Before the Law" (St. Louis: Democrat Book and Job, 1866), 13. For Langston's postwar speeches, see his papers in the Fisk University Franklin Library. The two quoted here are "former condition": "Address at the Meth-

odist Episcopal Church on 5th Street" (c. 1865), scrapbook in box 6; and "'Your hair'": "Our Emancipation; Our Progress; and Our Future . . . " (c. 1890), box 2, folder 15.

100. "The soldier": Dr. M. X. Corbin, "Surgeon's Certificate," February 27, 1901; "he has": General Affidavit, March 18, 1901; "inability": Pension Board ruling, all in Civil War Pension File.

101. "My father . . . by me": Deposition, Ella L. Hackett, March 28, 1903, Civil War Pension File.

102. "Pensioner Dropped," June 13, 1905, Civil War Pension File.

103. "Register of Enlistments, U.S. Army," ancestry.com. See also Thaddeus White's Compiled Military Service Record, NARA (file designation: White, Thaddeus M., Co. 8, Illinois Infantry [col'd] Spanish War).

104. FMC for 1910, Bonnette White and Alvin Miller Households, Georgia, Chatham County, Savannah.

CHAPTER 5 WILLIAM H. HOLTZCLAW

1. "Times": quoted in William Henry Holtzclaw, *The Black Man's Burden* (New York: Neale Publishing, 1915), 150 (hereinafter *BMB*). See also Theodore Rosengarten, *All God's Dangers: The Life of Nate Shaw* (New York: Knopf, 1972); and Charles S. Johnson, *Shadow of the Plantation* (Chicago: University of Chicago Press, 1934).

2. *BMB;* "The Negroes": Holtzclaw quoted in Emma C. Penney, "A Light in the Black Belt of Mississippi," *AM* (November 1907): 26; Rudyard Kipling, "The White Man's Burden," http://www.online-literature.com/Keats/922/ (accessed June 20, 2013); Neil R. McMillen, *Dark Journey: Black Mississippians in the Age of Jim Crow* (Urbana: University of Illinois Press, 1989); 97; "the most": R. Fulton Holtzclaw, *William Henry Holtzclaw: Scholar in Ebony* (Cleveland: Keeble Press, 1977), 48 (hereinafter *SE*); "You know": William H. Holtzclaw, "A School Principal's Story," in Booker T. Washington, ed., *Tuskegee and Its People: Their Ideals and Achievements* (New York: D. Appleton, 1905), 132; "possessed . . . would": William H. Holtzclaw (hereinafter WHH) to Emmett J. Scott, Snow Hill, Alabama, April 7, 1902, Part I: General Correspondence, 1882–1915, Booker T. Washington Papers, Library of Congress, Washington, DC. (Unless otherwise noted, the unpublished correspondence cited here between WHH and Scott and Booker T. Washington [hereinafter BTW] is taken from the General Correspondence of BTW Papers.) See also Robert R. Moton, "The Significance of Mr. Washington's Lecture Trip in Mississippi," *SW* (December 1908): 692.

3. Thomas Jesse Jones, *Negro Education: A Study of the Private and Higher Schools for Colored People in the United States* (Washington, DC: GPO, 1917), 348–349.

4. *BMB,* 168.

5. "Break Out in Newton County," *DCL,* September 27, 1908; "Farmers Union and the Night Riders," ibid., September 29, 1908; "As to Night Riders over Mississippi," ibid., October 6, 1908; "blind": "Law Enforcement League Takes Positive Action," ibid., April 2, 1909; "Prospects": ibid., January 26, 1909.

6. "If you": quoted in McMillen, *Dark Journey,* 120; *SE,* 171, 178; "moving": *BMB,* 167; William F. Holmes, "Whitecapping: Agrarian Violence in Mississippi, 1902–1906," *JSH* 35 (May 1969): 165–185.

7. *BMB,* 169–170.

8. Ibid.

9. "Was careful": ibid., 171; "watch": *SE,* 113.

10. For accounts of the tour and its participants, see *BMB,* 167–173; Moton, "Significance," 691–695; Hightower T. Kealing, "Booker T. Washington's Tour Through Mississippi: A New Form of University Extension," orig. pub. in the *A.M.E. Church Review* and reprinted in Louis R. Harlan and Raymond W. Smock, eds., *The Booker T. Washington Papers* (Urbana: University of Illinois Press, 1980), 9:674–681 (hereinafter *BTW Papers*); Booker T. Washington, "A Cheerful Journey Through Mississippi," orig. pub. in *World's Work* and reprinted in ibid., 10:60–68; August Meier, "Booker T. Washington and the Town of Mound Bayou," *Phylon* 15 (4th qtr., 1954): 396–401; and *Southern Notes* 4 (May 1907). For a description of Washington's suit, see *SE,* 114.

11. "Pacificator": Kealing, "Washington's Tour," 680; "Coliseum Gallery Fell on Booker's Big Meeting," *DCL,* October 7, 1908.

12. "I am not anxious": Vardaman quoted (on the closing of Alcorn College in Holly Springs) in Ray Stannard Baker, *Following the Color Line: An Account of Negro Citizenship in the American Democracy* (New York: Doubleday, Page, 1908), 248; Booker T. Washington, "The Rural Negro Community," *AAAPSS* 40 (March 1912): 84; Alfred Holt Stone, *Studies in the American Race Problem* (New York: Doubleday, Page, 1908); Alfred Holt Stone, "A Plantation Experiment," *QJE* 19 (February 1905): 270–287; "Charles Banks and the Bank of Mound Bayou," *CAM* 11 (June 1906): 419–422. Use of the term *Negro problem* was ubiquitous among whites desperate to find and maintain large numbers of subordinate black field-workers.

13. "Boldly": Kealing, "Washington's Tour," 677; "cheerful": Harlan and Smock, eds., *BTW Papers* (1981), 10:60; "on such": ibid., 67; McMillen, *Dark Journey,* 187.

14. "In every": Moton, "Significance," 695; "those fundamental": Washington, "Cheerful Journey," 68.

15. *BMB,* 172–173.

16. "He is always": Clarence H. Poe, "The Rich Kingdom of Cotton," *WW* (November 1904): 5493; "the mortgage": Lorenzo E. Hall, "My Reasons for Studying Agriculture," *SW* (July 1908): 398; "the more": *BMB,* 174; "sober": Montgomery quoted in McMillen, *Dark Journey,* 120. For the definitive biography of Washington, see Louis R. Harlan, *Booker T. Washington: The Making of a Black Leader, 1856–1901* (New York: Oxford University Press, 1972), and *Booker T. Washington: The Wizard of Tuskegee, 1901–1915* (New York: Oxford University Press, 1986).

17. "It was": *BMB,* 126; "serves": Vardaman quoted in McMillen, *Dark Journey,* 90; "God Almighty": *Vardaman's Weekly,* May 8, 1919; "Correspondence," *The Outlook* 75 (September 12, 1903): 139; Baker, *Following the Color Line,* 246; Clara S. Lopez, "James K. Vardaman and the Negro: The Foundation of Mississippi's Racial Policy," *SQ* 3 (January 1965): 155–180; Stuart Grayson Noble, *Forty Years of the Public Schools in Mississippi* (New York: Teachers College, 1918): 110–111; William F. Holmes, *The White Chief: James Kemble Vardaman* (Baton Rouge: Louisiana State University Press, 1970).

18. "A Governor Bitterly Opposes Negro Education," http://teachingamericanhistory .org/library/index.asp?document=2201 (accessed June 20, 2013); "The Good Old Fashioned People," in James Whitcomb Riley, *The Complete Works of James Whitcomb*

Riley in Ten Volumes, Including Poems and Prose Sketches (Ann Arbor: University of Michigan Library, 1916), 8:2068.

19. Harvey Wish, "Negro Education and the Progressive Movement," *JNH* 49 (July 1964): 188; Theodore DuBose Bratton, "The Christian South and Education," *Sewanee Review* 3 (July 1908): 296; Stone, *Studies,* 5, 43–44; "it had come": Baker, *Following the Color Line,* 248; Thomas Jesse Jones, "The Negroes of the Southern States and the U.S. Census of 1910," *SW* (August 1912): 464.

20. See, for example, Matthew Frye Jacobson, *Barbarian Virtues: The United States Encounters Foreign Peoples at Home and Abroad, 1876–1917* (New York: Hill and Wang, 2000); and Eric T. Lott, *Race over Empire: Racism and U.S. Imperialism, 1865–1900* (Chapel Hill: University of North Carolina Press, 2004).

21. See, for example, Thomas J. Woofter, *Landlord and Tenant on the Cotton Plantation,* Works Progress Administration, Division of Social Research, Monograph 5 (Washington, DC: GPO, 1936); Frank J. Welch, "The Plantation Land Tenure System in Mississippi," Mississippi Agricultural Experiment Station Bulletin No. 385 (State College: Mississippi Agricultural Experiment Station, June, 1943); Poe, "Rich Kingdom."

22. Erin Elizabeth Clune, "From Light Copper to the Blackest and Lowest Type: Daniel Tompkins and the Racial Order of the Global New South," *JSH* 76 (May 2010): 281, 307–309; Erin Elizabeth Clune, "Black Workers, White Immigrants, and the Postemancipation Problem of Labor: The New South in Transnational Perspective," in Susanna Delfino and Michele Gillespie, eds., *Global Perspectives on Industrial Transformation in the American South* (Columbia: University of Missouri Press, 2005), 199–228. See also Matthew Pratt Guterl, *American Mediterranean: Southern Slaveholders in the Age of Emancipation* (Cambridge, MA: Harvard University Press, 2008); and Andrew Zimmerman, *Alabama in Africa: Booker T. Washington, the German Empire, and the Globalization of the New South* (Princeton, NJ: Princeton University Press, 2010).

23. W. H. Holtzclaw, "The Growth of the Normal and Industrial School Idea," *CAM* 11 (August 1906): 115–118.

24. McMillen, *Dark Journey;* Grace Elizabeth Hale, *Making Whiteness: The Culture of Segregation in the South* (New York: Vintage Books, 1998), 21; J. William Harris, "Etiquette, Lynching, and Racial Boundaries in Southern History: A Mississippi Example," *AHR* 100 (April 1995): 387–410.

25. Booker T. Washington, *Up from Slavery, with Related Documents,* ed. by W. Fitzhugh Brundage (Boston: Bedford/St. Martin's Press, 2002), 251.

26. *SE,* 251.

27. Ibid., 117.

28. "I": ibid., 5; ibid., 3–6; *BMB,* 15; W. O. Atwater and Charles D. Woods, "Dietary Studies with Reference to the Food of the Negro in Alabama in 1895 and 1896," US Department of Agriculture Bulletin No. 38 (Washington, DC: GPO, 1897); Holtzclaw, "Principal's Story," 113 ("Hunger would sometimes drive us mad"). The family is not listed in the 1880 census; during the summers Jerry often sought wage work and Adaline worked as a cook for the landlord's family, probably taking her children with her during the day and leaving an empty cabin, which was therefore passed over by a census taker.

29. "Ordinary times . . . women riots": Petition of Randolph County Farmers to the Confederate President, in Ira Berlin, Barbara J. Fields, Thavolia Glymph, Joseph P. Reidy, and Leslie S. Rowland, eds., *Freedom: A Documentary History of Emancipation, 1861–1867,* Series 1, Vol. 1: *The Destruction of Slavery* (Cambridge: Cambridge University Press, 1985), 757; W. J. Spillman and E. A. Goldenweiser, "Farm Tenantry in the United States," *USDA Yearbook for 1916* (Washington, DC: GPO, 1916), Table 2.3.

30. "Was to . . . the year": *BMB,* 17; Harold D. Woodman, "Post–Civil War Southern Agriculture and the Law," *AH* 53 (January 1979): 319–387; Harold D. Woodman, "Postbellum Social Change and Its Effects on Marketing the South's Cotton Crop," *AH* 56 (January 1982): 215–230; Holtzclaw, "Principal's Story," 112; E. W. Hilgard, *Report on Cotton Production in the United States: Part 1: Mississippi Valley and the Southwestern States,* US Department of the Interior, Bureau of the Census (Washington, DC: GPO, 1884); Jacqueline Jones, *The Dispossessed: America's Underclasses from the Civil War to the Present* (New York: Basic Books, 1992), 13–166.

31. Compare the two accounts in *SE,* 9–10 and *BMB,* 18. On shifting, see Jones, *Dispossessed,* 104–126; Spillman and Goldenweiser, "Farm Tenantry," 344; J. A. Dickey and E. C. Branson, "How Farm Tenants Live," University of North Carolina Extension Bulletin 2, No. 6 (Chapel Hill: University of North Carolina Press, 1922); Woofter, *Landlord and Tenant.*

32. C. Vann Woodward, *Origins of the New South, 1877–1913* (Baton Rouge: Louisiana State University Press, 1951); Jones, *Dispossessed,* 127–166; Gavin Wright, *Old South, New South: Revolutions in the Southern Economy Since the Civil War* (New York: Basic Books, 1986), 34–42, 42–49; John Lee Coulter, "The Rural Life Problem of the South," *SAQ* 12 (1913): 60–71; *SE,* 2.

33. *BMB,* 16.

34. "Used to outgeneral": ibid., 30; "In this way": ibid., 30–31. See also Georgia Washington, "Condition of the Women in the Rural Districts of Alabama," *Proceedings of the Hampton Negro Conference* 6 (July 1902): 73–78; and Jacqueline Jones, *Labor of Love, Labor of Sorrow: Black Women, Work, and the Family, from Slavery to the Present,* 2nd ed. (New York: Basic Books, 2010), 77–101.

35. "Encouraged . . . work": *BMB,* 32; FMC for 1880, Alabama, Chambers County. The census taker recorded William's name as "Lawson" and Effie's as "Lola"; he probably misheard Will's name, and it is possible that Effie was a nickname for Lola.

36. *SE,* 27–30; "useless as . . . system": *BMB,* 35–36. See also Jones, *Dispossessed,* 73–4; and Glenn N. Sisk, "Diseases in the Alabama Black Belt, 1875–1917," *AHQ* 24 (Spring 1962): 52–61.

37. *BMB,* 23, 29–30.

38. *SE,* 13; "large numbers": Petition of Randolph County Farmers, 758; J. Morgan Kousser, *The Shaping of Southern Politics: Suffrage Restriction and the Establishment of the One-Party South* (New Haven, CT: Yale University Press, 1974). These data are drawn from a statistical profile of 520 households (112 black, 408 white) in Randolph County in 1880. See Jones, *Labor of Love,* 305–311 (Appendix C); and Peter Kolchin, *First Freedom: The Responses of Alabama's Blacks to Emancipation and Reconstruction* (Westport, CT: Greenwood Press, 1972), 13, 46–47.

39. "Come Sirs": quoted in Paul Horton, "Testing the Limits of Class Politics in Postbellum Alabama: Agrarian Radicalism in Lawrence County," *JSH* 57 (February 1991): 78; Samuel L. Webb, *Two-Party Politics in the One-Party South: Alabama's Hill Country, 1874–1920* (Tuscaloosa: University of Alabama Press, 1997), 4, 41, 92, 111; William Warren Rogers, *The One-Gallused Rebellion: Agrarianism in Alabama, 1865–1896* (Tuscaloosa: University of Alabama Press, 2001). On the bribing of black voters in Randolph County, see Sheldon Hackney, *Populism to Progressivism in Alabama* (Princeton, NJ: Princeton University Press, 1969), 36, 27.

40. "All the older": *BMB,* 38; "Der Book": *SE,* 35.

41. "Throbbing": *BMB,* 40; *SE,* 36–42; "I was dazed": Holtzclaw, "Principal's Story," 121.

42. *BMB,* 43–48.

43. Ibid., 50–51.

44. Ibid., 52–54.

45. "Appealed . . . aspired": ibid., 55; "Passing Club": ibid., 57; Kousser, *Shaping of Southern Politics,* 15, 41, 209–213.

46. "Liar": *SE,* 47, and *BMB,* 61; "the people": Holtzclaw, "Principal's Story," 129; ibid., 127

47. *BMB,* 60–61; *SE,* 46–47; FMC for 1900, Alabama, Randolph County.

48. "Render": *SE,* 48; "a southern . . . existence": *SE,* 48–49; *BMB,* 63; WHH to BTW, Snow Hill, Alabama, September 9, 1901, BTW Papers.

49. *BMB,* 66; "the first two": ibid., 64; *SE,* 49.

50. "Had married": *SE,* 51; Holtzclaw, "Principal's Story," 131.

51. "I": 43rd Day, "white": 2nd Day, *Official Proceedings of the Constitutional Convention of the State of Alabama, May 21st to Sept. 3rd, 1901,* 2069–2071, 8, http://www.legislature.state.al.us/misc/history/constitutions/1901/proceed ings/1901_proceedings_vol1/day43.html (accessed June 20, 2013). On the convention, see Michael Perman, *Struggle for Mastery: Disfranchisement in the South, 1888–1908* (Chapel Hill: University of North Carolina Press, 2001), 173–194.

52. "Practical direction": Aurelius P. Hood, *The Negro at Mound Bayou: Being an Authentic Story of the Founding, Growth, and Development of the "Most Celebrated Town in the South"* (Mound Bayou, MS: A. P. Hood, 1909), 5; "build": ibid., 7; "they sell": ibid., 116; Booker T. Washington, "A Town Owned by Negroes," *WW* 14 (July 1907): 9125–9134.

53. "Not only aroused": *BMB,* 66. Holtzclaw took the quotations from Orison Swett Marden, *Pushing to the Front: Or, Success Under Difficulties, a Book of Inspiration and Encouragement to All Who Are Struggling for Self-Revelation Along the Paths of Knowledge and Duty* (New York: Thomas Y. Crowell, 1894), 127.

54. J. William Harris, *Deep Souths: Delta, Piedmont, and Sea Island Society in the Age of Segregation* (Baltimore, MD: Johns Hopkins University Press, 2001), 41, 120. On the "great bear hunt," see Douglas Brinkley, *The Wilderness Warrior: Theodore Roosevelt and the Crusade for America* (New York: Harper Perennial, 2009), 431–449.

55. "The white man": quoted in Lopez, "James K. Vardaman," 166–167; E. A. Boeger and E. A. Goldenweiser, "A Study of the Tenant Systems of Farming in the Yazoo-Mississippi Delta," US Department of Agriculture, Bulletin No. 337 (Washington, DC: GPO, 1916); Nollie Hickman, *Mississippi Harvest: Lumbering in the Longleaf Pine Belt, 1840–1915* (Jackson: University of Mississippi Press, 1962).

56. "Wild": *BMB,* 69; "You cannot": ibid., 79; "What I want": ibid., 76; *SE,* 60; ibid., 81.

57. "I am not": WHH to Robert C. Bedford (Tuskegee financial agent), Utica, October 25, 1902, BTW Papers; WHH to BTW, Snow Hill, Alabama, June 30, 1902, ibid.; WHH to BTW, Utica, February 25, 1903, ibid.; FMC for 1900, Mississippi, Hinds County. A statistical study of 321 black households and 191 white households yields the demographic profile of this county. See also *BMB,* 79–80.

58. *BMB,* 82.

59. WHH to BTW, Snow Hill, Alabama, October 14, 1902, BTW Papers; *BMB,* 85.

60. "Dear fessor": *BMB,* 102; Arnold Cooper, *Between Struggle and Hope: Four Black Educators in the South, 1894–1915* (Ames: Iowa State University Press, 1989), 23. Holtzclaw's early local supporters included A. C. Carter, Oliver Brown, Tom Williams, Essex Gary, Henry Sampson, Dan Lee, Dan Griffins, Aaron Caldwell, Isaiah Marshall, Pleas McCadney, Zed McNeal, S. W. Harris, and Harrison Flanders.

61. *BMB,* 103–104.

62. "These highly": *SE,* 74; *BMB,* 112–113.

63. "Teachers' . . . condition": *BMB,* 129; "a *desire* . . . house": ibid., 136–137; Manning Marable, "The Politics of Black Land Tenure," *AH* 53 (January 1979): 142–152.

64. "Must follow": *BMB,* 131; "to shoulder": "Sensible Advice Given to Negro Farmers," *ST,* February 4, 1911.

65. *BMB,* 146–149.

66. Advertisements from *DCL* (Harry Hoyle ad from October 2, 1908); Hale, *Making Whiteness,* 123–197.

67. Gregory J. Renoff, *The Big Tent: The Travelling Circus in Georgia, 1820–1930* (Athens: University of Georgia Press, 2008); David Sehat, "The Civilizing Mission of Booker T. Washington," *JSH* 73 (May 2007): 323–362.

68. "That he": quoted in Rosengarten, *All God's Dangers,* xxi; ibid., 199, 354–355, 408–409; *BMB,* 124; "extra Sunday": *SE,* 145–147.

69. "Back . . . farm": "'Stay on the Farm' Slogan of Fifth Annual Session of the State Association of Teachers in Colored Schools Held at Utica, Mississippi," *ST,* August 5, 1911; "Well": Richard Wright, *Black Boy (American Hunger)* (New York: Harper Collins, [1945] 2005), 207.

70. *BMB,* 125–126, 153; Booker T. Washington, "Education Will Solve the Race Problem," *NAR* 171 (August 1900): 221–232; J. M. Stone, "The Suppression of Lawlessness in the South," *NAR* 158 (April 1894): 500–506; Khalil Gibran Muhammad, *The Condemnation of Blackness: Race, Crime, and the Making of Modern Urban America* (Cambridge, MA: Harvard University Press, 2010). Black crime was also a favorite topic of Theodore Roosevelt. See "President Roosevelt's Address," *SW* (July 1906): 403–407.

71. On Redmond, see McMillen, *Dark Journey,* 84, 95, 182, 312; *SE,* 86; and Cooper, *Between Struggle and Hope,* 87. For an account of the school in 1906, see "The Utica Normal and Industrial Institute," *CAM* (April 1906): 221–228.

72. See "Some Advice to Negros: Institute Held at Utica This Week. Right Living Was Theme," *Jackson Evening News,* February 15, 1907, BTW Papers; Scott to WHH, June 14, 1906, BTW Papers.

73. "Tuskegee's Twenty-Fifth Anniversary," *SW* (May 1906): 260–261; Gilson Willets, "After Forty Years of Freedom," *AM* (November 1905): 13; "We": quoted in *BMB*, 159; "all . . . ticket": ibid., 163; *SE*, 134–137; *Southern Notes* 4 (May 1906). See the fund-raising brochure, which features a map and description of the proposed parcel, signed by Holtzclaw (March 1907), box 57, reel 52, BTW Papers.

74. *SE*, 89; "all of which": Holtzclaw, "Principal's Story," 139.

75. *SE*, 239. Black newspaper accounts at times emphasized the "manly" nature of industrial schools. For example, an account of the annual Utica Negro Farmers Conference in the *Savannah Tribune* stressed the "manly discussion" among the participants and the "manly position" of the principal, who said he aspired to "measure up to the standards of a man, and if not he would have to get aside to make a place for a man." See "Mississippi Farmers Hold Successful Conference," *ST*, January 31, 1920.

76. "Demonstrating": Jackson *Daily News* article quoted in *BMB*, 220; "Odd . . . worked": William Pickens article pub. in *The Independent*, February 22, 1912, and most of it reprinted in *BMB*, 216–217; Wish, "Negro Education," 191; "Successful Negro Fair: Many Prizes Awarded at the Second Annual Fair of the Utica Normal and Industrial Institute—A Fine Lot of Exhibits," *ST*, December 2, 1911.

77. Penney, "Light," 25–27; Charles Alexander, "Down in Mississippi," *AM* (February 1909): 177–178; *BMB*, 221; "Office machines": *SE*, 205.

78. "The Negroes . . . schools": *BMB*, 202–205; McMillen, *Dark Journey*, 298.

79. *BMB*, 206, 209.

80. Ibid., 196.

81. Harlan and Smock, eds., *BTW Papers* (1982), 12:127–128.

82. "Throwing": Oswald Garrison Villard to BTW, New York, May 21, 1914, ibid., 13:27; WHH to BTW, May 7 and May 22, 1913, and Emmett Scott to WHH, November 20 and December 2, 1913, all BTW Papers.

83. "Conference of Negro Industrial Schools," *The Survey* 30 (May 10, 1913): 242.

84. "I am sure . . . years": BTW to WHH, Tuskegee, July 14, 1914, Special Correspondence, box 526, reel 395, BTW Papers.

85. "An elementary . . . industries": Jones, *Negro Education*, 2:347–349; Carter G. Woodson, "Personal: Thomas Jesse Jones," *JNH* 35 (January 1950): 107.

86. Pickens article quoted in *BMB*, 215, 217, 225.

87. WHH to BTW, Utica, August 9, 1912, BTW Papers; WHH to BTW, October 22, 1914, ibid.; BTW to WHH, Tuskegee, May 1, 1915, ibid.; "When the": *SE*, 117.

88. Holtzclaw, "Principal's Story," 111.

89. FMC for 1880, Chambers County: FMC for 1910, Randolph County; FMC for 1910, 1920, 1930, Mississippi, Hinds/Copiah Counties; *SE*, 223–227. On rural women in Alabama at the time, see Washington, "Condition of Women in the Rural Districts of Alabama," 73–78.

90. "She": Penney, "Light," 26; "I never . . . is?": *SE*, 223; McMillen, *Dark Journey*, 98.

91. The quotations are from letters Holtzclaw wrote to Mary Ella while he was on the road. "My very": sent from Boston on March 26, 1911; "My dear": sent from New York City, nd; "I have been thinking . . . students": ibid., all in William H. Holtzclaw Archives, Hinds Community College, Raymond, Mississippi. On Mary Ella's correspondence course with the American School of Home Economics in Chicago, see the

letter from Jessie F. Beadle, Chicago, November 19, 1909, WHH Archives, Hinds Community College; "the greatest": *BMB,* 224; "truly": ibid., 199.

92. *SE,* 223–227.

93. Henry S. Enck, "Black Self-Help in the Progressive Era: The 'Northern Campaigns' of the Smaller Southern Black Industrial Schools, 1900–1915," *JNH* 61 (January 1976): 86.

94. *SE,* 168–169.

95. R. H. Leavell, "Negro Migration from Mississippi," in J. H. Dillard, ed., *Negro Migration in 1916–17,* US Department of Labor, Division of Negro Economics (Washington, DC: GPO, 1919); James Grossman, *Land of Hope: Chicago, Black Southerners, and the Great Migration* (Chicago: University of Chicago Press, 1991), 17; Isabel Wilkerson, *The Warmth of Other Sons: The Epic Story of America's Great Migration* (New York: Random House, 2010); Carole Marks, *Farewell—We're Good and Gone: The Great Black Migration* (Bloomington: Indiana University Press, 1989); Neil Fligstein, *Going North: Migration of Blacks and Whites from the South, 1900–1950* (New York: Academic Press, 1981); Florette Henri, *Black Migration: Movement North, 1900–1920* (Garden City, NY: Anchor Press, 1976).

96. Nan Elizabeth Woodruff, *American Congo: The African American Freedom Struggle in the Delta* (Cambridge, MA: Harvard University Press), 2012; Grossman, *Land of Hope,* 43, 54–56, 70, 105; "'Scuse me": quoted in Johnson, *Shadow,* 98.

97. "American Congo": Woodruff, *American Congo,* 1; "Here": Letter of Henry E. Cobb, "A 'Near East' at Home," *NYT,* November 17, 1923.

98. "Considerable . . . violent": *SE,* 132–133; "America's shame": "Negro Farmers Hold Annual Conference," *ST,* February 9, 1922; McMillen, *Dark Journey,* 309–311; John M. Barry, *Rising Tide: The Great Mississippi Flood of 1927 and How It Changed America* (New York: Simon and Schuster, 1998); Robyn Spencer, "Contested Terrain: The Mississippi Flood of 1927 and the Struggle to Control Black Labor," *JNH* 79 (Spring 1994): 170–181.

99. "The explanation": "The Rural Negro on Relief," Research Bulletin No. 6950 of the Federal Emergency Relief Administration (Washington, DC: GPO, 1935).

100. "He was": *SE,* 218; "wan and tired": ibid., 228; "If my": *BMB,* 228–229.

101. *SE,* 229–233.

102. Ibid., 240.

103. Dunbar Rowland, "A Mississippi View of Race Relations in the South" (Jackson, MS: Harmon, 1903), 19, 20, 12, 16.

104. "Intelligence": Washington, *Up from Slavery,* 167; "strained": *BMB,* 125–126; McMillen, *Dark Journey,* 280. For an extended discussion of this theme, see Michael West, *The Education of Booker T. Washington: American Democracy and the Idea of Race Relations* (New York: Columbia University Press, 2008); and Karen E. Fields and Barbara J. Fields, *Racecraft: The Soul of Inequality in American Life* (London: Verso Books, 2012), 24, 39, 77, 117.

105. "A docile": Welch, "Plantation Land Tenure," 52; "Elaborate": ibid., 54; Woodruff, *American Congo.*

106. *SE,* 242–243; Walter Washington, "Utica Junior College, 1903–1957: A Half-Century of Education for Negroes" (EdD diss., University of Southern Mississippi, 1969), 73–78, 128.

CHAPTER 6 SIMON P. OWENS

1. Heather Ann Thompson, *Whose Detroit? Politics, Labor, and Race in a Modern American City* (Ithaca, NY: Cornell University Press, 2001), 185–186. For other accounts of the strike, see news articles in *DFP*, July 25 and 26, 1973; James A. Geschwender, *Class, Race, and Worker Insurgency: The League of Revolutionary Black Workers* (Cambridge: Cambridge University Press, 1977), 190–198; and Dan Georgakas and Marvin Surkin, *Detroit: I Do Mind Dying: A Study in Urban Revolution* (New York: St. Martin's Press, 1975), 101–133.

2. Thompson, *Whose Detroit?* 185–186.

3. "Capitulation . . . strikers": Fraser quoted in James Graham, "Walkout at Chrysler Plant Appears Ended," *DN*, August 13, 1973; Mark Lett, "2 Workers Idle Chrysler Plant," *DN*, July 24, 1973; Jack Crellin et al., "A Precedent in Chrysler Shutdown," *DN*, July 25, 1973; "They go": Paul M. Branzburg, "Chrysler Take-Over Eyed by Socialist," *DFP*, July 30, 1973. The photo of July 25, 1973, is on the front page of *DFP* with the headline "2 Angry Workers Shut Chrysler Plant."

4. Jack Crellin and Jack Burdock, "More Strikes Possible, Fraser Tells Chrysler Prior to Plant Tours," *DN*, August 10, 1973; Jo Thomas and Michael Orr, "New Wildcat Hits Chrysler," *DFP*, August 9, 1973; Jo Thomas and Douglas Williams, "Wildcatters Will Delay '74 Models: Chrysler," *DFP*, August 11, 1973; "It's Like": Wilson quoted in "Auto Union Is Threatening Big 3 to Get a Voice in Work Conditions," *NYT*, August 12, 1973; Thompson, *Whose Detroit?* 123, 174, 199–200. Frank Marquart, *An Auto Worker's Journal: The UAW from Crusade to One-Party Union* (University Park: Penn State University Press, 1975), 160, likens the auto plant to a cotton plantation.

5. Jack Crellin, Jack Burdock, Paul Bernstein, and Robert S. Wisler, "Police Oust Chrysler Plant Rebels," *DN*, August 15, 1973; Jack Crellin and Fred Manardo, "Key Chrysler Plant Is Struck," *DN*, August 8, 1973; Jack Crellin and Susan Fleming, "Wildcat Strike Continues at Chrysler Plant," *DN*, August 9, 1973; Jack Burdock and Jack Crellin, "Mack Stamping Is Forced to Close in New Chrysler Row," *DN*, August 14, 1973; "Chrysler Shuts Mack Plant After Rebels Launch Sit-In: Fired Worker Slugs Guards," *DFP*, August 15, 1973; Paul Branzburg, "Workers Holding Out Quietly," ibid.; William E. Farrell, "Chrysler Plant Shut in Assault," *NYT*, August 15, 1973.

6. "Shut": Gilbreth's wife, Sarah, quoted in Crellin, et al., "Police Oust Chrysler Plant Rebels"; "dedicated": Crellin and Manardo, "Key Chrysler Plant"; "There": Anthony McJennett quoted in Crellin and Fleming, "Wildcat Strike Continues."

7. Ralph Orr and Jo Thomas, "UAW Muscle Opens Plant: 1,000 Guard the Gates," *DFP*, August 17, 1973; Jim Schutze, "Fighting to Halt 'Sellout' by UAW, Radicals Claim," and Jo Thomas, "Young Workers Seeking 2d Revolution," *DFP*, August 19, 1973; Georgakas and Surkin, *Detroit*, 227–234; John Barnard, *American Vanguard: The United Auto Workers During the Reuther Years, 1935–1970* (Detroit: Wayne State University Press, 2004).

8. "Declaration . . . blackmail": Jack Burdock, Ronald L. Russell, and Anne Getz, "UAW Men Help Police Open Plant," *DN*, August 16, 1973; Ronald L. Russell, "'UAW Goons Won't Stop Us,' Chrysler Rebel Leader Vows," *DN*, August 19, 1973. See the dissident literature collected by UAW officials in UAW Region 1B, box 38,

folder 27, Walter P. Reuther Library, Wayne State University, Detroit, Michigan (hereinafter UAW Region 1B Archives).

9. "Fighting": B. J. Widick, "Work in the Auto Plants: Then and Now," in B. J. Widick, *Auto Work and Its Discontents* (Baltimore, MD: Johns Hopkins University Press, 1976), 6; "a Black": Charles Denby, *Indignant Heart: A Black Worker's Journal* (Detroit: Wayne State University Press, 1978), 273 (hereinafter *IH*).

10. David Gartman, "Dialectics of the Labor Process, Consumer Culture, and Class Struggle: The Contradictory Development of the American Automobile Industry," and Larry W. Isaac and Larry D. Christiansen, "Degradations of Labor, Cultures of Cooperation: Braverman's 'Labor,' Lordstown, and the Social Factory," both in Mark L. Wardell, Thomas L. Steiger, and Peter Meiksins, eds., *Rethinking the Labor Process* (Albany: State University of New York Press, 1999), 104, 125; Douglas Williams, "Workers Grab at Overtime but Ask Right to Say No," *DFP*, July 9, 1973. I am grateful to Michael Flug for providing me with a copy of the original typescript of "Indignant Heart" (hereinafter "IH"); it includes the real names of places and people, many of which were changed for the published version. See "IH," 20.

11. Raya Dunayevskaya, *Philosophy and Revolution: From Hegel to Sartre, and from Marx to Mao* (New York: Dell, 1973), 281; "To me": *IH*, 281; Michael Flug, e-mails, December 23, 2011, April 1, 2012, and June 24, 2013, describing the work routine of his friend and comrade Si Owens.

12. On the James Johnson Jr. case, see Thompson, *Whose Detroit?* "You see": "John Doe" interview, in Richard Feldman and Michael Betzold, eds., *End of the Line: Autoworkers and the American Dream: An Oral History* (Urbana: University of Illinois Press, 1990), 158; and Craig A. Zbala, "Sabotage in an Automobile Assembly Plant: Worker Voice on the Shopfloor," in Robert Asher and Ronald Edsforth, eds., *Autowork* (Albany: State University of New York Press, 1995), 209–225.

13. "This morning": "WJ," *N&L*, August–September 1973; "masterminds": *IH*, 276; "We did": Paul M. Branzburg, "Night in Captive Auto Plant: Unlikely Place for Drama," *DFP*, August 16, 1973.

14. "I wouldn't": "Police Oust Rebels," *DN*, August 15, 1973; "The workers": *IH*, 276; "American Airlines . . . class": Tom Dennis quoted in Pete Waldmeir, "Communists Disavow Wildcat Strike Pair," *DN*, August 24, 1973.

15. "Hurting": "IH," 75; David M. Lewis-Colman, *Race Against Liberalism: Black Workers and the UAW in Detroit* (Urbana: University of Illinois Press, 2008); Eileen Boris, "'You Wouldn't Want One of 'Em Dancing with Your Wife': Racialized Bodies on the Job in World War II," *AQ* 50 (March 1998): 77–108; Kevin Boyle, "The Kiss: Racial and Gender Conflict in a 1950s Auto Factory," *JAH* 84 (September 1997): 496–523.

16. See news accounts in the *DFP* throughout the summer of 1973. See also Thompson, *Whose Detroit?* 81–82, 90–94, 98–100, 143–152, 196–198, 204, 211.

17. Thompson, *Whose Detroit?*

18. "A Good": "WJ," *N&L*, May 1969; Lou Turner, "Charles Denby and the Idea of Marxist-Humanism," *N&L*, December 1997.

19. "There is": Raya Dunayevskaya, "Two Worlds: 'Black Power,' Race, and Class," *N&L*, January 1967; Dunayevskaya, *Philosophy and Revolution*, 291.

20. "IH," 7, 1, 6, 11.

21. "Were": "IH," 11; "It was": ibid., 9; Hasan Kwami Jeffries, *Bloody Lowndes: Civil Rights and Black Power in Alabama's Black Belt* (New York: New York University Press, 2009), 16–17.

22. "IH," 2, 3, 7.

23. Ibid., 10, 3, 4.

24. "What men": William Attaway, *Blood on the Forge* (New York: Monthly Review Press, [1941] 1987), 44; Lee Bidgood, "The Coming of Industry to the South," *AAAAPSS* 153 (January 1931): 151; Jeffries, *Bloody Lowndes,* 19; Lou Turner, "Charles Denby," in Jessie Carney Smith, ed., *Notable Black American Men* (Detroit: Gale, 1998), 291. Owens recounted his expulsion from Tuskegee in a conversation with Kevin Anderson. Kevin Anderson, e-mail, December 6, 2011.

25. "When": "IH," 14; Isabel Wilkerson, *The Warmth of Other Suns: The Epic Story of America's Great Migration* (New York: Random House, 2010); Elaine Latzman Moon, ed., *Untold Tales, Unsung Heroes: An Oral History of Detroit's African-American Community, 1918–1967* (Detroit: Wayne State University Press, 1994), 44–45.

26. "And I urge": Davis quoted in Keith P. Griffler, *What Price Alliance? Black Radicals Confront White Labor, 1918–1938* (New York: Garland, 1995), 54, Charles F. Holt, "Who Benefited from the Prosperity of the Twenties?" *EEH* 14 (July 1977): 277–289; Stanley Lieberson, *A Piece of the Pie: Blacks and White Immigrants Since 1880* (Berkeley: University of California Press, 1980), 339; Sterling D. Spero and Abram L. Harris, *The Black Worker: A Study of the Negro and the Labor Movement* (New York: Columbia University Press, 1931), 144–145.

27. "We had": "IH," 16; Richard W. Thomas, *Life for Us Is What We Make It: Building Black Community in Detroit, 1915–1945* (Bloomington: Indiana University Press, 1992), 29, 42–44; 53–67; Joyce Shaw Peterson, "Black Automobile Workers in Detroit, 1910–1930," *JNH* 64 (Summer 1979): 177–190; Moon, ed., *Untold Tales,* 43; John C. Dancy, *Sand Against the Wind: The Memoirs of John C. Dancy* (Detroit: Wayne State University Press, 1966).

28. "A man-killing . . . spot": "IH," 20; Peterson, "Black Automobile Workers"; Moon, ed., *Untold Tales,* 130, 150; August Meier and Elliott Rudwick, *Black Detroit and the Rise of the UAW* (New York: Oxford University Press, 1979), 3–19.

29. "IH," 22.

30. "Night mail": Robin D. G. Kelley, *Hammer and Hoe: Alabama Communists During the Great Depression* (Chapel Hill: University of North Carolina Press, 1990), 102; ibid., 53–55, 101–102, 161; Jeffries, *Bloody Lowndes,* 25; Theodore Rosengarten, *All God's Dangers: The Life of Nate Shaw* (Chicago: University of Chicago Press, 2000).

31. Kelley, *Hammer and Hoe,* 167. See also ibid., 163–168.

32. "IH," 27–30.

33. "Honey": ibid., 29; interview with Michael Flug, Chicago, January 6, 2012.

34. "That": "IH," 31. See also Hosea Hudson, *Black Worker in the Deep South: A Personal Record* (New York: International Publishers, 1972).

35. "IH," 32.

36. Ibid., 32–33. See also Robin D. G. Kelley, "'We Are Not What We Seem': Rethinking Black Working-Class Opposition in the Jim Crow South," *JAH* 80 (June 1993): 75–112.

37. "IH," 34, 37.

38. "Hoodoo . . . gazer": ibid., 41–42; "the most . . . scared": ibid., 50–51; "deteriorating": Charles Johnson, "The Present Status of Race Relations in the South," *JSF* 23 (1944–1945): 27.

39. "Our rights": Kevin Boyle, "Auto Workers at War: Patriotism and Protest in the American Automobile Industry, 1939–1945," in Asher and Edsforth, eds., *Autowork*, 123.

40. "IH," 52–57. For a general account of the riot, see Dominic J. Capeci Jr. and Martha Wilkerson, *Layered Violence: The Detroit Rioters of 1943* (Jackson: University Press of Mississippi, 1991); and Alan Clive, *State of War: Michigan in World War II* (Ann Arbor: University of Michigan Press, 1979), 130–169.

41. "IH," 56–57.

42. "Have": Stimson quoted in A. Russell Buchanan, *Black Americans in World War II* (Santa Barbara, CA: Clio Books, 1994); Thomas J. Sugrue, *The Origins of the Urban Crisis: Race and Inequality in Postwar Detroit* (Princeton, NJ: Princeton University Press, 1996), 17–31; "Negro Women War Workers," Women's Bureau Bulletin No. 205 (Washington, DC: GPO, 1945), 7; Herbert R. Northrup, "Unions and Negro Employment," *AAAPSS* 244 (March 1946): 54–56; Bernice Anita Reed, "Accommodation Between Negro and White Employees in a West Coast Aircraft Industry, 1941–1944," *Social Forces* 26 (October 1947): 76–84.

43. "One of": Martin Glaberman, *Wartime Strikes: The Struggle Against the No-Strike Pledge in the UAW During World War II* (Detroit: Bewick/Ed, 1980), 39; "I said . . . fields": "IH," 58; Robert C. Weaver, *Negro Labor: A National Problem* (New York: Harcourt, Brace, 1946); Nancy F. Gabin, *Feminism in the Labor Movement: Women and the United Auto Workers, 1935–1975* (Ithaca, NY: Cornell University Press, 1990), 212; Jacqueline Jones, *The Dispossessed: America's Underclasses from the Civil War to the Present* (New York: Basic Books, 1992), 233–235; Robert Korstad and Nelson Lichtenstein, "Opportunities Found and Lost: Labor, Radicals, and the Early Civil Rights Movement," in Eric Arnesen, ed., *The Black Worker: Race, Labor, and Civil Rights Since Emancipation* (Urbana: University of Illinois Press, 2007), 222–249.

44. "IH," 70, 63, 60.

45. Ibid., 61–63. On Bill Oliver, see Nelson Lichtenstein, *Walter Reuther: The Most Dangerous Man in Detroit* (Urbana: University of Illinois Press, 1995), 252, 317, 374–375.

46. Interview with James Boggs, in Moon, ed., *Untold Tales*, 152; Lichtenstein, *Walter Reuther*, 252, 310, 316–317, 323, 374, 375; Grace Lee Boggs, *Living for Change: An Autobiography* (Minneapolis: University of Minnesota Press, 1998); Stephen M. Ward, ed., *Pages from a Black Radical's Notebook: A James Boggs Reader* (Detroit: Wayne State University Press, 2011); Lewis-Colman, *Race Against Liberalism*, 25–28, 40–41, 51, 87–88; Thompson, *Whose Detroit?* 49–55, 66; Staughton Lynd and Alice Lynd, eds., *The New Rank and File* (New York: ILR Press, 2000), 203–204; Joyce Kornbluh interview with Lillian Hatcher, in "The Twentieth-Century Trade Union Woman: Vehicle for Social Change Oral History Project" (Ann Arbor: Institute of Labor and Industrial Relations, 1976); Dorothy Sue Cobble, *The Other Women's Movement: Workplace Justice and Social Rights in America* (Princeton, NJ: Princeton University Press, 2004), 5, 40–43, 52–53, 90, 107, 152, 200–201. Genora Johnson Dollinger is "Helen" in *IH*, 167, and "G" in "IH," 104.

47. "We must": Reuther quoted in Lichtenstein, *Walter Reuther,* 133; Glaberman, *Wartime Strikes,* 68; Boyle, "Auto Workers at War."

48. "Had . . . him": "IH," 101–103; Karen Tucker Anderson, "Last Hired, First Fired: Black Women Workers During World War II," *JAH* 69 (June 1982): 82–97; Jacqueline Jones, *Labor of Love, Labor of Sorrow: Black Women, Work, and the Family, from Slavery to the Present* (New York: Basic Books, 2010), 195–218.

49. "The best . . . the next": "IH," 64; Marquart, *Auto Worker's Journal,* 102; Lewis-Colman, *Race Against Liberalism,* 20, 33–34, 48–49. On the CIO's "culture of unity," see Lizabeth Cohen, *Making a New Deal: Industrial Workers in Chicago, 1919–1939* (Cambridge: Cambridge University Press, 1990).

50. "The end": "IH," 65; "Not . . . blank": ibid., 102–103; Marjorie McKenzie, "Against the Lean Years," *AWJ* 3 (Summer 1943): 7; Jones, *Labor of Love,* 210–213; Ruth Milkman, "Rosie the Riveter Revisited: Management's Postwar Purge of Women Auto Workers," in Nelson Lichtenstein and Stephen Meyer, eds., *On the Line: Essays in the History of Auto Work* (Urbana: University of Illinois Press, 1989):143–144.

51. "Negroes . . . Negroes": "IH," 66, 74; Christopher Phelps, "Introduction," to Max Shachtman, *Race and Revolution* (London: Verso Books, 2003), xxi.

52. "What": quoted in Moon, ed., *Untold Tales,* 181; Sugrue, *Origins,* 42–48; interview with Abson "Abe" McDaniel, in Feldman and Betzold, eds., *End of the Line,* 81–82; "Hitler": James Boggs, "The American Revolution" in Ward, ed., *Pages,* 133.

53. "IH," 105, 67–74.

54. Ibid., 76, 66, 94, 100, 110.

55. Ibid., 104–106.

56. Ibid., 106–107.

57. "I . . . party": ibid., 108; Scott McLemee, ed., *C. L. R. James on the "Negro Question"* (Jackson: University Press of Mississippi, 1996), 138–147; Boggs, *Living for Change,* 77.

58. C. L. R. James, "The Class Struggle," in C. L. R. James, *The Future in the Present: Selected Writings* (Westport, CT: Lawrence Hill, 1977), 128–151. See also Kent Worcester, *C. L. R. James: A Political Biography* (Albany: State University of New York Press, 1996); Frank Rosengarten, *Urbane Revolutionary: C. L. R. James and the Struggle for a New Society* (Jackson: University Press of Mississippi, 2008).

59. "State": Raya Dunayevskaya, "The Marxist-Humanist Theory of State Capitalism" (Detroit: News & Letters Committees, 1992); Raya Dunayevskaya, "A New Revision of Marxian Economics," *AER* 34 (September 1944): 531–537; "Raya Dunayevskaya Is Dead; Author Was Aide to Trotsky," *NYT,* June 13, 1987; Will Lissner, "Soviet Economics Stirs Debate Here," *NYT,* October 1, 1944; Will Lissner, "No Change Is Seen in Soviet Economy," *NYT,* July 29, 1945; "a class": Grace Lee Boggs, "Organizing in the U.S., 1938–1953," in Selwyn Reginald Cudjoe and William E. Cain, eds., *C. L. R. James: His Intellectual Legacies* (Amherst: University of Massachusetts Press, 1995), 167–168; "we Johnsonites": Boggs, *Living for Change,* 63; Anna Grimshaw, ed., *Special Delivery: The Letters of C. L. R. James to Constance Webb, 1939–1948* (Oxford: Blackwell, 1996).

60. "We": C. L. R. James, "Down with Starvation Wages in South-East Missouri," in James, *Future,* 89–90; Rachel M. Peterson, "Adapting Left Culture to the Cold

War: Theodore Ward, Ann Petry, and Correspondence" (PhD diss., University of Michigan, 2008), 229; Worcester, *C. L. R. James*, 81n78.

61. "The Negroes": "IH," 110; ibid., 108–110; "fight to": flyer in photo section following xvi; Ward, ed., *Pages*, 378n54; *IH*, 174–179; "I understood": "IH," 112.

62. "All theory": Raya Dunayevskaya to "Red," 1950, Raya Dunayevskaya Papers, reel 1, 1484, Walter P. Reuther Library, Wayne State University, Detroit, Michigan (available on microfilm) (hereinafter RD Papers with microfilm reel number and page number); A. H. Raskin, "Coal Strike Looms on Issue of Ending Pension Payments," *NYT*, September 18, 1949; Raya Dunayevskaya, *Marxism and Freedom: From 1776 Until Today* (New York: Bookman, 1958), 267; Charles Denby, "Workers Battle Automation" (Detroit: News & Letters Committees, 1960), 37–46; Herbert Northrup and Richard L. Rowan, *Negro Employment in Southern Industry: A Study of Racial Policies in Five Industries* (Philadelphia: University of Pennsylvania Press, 1971); Price Fishback, "Segregation in Job Hierarchies: West Virginia Coal Mining, 1906–1932," *JEH* 44 (September 1984): 755–774; James T. Laing, "The Negro Miner in West Virginia," *SF* 14 (March 1936): 416–422; Ronald Lewis, *Black Coal Miners in America: Race, Class, and Community Conflict, 1780–1980* (Lexington: University Press of Kentucky, 1987), 170–177.

63. "Ching to Bid for Peace in Steel as Layoffs Spread," *NYT*, October 19, 1949; 1983 Pre-Convention Discussion Bulletin No. 4, "The 1949–50 Miners Strike—and Labor Today," RD Papers, reel 4, 7867–7869; F. Forest, "Auto Union Relief Caravan Hailed in Coal Mining Town," RD Papers, reel 1, 1479–1481.

64. "Plodding": Letter from "Frank" to Andy Phillips, June 3, 1983, RD Papers, reel 4, 7873; Worcester, *C. L. R. James*, 123; Ward, ed., *Pages*, 37–41; Peterson, "Adapting Left Culture," 229–230; Grace Lee Boggs, "Thinking and Acting Dialectically: C. L. R. James, the American Years," *MR* 45 (October 1993): 38–46; James Edward Smethurst, *The Black Arts Movement: Literary Nationalism in the 1960s and 1970s* (Chapel Hill: University of North Carolina Press, 2005), 187–188.

65. "Strike": Constance Webb, *Not Without Love: Memoirs* (Hanover, NH: University Press of New England, 2003), 246–252; Boggs, *Living for Change*, 62, 110.

66. "I . . . refused": Webb, *Not Without Love*, 249; "felt . . . way": ibid., 266. Dunayevskaya used "indignant heart" in "Report on Organization," October 1959, RD Papers, reel 2, 2733; "And the people": "Presentation by Raya Dunayevskaya to the Black-Red Conference," January 12, 1969, RD Papers, reel 2, 4342. Dunayevskaya often used the word *indignant* to describe aggrieved workers and other groups.

67. "That he": Webb, *Not Without Love*, 266; Peterson, "Adapting Left Culture," 146, 246, 252, 261; Geschwender, *Class*, 41; Lichtenstein, *Walter Reuther*, 317; Lewis-Colman, *Race Against Liberalism*, 42–46; "to the point": Boggs, *Living for Change*, 100.

68. "Shameful": James quoted in Rosengarten, *Urbane Revolutionary*, 72; Kevin Anderson, "The Marcuse-Dunayevskaya Dialogue, 1954–1979," *SST* 39 (March 1990): 93; Webb, *Not Without Love*, 179; Boggs, *Living for Change*, 100; Anderson e-mail; "the rottenness ... things": "Our Organization" (1956), RD Papers, reel 2, 2666.

69. Interview with Flag.

70. Lou Turner, "Charles Denby and the Idea of Marxist-Humanism," *N&L*, December 1997; Turner, "Charles Denby," 291–292; Dunayevskaya, *Philosophy and Rev-*

olution, 291; "a question": *IH,* 225; Sugrue, *Origins,* 22–29, 242, 311–322; Barnard, *American Vanguard,* 307–308, 334; Geschwender, *Class,* 40–41; Boyle, "The Kiss," 507; Lewis-Colman, *Race Against Liberalism,* 41; Nancy McLean, *Freedom Is Not Enough: The Opening of the American Workplace* (Cambridge, MA: Harvard University Press, 2006), 56–57; Lichtenstein, *Walter Reuther,* 317, 373–375.

71. Denby, "Workers Battle Automation," 7. On mental and manual labor, see "WJ," *N&L,* March 1983.

72. "Revolution": *IH,* 181; "If violence": "WJ," *N&L,* January 22, 1957; "White and Negro Southerners Change Relations in the South," *N&L,* July 8, 1967; "Birmingham Negroes Show Way to Destroy Southern Humanity," *N&L,* May 1963; *IH,* 190–201.

73. "Report from the South," *N&L,* January 22, 1957; "It Is the Negro": "WJ," *N&L,* January 6, 1956; "American Civilization on Trial: The Negro as Touchstone of History" (Detroit: News & Letters Committees, 1963). See also Jo Ann Gibson Robinson, *The Montgomery Bus Boycott and the Women Who Started It: The Memoir of Jo Ann Gibson Robinson* (Lexington: University Press of Kentucky, 1987).

74. "The good": "Way of the World" column, *N&L,* February 1964; "I have . . . life": ibid., June–July 1963.

75. "The feeling": *IH,* 196; Moon, ed., *Untold Stories,* 263; Sugrue, *Origins;* Thompson, *Whose Detroit?*

76. "We have": police chief quoted in Jeffries, *Bloody Lowndes,* 49; Pete Daniel, "African American Farmers and Civil Rights," *JSH* 73 (February 2007): 16.

77. Jeffries, *Bloody Lowndes,* 39–80; "totalitarian . . . darkness": Andrew Kopkind, *The Thirty Years' Wars: Dispatches and Diversions of a Radical Journalist, 1965–1994* (London: Verso Books, 1995), 48–49.

78. "For White": "Labor, Negro Movement Make New Links to Change Society," *N&L,* March 1966; "comes out": John Hulett, "Creating the Black Panther Movement," in Herbert Aptheker, ed., *A Documentary History of the Negro People in the United States, 1960–1968* (New York: Citadel Press, 1951), 7:404; "a bold": Carmichael quoted in Peniel Joseph, *Waiting 'Til the Midnight Hour: A Narrative History of Black Power in America* (New York: Henry Holt, 2006), 164; "The Snick": John Corry, "The Changing Times in Lowndes County: An All-Negro Ticket," *NYT,* October 31, 1966; Jeffries, *Bloody Lowndes,* 143–178.

79. "My": Glover quoted in Gene Roberts, "'Tent' City Rising in Alabama Field," *NYT,* January 1, 1966; Cheryl Greenberg, ed., *Circle of Trust: Remembering SNCC* (New Brunswick, NJ: Rutgers University Press, 1998), 99; Jeffries, *Bloody Lowndes,* 30, 109–111; *IH,* 215; "200 Acres of Land Purchased in Lowndes County, Alabama," *Community Views,* February 1, 1968, 1; Charles Denby, "Trip Down South Reveals Negro Revolution Keeps Moving Forward," *N&L,* April 1967; "Northern guardian angel": "Factory Worker Helps Lowndes County Poor," *Jet,* March 16, 1966, 6; Mississippi Department of Archives and History Sovereignty Commission online, files 1-114-0-4-1-1-1 and 10-86-049-6-1-1 (page from the *Congressional Record,* House of Representatives, February 9, 1966, 2653), http://mdah.state.ms.us/arrec/digital_archives /sovcom/result.php?image=/data/sov_commission/images/png/cd09/070362.png& otherstuff=10|86|0|49|6|1|1|69450|# (accessed June 20, 2013).

80. "We are": "WJ," *N&L,* March 1965; "The Negro Nationalists": ibid., August–September 1967; Corry, "Changing Times"; Jeffries, *Bloody Lowndes,* 179–206; Dunayevskaya, "Two Worlds"; "made": *IH,* 212.

81. "The Negro . . . work": *IH,* 214–215; "The movement": "200 Acres," 1–2; Denby, "Trip Down South"; "It hasn't": Charles Denby, "Trip Down South," *N&L,* June 1967.

82. "Law": *IH,* 223; "power structure": ibid., 227; Sidney Fine, *Violence in the Model City: The Cavanagh Administration, Race Relations, and the Detroit Riot of 1967* (Ann Arbor: University of Michigan Press, 1989), 463; Georgakas and Surkin, *Detroit,* 15.

83. "A Summary of the National Editorial Board Meeting of News and Letters Committees," September 3–4, 1977, RD Papers, reel 3, 5779.

84. "WJ," *N&L,* May 1980; MacLean, *Freedom,* 89–108; James J. Heckman and Brook S. Payner, "Determining the Impact of Federal Antidiscrimination Policy on the Economic Status of Blacks: A Study of South Carolina," *AER* 79 (March 1989): 138–177; Herbert Hill, "The AFL-CIO and the Black Worker: Twenty-Five Years After the Merger," *JIR* 10 (Spring 1982): 5–78; James Geschwender, "Marxist-Leninist Organization: Prognosis Among Black Workers," *JBS* 8 (March 1978): 291; John J. Donahue III and James Heckman, "Continuous Versus Episodic Change: The Impact of Civil Rights Status of Blacks," *JEL* 29 (December 1991): 1603–1643.

85. Lichtenstein, *Walter Reuther,* 413–414; Lauren Ray, "The League of Revolutionary Black Workers, Arab Americans, and Palestine Solidarity," *PSR* (Fall 2003), http://psreview.org/content/view/18/70/ (accessed June 18, 2013); Gartman, "Dialectics," 103–104; "the last": "WJ," *N&L,* June 1978.

86. "WJ," *N&L,* November 1968.

87. "Black Workers Uprising," *Inner City Voice* 1 (June 1968): 1; Thomas R. Brooks, "Workers, Black and White: DRUMbeats in Detroit," *Dissent,* January–February 1970, 16–25.

88. Thompson, *Whose Detroit?* 103, 109–114, 116–122, 160–168, 170, 179, 185; Geschwender, *Class,* 91; Geschwender, "Marxist-Leninist Organization."

89. "Capitalism": *The South End,* January 23, 1969, 6; "The Union": ibid., 10; Thompson, *Whose Detroit?* 199; "U-ain't": elrum Newsletter, August 14, 1970, UAW Region 1B, series iii, box 237, folder 30, Reuther Library; "calling": "League of Revolutionary Black Workers: The U.A.W. Must End All Racist Practices," *ICV,* November 1969, 12; "Be-Head": *The South End,* January 23, 1969, 4. Other plant newsletters included "Lynch Road Rumblings," "drum," "Eldon Wildcat," and "jarum."

90. "It is . . . department": "Mack Stinger," UAW Region 1B, series 1 box 18, folder 16; *IH,* 265.

91. "Tell": "WJ," *N&L,* August–September 1970; "vulgar": *IH,* 267; "an Old . . . true": ibid., 268.

92. Brooks, "Workers, Black and White; "specialize": "Common Sense or Chaos?" UAW communication to members, c. October 1968, UAW Region 1B, box 237, folder 30; Thompson, *Whose Detroit?* 190; "WJ," *N&L,* October 1969 and March 1970; Geschwender, *Class,* 182–187; "unions . . . management": "Black U.A.W. Workers Caucus Formed," *The South End,* November 12, 1971, 6.

93. "Concretizing": "A Summary of the Plenum of News and Letters Committees," September 1–2, 1979, RD Papers, reel 3, 5965; "the first": "WJ," *N&L*, May 1970; "A Report on the Black-Red Conference, Detroit, Mich., Jan. 12, 1969," RD Papers, reel 2, 4350; "international": John Alan, "Elitism Takes Its Toll," *N&L*, April 1971; Lou Turner, "Toward a Black Radical Critique of Political Economy," *BS* 40 March 22, 2010): 7–19.

94. "With": "WJ," *N&L*, March 1968; "white": Paul Delaney, "Era of Routine Violence Against Blacks by Whites in the South's Black Belt Appears Ended," *NYT*, September 19, 1973.

95. "It": "WJ," *N&L*, June 1974; Thomas A. Johnson, "Poverty Still Pinches Rural Alabama Blacks," *NYT*, December 30, 1975; Andrew Kopkind, "Lowndes County, Alabama: The Great Fear Is Gone," in Kopkind, *Thirty Years' Wars*, 259–266.

96. "Paramilitary": Larry W. Isaac and Larry D. Christiansen, "Degradations of Labor, Cultures of Cooperation," in Wardell et al., eds., *Rethinking the Labor Process*, 127; "Worker Alienation, 1972," Hearings Before the Subcommittee on Employment, Manpower, and Poverty of the Committee on Labor and Public Welfare, United States Senate, 92 Cong., 2nd sess., S3916.

97. Thompson, *Whose Detroit?* 182–184.

98. "WJ," *N&L*, July 1977; Georgakas and Serkin, *Detroit*, 234–235.

99. "Black people": "Way of the World," *N&L*, December 1973; "If": "Fleetwood Workers Speak," February 1974, mimeograph, personal collection of Michael Flug.

100. "You": "WJ," *N&L*, August–September 1978; Widick, ed., *Auto Work*, 59; Robert Reich, "The Limping Middle Class," *NYT*, September 4, 2011; "Draft Perspectives Thesis, 1977–1978: Time Is Running Out," *N&L*, August–September 1977; Thomas Borstelmann, *The 1970s: A New Global History from Civil Rights to Economic Inequality* (Princeton, NJ: Princeton University Press, 2011), 62–63, 133.

101. Anderson e-mail.

102. See the "WJ" columns for August–September, October, and November 1979 and for June 1981. I am grateful to Michael Flug for his assessment of the theoretical significance and implications of *IH*.

103. "Reagan's": "WJ," *N&L*, August–September 1981; David Halberstam, *The Reckoning* (New York: William Morrow, 1986); "Chrysler to Convert Detroit Stamping Plant," *Chicago Tribune*, November 2, 1988; "Chrysler's Mack Avenue Engine Plant History," *Automotive Intelligence*, April 30, 1999, http://www.autointell.net/nao_companies/daimlerchrysler/dc-manufacturing/chrysler-mfg-mack-ave-03.htm (accessed June 25, 2013). In 1990 Chrysler cleared the debris from "Old Mack" and constructed a new, larger factory on the site.

104. Jacqueline Jones, "The Late-Twentieth-Century War on the Poor: A View from Distressed Communities Throughout the Nation," *BCTWLJ* 16 (Winter 1996): 1–16; Fine, *Violence*, 462–463.

105. "About racism": Charles Denby, "The Black Dimension in the South Today," September 1982, RD Papers, reel 4, 7585; "The crisis": Lou Turner, "Black World" column, *N&L*, December 1985, 1; Antonio Gramsci, *Selections from the Prison Notebooks*, ed. by Quintin Hoare and Geoffrey Nowell Smith (New York: International Publishers, 1971), 275–276.

106. "An idea . . . job": Denby, "Black Dimension," 7585–7586; Jeffries, *Bloody Lowndes,* 238–234; Kopkind, "Lowndes County," 263; Jeffries, *Bloody Lowndes,* 207–246. For an example of modern thinking on the role of genetics in constructions of "race," see Richard J. Herrnstein and Charles Murray, *The Bell Curve: Intelligence and Class Structure in American Life* (New York: Free Press, 1996); and Steven Fraser, ed., *The Bell Curve Wars: Race, Intelligence, and the Future of America* (New York: Basic Books, 1995).

107. "I was . . . level": Denby, "Black Dimension," 7588–7589; "WJ," *N&L,* October 1982.

108. Interview with Flug.

109. *N&L,* November 1983, 1.

110. For the funeral ("Eulogistical Services for the Late Simon Owens, Sr.") and memorial service programs I am grateful to Michael Flug.

111. See the obituary for Effie Owens by Olga Domanski, *N&L,* October 1993.

EPILOGUE

1. Jackson quoted in Kathryn Marie Dudley, *The End of the Line: Lost Jobs, New Lives in Postindustrial America* (Chicago: University of Chicago Press, 1994), 145–146.

2. Catherine Rampell, "Big Income Losses for Those Near Retirement," *NYT,* August 23, 2012.

3. "There": Kindle quoted in Timothy Williams, "As Public Sector Sheds Jobs, Blacks Are Hit Hardest," *NYT,* November 28, 2011; "the permanent": *N&L,* September–October 2011, 3; Jonathan Mahler, "G.M., Detroit, and the Fall of the Black Middle Class," *NYT Sunday Magazine,* June 28, 2009; US Department of Labor, "The African-American Labor Force in the Recovery," February 29, 2012, http://www.dol.gov/_sec/media/reports/blacklaborforce/ (accessed May 28, 2013).

4. Roberts quoted in Nelson D. Schwartz and Michael Cooper, "Racial Diversity Efforts Ebb for Elite Careers, Analysis Finds," *NYT,* May 28, 2013.

5. Elizabeth Renuart, "An Overview of the Predatory Mortgage Lending Process," *Housing Policy Debate* 15 (2004): 467–502; Testimony of James H. Carr, "Predatory Lending and Reverse Redlining: Are Low-Income, Minority, and Senior Borrowers Targets for Higher Cost Loans?" submitted to the US Joint Economic Committee, Thursday, June 25, 2009; "Predatory Lenders," *NYT,* April 29, 2013; National Council of Negro Women, "Income Is No Shield, Part III: Assessing the Double Burden: Examining Racial and Gender Disparities in Mortgage Lending," c. 2010, http://www.ncnw.org/images/double_burden.pdf (accessed June 25, 2013). On persistent discrimination against blacks looking for housing, see Shaila Dewan, "Discrimination in Housing Against Nonwhites Persists Quietly, U.S. Study Finds," *NYT,* June 12, 2013.

6. Rakesh Kochhar, Richard Fry, and Paul Taylor, "Wealth Gaps Rise to Record Highs Between Whites, Blacks, and Hispanics," Pew Research Center Social and Demographic Trends Publications, July 26, 2011; Annie Lowrey, "Wealth Gap Among Races Has Widened Since Recession," *NYT,* April 29, 2013.

7. Taylor Branch, "The Shame of College Sports," *The Atlantic,* October 2011, 102.

8. American Civil Liberties Union, "The War on Marijuana in Black and White," http://www.aclu.org/criminal-law-reform/war-marijuana-black-and-white-report (ac-

cessed June 25, 2013); "to meet": Dr. Phillip A. Goff quoted In Ian Urbina, "Blacks Are Singled Out for Marijuana Arrests, Federal Data Suggests," *NYT,* June 4, 2013; Michelle Alexander, *The New Jim Crow: Mass Incarceration in the Age of Colorblindness* (New York: New Press, 2010); Becky Pettit, Bryan Sykes, and Bruce Western, "Technical Report on Revised Population Estimates and NLSY79 Analysis Tables for the Pew Public Safety and Mobility Project" (Cambridge, MA: Harvard University, 2009); Becky Pettit, *Invisible Men: Mass Incarceration and the Myth of Black Progress* (New York: Russell Sage Foundation, 2012); Tyjen Tsai and Paola Scommegna, "U.S. Has World's Highest Incarceration Rate," Population Reference Bureau, August 2012, http://www.prb.org/Articles/2012/us-incarceration.aspx (accessed June 25, 2013).

9. See, for example, Angela Y. Davis, *The Meaning of Freedom* (San Francisco: City Lights, 2012); and Richard C. Fording and Sanford F. Schram, *Disciplining the Poor: Neoliberal Paternalism and the Persistent Power of Race* (Chicago: University of Chicago Press, 2011).

10. Nadya Labi, "Misfortune Teller," *The Atlantic,* January–February 2012, 19; Jeffrey Fagan, "The Contradictions of Juvenile Crime and Punishment," *Daedalus* (Summer 2010): 43–62; Loic Wacquant, *Deadly Symbiosis: Race and the Rise of the Penal State* (Cambridge: Polity Press, 2010).

11. Ari Berman, "The GOP's New Southern Strategy," *The Nation,* February 20, 2012, 11–17.

12. "I guess": Darrel Rowland, "Voting in Ohio: Fight over Poll Hours Isn't Just Political," *Columbus Dispatch,* August 19, 2012; Ethan Bronner, "Legal Battles Erupt as Voters Fear Exclusion by Tough ID Laws," *NYT,* July 20, 2012.

13. "Learn how to be": Rachel Weiner, "John Sununu, Mitt Romney's Best/Worst Surrogate," *Washington Post,* July 17, 2012; "food stamp": James Oliphant, "Gingrich Defends Calling Obama 'The Food Stamp President,'" *LAT,* January 16, 2012; "deepseated": "Beck: Obama Has 'Exposed Himself as a Guy' with 'a Deep-Seated Hatred for White People," *Fox & Friends,* Fox News, July 28, 2009, http://mediamatters.org video/2009/07/28/beck-obama-has-exposed-himself-as-a-guy-with-a/152551 (accessed June 19, 2013); Dan Halperin, "Fifty Shades of Gray," *Harper's Magazine*, September 2012, 42; Ta-Nehisi Coates, "Fear of a Black President," *The Atlantic,* September 2012, 76; Karen E. Fields and Barbara J. Fields, *Racecraft: The Soul of Inequality in American Life* (London: Verso Books, 2012), 264; Seth Stephens-Davidowitz, "The Effects of Racial Animus on a Black Presidential Candidate: Using Google Search Data to Find What Surveys Miss," 2009, http://www.people.fas.harvard.edu/~sstephen/papers/Racial AnimusAndVotingSethStephensDavidowitz.pdf (accessed June 20, 2013); Sarah Netter, "Racism in Obama's America One Year Later," ABC News, January 27, 2010, http:// abcnews.go.com/WN/Obama/racism-obamas-america-year/story?id=9638178 (accessed June 25, 2013); "Are You Impartial to a Certain Race? Take the Implicit Association Test," April 17, 2012, http://www.andersoncooper.com/2012/04/17/are-you-impartial -to-a-certain-race-take-the-implicit-associate-test/ (accessed June 25, 2013); "[AP-Yahoo] Poll: Racial Views Steer Some Away from Obama," September 20, 2008, http://www .politico.com/news/stories/0908/13658.html (accessed June 20, 2013). "Romney Adopts Harder Message for Last Stretch: Nod to White Workers," *NYT,* August 26, 2012.

14. Frederick C. Harris, "The Price of a Black President," *NYT,* October 28, 2012; Fields and Fields, *Racecraft,* 264.

15. Randall Kennedy, *The Persistence of the Color Line: Racial Politics and the Obama Presidency* (New York: Vintage Books, 2011), 73.

16. Douglas Quenqua, "How Well You Sleep May Hinge on Race," *NYT,* August 21, 2012.

17. Richard J. Herrnstein and Charles Murray, *The Bell Curve: Intelligence and Class Structure in American Life* (New York: Free Press, 1996); Fields and Fields, *Racecraft,* 16, 100. In 2013 a researcher with the conservative Heritage Foundation argued against proposed national policies that would allow undocumented immigrants to remain in the United States, claiming that members of the Hispanic "race" had a lower IQ than native-born whites. His argument was notable in two respects: first, the notion that Spanish-speaking people representing many different ethnicities and regions of the world constitute a "race," and second, his time-honored attempt to invoke the idea of race to further a specific political agenda. See Jason Richwine, "IQ and Immigration Policy" (PhD diss., Harvard University, 2009); and Jon Wiener, "Why Did Harvard Give a PhD for a Discredited Approach to Race and IQ?" *The Nation,* May 11, 2013, http://www.thenation.com/blog/174291/harvard-phd-and-hispanics-iq-how -jason-richwines-dissertation-got-him-fired-heritage-fou#axzz2XFGCwAU5 (accessed June 25, 2013).

18. David Brooks, "The Party of Work," *NYT,* November 9, 2012.

19. Sam Dillon, "Lines Grow Long for Free School Meals, Thanks to Economy," *NYT,* November 30, 2011; "The School Lunch Barometer," *NYT,* December 30, 2011.

INDEX